D0891722

Desecrating the American Flag

Desecrating the American Flag

Key Documents of the Controversy
from the Civil War to 1995

Edited by

Robert Justin Goldstein

Syracuse University Press

The paper used in this publication meets the minimum requirements of American National Standard for Information Sciences—Permanence of Paper for Printed Library Materials, ANSI Z39.48-1984. ♾™

Library of Congress Cataloging-in-Publication Data

Desecrating the American flag : key documents of the controversy from the Civil War to 1995 / edited by Robert Justin Goldstein. — 1st ed.
p. cm.
Includes index.
ISBN 0-8156-2702-5 (cloth : alk. paper). — ISBN 0-8156-2716-5 (pbk. : alk. paper)
1. Flags—Desecration—United States—History—Sources. 2. Flags—Law and legislation—United States—Criminal provisions—History—Sources. I. Goldstein, Robert Justin.
KF5150.D47 1996
364.1′31—dc20   96-19990

Manufactured in the United States of America

For Sydney and her cats,
who desecrate only couches

ROBERT JUSTIN GOLDSTEIN is professor of political science at Oakland University in Rochester, Michigan. He is the author of *Political Repression in Modern America, Censorship of Political Caricature in Nineteenth-Century France, Saving "Old Glory": The History of the American Flag Desecration Controversy,* and *Burning the Flag: The Great 1989–1990 American Flag Desecration Controversy.*

Contents

Documents

Preface

During 1989–90, a controversy over whether it should be legal to damage the American flag to express political protest received massive media attention and became a dominant political issue in Washington. This dispute involved, at a minimum, patriotism, politics, and democratic theory; it engulfed all three branches of the federal government. In 1989–90 alone, it engendered two major Supreme Court decisions, filled several thousand pages of congressional hearings and floor debates, and led President George Bush to urge twice a constitutional amendment that most observers and experts agreed would amend the Bill of Rights for the first time in American history. Although the flag desecration issue disappeared from the news headlines and from general public attention for five years after the 1990 (second) defeat of the proposed Bush constitutional amendment, in 1995 the issue was revived in Congress and the amendment was handily endorsed by the House of Representatives in June before being barely defeated in the Senate in December.

Amidst the 1989–90 controversy, only Americans old enough to remember anti-Vietnam war protests recalled that a similar, although less intense and less massively publicized, debate raged during the Vietnam era; few were aware that the flag desecration controversy actually originated in the late nineteenth century, when organized pressure by veterans and patriotic-hereditary groups led to passage (by all of the states by 1932, although not until 1968 by the federal government) of flag desecration laws (which eventually led to the Vietnam-era flag prosecutions and to the 1984 Texas prosecution of Gregory Lee Johnson, which spurred the 1989–90 dispute).

Although the 1989–90 controversy temporarily disappeared from the press and from political discussion with startling rapidity after the failure of President Bush's proposed constitutional amendment in 1990 left in force Supreme Court rulings that upheld the legality of symbolic flag protests, and a similar phenomenon occurred immediately after the revived amendment was again defeated in 1995, this one-hundred-year history of intense controversy in America over flag desecration suggests that sooner or later this dispute will again return to the forefront of American attention. Even if this proves not to be the case, the enormous amounts of time, energy, and ink that have been devoted to the controversy in the past suggest that a collection of documents covering the entire history of this dispute could prove helpful to constitutional lawyers, historians, political scientists, journalists, and others with an interest in civil liberties, flags, democratic theory, and American politics.

In this volume, therefore, I have provided a selection of documents related to this subject that range over one hundred years and that are presently scattered in hundreds of different sources. My primary goal has been to produce a collection of materials that is reasonably comprehensive and balanced—in time periods covered and point of view—and to particularly emphasize documents that are unusually interesting, historically important, and/or rare (many of the pamphlets quoted from the 1895–1910 period are extremely scarce, in some cases apparently existing today only in single copies). From literally thousands of documents, whose bulk easily exceeded twenty thousand pages, I have selected 147 key documents.

It would perhaps be helpful to the reader for me to outline my own views about the flag desecration issue. During the six years in which I have researched this controversy, I have interviewed hundreds of people who were involved in it in one way or another and I rarely met anyone who lacked strong, unchangeable, and uncompromising views on the issue (in this sense it somewhat resembles the abortion controversy). Like most people, I do have my own views on this subject, and although I have tried to keep them out of this book and tried not to let them influence my choice of documents—in fact, the majority of documents included herein express views with which I disagree—no doubt they have crept in here and there, and I consider it only fair to my audience to alert them to my biases.

In short, although I think it is clear that flag desecration only alienates people, and for that reason is generally an unwise political tactic, I also believe that it is a form of pure expression (as is almost anything involving the flag, which is a symbol without any other functional purpose) and therefore is protected by the First Amendment. Although some have argued that the First Amendment refers only to "speech" and "press" and not to "expression," any attempt to exclude flag desecration from the protection of the First Amendment on such grounds would also exclude from constitutional protection all nonverbal communication such as sign language, dance, paintings, sculpture, and all gestures, including even waving the American flag.

Furthermore, in my view, any attempt to argue that a "special" exception to the First Amendment should be carved out for flag desecration shows a lack of understanding of what the Bill of Rights, and indeed democracy, are all about. Above all what differentiates democracy from authoritarianism is precisely that all points of view, even the detestable, offensive, and unpopular, may be expressed, so that the public can freely choose from all possible alternatives (after all, medieval religious authorities sought to suppress circulation of ideas about the heliocentric theory of the solar system on grounds of their obvious falsity and offensiveness). Finally, although flag desecration usually backfires as a political tactic, I do not find it difficult to imagine circumstances in which it might serve a useful purpose. For example, had two hundred prominent Americans collectively burned flags to protest the forced expulsion and detention without trial of Japanese Americans during World War II, or to protest the excesses of McCarthyism, I can at least imagine that there is a small chance that American history might not bear those stains today. Similarly, if, instead of fringe groups, two hundred prominent Americans had burned flags to protest the deepening American involvement in Vietnam in 1965, perhaps there is a small chance that there might not be a wall today in Washington, D.C., with fifty-eight thousand names carved in it.

Ann Arbor, Michigan   ROBERT JUSTIN GOLDSTEIN
April 1996

A Note on the Texts

The documents I have chosen for inclusion (usually in excerpted form owing to considerations of space) have been organized in fourteen chapters, each of which is introduced by a short essay designed to provide a context for the documents that follow. These essays are designed to be self-contained, so that the reader who consults them may examine all, some, or even none of the documents they introduce, while still understanding key issues and developments in the flag desecration controversy.

Document sources appear immediately before each document. Substantive material that I have deleted from original documents is replaced by ellipses (. . .); when the original documents themselves delete material quoted from other sources this is indicated with asterisks (* * *). In the reprinted documents, I have routinely corrected obvious typographical and spelling errors (or, in some cases, anachronistic spelling), and, as is often done in reprinting legal materials, footnotes and citations within reprinted documents to other materials not reproduced in this book have been omitted without individual indications of such peripheral deletions. All material published in italics or in capital letters in the documents appeared that way in the original.

Material enclosed in parentheses in documents appeared in the original in that form; material I have interpolated into the documents for purposes of clarification are enclosed in brackets [ ]; on those occasions where material appeared in brackets in the original documents, they appear as angle brackets ⟨ ⟩. To avoid confusion, the endnotes to my introductory essays are sequentially numbered by chapter and printed at the end of the book, while the relatively few notes that are reproduced from the original documents are printed at the end of each document, with the note numbering scheme in the document retained (thus, if some footnotes included in the original documents have been deleted in the editing process, as is invariably the case, the retained notes may neither begin with footnote one nor be numbered sequentially). Because most of the information in my essays is documented in the referenced materials included in this book, and because Kent State University Press and Westview Press have already published my very lengthy and completely footnoted narrative account of the flag desecration controversy (see notes for full citations), I have deliberately kept my own notes to a minimum in this volume.

Abbreviations

ABA	American Bar Association
AFA	American Flag Association
CFA	Citizens Flag Alliance
DAR	Daughters of the American Revolution
FPA	Flag Protection Act (1989 Federal law)
FPM	Flag Protection Movement
GAR	Grand Army of the Republic
HJC	House Judiciary Committee
NCCUSL	National Conference of Commissioners on Uniform State Laws
RCP	Revolutionary Communist Party
RCYB	Revolutionary Communist Youth Brigade
SAIC	School of the Art Institute of Chicago
SAR	Sons of the American Revolution
SCW	Society of Colonial Wars
SJC	Senate Judiciary Committee
WFM	Western Federation of Miners

Desecrating the American Flag

A Civil War Execution for Flag Desecration

Until the eve and onset of the Civil War, the American flag played only a small part in the life of the United States. It was generally displayed only at federal buildings and military bases and rarely, if ever, by private citizens or even at schoolhouses or other local governmental installations. Only as the Civil War approached did the flag (in the North only, of course) become a wildly popular symbol of the country. For the same reason, only then did the flag become, for the first time, an object used for popular symbolic political protest, as supporters of the Confederacy on several occasions destroyed American flags or in other ways (such as hauling it down from federal installations or bombing it at Fort Sumter) used it to express their opposition to the North.[1]

Even before the formal outbreak of the war, President James Buchanan's secretary of the treasury, John Dix, in response to a threatened seizure of a federal ship by secessionist forces in Louisiana, telegraphed to a New Orleans treasury clerk on January 29, 1861, "If any one attempts to haul down the American flag, shoot him on the spot."[2] On June 7, 1862, in New Orleans, William B. Mumford was hung for committing this offense, after being convicted of treason by a military court for, on April 27, 1862, pulling down, dragging in the mud, and shredding an American flag that had been hoisted over the New Orleans federal mint amidst the federal re-occupation of the city. Mumford was retroactively punished in accordance with a decree issued on May 1, 1862 by Union general Benjamin Butler that ordered "severe punishment" for anyone who failed to treat the American flag and other federal emblems with "the utmost deference" (document 1.1). On June 5, 1862, Butler, whose harsh rule made him known as the "Beast of New Orleans" and led to his removal by President Lincoln several months later, confirmed the death sentence pronounced upon Mumford by the military tribunal in a "special order" (document 1.2).

The execution of Mumford, who met his death with composure, stating that he had wronged no one but was prepared to die, made him a martyr in the eyes of the South. Thus, in an 1862 proclamation, Thomas O. Moore, the deposed and by then fugitive governor of Louisiana, saluted Mumford for refusing to disavow the Confederacy in order to save his life, hailed his example as that of an "heroic soul" inspired by "fervid patriotism," and swore not to let Mumford's "murder" pass "unatoned" (document 1.3). Similarly, in another 1862 proclamation, Confederate president Jefferson Davis termed the Mumford execution an "outrage" and a "deliberate murder" and cited it as the primary justification for declaring Butler "an outlaw and common enemy of mankind," to be "immediately executed by hanging" if captured by Confederate forces (document 1.4).

Document 1.1

Gen. Benjamin Butler's decree concerning emblems of the United States, New Orleans, May 1, 1862.

Source: George H. Preble, *Origin and History of the American Flag* (Philadelphia: Nicholas Brown, 1917), vol. 2, 472.

All ensigns, flags, or devices tending to uphold any authority whatever, save the flags of the United States and those of foreign consulates, must not be exhibited, but suppressed. The American ensigns, the emblem of the United States, must be treated with the utmost deference and respect by all persons, under pain of severe punishment.

Document 1.2

Gen. Benjamin Butler's "special order" confirming the death sentence of William B. Mumford for hauling down a United States flag, New Orleans, June 5, 1862.

Source: George H. Preble, *Origin and History of the American Flag* (Philadelphia: Nicholas Brown, 1917), vol. 2, 473.

William B. Mumford, a citizen of New Orleans, having been convicted before a military commission of treason, and an overt act thereof in tearing down the United States flag from a public building of the United States, for the purpose of inciting other evil-minded persons to further resistance to the laws and order of the United States, after said flag was placed there by Commodore [David] Farragut, of the United States navy. It is ordered that he be executed according to the sentence of the said military commission, on Saturday June 7th inst., between the hours of eight A.M. and twelve M. [midnight] under the direction of the provost-marshal of the district of New Orleans; and for so doing, this shall be sufficient warrant.

Document 1.3

Proclamation by deposed Louisiana governor Thomas Moore, 1862, hailing the executed flag desecrator William Mumford as a martyr.

Source: James Parton, *General Butler in New Orleans* (New York: Mason Brothers, 1864), 352–53.

The noble heroism of the patriot Mumford has placed his name high on our list of martyred sons. When the federal navy reached New Orleans, a squad of marines was sent on shore, who hoisted their flag on the mint. The city was not occupied by United States troops, nor had they reached there. The place was not in their possession. William B. Mumford pulled down the detested symbol with his own hand, and for this was condemned to be hung by General Butler after his arrival. Brought in full view of the scaffold, his murderers hoped to appall his heroic soul by the exhibition of the implements of ignominious death. With the evidence of their determination to consummate their brutal purpose before his eyes, they offered him life, on the condition that he would abjure his country [the Confederacy] and swear allegiance to her foe. He spurned the offer. Scorning to stain his soul with such foul dishonor, he met his fate courageously, and has transmitted to his countrymen a fresh example of what one will do and dare under the inspiration of fervid patriotism. I shall not forget the outrage of his murder, or shall it pass unatoned.

Document 1.4

Proclamation by Confederate president Jefferson Davis, December 23, 1862, calling for the execution of Union general Benjamin Butler for the hanging of William Mumford.

Source: James Parton, *General Butler in New Orleans* (New York: Mason Brothers, 1864), 607–9.

Whereas, a communication addressed on the 6th day of July last, 1862, by [Confederate] General Robert E. Lee . . . to General H. W. Halleck, commander-in-chief of the United States army, informing the latter that a report had been received this government that Wm. B. Mumford, a citizen of the Confederate States, had been executed by the United States authorities at New Orleans for having pulled down the United States flag in that city before its occupation by the United States forces, and calling for a statement of the facts, with a view of retaliation if such an outrage had really been committed under the sanction of the authorities of the United States. . . . And whereas [despite the failure of U.S. officials to respond to this and subsequent letters], . . . I have received evidence fully establishing the truth of the fact that the said William B. Mumford, a citizen of the Confederacy, was actually and publicly executed, in cold blood, by hanging, after the occupation of the city of New Orleans by the forces under General Benjamin F. Butler, when said Mumford was an unresisting and non-combatant captive, and for no offense even alleged to have been committed by him subsequent to the date of capture of the said city;

And whereas, the silence of the government of the United States, and its maintaining of said Butler in high office under its authority for many months after his commission of an act that can be viewed in no other light than as a deliberate murder, as well as of numerous other outrages and atrocities hereafter to be mentioned, afford evidence too conclusive that the said government sanctions the conduct of the said Butler, and is determined that he shall remain unpunished for these crimes;

Now, therefore, I, Jefferson Davis, President of the Confederate States of America, and in their name, do pronounce and declare the said Benjamin E. Butler to be a felon, deserving of capital punishment. I do order that he shall no longer be considered or treated simply as a public enemy of the Confederate States of America, but as an outlaw and common enemy of mankind, and that, in the event of his capture, the officer in command of the capturing force do cause him to be immediately executed by hanging. . . .

Origins of the Controversy, 1890–1942

At least in the North, the American flag retained its newfound popularity in the aftermath of the Civil War. However, at first this popularity was primarily manifested in an explosion of flag use for commercial purposes as advertising became a major industry for the first time amidst the rapid industrialization of the United States; flags were not widely flown over schoolhouses until about 1900 and the ancestor of the modern Pledge of Allegiance was only written in 1892.[1] What will henceforth be termed the Flag Protection Movement (FPM) gradually emerged during the 1890s and sought to forbid all uses of the flag except in strictly regulated patriotic ceremonies, in an effort to surround the emblem with the aura of a holy relic, above all as a reaction to the post–Civil War commercialization of the flag. Thus, when the House of Representatives, without hearings or floor debate, passed a bill to prevent flag "desecration" in 1890, in what amounted to the first public evidence of the FPM, it acted in response to a House Judiciary Committee (HJC) report that clearly indicated that the bill's purpose was solely to ban advertising use of the flag (document 2.1). Since the Civil War, no reports of physical destruction of the American flag had surfaced, and no mention was made in the proposed bill or in the committee report of any need to forbid symbolic political protests that involved such acts.

The first major public statement of the FPM came in a pamphlet (document 2.2) that was published (officially on July 4, 1895, although in fact later that year) and widely distributed by the National Flag Committee of the Illinois Society of Colonial Wars (SCW). The group's flag committee was one of the earliest of many flag committees appointed by various patriotic and hereditary groups in the middle and late 1890s to seek congressional passage of a national flag desecration law. Two of the three signers of the 1895 pamphlet were among the key FPM leaders: Capt. Philip Reade, a Union army veteran and career officer who in 1895 was governor (president) of the Illinois SCW and who worked tirelessly, although usually behind the scenes, to line up support for the FPM among a wide variety of organizations; and Charles Kingsbury Miller, a wealthy retired advertising executive who subsequently served as chairman of the flag committees of both the Illinois SCW and the Illinois Sons of the American Revolution (SAR) and became one of the most prolific FPM pamphleteers.

As had been the case with the 1890 HJC report, the major focus of the 1895 pamphlet that Reade and Miller helped coauthor was upon commercial and advertising misuses of the flag; however, the pamphlet also refers to partisan political use of the flag as an additional form of desecration, and this further form of flag "desecration" subsequently attained major importance to the FPM as a result of developments during the 1896 election (see text below and documents 2.3 and 2.4). Furthermore, scattered throughout the pamphlet were indications of concern over perceived growing threats to American political stability, American political institutions, and the role of traditional elites such as those represented in the FPM. These perceived threats were clearly associated with rapid changes in late-nineteenth-century America such as increasing urbanization, immigration, and industrialization, and concomitant with signs of rising radicalism such as the 1894 Pullman Strike. After 1900, the FPM, which originally focused largely on threats to the flag posed by commercialism, increasingly stressed supposed threats to the flag, and by implication to the nation, by symbolic protests by immigrants and radicals. This development suggests that the FPM quickly became, above all, a reflection of fears by traditional elites that their power was threatened by new and strange political forces (see text below and, for example, documents 2.5, 2.6, 2.7, and 2.8). Like many FPM statements, the 1895 pamphlet was filled with rhetoric that idealized and idolized the flag as a representation of all that was "sacred" and good.

The FPM received a considerable boost because of several incidents of physical flag desecration that were associated with the 1896 presidential campaign. As had occurred during previous elections, but to a much greater extent in 1896, the Republican candidate, William McKinley, identified himself both literally and figuratively with the flag. As in past campaigns, both parties sometimes campaigned with flags that featured partisan slogans and pictures attached to them. The climax of the Republican strategy came during the weekend before the election; campaign officials proclaimed October 31, 1896, to be a national flag day in honor of McKinley, and the day featured huge parades throughout the country on his behalf, festooned with thousands of flags. In a number of incidents, Democrats who were enraged by McKinleyite suggestions that their patriotism was suspect responded to such displays by tearing down or otherwise assaulting flags displayed by Republicans. One such incident was a flag burning reported in the November 1, 1896, *New York Times* (document

2.3), which, like much of the press, was bitterly hostile to Democratic-Populist presidential candidate William Jennings Bryan.

The incidents of flag desecration associated with the 1896 campaign considerably increased the FPM's appeal and led to a change in its focus, as thereafter the movement stressed opposition to physical flag desecration as well as to commercial use of the flag. Although at first the stress on desecration was in opposition to the traditional placing by mainstream political parties of partisan campaign slogans and pictures on the flag, after 1900 the focus shifted to outlawing physical desecration as a form of political dissent supposedly used or threatened by radicals and immigrants. The events of 1896 were largely responsible for the prominent role in the FPM taken thereafter by the Daughters of the American Revolution (DAR), under the leadership of its Milwaukee chapter and its local activist, Frances Saunders Kempster. In 1896, the Milwaukee chapter sponsored a petition to Congress calling for a national flag desecration law, which was subsequently endorsed by the national DAR in 1897 and which focused exclusively on the 1896 campaign incidents of flag desecration (document 2.4).

Between 1898 and 1902, the leading FPM publicist was Charles Kingsbury Miller, the retired newspaper advertising executive who served as chairman of the flag committees of the Illinois chapters of the SCW and the SAR, and who was also one of the original members of the executive committee of the American Flag Association (AFA), an organization formed in 1898 to coordinate the efforts of the various flag committees that sought flag desecration legislation. Miller published numerous articles and pamphlets (documents 2.5, 2.6, and 2.7), which often suggested that congressmen who failed to support flag desecration legislation were lacking in courage and patriotism. Miller painted an apocalyptic picture of a nation threatened with mobs of flag desecrators that included mercenary businessmen, savage immigrants, bloodthirsty trade unions, and revolutionary anarchists and radicals, all of whom could be checkmated if only flag desecration were outlawed.

Miller repeatedly blamed Rep. David Henderson (R., Iowa), HJC chairman during the 1890s and later briefly Speaker of the House, for blocking House action on a national flag desecration law. His often venomous attacks on Henderson, as well as what AFA president Ralph Prime regarded as Miller's exaggerated claims of credit in connection with the passage of state flag desecration laws, led Prime to denounce him and, apparently, to oust him from the AFA executive committee after 1901. Despite Prime's views of Miller, Philip Reade, who was perhaps more responsible that any other person for the FPM's creation, publicly declared in 1903 that the successes of the movement had been due more to Miller's efforts "than those of any one man."[2]

The most important founding organizations involved in the FPM were the SAR and the DAR; a less important role was played by veterans organizations, especially groups composed of Union Civil War veterans, such as the Grand Army of the Republic (GAR) and the Loyal Legion, the latter of which was restricted to Union Civil War officers. Beginning in the late 1890s, most of these organizations created national and local flag committees that were dedicated to encouraging passage of national and state flag desecration laws. Although in 1900 the various flag committees of these groups formed the AFA to coordinate their efforts, the constituent organizations of the AFA generally retained their own flag committees, which sometimes competed with one another in drawing up draft legislation and claiming credit for obtaining the passage of state flag desecration laws.

Although the rhetoric of most flag committees was usually less hysterical and exaggerated than that of Charles Kingsbury Miller, all of the themes that he touched on were included by them in a more muted form, as can be clearly seen in the 1899 report of the DAR Flag Committee (document 2.8). Much of the flag committee reports after 1900 were devoted to reporting progress in obtaining passage of state flag desecration legislation, while puzzling over and lamenting the inability to obtain such legislation from Congress. In the 1903 report of the SAR Flag Committee (document 2.9), chairman Ralph Prime, who also chaired the AFA, alludes to two of the difficulties: the apparent opposition of southern congressmen and competition between the various flag committees (in document 2.8, DAR chairwoman Frances Saunders Kempster alludes to the fact that in 1899 only the DAR's proposed flag bill banned physical flag desecration as well as advertising use of the flag, although subsequently the SAR and the AFA endorsed a similar measure and, after earlier complaining that the DAR version was too harsh, they then complained that it was too "soft"). The comparatively passive role of the GAR is clearly indicated in the 1903 report of its flag committee (document 2.10), which essentially defers to the AFA (while also alluding to the complications caused by competition between the AFA's constituent groups).

Between 1898 and 1912, the AFA was the most influential organization in the FPM. Although the AFA was designed to be a coordinating and unifying body composed of representatives of the flag committees of the various patriotic, hereditary, and veterans organizations that sought flag desecration legislation, in practice it appears to have been dominated by the SAR, and especially by the Empire State (New York) SAR. Throughout most of the period of the AFA's greatest influence, for example, Ralph Prime, Empire State SAR leader, served also as national SAR Flag Committee chairman and AFA president and thoroughly dominated all three of these groups. Despite the AFA's intended role as coordinator and unifier, in practice there were frequent conflicts over both goals and tactics between the AFA (which in effect meant Prime) and some of its component groups and leaders, in particular Chicago FPM leader Charles Kingsbury Miller and Milwaukee DAR FPM leader Frances Saunders Kempster.

Between its organization in 1898 and its departure from the national stage in about 1912 (which seems to have reflected Prime's advancing age and declining energies), the AFA published six "circulars of information." Although Prime's bias must be taken into account, these circulars provide by far the most detailed information about the FPM's work and progress during its formative and most influential years, which resulted in the passage of state flag desecration laws in over thirty states and territories between 1897 and 1912. In addition, as a result of the FPM's efforts, congressional hearings on federal flag desecration legislation were held during at least six years between 1898 and 1918, and flag desecration bills passed the Senate (although not the House) in 1904, 1908, 1913, 1914, and 1918.

Documents 2.11, 2.12, and 2.13 reprint portions of three of the AFA's published "circulars of information." The material reprinted from the 1900 circular (document 2.11) consists of the text of the AFA's model flag desecration law, which influenced many of the state laws to which Prime refers in his addresses to the AFA excerpted in documents 2.12 and 2.13. Document 2.12 contains portions of the AFA's 1905–6 circular of information, including a list of all states that had passed flag desecration legislation by 1905 (with date of passage), an explanation of the intent of the AFA's model law, a listing of examples of flag desecration objectionable to the AFA, a listing of provisions in foreign countries concerning flag desecration, and excerpts from Prime's 1904 and 1905 addresses to the AFA's annual meeting. Document 2.13 includes excerpts from Prime's 1907 address, which was published in the AFA's circular for 1907–8. Although listing with pride the states in which flag desecration laws had been passed, in his various addresses Prime laments the failure to obtain such measures in the South, which he declares is "impossible to understand," and the concomitant AFA failure at the national level, which is attributed to a combination of states' rights sentiments, opposition to criminal penalties for flag desecration, and undemocratic procedures in the House of Representatives.

The FPM's distaste for the crass "commercialism" of the new industrial society, with its willingness to use the flag for advertising purposes, and for the "lawless leaders of union labor," who are accused of using the flag as a background for strike propaganda, come through clearly in Prime's remarks. As one means of protesting advertising use of the flag, Prime proposes refusing to buy any merchandise advertised by the flag, but he unconvincingly hastens to declare that such merchandise boycotts have nothing in common with the "reprehensible boycotting of a merchant [as opposed to particular items]" then used by labor unions to protest perceived unfair labor policies, which was widely viewed in "respectable" circles as a subversive interference with freedom of trade.

In both his 1904 and 1905 remarks, Prime attacks those in the FPM who, he alleges, seek personal glory (meaning Miller) and claim credit for results they did not create (meaning Miller and the DAR). In his 1907 remarks, Prime begins with a short history of the FPM, and at the conclusion he discusses recent court cases involving state flag desecration laws, culminating with the Supreme Court's 1907 ruling in *Halter v. Nebraska* upholding such legislation (document 3.10).

Although the original impetus for the FPM in the mid-1890s was concern over perceived advertising misuse of the flag and perceived partisan misuse of the flag by "mainstream" political parties, after about 1900, and especially after the Supreme Court's 1907 *Halter* decision, the FPM's rhetoric increasingly stressed the need to suppress radical political groups who might seek to damage the flag as expressions of symbolic political dissent. In short, whereas the FPM originally focused on alleged flag misuse by "mainstream" business and political groups, who sought to use the flag not to express dissent but to gain benefits from its patriotic resonance, it soon began to focus primarily on political dissenters who might seek to use the flag to disassociate themselves from the political mainstream. Thus, although the FPM was originally motivated by a desire to protect the flag from *any* source of perceived "contamination" by impure motives, it soon became dominated by a desire to suppress views attributed to those who might use the flag to express political dissent.

This evolution in the FPM's stress can be traced by examining the changing rhetoric used in congressional hearings and floor discussion of the flag desecration issue between 1902 and 1943 (documents 2.14–2.17, 2.21–2.25), as well as in the provisions of the 1918 Sedition Act and proposed flag desecration bills, and in the language used to endorse flag desecration legislation proposed during World War I by the National Conference of Commissioners on Uniform State Laws (NCCUSL) and by the American Bar Association (ABA). In general, during Congressional hearings and floor debate before 1910, considerable stress was placed on alleged commercial desecration of the flag, but after then, and especially after World War I, the main stress was on the threat posed to the flag by political dissidents, as is reflected in the provisions of the 1918 Espionage Act (document 2.18). After 1910, most proposed federal flag desecration laws excluded from their provisions all clearly "patriotic" uses of the flag, and by 1943 interest in advertising use of the flag had diminished so greatly that when the Senate that year passed a proposed federal flag desecration bill all provisions related to advertising use of the flag, previously included in most proposed bills, were deleted (see documents 2.16, 2.23, 2.25). In 1917, when the NCCUSL, an organization of representatives of state governments, urged passage by all states of a uniform flag desecration law based on the AFA's model law of 1900 (document 2.11), it adopted a committee report that above all stressed the need for laws to suppress "malicious outrages" committed against the flag by the "labor element" and other representatives of the "red flag of anarchy" (document 2.19). Similarly, in 1918 the ABA urged endorsement of the NCCUSL model law on the grounds that such action was "essential" to the maintenance of American "power and prestige" and to "speedily and effectively" suppress "the insidious encroachments of treason" that might seek to "strike at the symbol and at the sovereignty symbolized" (document 2.20).

Document 2.1

1890 House Judiciary Committee report in support of federal flag desecration legislation.

Source: House of Representatives, *To Prevent Desecration of the United States Flag.* 51st Cong., 1st sess., 1890. Report accompanying H.R. 10475 (subsequently passed by the House of Representatives in 1890 [*Congressional Record*, 10697]).

. . . The flag of our country is the symbol of our national existence, power, and sovereignty. It is the emblem of freedom and equality and representative of the glory of the American name. It is a reminder of American fortitude, courage, and heroism, and of the suffering and sacrifices on land and sea which have been endured for its preservation and for the preservation of the country it represents. It is the shield and protection of the citizen at home and abroad and should be honored and reverenced by every American who is a lover of his country. It should be held a thing sacred, and to deface, disfigure, or prostitute it to the purposes of advertising should be held to be a crime against the nation and be punished as such.

We therefore favor the proposition of the accompanying bill, . . .

That any person or persons who shall use the national flag, either by printing, painting, or affixing on said flag, or otherwise attaching to the same any advertisement for public display, or private gain, shall be guilty of a misdemeanor, and on conviction thereof in the district court of the United States shall be fined in any sum not exceeding fifty dollars, or imprisoned not less than thirty days, or both, at the discretion of the court.

Document 2.2

1895 pamphlet in support of federal flag desecration legislation.

Source: "The Misuse of the National Flag of the United States: An Appeal to the Fifty-Fourth Congress of the United States" (Chicago: National Flag Committee of the Society of Colonial Wars in the State of Illinois, 1895).

At a court of this society, held in Chicago, Ill., on February 23, 1989, . . . the following resolutions, presented by Captain Philip Reade, U.S Army were adopted, . . .

"The Society of Colonial Wars, in the state of Illinois, solicits its representatives in Congress . . . to pass a bill which shall provide that any person or persons who shall manufacture or use the national flag, or the national coat-of-arms, or a pattern thereof, either by printing, painting, or otherwise attaching to the same any advertisements for private gain by public display or distribution, shall be guilty of a misdemeanor, and, on conviction, be fined in a sum not exceeding $1,000, or be imprisoned for a term not exceeding 100 days, or both, . . . It further solicits in support of this proposed enactment the co-operation of every military, loyal, patriotic and hereditary-patriotic society in the United States." . . .

Captain Philip Reade, U. S. Army, Governor of the Society, appointed as his colleagues [to form a National Flag Committee under this resolution] Mr. Charles Kingsbury Miller and Colonel Henry Lathrop Turner, Illinois National Guard. . . .Captain Reade and Mr. Miller then began recording the name and address, location, etc., of every corporation and organization, firm or individual known and observed by them to use the national flag, coat-of-arms, or a pattern thereof, for private gain by public display or distribution.

Violations of the proposed law were found to be so numerous, flagrant, ingenious and startling in Chicago alone that it was determined for the purposes of this report to name only about one hundred of them. . . . Here are some of the occupations, appliances, stores, uses, persons, articles, occasions, places, trade marks, organizations, firms, advertisements in which, by which, where, how or by whom Old Glory, whereof poets rhapsodize, musicians sing, politicians declaim, historians write and patriots die, the national flag of this country or its pattern, is treated with grave disrespect or used for mercenary purposes in the city of Chicago, viz:

Auction Stores,	Exchange Saloons,	Refrigerator Cars,
Awning Makers,	Festival Halls,	Restaurants,
Bicycles,	Fire Works Stores,	Roof Gardens,
Belts,	Fancy Photographs,	Real Estate Booths,
Breech-clouts,	Furriers,	Regalia Companies,

Boat-houses,
Bock-beer Advertisements,
Bar-rooms,
Barbers' Poles,
Barber Shops,
Banner decorations,
Base-ball Grounds,
Breweries,
Beer Gardens,
Beer Saloons,
Bottling Companies,
Blotting Pads,
Burlesque Shows,
Bill-board Posters,
Circus Clowns,
Cigar Makers,
Carriage Cushions,
Chewing Gum,
Charity Balls,
Chimney Sweeps,
Christian Endeavor Badges,
Cuff Buttons,
Coat Racks,
Confectionery Boxes,
Covers for S't Venders Stands
Cotton Mills Trade-mark,
Decoration—Dept. Stores,
Dime Museums,
Dental Associations,
Door Mats,
Dress for Ballet Dancers,
Drug Stores,
Drapery,
Dry Goods,

Fish Houses,
Figure-heads for Vessels,
Furniture Vans,
Grocery Stores,
Hat Booths,
Hardware Stores,
Hotel Attractions,
Ice Companies,
Japanese Auction Store,
Japanese Goods,
Labels on Cigar Boxes,
Lapel Buttons,
Laundry Wagons,
Lemon Wrappers,
Liquor Stores,
Lemonade Stands,
"Living Pictures,"
Music Covers,
Mineral Water Labels,
"Old Glory" Saloons,
"Old Glory" Lunch Room,
Piano Makers,
Picnic Grounds,
Patent Medicines,
Personal Adornments,
Political Clubs,
Partitioning Rooms,
Polo Games,
Poolrooms,
Pails,
Pocket Handkerchiefs,
Panoramas,
Pillow Covers,
Paper Napkins,
Portieres,
Pyrotechnic Advertisements,
Prize Fighters,

Railroad Advertisements,
Salvation Army Meetings,
"Street Fakirs,"
Sashes,
Shoe Stores,
Sample Rooms,
Sign Painters,
Soap Makers,
Scenic Decorations,
Storage Warehouses,
Saloons,
Soda Water Fountains,
Society Pins,
"Shooting the Chutes,"
Shooting Galleries,
Stage Display,
Steamship Companies,
Tar Soap,
Tailoring Establishments,
Tent Makers,
Theatres,
Theatrical Plays,
Toy Manufacturers,
Tobacco Dealers,
Transom Screens,
Trade Mk's Domestic Fabr's,
Variety Halls,
Vaudeville Shows,
Warehouse Advertisements,
Wagon Decorating,
War Dramas,
War Museums,
Water Carnivals,
Window Shades,
Whisky Barrels,
Whisky Bottles,

This society desires to show that it believes the national flag to be the noblest ensign ever floated. We believe that it should not be desecrated to party uses. It should be kept uncontaminated by politics as by trade. The people who would use it for either for selfish purposes are not true Americans in fact or in spirit. They would be just as ready to prostitute any sacred emblem to their selfish partisan ends. Old Glory is too sacred a symbol to be misused by any party, creed or faction. At the various meetings of our society the sentiments have been enthusiastically endorsed. . . .

On June 14th, '95, the daily *Inter Ocean*, of Chicago, editorially published an article with the right ring in it, and we give it below . . . :

" . . . It is too often a source of annoyance and humiliation to every true American citizen to see the national stars and stripes desecrated with the advertisements of merchants and mountebanks of every description, mostly ignorant and foolish folk who fancy this singular method of announcing their wares attracts favorable public attention, whereas, on the contrary, it evokes the indignation and disgust of all who have the honor of the Nation at heart and often materially injures the business of the flag-desecrators.

"Among the patriotic societies which are actively working toward the abolition of this national scandal and the protection of the flag from sordid business sharks of every kind, is the Society of Colonial Wars, of this city. . . .

"The Grand Army of the Republic (Department of Illinois), the Sons of the Revolution, . . . Sons of the American Revolution, Regular Army and Navy Union, and various other organizations have passed resolutions promising their active co-operation in the matter. . . ."

A principle is at stake. We cannot believe that there is indifference. We believe that a part of the problem of self-government is to show respect for the national flag by protecting it from the selfish mercenary hucksters and tricksters who use it for purposes of private and commercial gain, and who thus divorce it from the legitimate place and uses, all for individual or corporate emolument.

Whether you be of the rich or the poor, whether Catholic or Protestant, whether your parents be native born Americans or foreign born, whatever be the character of the homes from which you come, the first great duty of every citizen is loyalty to the flag and the principles for which it stands. The responsibility of citizenship is upon all who read these lines. The flag is a part of the history of this nation. It is an inspiration. Be staunch to it. It is our greater self. We violate a sacred trust if we do not cherish and protect it. It is the obligation of American citizenship. The multisms of anarchy and unrest in our midst to-day are evidence of a disregard for law and a yearning for the kind of liberty that knows no bounds. . . .

Every people has some emblem which is the symbol to them of all that is good and great in their country, the embodiment of all the principle and institutions which place their native land far above all other lands in the love and veneration of its inhabitants. In modern nations this patriotic love and reverence is centered in the flag. In this country there is more than common reason why our starry flag should be honored and admired. It is intrinsically beautiful, with its brilliant colors and simple, expensive design, which cannot be said of many of the world's flags. Its history is clear; it is a flag of peace; it has never been carried by any army of oppression, which went forth for conquest, animated only by greed of gain; it has never floated cruelly over scenes of ruin, plunders and carnage for the sake of ministering to the ambition of kings. But where high principles were in danger, where the liberty of its humblest subject was touched, where oppression or tyranny dared intrude, there its stars have always blazed with a wrathful flame and its red stripes have symbolized the punishment our country's enemies should receive at our hands.

It means all that is good and true and pure and beautiful in a land of freedom. It is far worthier of self-sacrifice and heroic devotion than any goddess of the olden time. . . .

We like to see "Old Glory" flutter everywhere in the breeze provided it is not accompanied by any sign, lettering, printing or painting to indicate that the display is to attract attention to any matter of profit, meretricious object, political purpose or private gain. . . .

We solicit state legislators to, by formal resolution, take action regarding the passage by Congress of a law that will protect the national flag, the national coat-of-arms and their patterns from the disrespectful uses that we have, in part, pointed out. . . .

Document 2.3

Report of flag desecration during the 1896 presidential campaign.

Source: New York Times, Nov. 1, 1896.

THE FLAG BURNED

A BRYAN CROWD IN MISSOURI INSULTS THE NATIONAL COLORS

Sedalia, Mo., Oct. 31–The Stars and Stripes were burned at Pleasant Hill, Cass County, this afternoon, by the followers of William J. Bryan.

A Bryan demonstration was being held in the town, and the sight of a sound-money [McKinley] excursion from Harrisonville set the Bryanites wild with rage. Little "Ollie" Wheeler, the five-year-old daughter of Samuel Wheeler, who had been singing sound-money songs on the trip, stepped upon the rear platform of the coach, bearing in her hands a small flag. Almost instantly a man carrying a Bryan banner snatched the flag and carried it a few feet distant to a spot where they were burning the sound-money literature that had been distributed, and the flag was consigned to the flames.

One wearer of a Bryan button, however, tore it from his coat and threw it to the ground, remarking, "This is a disgrace and I'll never be caught in another Bryan crowd."

Document 2.4

1897 petition to Congress, organized by the Milwaukee Daughters of the American Revolution and endorsed by the national DAR, calling for passage of a national flag desecration law.

Source: National Archives, Record Group 233, HR 56A-19.2.

The following circular, and the draft of a "Bill to prevent desecration of the National Flag," which will come before Congress this winter, with a brief statement concerning the necessity for such a bill, are herewith presented for your careful consideration. The strong sentiment upon this matter, which exists among earnest and patriotic men and women, is united in support of Congressional action. Patriotism is more than a mere catchword, and as surely as the love of country burns deep in the hearts of the people, just as surely do acts of vandalism and insult to the National flag arouse feelings of anger and resentment. The sense of shame and indignation spreads and deepens, and voices have been heard in all parts of our land demanding that these outrages and indignities should cease. Military and patriotic societies have come forward with urgent requests for the action of the National Government to protect its emblem from desecration. The veterans of the Grand Army of the Republic and the Loyal Legion, the ex-Confederate Veterans, the younger men of the National Guard who are sworn to preserve it, and the various societies of descendants of the early patriots who gave it to us, all unite in a ringing call for protection for the flag.

It should hardly be a question for argument whether a man may wantonly and maliciously tear our country's flag to shreds or trample it into the mire; hardly less of a question whether it ought to be used as a vehicle of advertisement for patent nostrums or intoxicating liquors, yet instances of such misuse are too well known; and with such associations may also be classed those of political partisanship with their accompaniments of intense and bitter feeling, rancor and turbulence. All of which bring neither glory nor benefit to the flag, or to those who are bound to honor and protect it.

The last presidential campaign forced upon many the unwelcome recognition of the fact that although in time of war our flag was a sacred emblem to be treated with respect by all even upon penalty of death, in the piping times of peace it might be treated with any conceivable indignity, like the veriest rag of the street. That this statement may not be considered exaggeration, the following instances are given, which were matters of public knowledge . . . notices of which were wide-spread in the newspapers at the time of the occurrences:

In the rooms of the Madison Circuit and district Court of Anderson, Ind., paper flags bearing pictures of political candidates were torn down and trampled upon.

A stranger in Council Bluffs, Iowa, rode up to a large American flag bearing a partisan banner and fired upon it with a shotgun. A soldier shot at the mounted assailant of the flag, killing the horse and wounding the man, who escaped. . . .

A large American flag, bearing a banner with a partisan motto, the property of a citizen, was suspended across the principal street of Hammond, Ind., from a private residence. After having been repeatedly threatened the flag was torn down in the early morning and trampled into the mud.

Clubs of opposing political parties met at the railroad station at Janesville, Wis., with the result that a National flag was rotten-egged and torn.

At Waukeshau, Wis., a large silk flag, bearing no emblem whatever, flying from a flag-staff upon a street corner, the property of a political club, was pulled down, torn to shreds, and the fragments trampled into the mud.

In Chicago, a large number of the flags bearing pictures of political candidates were spread over the floor of the headquarters of an opposing party and ostentatiously used for wiping muddy boots, and for the reception of tobacco juice. . . .

A procession marched unmolested through the streets of Lafayette, Ill., bearing the red flag and trailing the American flag through the filth of the street. . . .

Many similar occurrences are known to have taken place in other states than those named. The evil is widespread, not local, and the feeling is apparent everywhere that the flag can be treated with disrespect, intentionally, and without fear of punishment. . . .

It is necessary that the United States Government should hold the National Standard in its strong grasp and warn off all those who would treat it with indignity. . . .

Document 2.5

Address delivered by Charles Kingsbury Miller at an Illinois SAR banquet, Chicago, November 2, 1898.

Source: Pamphlet, "Desecration of the American Flag and Prohibitive Legislation."

Among all the nations of the earth we present the unique example of a people permitting its national flag—the emblem of their civil, political and religious liberty—to be pulled down, torn into shreds, spat upon, dragged in the dust, trampled under foot and otherwise treated with contumely, without legal means to prevent or punish the perpetrators of these offenses against patriotic respect. . . .

In our young republic, devoid of traditions, with a mixed population, augmented by constant arrivals from foreign shores, our government needs a national law to teach these newcomers to this land of liberty, as well as to remind our thoughtless but well-meaning citizens that they must treat with public respect the flag which represents all that makes us noble as a nation. . . .

Political parties of every faction use the American flag as a floating signboard, bearing the names of candidates, hanging it over the streets, in front of saloons, in the precincts of slums, and from businessmen's clubs in the most prominent thoroughfares, while commercial piratism has seized the flag and made it a universal agent for advertising their wares and patent nostrums, until the leperized taint of private gain seems to have blighted the sentiment of patriotic reverence. . . .

The national flag is converted into grotesque coats for negro minstrels, decorative skirts for ballet dancers, manufactured into picture mats with openings cut to admit different size photographs, and is used as fancy dog blankets and equine fly nets in civic celebrations. . . .

The first misuse of the flag began in thoughtlessness. Its sacredness encroached upon by the great political parties and the janizaries of trade, is a wrong to our nation. It sets a bad example to the lower classes, who degrade the flag to its nadir; and has deadened the sentiment that the emblem of our republic should be kept as inviolate as was the Holy of Holies in King Solomon's temple. . . .

The multitude of uneducated foreigners who land upon our friendly shores are ignorant of everything pertaining to American institutions, even after many years' residence, coming solely to better their condition, while the world's enemies, the anarchists, flock to this country to find a safe and free asylum. As a result of these changes, we observe our flag no longer protected by the sentiment of a century ago, but treated with open disrespect; . . . In the sunshine of peace, the soldiers in the ranks of commerce, waging their mercenary warfare for the capture of the almighty dollar, do not seek their inspiration in looking up to the national colors flying above them, but in gazing down at the flag, printed on their trade-marks, which booms their wares, gains the coveted dollar, and is then flung like an outcast into the dust of disrespect. . . .

Our patriotism must not be endangered, nor our national pride humiliated by the widespread desecration of the flag. Those three sacred jewels, the Bible, the Cross and the Flag, command our national reverence. . . . Expansive America—the growing power of civilization—absorbing new races, needs a flag law. Our public officials, acting under a flag openly degraded, battle with the lath of a manikin against the spirit of lawlessness and license, which this disrespect encourages in the leaders of mobs and misguided strikers of labor unions. . . . The seeds of contempt sown by public disrespect have already sprung up and grown into plants, manifested in part in anarchy and murderous labor riots. . . .

Document 2.6

Article by Charles Kingsbury Miller.

Source: "A Nation's Disgrace," *The Spirit of '76,* Apr. 1899.

A few years since the battle-cry of the great [1894] railroad strike in Chicago was, "To hell with the American government and its flag," Judge Waterman of the criminal court in the same city recently said in a public address, "There is not another country on the globe where the children are so lawless and degenerate as in the United States." . . .

The unusual liberty in this country is understood as license, by the lowest class of the foreign born. . . . We may have to grapple with a social problem that will bear a very ugly resemblance to the social upheavals with which Monarchial governments have to struggle. The beginning of a conflagration is easily extinguished—the time has come for this nation to teach its first lesson in domestic respect—the text of which we will find in a national law protecting the national colors.

The United States has now taken her place as one of the Family of Nations, but unlike all other nations, she permits her national flag to be insulted within her own borders—and through the open opposition of [Senate Judiciary Committee Chairman] Senator Hoar and the concealed opposition of [House Judiciary Committee Chairman] Representative Henderson, our societies feel that while these chairmen block the doors of their respective judiciary committees, none of the various flag bills which have been trapped there, as flies in the spider's web, will ever be able to struggle out. . . .

[Henderson] expressed his sentiments one day in the committee room, saying . . . that "he hoped the American people would continue to wrap hams in the flag, not to teach patriotism but to teach ham eaters to eat American hams." . . . How will the suggestion of Congressman Henderson, to use our national flag for ham wrappers, fall upon the ears and sink into the hearts of our soldiers in the Philippine Islands—in Cuba—in Puerto Rico—and the soldiers at home. . . .

Those who are working for flag legislation will welcome a change in the House Chairmanship, which will relieve them of Dictator Henderson

. . . [who has] stifled and entombed [all flag legislation] in the judiciary committee—which Congressman Henderson holds by the scruff of the neck. . . .

Document 2.7

Pamphlet by Charles Kingsbury Miller.

Source: "The United States Flag Dishonored and Disgraced in America, Cuba and the Philippine Islands," Dec. 3, 1901.

The red flag of danger flies in America. Anarchy is rampant, striking down the chief magistrates of our nation [a reference to the assassination of President McKinley]—increasing pauper immigration is deteriorating our citizenship—railroad trains are robbed from the Atlantic to the Pacific slope—a scattered army of two hundred thousand tramps commit depredations [a reference to "Coxey's Army" of the unemployed during the 1894 depression?]—gigantic trusts and combinations stifle competition in every State in the Union—the emblem of our country is desecrated by commercial vandalism, and treated with the utmost disrespect in our own land by our own citizens, our national government knowingly permits its degradation, and is stolidly indifferent to public appeals for protection of the flag from domestic assaults on its sacred character. . . .

Had Congress heeded the voice of our people, by enacting a moderate law in 1894, to exclude anarchists from our country the assassination of President McKinley would not have occurred [in fact, McKinley's assassin was neither an alien nor an anarchist]. A flag law is similarly needed to end the abuses of our nation's emblem, which inoculates the minds of our large and mixed population, unable and untrained, to discriminate between the government and its symbol, with contemptuous disrespect of the government which permits the desecration of its national flag. What will the present Congress do with the red flag of anarchy and what action will they take for protecting the honor of the American flag?

Document 2.8

Report of the DAR Flag Committee, chaired by Frances Saunders Kempster, to the 1899 DAR National Convention.

Source: American Monthly Magazine, Apr. 1899, 903–7.

First let me say for all the workers in this effort for a law, that we want the flag used as freely as possible. We want it upon the school houses and national buildings. We want the flag with its symbolism of loyalty and fidelity—like the unchanging stars in the sky—with its purity of devotion, with all it typifies of agony and of sublime self-sacrifice, held free and pure and sacred as the cross. It has been contaminated by the greed of gain until it has been dragged down to the vilest associations. It has been used as a trade mark of party patriotism. It has been a frequent participant of street broils and riots, and the recipient of rotten eggs, tobacco juice and street filth. . . . We shed tears of sympathy as we hear of the deeds of the lion-hearted of our land, and then do we look on serene and unmoved at the daily and hourly mockery and degradation of the emblem of all the blood-shed and glory of our national history? . . .

At the present time there are few great nations but have laws to pre-serve their flag from desecration, and all consider their national ensign sacred, not to be sullied by love of gain, not to be at the mercy of the reckless, the evil-minded nor the anarchist. . . .

In 1896, during the political campaign, . . . [the daily press reported] various forms of insult and vandalism offered the national flag. . . . [T]o stand by, indifferent to such maltreatment, was like watching undisturbed while sacred altars were being dishonored, for upon what altar has greater, richer sacrifices been poured than upon this altar of our country, in de-fense of this flag of freedom? . . .

The flag bill endorsed by the National Society, Daughters of the Amer-ican Revolution, will be introduced into the United States Congress at its session next winter and the Flag Committee asks you to bring every possi-ble influence to bear upon your members of Congress. . . . The Daughters ask for a law "to prevent the use of the flag for advertisement, to prevent placing upon it or attaching to it, devices and inscriptions, and to punish those who treat it with indignity, or wantonly injure or destroy it." The Flag Committee for the Daughters appeals to you for your interest in this bill, not because it is a work begun by the Daughters, but because no other flag bill before Congress, or indeed, ever presented to Congress, has pro-vided against the three forms of desecration which prevail, and without these three provisions, no law can preserve our flag from desecration.

The terms in which it is expressed are of small moment. We ask for the substance; we do not care for its shadow; we ask Congress to take our flag, held in such reverence by our soldiers and sailors, out of the depths to which it has been dragged by the various forms of advertisement; out of the associations which invite wanton insult. We ask them to declare to the fomenter of sedition and to the anarchist, that the flag must be respected, and to show to the children of those new to our country and its institu-tions that it is a standard to be loved and honored. . . .

Let us keep pure and uncontaminated that which has been christened and hallowed by such prodigal outpouring of noble blood. We ask you to rescue our flag from its position, as a coiner of patriots' blood into traders'

gold, to shield it from indecent and insulting treatment which follow its
seizure for political profit and which are unavoidable when the Nation's
banner is brought into street fights, and used as a trade-mark of party
patriotism.

We plead with you as Daughters descended from those who kept all
sacred things pure and holy, who suffered and endured all things to give us
a flag and a country, that you go back to all parts of this great land and
arouse your people in each corner and district of your State with such
ardor, that our representatives in Congress cannot another year refuse to
grant our prayer, that the Government itself shall respect the dignity of our
flag, shall hold aloof its ensign, pure and unsullied, demanding respect and
honor from all who are sheltered by its folds.

Document 2.9

Report of the SAR Flag Committee, chaired by Col. Ralph Prime, to the
1903 SAR Convention.

Source: 1903 National Year Book, National Society of the Sons of the American
Revolution, 114–16.

COLONEL PRIME: . . . You have heretofore been informed that the Sons of
the American Revolution started the campaign in the defense of the American Flag from desecration. . . . Almost immediately other Flag Committees
were appointed by the different patriotic societies, and in the month of
August [1897], at a convention held in New York the American Flag Association was formed, consisting of the members of the Flag Committees of
all the patriotic societies. Since that time the American Flag Association
has been engaged in obtaining legislation to protect the Flag from desecration in the different states of the Union. Down to this time we have obtained legislation in twenty-five states. . . .

[W]e have had, for the last five or six years, before every Session of
Congress, a National bill to reach the evil in all of the states and territories
and in the District of Columbia; but we have been unable, on account of
great political questions which have crowded out everything except those
political questions, to obtain any action on the part of the National Congress. But within a few months past the Commissioner of Patents made a
decision in which he reviewed the subject of the use of the Flag and decided that thereafter no copyrights would be permitted or registered by the
United States Government which used the Flag, or anything like the Flag,
in any registration of a copyright, so that we have, to that extent, the
National Government with us. (Applause.)

I need not recite to you what are the abuses of the Flag which have been understood to be included in the expression desecration of the Flag, but when you come to remember that the use of the Flag upon the label of a whiskey bottle, or as the covering to the bung-hole of a lager beer cask, or painted as an advertisement upon the side of the wagon that conveys lager beer barrels around through our cities, or that puts the Flag as a means of advertising any merchandise, you will see at once many of the desecrations to which the Flag is put; and I could name others to you which are simply disgracing and are literally unmentionable. It is to reach all of these, as well as the desecration of the Flag itself, that we are endeavoring to obtain legislation. You will see how necessary it is not to confine the legislation to simply the word "Flag," but that it should be described in some inclusive way so as to take in that which we recognize as the Flag and yet which, by reason of the absence of a star or the use of different material from the legal material, is not in fact the legal flag. . . .

I might, as I say, mention many of the evasions which there are all over the country in the use of so popular a symbol as the United States flag in order to draw attention to and advertise merchandise and the receptacles of merchandise. Now you will see, Compatriots, that we have list of twenty-five of the states which you may call the Northern states, that have already enacted legislation . . . and we would that our Southern brethren would come in with us and take hold of the matter and obtain the same legislation in the Southern States. We are engaged in this campaign, all of the Flag Committees, the Flag Committee of the Congress of the National Society of the Sons of the American Revolution as well as others, not out of any personal desire or society desire to have any credit to ourselves; and yet we regret that there are those who at once take to themselves the credit of having procured legislation which they have had nothing whatever to do with. . . .

Document 2.10

Report of the GAR Flag Committee to the 1903 GAR Convention.

Source: Journal of the 37th National Encampment of the GAR, 1903, 183–84.

It is difficult for a committee so widely separated and unable to meet together to accomplish much as a body, but I think each individual member has tried to do all in his power to help the American Flag Association, of which our committee is a part, to obtain Flag Legislation. . . . It is unfortunate that a proper flag law to prevent the desecration of the American Flag has not yet been passed by the Congress of the United States. Too many forms have been presented which have not helped to obtain legislation. A bill has been prepared by the American Flag Association which, I think, covers all points necessary and all should unite on this bill. Surely, those who followed " Old Glory" in war and were willing to die for it and what it represented should now use all the influence in their power and urge the Senators and members of Congress from their States to pass this bill without delay.

Document 2.11

1900 *Circular of Information* of the American Flag Association.

Form of Legislative Act recommended by the Executive Committee of the American Flag Association, to be used to obtain legislation to protect the flag from desecration. . . .

Section I. Any person who in any manner, for exhibition or display shall place or cause to be placed, any words or marks or inscriptions or picture or design or device or symbol or token or notice or drawing or advertisement of any nature whatever upon any flag, standard, color or ensign of the United States, or shall expose or shall cause to be exposed to public view any such flag, standard, color or ensign of the United States upon which shall be printed, painted or otherwise placed or which shall be attached, appended, affixed or annexed any words, or figures, or numbers or marks, or inscriptions or picture or design or device or symbol or token or notice or drawing or any advertisement of any nature or kind whatever, or who shall expose to public view or shall manufacture or sell or expose for sale or have in possession for sale or for use any article or thing or substance being an article of merchandise or a receptacle of merchandise upon which shall have been printed, painted or otherwise placed, a representation of any such flag, standard, color or ensign of the United States, to advertise or call attention to or to decorate or to ornament or to mark or to distinguish the article or thing on which so placed, or shall publicly mutilate, trample upon or publicly deface, or defy, or defile, or cast contempt, either by words or act, upon any such flag, standard, color or ensign of the United States shall be guilty of a misdemeanor.

Section 2. The words flag, standard, color or ensign of the United States as used in this act shall include any flag, any standard, any color or any ensign or any representation of a flag, standard, color or ensign or a picture of a flag, standard, color or ensign made of any substance whatever or represented on any substance whatever, and of any size whatever evidently purporting to be either of said flag, standard, color or ensign of the United States or a picture or a representation of either thereof, upon which shall be shown the colors, the stars and the stripes in any number in either thereof or by which the person seeing the same without deliberation may believe the same to represent the flag or the colors or the standard or the ensign of the United States of America. . . .

Document 2.12

1905–6 *Circular of Information* of the American Flag Association.

Since 1897 legislation to preserve the flag from desecrating uses has been obtained in Maine (1899), New Hampshire (1899), Vermont (1898), Massachusetts (1899), Rhode Island (1903), Connecticut (1905), New York (1905), New Jersey (1904), Pennsylvania (1897), Delaware (1903), Maryland (1902), Ohio (1902), Michigan (1901), Indiana (1901), Illinois (1899), Wisconsin (1901), Minnesota (1899), North Dakota (1905), South Dakota (1901), Montana (1905), Idaho (1905), Iowa (1900), Missouri (1903), Kansas (1905), Nebraska (1903), Colorado (1901), Utah (1903), Wyoming (1905), New Mexico (1903), Arizona (1899), California (1899), Oregon (1901), Washington (1904), and Puerto Rico (1904). The statutes of the United States have also forbidden the use of the Flag in registration of trade marks. . . .

The form of legislative act printed in this pamphlet [see document 2.11] . . . has been prepared and approved by the Executive Committee of the American Flag Association as a result of the study of the whole subject, . . . and observations of the evils to be prevented and such form of bill is drafted to prevent:

1. Attaching to or writing anything whatever on the flag; or

2. Using pictures of the flag for any purpose of advertising.

3. The bill also is drafted so as to reach and prevent the use of flags varying in the number of stars from the actual number of States (thus ceasing to be the legal flag) or varying from the legal size and legal material. Each of these is claimed to remove the flag from the name of the flag of the United States of America, . . .

Some of the desecrations of the flag which have come to the notice of the Association are:

1. Attaching to the flag political tickets.

2. Attaching to the flag advertisements.

3. Writing or printing commercial advertisements upon the white stripes of the flag.

4. Attaching to the flag advertisements, or writing on the white stripes of the flag advertisements, some of which are of bicycles, bock beer, whiskey, fine cambric, bone knoll, sour mash, tar soap, American pepsin chewing gum, theatres, tobacco, Japan tea, awnings, breweries, cigars, charity

balls, cuff buttons, dime museums, floor mats, fireworks, furriers, living pictures, picnic grounds, patent medicines, poolrooms, prize fights, restaurants, roof gardens, real estate agencies, sample rooms, shoe stores, soap makers, saloons, shooting galleries, tent makers, variety shows, venders of lemon acid, and for awnings and a host of others.

5. Printing the flag on thin paper and using for wrapping of lemons, oranges, fruits, small cheeses, hams, spools of thread, soap, chewing gum, fireworks, cigars, etc.

6. Printing the flag on paper and pasting upon casks of beer and ale, and bottles of whiskey and other liquors.

7. Printing the flag on the back of trolley transfer tickets to advertise brewing companies and placing upon the white stripes the words, "Stands for the best beer."

8. Printing the flag on confectionery boxes, boxes of chewing gum, trolley car transfer tickets, pillow covers, door mats, paper napkins, handkerchiefs, blotting pads, water-closet paper, etc.

9. Printing the flag on the sides of wagons with advertisements of business.

10. Printing upon and burning pictures of the flag into porcelain or crockery water closets and urinals.

11. Using the flag for clouts of prize fighters, and of contestants in foot races and bicycle races.

12. Making clothing of the flag for clowns, representations of Uncle Sam and of Columbia.

13. The flag has been used for sacks to contain coal and other merchandise.

14. The flag has been stripped from the staff and torn in shreds and stamped upon by anarchists and others in excitement and in anger. . . .

Regulations of Foreign Countries.

It seems to us that there is no reason for looking for a precedent in the legal regulations of foreign countries as to their flag. Our people are not like the people of other lands. The freedom we enjoy induces the abuses with us which we do not observe abroad. Commercialism run wild with us tends to these abuses unless restrained.

Yet so far as we are informed and as far as we are able to learn as to the regulations of other countries, the following are said to be some of the penal provisions of other countries as to the misuse of flags of those countries:—

Italy.—Law of June 30, 1889, article 15, 115: "Whoever with intention of contempt should take same, destroy or insult in a public place, or in a place open to the public, the flag, or any other emblem of the state, will be punished by detention from three to twenty months."

Austria-Hungary.—The Hungarian criminal law, 50, of 1879, paragraph 37, says: " No more than two months arrest and not more than 300 florins fine should be inflicted upon any one * * * who, with intent to insult, defiles, damages or tears down the flag or coat of arms publicly, used as the insignia of either civil or military authority."

Germany.—Articles 135, 303, inflict a fine up to 300 thalers, or punished with imprisonment up to two years.

Greece.—Act 141 of the penal code provides imprisonment and prosecution by the district attorney of the place in which the outrage to the flag is committed, with incarceration for three months maximum.

Russia.—Penalty is two to nineteen years in jail.

Brazil.—Article 100 of penal code, for desecration of national colors, has a penalty of imprisonment for not less than six months to one year. Decree number 3346, of the fourteenth of October, 1887, places the penalty of insult to the flag at $100 to $500.

Mexico.—Has a legal provision against the desecration of or insult to the national colors.

China.—Punishment under one of the laws relating to the desecration of insignia.

Spain.—The penal code provides a penalty for insult to or desecration of the national flag.

Portugal.—Penal code, articles 424, 181, Six months to one year's imprisonment.

France.—Desecration of the national flag, punishable under sections 257, 379 and 475 of penal code.

Great Britain.—Outrages to the national colors can be dealt with under the laws dealing with sedition or treason. . . .

Chile, Peru, Bulgaria, Rumania, Belgium and all other foreign governments which have no special legal provision can bring an action before either the civil or military tribunals for any injudicious use of its national flag under a general provision of the code. . . .

1904. President's Address [by Col. Ralph Prime]

Our work has gone on during the past year not without some successes. . . . So that we now have flag legislation written upon the statute books of [twenty-six states and two territories] forming a continuous and unbroken chain from the Atlantic to the Pacific, and embracing every Northern State excepting only North Dakota, Montana, Wyoming, Kansas and Nevada. . . .

But what am I to say about the so-called Southern States. Are they to remain out of this patriotic column? In none of them have we yet succeeded in making an impression. There is nothing political in the question, nor anything sectional, and yet . . . none of them have listened to our appeal. I seriously suggest to you that at this meeting you consider this subject and devise some means by which we can reach the patriotic sentiment of the patriotic people in those thirteen Southern States. . . .

Your President, with a committee consisting of representatives from the different societies, appeared on February 20, 1902, before the Military Committee of the United States Senate, and argued in behalf of legislation by Congress [document 2.14]. . . . [The legislation] slept a sleep of two years, but] on March 1, 1904, a Flag Bill was passed by the Senate of the United States. It was not as comprehensive and clear a bill as we could have desired, but it nevertheless was a most material step in advance. . . .

Instances of desecration of the flag in other States have come to our attention. A gross and outrageous act of desecration came to our notice from the Territory of Arizona. As a part of the union labor troubles in that State, a large print or placard of the flag was largely posted; the forty-five stars being replaced with descriptions of men labeled as "scabs," and the stripes of the flag were used upon which to print offensive, opprobrious, and to some extent obscene and ribald attacks upon the men named as "scabs." It was a dastardly attempt to drag into the union and non-union controversies the flag of our country, and to cover it with obloquy; this at the hands of the representatives of union labor. Such acts can never redound to the benefit of the labor element. They will most certainly alienate further and further all sympathy for the lawless leaders of union labor. It is to be regretted that such acts are very hard to disassociate from individuals who are leaders in the labor troubles, and they must necessarily fall to the act of the whole of the labor element, when the flag comes to be used in that way by any labor leaders. We are glad to learn that the authorities of Arizona were with all their energy seeking to arrest and punish under the Flag Law of that Territory the perpetrators of the outrage.

Another very like act of desecration we learn of from Colorado. There too the labor element undertook to use the flag for purposes of abusing the non-union element and citizens generally who did not join in the ranks of the union labor leaders in their campaign of violence. A large placard of the flag printed in colors was used, upon the stripes of which were printed in violent, outrageous and threatening language attacks against the press, the militia, the courts, the Citizens' Association, and in fact every ministry of law and order [document 3.11]. . . .

A statute of such wide-spread application as the Flag Law we must expect will apply with great force upon many people who have been accustomed to ride rough shod over the patriotic sensibilities of our American people, and will find much opposition among that class among whom commercialism is higher than patriotism.

I may also say that it behooves us as patriotic citizens never to buy, or traffic in, nor to give our consent to the traffic in merchandise, upon which the flag is imprinted, or which is advertised by the flag. This is not the reprehensible boycotting of a merchant [a reference to labor boycotts in trade union disputes], and is but the patriotic and justifiable refusal to purchase from him the particular article which he advertises with the flag. Surely a vast difference is apparent between the boycotting of a merchant and the refusal to purchase a particular article that he thus offensively thrusts upon us. . . .

It is with exceeding regret that I find so many who are far more anxious to be acknowledged to be first in this good work than to be very influential and potent in the work. The strife in such a patriotic matter to be first and to put the personal pronoun I above everything else, is quite as lamentable as the commercialism which desecrates the flag is despicable. Let us go forward and insist upon all others going forward with us to attain the one object, without any satisfaction to be obtained by any personal honor or glory. . . .

1905. President's Address [by Col. Ralph Prime]

. . . During the first session of the last Congress a bill was passed by the United States Senate in the line of preventing flag desecration. . . . But when the bill reached the House of Representatives, by reason largely of the un-American and modern way of conducting business in that House, so utterly subversive of the genius of our country, and quite like the influence exercised by the Czar of Russia over the people of his country, and by which the elected representatives of the people in the popular house of Congress are throttled and silenced, and not permitted to be heard or to move legislation, this subject could never be brought to the front, and congressional legislation, as in other years, failed. . . .

For several years the Department of the Interior has refused to register trade-marks which contain pictures of the flag, or parts of the flag, or the stars or the stripes, or even the use in combination of the colors of the flag, . . . the acts being held to be contrary to public policy and good citizenship and national honor. These decisions of the Department, judicial in their nature, were at the last session of Congress supplemented by a new general act concerning the registration of trade-marks, broadly forbidding the registration of a trade-mark containing as a part of any device a picture of the flag of the United States. This legislation is a step forward, and must sooner or later be succeeded by the very legislation which we desire to obtain from Congress in the shape of a Federal statute.

In connection with this matter of legislation, I fervently wish that we could be content to work as patriots for the cause and for love of it, without the vain glory of any desire for credit to any man for what he does over another. . . . Let us be ashamed to be classed with one of our patriotic societies which year after year publicly lays claim to credit for every statute no matter when passed, and no member of which society has ever lent the slightest aid to obtaining that which they claim was wholly done by them alone. . . .

Document 2.13

1907–8 Circular of Information of the American Flag Association.

The finances of the Association require some attention. The expense of the odd years amounts to about $100 per year, and of every other year to about $300 per year. This small sum in each case covers the expense of printing, of postage, of expressage and other necessary and incidental expenses in the carrying on of the work, and in the year requiring the larger sum, it covers also the issuing every two years of your circular of information. . . . Some patriotic societies make a contribution each year; others do not. Please give your attention and thought to this matter and inaugurate a movement which shall keep our treasury supplied with the small sum necessary to carry on the work of the Association.

ANNUAL ADDRESS by the PRESIDENT, Col. Ralph E. Prime, June 14, 1907

Ladies and Gentlemen, members of the American Flag Association.—I congratulate you upon this, the eleventh annual meeting of the Association, completing ten years of successful work. When we met and organized the Association in the City Hall [in 1897], in the city of New York, none of us probably had any conception of what there was before us to do, nor any defined plan of work. I would not for a moment assume but that the mass of our fellow citizens who have preceded us, during the life of our country, had less reverence and respect for, and love of, that flag, the emblem of our nationality, but in those times, . . . the greed of gain and the passions of men had not led them to forget what was due to the country that protected them, their lives, their property and their families, as to do outrageous acts of desecration, such acts as we have come to be accustomed to see. The situation culminated in the presidential campaign of 1896, when political rancor ran so high, and political excitement knew no bounds, and both at the east and at the west of our country, infuriated partisanship was manifested in tearing down the Flag, tearing it in pieces, and trampling it in the dust; when eastern and western political parties, each assuming that they alone represented the patriotism of the country, advertised their political candidates by attaching their names and pictures to the Flag, or writing their names upon the white stripes of the Flag, when our country was flooded with merchandise advertised by pictures of the flag, and in some instances indelibly burned into the material of which the merchandise was made. Such a condition of things called forth a resentment which roused liberty-loving and patriotic people to put an end to such forms of desecration. . . .

Congress was open to listen to us, but there was no money in our quest, and no politics in it, and the hearings that we obtained came to no practical result. We then turned to the several states and began to obtain flag legislation in the States, and during the last ten years we have obtained legislation in every State north of the Potomac and the Ohio, and north of Arkansas and Texas, and of the Mexican boundary, and the galaxy of Northern States that stand in one band, all of them, making criminal such acts of desecration, was completed this year . . .

We regret with all our hearts that south of that line we have not succeeded in making any impression, and have failed time and time again to obtain any legislation in that direction. . . . I do not believe that this state of things is due to any disloyalty, but it is to be laid to the account of some other failing, which it is impossible to understand.

We have not ceased during this period, every year, to besiege Congress with our requests and our petitions. . . . Why so patriotic a project should have as practical enemies and not as friends every Senator and Member of Congress it is impossible to understand. . . .

During the period of our work, some of the statutes passed in the different States have been the subject of judicial consideration. First came the Illinois statute, which in 1899 was declared unconstitutional by the Supreme Court of Illinois [document 3.9]. . . . In New York it was the subject of attack by the cigarmakers, and in 1904 the New York statute was decided to be, part of it, unconstitutional, but only because it made no distinction between the desecration of flags which existed and were property at the time of the passage of the act and those which were made and created after the act took effect, the court holding that the Legislature could not destroy property already in existence which was protected by the Constitution [document 3.2]. The New York act was accordingly amended, so as to make clear the distinction, by making it apply solely to the property which came into being after the act took effect. . . .

But by far the most important of all the judicial decisions grew out of the law of the State of Nebraska. In that case the accused party had exposed for public view and sale a bottle of beer on which for the purposes of advertisement was printed or painted a representation of the flag. The arrest of the offender took place, and he was found guilty after trial. . . .

[On appeal to the United States Supreme Court,] the highest court in our land decided that the legislation that we have obtained in so many states was constitutional [document 3.10]. . . .

We are now placed upon firm ground. Our legislation is approved as to principle and form, and also as to the criminal penalty and punishment which follows, and is so approved by the highest court in our land, and there cannot be any longer any question about the effectiveness of our work.

Document 2.14

Testimony by AFA president Col. Ralph Prime, February 20, 1902.

Source: The American Flag: Hearings Before the Senate Committee on Military Affairs, 57th Cong., 1st sess., 1902, S. Doc. 229.

The CHAIRMAN [of the Committee]. I heard the story of a fellow in Boston who made a rag bag of the flag and they fined him $20.

Colonel PRIME. Yes. I have a newspaper clipping of that case here. He sewed a copy of the flag on the outside of a burlap bag in which he gathered coals from ash barrels, and then went through the streets of Boston carrying this on his back. He was arrested at the instance of one of our flag committees, taken before a criminal magistrate, and fined $20. I am glad to say he was not an American-born citizen, if he was a citizen at all. He was a Russian.

Senator BURROWS. One of the latest uses to which the flag has been put is for the ornamentation of water-closets.

Colonel PRIME. I am glad you have seen that, because I have been disgusted with it myself. They not only use the flag for purposes of desecration, but they print it on papers which are used to wrap up packages, . . . to wrap up cheese, hams, and things of that kind. If you lived in the Far East, you would see that water-closet paper is wrapped in the American flag. I believe that is not manufactured in the state of New York, but they imprint the picture of the flag upon the urinal and the water-closet.

The CHAIRMAN. Put it on the porcelain?

Colonel PRIME. Burn it into the porcelain. . . . [W]hat we want to reach is not only the use of the flag itself for desecration purposes, but the printing of the flag upon paper and using that for desecrating purposes. . . .

I have negatives of pictures taken in Honolulu and in Manila showing the use of the flag permanently nailed up as an advertisement of houses of ill fame. That is a more common use, on liquor saloons and houses of ill fame, in the new possessions, a more common use than any other.

Document 2.15

April 27, 1908, hearing before the Senate Committee on Military Affairs.

Source: American Flag: Hearings Before the Committee on Military Affairs, 60th Cong., 1st sess., Apr. 1908.

Statement of Mrs. George T. Smallwood: . . . I come to appeal to you from the standpoint of sentiment, and to voice the feelings of the 65,000 Daughters of the American Revolution who claim this flag by inheritance and who venerate every star in its azure field and every stripe of red and white. Our flag, like our country, was born in sentiment, as noble as ever emanated from the soul of man. It has been baptized in sentiment by the fire and blood and battle; heroes have given their lives for it, they have raised their dying eyes to its glorious colors, have clasped it to their heaving breasts, and it has been draped over many a still form from whose tenant has perished willingly to preserve it from pollution. We, the Daughters of the American Revolution, come to appeal to you to save their flag and yours and ours from desecration. . . . Once more our great society appeals to you, its honored statesmen, to make that flag, for which they have given fathers, husbands and sons, an ensign of our glorious country alone; an emblem of purity, liberty and protection, the flag of your fathers, the flag of your heroes, your flag, their flag, my flag. . . .

Statement of Mrs. Isabel Worrell Ball [chairman of the national committee of the Woman's Relief Corps]: . . . I stand before you today representing 150,000 women banded together for the patriotic purpose of teaching love of the flag and of the Government to a rising generation. . . . we join with every other patriotic organization in desiring that some bill be passed; whose bill, what bill, we care not, so some bill that will protect the flag from the contaminating influences of the commercial interests of the country may be passed. . . . When General Ruggles took charge of the Soldiers' Home in this city, he found all of the lavatory arrangements bearing the British and the American flags crossed; in the bottoms of the washbowls, in the urinals, and everything else in the Soldiers' home. . . .

You will find over here in Georgetown today, in a plumber's institution, rolls of toilet paper, every piece of it with the American flag on it. You will find it used as a decoration for saloons; you will find it on beer bottles named "Old Glory"; you will find it on whisky bottles. . . . I am afraid that if you will walk over to the House of Representatives you will find that to get into it you must walk over the great seal of the United States. . . . The commercial interests of the country are absolutely against the passage of such a bill by Congress.

Document 2.16

Senate debate preceding passage of a flag desecration law, 1908.
Source: Congressional Record, May 15, 1908, 63170.

Mr. Warren [of Wyoming, on behalf of the Senate Military Affairs Committee, which had favorably reported out a flag desecration proposal]: . . .
I want to say, generally speaking, that any flag or any use of the flag devoted to patriotic or loyal purposes would not be complained against, nor proceeded against under the law. It is not the intent of the law to do that. [Before final passage, the bill was amended to state that it would "not apply to banners or flags carried by military or patriotic organizations authorized by law"; similar provisions were included in bills passed by the Senate in 1913, 1914 and 1918 (*Congressional Record,* May 20, 1908, 6600; Feb. 27, 1913, 4158; July 9, 1914, 11882; March 23, 1918, p. 3753).]

Document 2.17

January 23, 1918, hearings before the House Judiciary Committee.

Source: House Judiciary Committee Subcommittee No. 1, *To Preserve the Purity of the Flag,* 62nd Cong., 2nd sess., 1918.

Statement of Hon. [Representative] J. M. C. Smith [of Michigan]. . . .
[T]his is absolutely a time [during World War I], above all times, when I think that sedition should be suppressed. . . .
Mr. [John] Nelson [Representative of Wisconsin]. There are two offenses [in the bill supported by Rep. Smith]. First to mutilate it [the flag]—that is, to do something to injure it in some way; and then casting contempt by word or act? . . . How would you define "contempt" by word? . . .
Mr. Smith. Swearing at it and expressing contempt for it, saying that the German flag is a better flag than ours, or expressing loyalty to another flag in preference to our flag. . . . You will notice that my bill does not cover advertisements. Why? Because here are a number of cases. For instances, I saw a very beautiful emblem of the flag put on a piece of paper advertising that paper for sale, and I would not want, where it is thoroughly for patriotic purposes, to prevent that. . . . I do not think it should be prohibited for advertising if the purpose of the advertisement is a patriotic one. . . .
Mr. Wheeler. Do you not believe that a man who would wipe his hands on the flag is an enemy of this country? . . . In my judgment, either one of two things ought to be done to him; either shoot him or lock him up. . . .

Mr. Smith. . . . Over in an automobile factory in Lansing, 18 miles from my own home, a man wiped his hands on the flag, or spoke disrespectfully of the flag, and I am told by a good citizen of Lansing that they tied a clothesline around his foot, broke a hole in the ice, threw him in the Grand River, and pulled him out, and he in that way made amends. . . .

Document 2.18

The Sedition Act of 1918, outlawing verbal criticism of the flag and providing for the dismissal of federal employees engaging in such criticism.

Source: U.S. Code, 40 *Statutes* 555.

. . . [W]hoever, when the United States is at war, shall willfully utter, print, write or publish any disloyal, profane, scurrilous, or abusive language about the form of government of the United States, or the Constitution of the United States or the military or naval forces of the United States, or the flag of the United States, or the uniform of the Army or Navy of the United States, or any language intended to bring [such] into contempt, scorn, contumely, or disrepute, . . . shall be punished by a fine of not more than $10,000 or imprisonment for not more than twenty years, or both: Provided, that any employee or official of the United States Government who commits any disloyal act or utters any unpatriotic or disloyal language, or who, in an abusive and violent manner criticizes the Army of Navy or the flag of the United States shall be at once dismissed. . . .

Document 2.19

Report of a 1913 Committee of the National Conference of Commissioners on Uniform State Law (NCCUSL) urging the states to pass a uniform flag desecration law.

Source: Proceedings of the 23rd Annual Conference of the NCCUSL, 1913, 157–74. This report was subsequently endorsed by the 1917 NCCUSL conference and declared obsolete by the 1966 NCCUSL Conference (*Handbook of the NCCUSL and Proceedings of the 1966 Conference,* 427).

. . . It seems somewhat peculiar that even patriotic and thoughtful people are constantly endeavoring to use the flag for advertising purposes, and they fail to realize the effect of what they are doing. . . . It is a fact that within a comparatively short time malicious outrages have been committed against the flag by organizations existing in this country. The flag has been torn down and the red flag of anarchy run up in its place. This spirit is not confined to any particular section of the country, but exists from coast to coast. These acts have been largely connected with meetings and demonstrations of the labor element. It is the plain and imperative duty of those connected with the labor movement of our country to have a thorough understanding of the situation and to eliminate from their membership from one end of the land to the other all flag desecrators of every name and nature. The labor element must be a patriotic element, if they are to have the sympathy of the American people. The laborer must not only toil with his hands or his brain for the bread of life, but he must sustain his country and respect the flag that stands as an emblem of all that it is.

Document 2.20

1916 report of an American Bar Association committee recommending endorsement of the 1917 NCCUSL Uniform Flag Law.

Source: ABA Journal, 1916, 538. The report was endorsed by the 1918 ABA annual meeting (Report of the 41st Annual Meeting of the ABA, 1918, 82).

. . . We cannot refrain from noting the exceeding timeliness of the proposed legislation. The flag is the symbol of sovereignty, and at no time has the sovereignty of this government been so assertive and conspicuous, in the place which it occupies in the sun which lights the world. It is essential to the maintenance of its power and prestige among the nations of the world, that it shall be respected among the peoples at home, and that the insidious encroachments of treason which strike at the symbol and at the sovereignty symbolized, shall be speedily and effectively suppressed, to the end that this nation, self-respecting and respected, shall, with the other forces of righteousness, with which it is now allied, secure that, "peace which passeth (the) understanding," of the Germans lords, and over-lords, who know no peace, save that of abject subjection to the tyranny of force.

Document 2.21

January 31, 1927, hearing before the House Judiciary Committee.

Source: To Prevent Desecration of the Flag, 69th Congress, 2nd sess., 1927, serial 29.

Statement of Capt. Paul V. Collins, Washington, D.C.: . . . New York is honeycombed with treason, and so is Washington, D.C. Not very long ago, on Fourteenth Street, I saw the American flag draped around the cushion of a truck on which two negroes were riding. Over and over again we see such desecration. . . . These insidious influences are permeating everywhere. The churches are being poisoned with it. They are being led aside by a sentimentalism until they are really standing with the Bolsheviks. The American Legion itself is not free from that poison. . . .

Statement of Mrs. Lowell F. Hobart, Representing the National Society, Daughters of the American Revolution: . . .[R]eference has been made here to unpatriotic propaganda and I want to say to you that right here in Washington the Young Workers party holds meetings at which young children recite poems that incite them to love and honor the international flag and not the flag of the country. The Young Workers Party has been asking all young people to come in and join with the people of Russia in overthrowing this Government having labor put in command of everything. . . .

Mr. [William] Bowling [Representative from Alabama]. How many of you are in favor of the legislation that proposes to admit 268,000 of these foreign people into the country, outside of the quotas?

Mrs. Hobart. I am against immigration entirely. . . .

Statement of Mr. Frank L. Peckham, Commander, National Patriotic Council, Washington, D.C.: . . . [A]ny person fit to be an American and to live in America has a reverential love for the American flag, and no laws that we can pass, no statutes that were ever put on the books, will make anybody who does not love the American flag love and revere the flag, but we can and ought to put on the statute books laws that will punish that type of individual for desecration of the American flag.

Document 2.22

House of Representatives floor address by Rep. Mayhew Wainwright of New York, the leading congressional advocate of federal flag desecration legislation in the 1925–30 period, March 4, 1927.

Source: Congressional Record, 1927, 5931–32.

Many States have adopted laws to protect the national and their own State flags but surely no statute can carry the same authority, the same weight, the same impressive mandate as a Federal statute with uniform and equal application throughout the country declaring all so evilly or carelessly disposed within our borders, in the name of 48 sovereign States that it is the will, the express command, of the sovereign people . . . that open disrespect or irreverence and any disrespect or irreverence and mutilation or misuse of the flag will be surely punished. . . .

That banner stands for all that his country means to the loyal American, the true patriot—his pride in the glorious past, his hope for a still more glorious future, the principles of human liberty and justice on which his Government rests, the blessings that God has bestowed on those who have been privileged to live in this country, the valor of her sons, his pride in her matchless beauties and awe-inspiring wonders, his religious faith, his high ideals, his home, his dear ones, all that life holds dear. . . .To fail to treat it with respect in his presence is a personal offense. To use it for selfish or debasing purpose fills him with wrathful indignation; to mutilate, defile, deface, or speak of it in contempt or derision is to him a mortal affront. So desecration of the flag has become not only an offense to the strongest public sentiment, but, in fact, a positive incitement to disorder. But may it not be much more? May it not be evidence of a treacherous, treasonable, disloyal state of mind in the one who dares to defile or defame this country's flag? Unless restrained, repressed, and punished will not such actions lead to similar evil tendencies in others, to the spread of pernicious doctrines? Surely, unless repressed and punished, they will serve as an encouragement to those of revolutionary tendencies, of whom, alas, there are already too many among us, too many blackhearted or light-headed people who would tear down the whole structure of our Government and our institutions; not only our Constitution, but the family relation, personal morality, religion, private property—in fact, all those things upon which our civilization rests. . . .

Particularly proper it would seem at this time, when there is so much radical and revolutionary activity, when sentiments of disloyalty to our institutions and form of government are so prevalent, taking the form too often of insult or irreverent expressions or actions towards the flag, that the proposal for a national flag law should at last be realized.

Document 2.23

March 2, 1928, House Judiciary Committee report in support of a federal flag desecration law.

Source: Prevent Desecration of the Flag, 70th Cong., 1st sess., 1928, H. Rep. no. 823.

. . . The legislation has the endorsement of numerous patriotic societies and the committee feels it should receive the prompt approval of Congress. The necessity for the legislation is set forth in full in an address by Hon. J. Mayhew Wainwright, the author of this bill, to be found in the *Congressional Record* of March 4, 1927 [document 2.22]. [Identical language is used in a January 29, 1930 report from the House Judiciary Committee in support of the same legislation, printed as "Prevent Desecration of the Flag" (H. Rep. no. 561, 71st Cong., 2d sess.). The House passed

Wainwright's bills in both 1928 and 1930; in both cases the bills provided exemptions whenever the flag was depicted on "any" article or "in any position where its use is purely and obviously for ornamental or patriotic purposes" (*Congressional Record*, Mar. 19, 1928, 5000; Feb. 5, 1930, 3107).]

Document 2.24

House of Representatives debate of March 19, 1928, preceding passage of the Wainwright federal flag desecration bill.

Source: Congressional Record, 1928, 5002.

Mr. GILBERT. Mr. Speaker, it appears from the discussion that Kentucky is the only State that has not already a law identical with the one sought to be enacted. In Kentucky we have no revolutionists, we have no reds. If there ever had been occasion for a law of this kind, Kentucky certainly would have enacted it. If one in Kentucky should purposely and wantonly insult the flag, he probably would never reach the court house. I am not opposed to the legislation. I simply want to inform the House that it has never been necessary and never will be in Kentucky to have a law to protect the national emblem from desecration.

Document 2.25

Remarks by Rep. Bertrand Gearhart of California in the House of Representatives, July 27, 1942.

Source: Congressional Record, 1942, A30120.

. . . Though American soldiers, sailors and marines are, on land and sea and in the air, laying down their lives in far corners of the world in defense of the glorious banner of this Republic, our Federal courts, their judges and their marshals remain powerless to visit punishment upon or even to hale to the bars of justice for castigation those who desecrate, yea, even spit upon the flag of our country—simply because Congress fails to act to end this crying deficiency in our laws. . . . [In 1941 and again in 1943 the Senate, but not the House, passed a flag desecration bill; the 1943 bill was amended in the Senate Judiciary Committee to strike the provision, which had been included in all previous proposals which had passed either House or Senate, which forbade using depictions of the flag for advertising purposes. *Congressional Record*, Apr. 4, 1941, 3044; June 15, 1943, 5874]

Enforcement and Adjudication
of State Laws
1899–1942

Evidence concerning the enforcement of state flag desecration laws during the pre-Vietnam War era is extremely difficult to obtain, as most prosecutions were not considered important enough to be reported in standard legal sources and the lack of newspaper indexing (with the major exception of the *New York Times*) makes it virtually impossible to track such cases in the general press. However, the limited evidence available suggests that enforcement varied widely from state to state, and even from city to city, especially in the very early period. Thus a news story from the *Chicago Daily Inter-Ocean* newspaper of December 6, 1899 (document 3.1) reports massive prosecutions in Chicago, spurred by rewards provided to "informers" by the 1899 Illinois state law, while a *New York Times* story of July 22, 1900 (document 3.2) suggests, conversely, that at least until that date, the 1899 New York state law was, at most, loosely enforced in New York City.

Almost all reported prosecutions during 1900–1907 involved advertising use of the flag (documents 3.1–3.10). Several of these prosecutions were thrown out by state courts, often on grounds that cast doubt upon the fundamental wisdom and/or constitutionality of flag desecration laws (documents 3.5–3.9). By far the most important of these rulings was a 1900 decision of the Illinois Supreme Court in the case of *Ruhstrat v. People*, involving the depictions of flags upon cigar-box labels (document 3.9). The Illinois court declared that the personal liberty protections of both the state and federal constitutions included the right to pursue an occupation, encompassing the right to advertise a business "in any legitimate manner," including the use of pictures. The decision also held that the general police power that authorized the passage of state legislation only extended to laws necessitated by threats to the "public health, safety, comfort or welfare," and that no such need authorized the state to "arbitrarily invade the personal rights and personal liberty" of citizens by forbidding the practice of placing pictures of flags on advertising labels, an exercise that the court termed "harmless" and no more desecrating of the flag than flying one to identify an American ship on the high seas. Furthermore, the Illinois court suggested that, because the national flag was a creation of the national legislature, only the Congress and not the states could restrict its use.

The threat to state flag desecration laws posed by the Illinois ruling and similar holdings by several other courts was quashed, however, when the U.S. Supreme Court, in the 1907 case of *Halter v. Nebraska* (document 3.10), upheld, by an 8–1 vote, a 1905 decision of the Nebraska Supreme Court that had found the state's flag desecration law constitutional. Like the 1900 AFA model flag law (document 2.11), most of the state flag laws, including the Nebraska law, barred three types of activities: placing any kinds of marks or pictures on the flag; using depictions of the flag in any way for advertising purposes; and acting to "mutilate, deface, defile or defy, trample upon or cast contempt, either by words, or act, upon any such flag." Again, like most state flag laws, the Nebraska law defined "flag" in extraordinarily expansive terms, including any representation that depicted "the colors, the stars and the stripes, in any number of either thereof," as well as any depiction that a person "seeing the same, without deliberation, may believe the same to represent" the flag.

In what amounted to a lengthy and point-by-point rebuttal to the Illinois Supreme Court, the U.S. Supreme Court, in a decision filled with patriotic oratory, rejected the suggestion that Congress's failure to ban flag desecration prevented state legislatures from doing so. Banning the commercial use of the flag was held to be aimed at a usage that would "degrade and cheapen" it and thus reflected a proper state intent to "encourage love and patriotism" among its people. While the *Halter* ruling explicitly dealt solely with advertising use of the flag, the entire tone of the ruling clearly suggested that banning flag desecration used to express political dissent would be equally valid; thus the court noted that just as encouraging "love and patriotism" was a proper state legislation motivation, that such emotions "will diminish in proportion as respect for the flag is weakened."

Just as the rhetoric urging the adoption of flag desecration laws rapidly shifted away from the original impetus of seeking to ban advertising use of the flag (to the point where such provisions were entirely omitted from the bill passed in the Senate in 1943) and increasingly reflected a desire to suppress political dissent, a similar pattern was reflected in reported flag desecration prosecutions. After the Supreme Court's 1907 *Halter* ruling, prosecutions under these laws for advertising or commercial use of the flag virtually disappeared (although groups such as the DAR frequently complained about the failure of authorities to act in such cases, indicating that such uses by no means ended); almost all prosecutions that ensued related to perceived uses of the flag for symbolic political dissent.

Perhaps the first such case occurred during a 1903–4 strike in Colorado led by the militant Western Federation of Miners (WFM), when WFM official "Big Bill" Haywood (later of Industrial Workers of the World fame) was prosecuted for protesting repressive actions taken by Colorado officials during the strike with posters of the flag that had political comments printed across the stripes (document 3.11). The prosecution was thrown out of court when Haywood's lawyers submitted evidence of numerous cases of commercial flag uses that seemingly violated the Colorado law but had not been prosecuted. Probably the most widely publicized flag desecration incident until the Vietnam War era, as well as the first flag-burning prosecution in American history, arose in 1916. Amidst the tension aroused in the United States by the outbreak of World War I in Europe, a socialist-pacifist New York City clergyman, Bouck White, pastor of the Church of the Social Revolution, was prosecuted for burning a flag on the eve of his already-pending flag desecration trial for circulating an antimilitarist caricature that had portrayed the flag as entwined with money and war. White was found guilty and sentenced to the maximum New York penalty of thirty days in jail and a $100 fine each in separate prosecutions for both the caricature and the burning, events that received national and, in some cases, front-page press attention (document 3.12).

Immediately preceding and during American involvement in World War I, there were numerous other flag desecration prosecutions, almost invariably involving perceived political protests; in many other wartime incidents, Americans who were judged to be insufficiently patriotic were forced by mobs to kiss the flag (documents 3.13–3.26). In at least three states, penalties for flag desecration were increased during the war from modest punishments like New York's maximum to the draconian terms of five years in jail (Louisiana) or even twenty-five years in jail (Texas and Montana); at the start of the war, the Justice Department announced that aliens who engaged in "tearing down, mutilating, abusing or desecrating the United States flag in any way" would be subjected to "summary arrest and confinement" under wartime presidential emergency regulations (document 3.24).

By far the harshest penalty for "flag desecration" in American history was handed out during World War I to a Montana man, E. V. Starr, who under the 1918 Montana law, which became the model for the 1918 federal Sedition Act (document 2.18), was given a $500 fine and a jail term of ten to twenty years at hard labor for refusing a mob's demands to kiss a flag and for terming it "nothing but a piece of cotton" with a "little paint" and "some other marks" on it which "might be covered with microbes." Considering the case on appeal, Federal district court judge George Bourquin termed the sentence a "horrifying" one that justified George Bernard Shaw's comment that American courts had gone "stark, staring, raving mad" during the war; Bourquin also labeled the mob that had assaulted Starr "heresy hunters" and "witch burners." Nonetheless, he concluded that he was powerless to intervene, because the Montana state law was clearly constitutional under the *Halter* precedent (document 3.25).

Between World War I and the Vietnam War era there were relatively few flag desecration prosecutions, with the exception of a small upsurge between 1939 and 1945 associated with World War II and its accompanying tensions. Almost invariably such prosecutions were upheld on appeal, even in cases, like Starr's, involving oral "desecration" of the flag. For example, in 1918 the Kansas Supreme Court upheld the conviction of a man who had "expressed a very vulgar and indecent use of the flag" while visiting a blacksmith shop, on the grounds that such a shop was a "public place" (the Kansas law, like most state flag laws, outlawed "public" acts or words that desecrated the flag) and that the man's language suggested a lack of "respect" for the flag, which "should be found in the breast of every citizen of the United States" (document 3.26). In one of the few cases in which a flag desecration conviction was overturned on appeal, in 1942 the Maine Supreme Judicial Court held that the actions of a man who, while visiting a friend at his house, termed the flag a "rag" and said that he would tear it up and trample it while making hand motions, did not break the law as they did not occur in "public" (document 3.27).

Document 3.1

Chicago Daily Inter-Ocean, October 20, 1899.

FLAG LAW A HARDSHIP—ONE THOUSAND CITIZENS ARRESTS FOR ALLEGED VIOLATIONS—ALL LIABLE TO FINE—PROVISIONS SO SWEEPING THAT INNOCENT PERSONS SUFFER—BUSINESS OF MAKING COMPLAINTS PROVIDES GOOD INCOME FOR INFORMERS—STATE'S ATTORNEY ON ABUSES

Chicago is terrorized, in some parts at least, by the prosecutions begun under the new flag law, which became operative July 1. It is said on good authority that more than 1,000 persons in the city, who did not dream that they had violated this law, have been arrested. . . .

The law is already regarded as one of the most odious that ever crept into the Illinois statute book. [On June 14, 1895, the *Inter-Ocean* had become one of the earliest newspapers to call for such a law, deeming it "necessary" and "eminently desirable" to "have a law protecting our national colors from vulgar desecration," such as in "the use of the flag for advertising purposes," if "the youthful mind is to be imbued with a respect that in the mature citizen shall be honor for the flag," an object that "should be used honorably and holily," as "apart from religion, the flag of one's country is the most sacred of symbols."] It forbids any one virtually to have in his possession any print or any photograph of any "national flag or emblem" connected with any sort of advertising matter, such as a show bill or a label on a box or bottle. The penalty is a fine of from $10 to $100. . . .

And then, to stimulate prosecutions, it is provided that any one who begins suits [i.e., brings a complaint] shall receive one-half of the fines inflicted. Already dozens of men are engaged in making lists of persons who have such flags or emblems on their premises and having them arrested for it. Some of the complainants are making large sums of money by this practice, and as they prosecute none but the poor and helpless the amount of suffering inflicted is immense. . . . There is not a person in Chicago who is safe from prosecution under this flag law. The pictures of United States flags of various kinds . . . are really omnipresent in business places and in homes. They are often on labels or showbills, or calendars, or the wrappers of goods which have been bought. . . . In all of these cases the person who displays the flag or emblem is liable to arrest for a misdemeanor.

Justice Rhoades . . . tried and convicted several persons for violation of this law, while the very [courtroom] walls around him were covered with flags [on calendars or other printed matter] used for advertising purposes. . . . State's Attorney Deneen was asked yesterday what he thought of the law, and what his experience had been with it, and he said: "I have conducted three prosecutions under this law, because I was threatened with prosecution for malfeasance in office unless I did it. But I think it susceptible of being made a terrible curse to the people, and I feel more anxious to protect the public from unjust prosecution under it than to start prosecutions."

Document 3.2

New York Times, July 22, 1900.

FLAG MUST BE RESPECTED—ADVERTISING ON NATIONAL AND STATE EMBLEMS TO BE STOPPED—POLICE MUST ENFORCE LAW—CHIEF DEVERY ACTS UPON COMPLAINT BY DISTRICT ATTORNEY GARDINER—CAMPAIGN BANNERS AFFECTED

An order has just been issued by Chief of Police Devery under which all American flags, whether of cotton, silk, printed, painted, illuminated in electric lights, or of any other kind which contain anything in the way of inscription or advertisement will be hauled down by the police because they violate a section of New York's Penal Code. . . .

This order includes all campaign banners and advertising devices except barbers' poles, which latter, it is explained, do not resemble closely enough the National emblem. The police will frown upon advertisements of certain mercantile and manufacturing firms who attempt to gain the confidence of the public by decorating their stores, factories and innumerable billboards with American banners, inscribed with advice of this kind: "Use of Yankee Doodle Toothpicks," "Try Star-spangeline for the bath," "Uncle Sam Pills cure all ills," &c. Such frivolities will be dealt with summarily. Then the illustrated dailies will not be permitted to announce in red letters, on a background of American flags, the victories of our troops over the Chinese [during the Boxer rebellion]. . . .

At Police Headquarters it was said yesterday that this law covered American banners to which a piece of cloth had been attached, with the names of candidates printed upon it. Of such flags and devices for political purposes there are a great many displayed in this city at the present time. All these will have to be taken down. An attempt to evade the law by changing the number of stripes or stars, say the police, will not be effectual because the law makes provision for flags which evidently purport to be United States flags. . . .

Document 3.3

New York Times, August 5, 1899.

FLAG LAW TO BE TESTED

Chicago—By the arrest of F. L. Rossbach, manager of the Washington Shirt Company, at Dearborn and Washington Street, who is charged with using the American flag for advertising purposes there promises to be a thorough test of the flag law in the courts. . . . Charles A. Warren requested that a fine be imposed on his client that he might carry it to a higher court and make a test case of it. A fine of $10 was imposed and the case was appealed. . . .

Document 3.4

New York Times, August 5, 1899.

ARRESTED UNDER THE FLAG LAW—PRESIDENT OF A TELEPHONE COMPANY ADVERTISED ILLEGALLY

Chicago—Violation of the State law prohibiting the using of the National flag for advertising purposes is the charge on which P. C. Burns, President

of the American Electric Telephone Company, was arrested here today. . . .
The complainant is J. G. Nolan, and the use of the flag on letterheads,
envelopes, and in newspaper advertisements was the evidence on which
Mr. Nolan secured his warrant. "As soon as we use up these stamped
envelopes bearing the flag we will order something different," said Mr.
Burns. "The red-white-and-blue shield device, to which objection has also
been made, is not a representation of the flag, in my opinion."

Document 3.5

New York Times, October 5, 1899.

DECLARES THE FLAG LAW VOID—CHICAGO JUDGE HOLDS THAT NATIONAL
EMBLEM IS A LEGITIMATE TRADE MARK
Chicago—[Illinois Circuit Court] Judge Gibbons today declared that the
flag law was void because it deprived the Governor of his constitutional
prerogatives of pardon or reprieve [as in conflict with the flag law provision guaranteeing to informers a share of the fine]. He then said: "Wherein
is the flag desecrated by making a lithograph or a picture thereof as a
trademark? If the common use of the flag is to abate veneration for it, why
did our Solons [state legislators] pass a law making it compulsory to fly
the National emblem from the flagstaff of every schoolhouse? We need no
flag law in the State of Illinois to make men patriotic or to prevent men
from desecrating the flag. Every man in all this land vies with his neighbor
in showing devotion, loyalty and reverence to the flag, and it is a reflection
upon the names of Illinois's patriotic dead to have enacted such a law."

Document 3.6

New York Times, February 6, 1904.

AMERICAN FLAG AS TRADE MARK—APPELLATE DIVISION DECIDES IT IS NO
CRIME TO SO USE IT
  "The interdiction by the State," said the [New York State] Appellate
Division yesterday by Justice Patterson, "of the use of a picture or representation of the American flag as a trade mark or upon trade labels, or in
connection with the advertisement of merchandise, in no way relates to
any one of the legitimate subjects to which the police power of the state
extends. . . . There is nothing in the use of a representation of the American flag as a trade mark," said Justice Patterson, "or in connection with a
trade mark or trade label, that inspires the idea that the flag is degraded or
belittled [in a case involving selling cigar boxes imprinted with depictions
of the flag]." [This case, *People ex rel. McPike v. Van De Carr,* is reported
at 86 *New York Supplement* 644, 1904.]

Document 3.7

New York Times, May 18, 1904.

Albany—The Court of Appeals [New York's highest court] today, in [an appeal of the case discussed in document 3.6] declared unconstitutional that portion of the flag law enacted by the legislature of 1903 which prohibits the use of the American flag or any representation of it for advertising purposes. . . . [T]he opinion written by Chief Judge Parker says: "The statute in express terms applies as well to articles manufactured and in existence when it was lawful to manufacture them and have them in possession as to those thereafter manufactured or acquired. It attempts, therefore, to destroy existing property rights, . . . the Legislature is powerless to effectuate such a result. It follows that so much of the statute [that applies to pre-existing property] is void." [This case, *People ex rel. McPike v. Van De Carr,* is reported at 70 *Northeastern Reporter* 965, 1904.]

Document 3.8

New York Times, July 31, 1904.

COURT DEFINES U.S. FLAG—STARS AND STRIPES DO NOT CONSTITUTE STANDARD UNLESS PROPERLY ARRANGED

Boston—Stars and stripes do not constitute a United States flag unless arranged according to the form authorized by the United States government, according to a decision of Judge Adams, announced in the Municipal Court today. The opinion was given in the case of two persons who recently opened a store for the sale of decorations for the coming Grand Army of the Republic National encampment here, and who had been arrested on the charge of desecrating the United States flag by selling a lettered emblem with the usual stripes, but with the stars covering the entire third of the flag nearest the staff. Judge Adams, ruling that this was not a United States flag, discharged the respondents.

Document 3.9

Ruling of the Illinois Supreme Court, April 17, 1900, declaring the Illinois flag desecration law unconstitutional.

Source: Ruhstrat v. People, 57 *Northeastern Reporter* 41.

A. Ruhstrat was convicted of violating Act April 22, 1899, prohibiting the use of the national flag for commercial or advertising purposes, and brings error. Reversed. . . .

Plaintiff in error, A. Ruhstrat, and his partner, Allen S. Curlett, are co-partners under the firm name of Ruhstrat & Curlett in the wholesale and retail cigar business in the city of Chicago. They used pictures of the national flag upon cigar-box labels for the purpose of advertising [and were subsequently convicted and fined, first before a justice of the peace and then on appeal before the Cook County Criminal Court, and thereupon have appealed to this court on the grounds] that the act in question was illegal and void, as being in violation of the constitutions of the state of Illinois and of the United States. . . .

Under the provisions of the Illinois and federal constitutions which guarantee the right to life, liberty and property unless regulated with due process of law and prior court interpretations of these provisions, plaintiff in error had not only the right to choose the business in which he was engaged in his occupation, but he had the right to pursue and carry on that business in any way and by any methods which were lawful and proper. . . . In these days of commercial enterprise, advertising is an important factor in business pursuits. It cannot be denied that plaintiff in error had a right to advertise his business in any legitimate manner, so as to attract the attention of the public. . . .

It is claimed that the law tends to elevate the morals and promote the welfare of the public, and that, as such, is a valid exercise of legislative power. The police power is limited to enactments which have reference to the public health or comfort, the safety or welfare of society. . . . It is difficult to see how the flag law of April 22, 1899, tends in any way to promote the safety, welfare, or comfort of society. The use of a likeness of the flag upon a label or as part of the trademark of a businessman in the lawful prosecution of his business cannot be regarded otherwise than as an act which is harmless in itself. It may violate the ideas which some people have of sentiment and taste, but the propriety of an act, considered merely from the standpoint of sentiment and taste, may be a matter about which men of equal honesty and patriotism may differ. The act in question is severe in its terms. . . .

What is the offense for which these penalties are imposed? . . . It is not clear that the prohibition leveled against the use or display of the flag tends in any way to elevate the morals or promote the welfare of the public. The flag is used, in the prosecution of commerce upon the high seas, as a symbol of nationality. . . . It is difficult to see why, if, in the presentation of foreign commerce or trade, the flag is used to protect a ship and cargo and designate its character, it should be a desecration of the same flag to use a likeness of it upon a label or trademark in the prosecution of domestic trade or business. . . .

Presumably the national flag was adopted [by Congress] for the use of the citizens of the United States. . . . The usage and practice of employing a flag for commercial purposes have been indulged in by citizens of the United States with the knowledge of the national government. The absence of congressional prohibition against the usage and practice thus indulged in with the knowledge of the general government has created a "privilege" in the citizen of the United States. . . .

An act of legislation, passed by a particular state, which deprives the citizen of such privilege, contravenes that clause of the [Fourteenth] amendment to the national constitution which forbids any state to abridge the privileges and immunities of a citizen of the United States. . . . We are of the opinion that this law is unconstitutional, not only as an infringement upon the personal liberty guaranteed to the citizen by both the federal and state constitutions, but also as depriving a citizen of the United States of the right of exercising a privilege implicitly, if not expressly, granted to him by the federal constitution.

Document 3.10

U.S. Supreme Court ruling upholding the Nebraska flag desecration law, March 4, 1907.

Source: Halter v. Nebraska, 205 United States Reports 34.

MR. JUSTICE HARLAN delivered the opinion of the court.

This case involves the validity, under the Constitution of the United States, of an act of the State of Nebraska, approved July 3d, 1903, entitled "An act to prevent and punish the desecration of the flag of the United States."

The act, among other things, makes it a misdemeanor, punishable by fine or imprisonment, or both for any one to sell, expose for sale, or have in possession for sale, any article of merchandise, upon which shall have been printed or placed, for purposes of advertisement, a representation of the flag of the United States. It expressly excepted, however, from its operation any newspaper, periodical, book, etc., on which should be printed, painted or placed a representation of the flag *"disconnected from any advertisement."*

The plaintiffs in error were proceeded against by criminal information upon the charge of having, in violation of the statute, unlawfully exposed to public view, sold, exposed for sale, and had in their possession for sale a bottle of beer, upon which, for purposes of advertisement, was printed and painted a representation of the flag of the United States.

The defendants pleaded not guilty, and at the trial insisted that the statute in question was null and void, as infringing their personal liberty guaranteed by the Fourteenth Amendment of the Constitution of the

United States, and depriving them, as citizens of the United States, of the right of exercising a privilege, impliedly if not expressly guaranteed by the Federal Constitution; also, that the statute was invalid in that it permitted the use of the flag by publishers, newspapers, books, periodicals, etc., under certain circumstances—thus, it was alleged, discriminating in favor of one class and against others. These contentions were overruled and the defendants having been found guilty by a jury were severally adjudged to pay a fine of $50 and the costs of the prosecution. Upon writ of error the judgments were affirmed by the Supreme Court of Nebraska. . . .

The importance of the questions of constitutional law thus raised will be recognized when it is remembered that more than half of the States of the Union have enacted statutes substantially similar, in their general scope, to the Nebraska statute. That fact is one of such significance as to require us to pause before reaching the conclusion that a majority of the States have, in their legislation, violated the Constitution of the United States. Our attention is called to two cases in which the constitutionality of such an enactment has been denied—*Ruhstrat v. People* [document 3.9]; *People ex rel. McPike v. Van De Carr* [document 3.7]. . . .

In our consideration of the questions presented we must not overlook certain principles of constitutional construction, long ago established and steadily adhered to, which preclude a judicial tribunal from holding a legislative enactment, Federal or state, unconstitutional and void, unless it be manifestly so. Another vital principle is that, except as restrained by its own fundamental law, or by the Supreme Law of the land a State possesses all legislative power consistent with a republican form of government; therefore each State, when not thus restrained and so far as this court is concerned, may, by legislation, provide not only for the health, morals and safety of its people, but for the common good, as involved in the well-being, peace, happiness and prosperity of the people.

Guided by these principles, it would seem difficult to hold that the statute of Nebraska, in forbidding the use of the flag of the United States for purposes of mere advertisement, infringes any right protected by the Constitution of the United States or that it relates to a subject exclusively committed to the National Government. . . . For that flag every true American has not simply an appreciation but a deep affection. No American, nor any foreign born person who enjoys the privileges of American citizenship, ever looks upon it without taking pride in the fact that he lives under this free Government. Hence, it has often occurred that insults to a flag have been the cause of war, and indignities put upon it, in the presence of those who revere it, have often been resented and sometimes punished on the spot.

It may be said that as the flag is an emblem of National sovereignty, it was for Congress alone, by appropriate legislation, to prohibit its use for illegitimate purposes. We cannot yield to this view. If Congress has not chosen to legislate on this subject, and if an enactment by it would super-sede state laws of like character, it does not follow that in the absence of national legislation the State is without power to act. . . . So, a State may exert its power to strengthen the bonds of the Union and therefore, to that end, may encourage patriotism and love of country among its people. When, by its legislation, the State encourages a feeling of patriotism to-wards the Nation, it necessarily encourages a like feeling towards the State. One who loves the Union will love the State in which he resides, and love both of the common country and of the State will diminish in propor-tion as respect for the flag is weakened. . . . By the statute in question the state has in substance declared that no one subject to its jurisdiction shall use the flag for purposes of trade and traffic, a purpose wholly foreign to that for which it was provided by the Nation. Such a use tends to degrade and cheapen the flag in the estimation of the people, as well as to defeat the object of maintaining it as an emblem of National power and National honor. And we cannot hold that any privilege of American citizenship or that any right of personal liberty is violated by a state enactment forbid-ding the flag to be used as an advertisement on a bottle of beer. It is familiar that even the privileges of citizenship and the rights inhering in personal liberty are subject, in their enjoyment, to such reasonable re-straints as may be required for the general good. Nor can we hold that any one has a right of property which is violated by such an enactment as the one in question. If it be said that there is a right of property in the tangible thing upon which a representation of the flag has been placed, the answer is that such representation which, in itself, cannot belong, as property, to an individual has been placed on such thing in violation of law and subject to the power of Government to prohibit its use for purposes of advertisement. . . .

[W]e are of opinion that those who enacted the statute knew, what is known of all, that to every true American the flag is the symbol of the Nation's power, the emblem of freedom in its truest, best sense. It is not extravagant to say that to all lovers of the country it signifies government resting on the consent of the governed, liberty regulated by law; the pro-tection of the weak against the strong; security against the exercise of arbi-trary power; and absolute safety for free institutions against foreign aggression. As the statute in question evidently had its origin in a purpose to cultivate a feeling of patriotism among the people of Nebraska, we are unwilling to adjudge that in legislation for that purpose the State erred in duty or has infringed the constitutional right of anyone. On the contrary, it may reasonably be affirmed that a duty rests upon each State in every legal way to encourage its people to love the Union with which the State is indissolubly connected.

Another contention of the defendants is that the statute is unconstitu-tional in that, while applying to representations of the flag placed upon articles of merchandise for purposes of advertisement, it does not apply to a newspaper, periodical, book, pamphlet, etc., on any of which shall be printed, painted, or placed the representation of the flag disconnected from any advertisement. These exceptions, it is insisted, make an arbitrary classification of persons which, in legal effect, denies to one class the equal protection of the laws.

It is well settled that when prescribing a rule of conduct for persons or corporations a State may, consistently with the Fourteenth Amendment, make a classification among its people based "upon some reasonable ground—some difference which bears a just and proper relation to the attempted classification—and is not a mere arbitrary selection." . . .

Now, no one can be said to have the right, secured by the Constitution, to use the country's flag merely for purposes of advertising articles of merchandise. If everyone was entitled of right to use it for such purposes, then, perhaps, the State could not discriminate among those who so used it. It was for the state of Nebraska to say how far it would go by way of legislation for that protection of the flag against improper use—taking care, in such legislation, not to make undue discrimination against a part of its people. It chose not to forbid the use of the flag for the exceptional purposes specified in the statute, prescribing the fundamental condition that its use for any of those purposes should be "disconnected from any advertisement." All are alike forbidden to use the flag as an advertisement. It is easy to be seen how a representation of the flag may be wholly disconnected from an advertisement and be used upon a newspaper, periodical, book, etc., in such way as not to arouse a feeling of indignation nor offend the sentiments and feelings of those who reverence it. In any event, the classification made by the State cannot be regarded as unreasonable or arbitrary or as bringing the statute under condemnation as denying the equal protection of the laws.

It would be going very far to say that the statute in question had no reasonable connection with the common good and was not promotive of the peace, order and well-being of the people. Before this court can hold the statute void it must say that and, in addition, adjudge that it violates rights secured by the Constitution of the United States. We cannot so say and cannot so adjudge. . . .

Document 3.11

New York Times, March 29, 1904.

Secretary Haywood of the Western Federation of Miners is to be arrested for desecration of the flag. The same charge was preferred against President Moyer, who has been in jail at Telluride since Saturday, being unable to find bondmen.

The desecration of the national flag consisted in the printing of thirteen sentences on the thirteen bars on the flag, the sentences in order being as follows:

> "Martial law declared in Colorado.
> Habeas Corpus suspended in Colorado.
> Free Press throttled in Colorado.
> Bull pens for union men in Colorado.
> Free speech denied in Colorado.
> Soldiers defy the court in Colorado.
> Wholesale arrests without warrant in Colorado.
> Union men exiled from homes and families in Colorado.
> Constitutional right to bear arms questioned in Colorado.
> Corporations corrupt and control administration in Colorado.
> Right of fair, impartial, and speedy trial abolished in Colorado.
> Citizens Alliance resorts to mob law and violence in Colorado.
> Militia hired to corporations to break the strike in Colorado."

Document 3.12

Articles from the *New York Times* reporting on the prosecutions and conviction of New York clergyman Bouck White for flag desecration, for circulating a caricature of the flag, and for burning the flag.

Source: New York Times, June 2, 3, 1916; Mar. 15, 16, 1917.

[June 2, 1916] SOCIAL REBELS BURN ALL FLAGS—BOUCK WHITE'S FOLLOWERS PELTED AS THEY DESECRATE AMERICAN AND OTHER EMBLEMS—A REAR-YARD CEREMONY—COLORS DROPPED IN KETTLE AND SET ABLAZE AS A CEREMONY OF CHURCH REVOLUTION—LEADER ON TRIAL TODAY—ACCUSED OF VIOLATING LAW BY USING STARS AND STRIPES FOR ADVERTISING PURPOSES

An American flag, with the emblems of other nations, was deliberately burned last night as part of the exercises connected with a general meeting of the Church of the Social Revolution held on the eve of the trial of its leader, Bouck White, which will begin today in Special Sessions. The ceremony was held in the back yard of the house the organization maintains. . . .

While the flags were being burned, hisses and catcalls resounded, and missiles were thrown from the rear windows of neighboring houses. . . .

The flag-burning in the back yard followed a long meeting in the rooms of the organization. The question of flags was raised by the prospective trial of White as the result of the publication of a cartoon by him which the complainant considers desecration of the Stars and Stripes. The charge is that he violated the penal law by using the United States flag for advertising purposes. . . .

[A]fter the meeting at the Church, members adjourned to the back yard where a sort of altar, shrouded in red cloth, was revealed . . . and in front of this was a large kettle swung on a tripod. . . . Finally, a signal was given and a man stepped into the circle of light near the tripod and kettle, which was marked "Melting Pot." . . . He said that at this time when the armies of Europe were burning and destroying it was particularly fitting that an act typifying international brotherhood should be done.

A man came forward from the house carrying a small British flag. He advanced before the tripod and kettle, which was now flaming with kerosene that had been poured in, and in droning tones recited a formula that was to be heard many more times, with occasional slight variations. It was like this:

"I, Robert W. Davis, a native of Great Britain, cast the flag of my native country into this melting-pot as a symbol of international renunciation in favor of internationalism and universal brotherhood."

Then the flag was thrown into the burning pot. After this each flag-bearer delivered a prayer in his native language. . . . Then a gasp went up from the crowd when the last man advanced and it was seen that he carried an American flag. . . . As soon as they saw the American flag the people in the nearby houses began to [utter] hisses and catcalls . . . and half a dozen missiles fell among the crowd about the melting pot.

[Albert] Henkel [the bearer of the American flag] dramatically broke the staff of the flag and threw it into the pot. . . . As it blazed up, a large red flag bearing the word "Internationalism" was broken out above the red altar. . . .

[June 3, 1916] SWANN WILL JAIL THE FLAG-BURNERS—DISTRICT ATTORNEY ANNOUNCES THAT SOCIAL REBELS WILL BE PUNISHED FOR DESECRATION—BOUCK WHITE SENTENCED—PROMINENT WOMEN WILL APPEAL TO CONGRESS TO DEPRIVE HIM AND HIS FOLLOWERS OF CITIZENSHIP

While Bouck White, leader of the Church of the Social Revolution, was being tried in Special Sessions yesterday on an old charge of desecrating the American flag, on which he was found guilty and received the sentence of 30 days in the penitentiary and a fine of $100, several movements were put under way to punish him and his follower for having burned an American flag on the eve of this trial. It was made apparent that the flag burning had roused considerable public indignation.

Police Commissioner Wood ordered an investigation into the flag burning. District Attorney Swann said he would have everyone who had participated in it in jail within a week, and several women's organizations began a nationwide movement to induce Congress to deprive White [and other] principal actors in the scene of their citizenship and provide similar punishments in the future for similar offenses. . . .

In his trial in Special Sessions the social revolutionist pastor continually attempted to deliver harangues on the ideals which he and his followers represented. [The trial resulted from] the distribution in last March of circulars on which there was a cartoon portraying the American flag as the resting place for an uncouth beast in human semblance, with a hand reaching out towards a pot of money. . . .

"Why don't you go and live in some other country," asked Judge McInerney [of White]. "Why don't you find a country that likes to have its flag desecrated?"

[March 15, 1917] JURY IN FLAG CASE FINDS WHITE GUILTY. . . .

After deliberating five hours, a jury before Judge McIntyre in General Sessions at midnight last night adjudged the Reverend Bouck White, pastor of the Church of the Social Revolution . . . [and] two of his followers guilty of desecrating the American flag. Charles Y. Meighan, the foreman, recommended clemency for the three men. . . .

"Gentlemen of the jury," Judge McIntyre said to the twelve men in the jury box, "your verdict goes out to the world and shows to the people that the American flag must be revered and respected. It is a warning to the aliens in this country that American institutions must be accorded proper respect, especially in these momentous days in the nation's history. . . ."

In summing up to the jury, White declared that, "Instead of desecration, the flag never had received a more profound and mighty consecration" as at the service, when, he said, it was "melted" with the emblems of other nations symbolic of world brotherhood.

"The news of your verdict will go into the trenches of Europe, . . . If you find me guilty, you will have set the world in a backward direction. Years from now you will experience a gnawing sensation of regret when you hear the word brotherhood if you do not do your share toward bringing it into being."

Assistant District Attorney Alexander Rorke characterized White as an "egotistical humbug. . . . If an American in his indignation had shot White dead on the night of the flag burning, I doubt if you could find a juryman who would vote to convict him."

[March 16, 1917] BOUCK WHITE GETS 30 DAYS—TWO OTHERS WHO DESECRATED THE FLAG ALSO SENT TO THE WORKHOUSE

The Rev. Bouck White, pastor of the Church of the Social Revolution . . . was yesterday sentenced by Judge McIntyre in General Sessions to 30 days in the workhouse and to pay a fine of $100 [for the desecrating the flag by burning it in June, 1916. Edward] Ames, who was the master of ceremonies [during the flagburning incident] and [August] Henkel, who cast the American flag into the "melting pot," were also sentenced to 30 days.

"If there ever was a time in this great Republic," Judge McIntyre said, in passing sentence, "when every American should be true and loyal to the flag, it is now. I regret that I haven't the power to make this sentence a matter of years. In recent years there has been coming into our country certain elements from lands where there has been oppression. Instead of enjoying the opportunities afforded by America, they have dared to suggest destruction to our institutions. To these and all others this court sends the warning that hereafter it must be 'hats off to flag.'" . . .

Document 3.13

New York Times, June 22, 1916.

SUSPENDED FOR ALLEGED FLAG INSULT

Joseph Brandon of 1409 Prospect Avenue, the Bronx, who was arrested Monday night and taken before Magistrate Simms in the Morrisania Court, on Tuesday, charged with insulting the American flag and reviling United States soldiers at a recruiting station in the Bronx, has been suspended by Secretary James H. Walker of the Public Service Commission, where Brandon has been employed as a clerk. . . .

Document 3.14

Chicago Tribune, April 3, 1917.

CRIES "HOCH DER KAISER" AND UP HE IS STRUNG

Thermopolis, Wyo.—A stranger, believed to be a German, who shouted "Hoch der Kaiser," as he stood drinking at a saloon bar here, narrowly escaped lynching. A miner knocked him down, a rope appeared as if by magic, and in a moment the dazed man was hanging from a beam. Before life was extinct, however, he was cut down by the city marshal. Revived with cold water, he was forced to kneel and kiss the American flag. He then was warned to get out of town. He did.

Document 3.15

New York Times, April 9, 1917.

$1,000 TO BACK LOYALTY

BAKER OFFERS TO PAY FOR PROOF HE EVER INSULTED FLAG

Jacob Guth, a baker at 1776 Broadway, Brooklyn, yesterday offered to pay $1,000 to anyone who could prove that he had ever offered insult of any kind to the American flag. Last night Guth's store window showed the sign announcing the offer, which was pasted on the window between two American flags and lighted by an electric bulb. Guth, who was born in Alsace-Lorraine . . . became an American citizen in 1895. He says he made the offer on the advice of his attorney and [Police] Captain David King . . . after gossip started the rumor that he was disloyal, greatly to his embarrassment.

Document 3.16

New York Times, April 10, 1917.

20 DAYS FOR INSULT TO FLAG

Wearing an American flag in his buttonhole, Louis Stoltz, native-born, but of German descent, . . . was sentenced yesterday to twenty days in the county jail by Magistrate Handy for using profane language in reference to the American colors. Stoltz, who had served four years in the army, denied the charge.

Document 3.17

Chicago Tribune, April 10, 1917.

MILZACK KISSES THE FLAG, BUT NOT FOR LOVE

Lawrence Milzack, a farmer, West One Hundred and Third Street and Crawford avenue, made the mistake, in the presence of a gathering in the saloon of Nicholas Finley, 4701 South Halstead, yesterday, by declaring, "the Kaiser will get President Wilson and the country, too." An American flag was spread on the floor and Milzack made to kneel and kiss it. Then he was booted into the street, where Patrol Sergeant Sandstrom nailed him and locked him up for federal investigation.

Document 3.18

New York Times, April 15, 1917.

HELD FOR DESECRATING THE FLAG

Dunellen, N.J.—Joseph Braick, a Slav, was arrested here this afternoon charged with desecrating the American flag. . . . He is alleged to have cut a flag to pieces and then stamped upon it.

Document 3.19

New York Times, April 25, 1917.

FLAG DESPOILERS GUILTY

Miss Helen Boardman of 28 Grove Street, and Miss Katherine Anthony of 36 Grove Street, arrested at Broadway and Eleventh Street on Monday, charged with sticking anti-conscription buttons and posters to American flags that hung from buildings [have been] found guilty of disorderly conduct. The court held them under $50 bonds each to keep the peace for six months and to serve five days in prison if the paroles were not observed.

Document 3.20

New York Times, May 11, 1917.

FLAG INSULTER GETS 30 DAYS

For making improper remarks about the American flag, Joseph Sadokierski, . . . Russian machinist . . . was sentenced to the workhouse for one month by Magistrate Simms in Harlem Court yesterday.

Document 3.21

New York Times, June 2, 1917.

INSULT TO FLAG COST $50

On complaint of Miss Charlotte Fairchild of 5 East 47th St., William Meyre, 45 years old, of 25 West 46th St., a lace importer was fined $50 by Magistrate Corrigan in the Men's Night Court last night for having written across an American flag printed on a placard and displayed in a shop at Fifth Avenue and 45th St. the words, "Look at the German flag above it." . . . He pleaded guilty to a charge of disorderly conduct.

Document 3.22

New York Times, June 21, 1917.

HELD FOR SHOOTING FLAG

Ossining—Charged with shooting the American flag at the country home of V. Everit Macy in Ossining, two Scandinavian butlers employed there were arrested and held in $100 bail each. . . .

Document 3.23

Detroit Free Press, October 12, 1917.

THREE PAY FINES FOR SLIGHT TO THE FLAG

Three self-styled "internationalists" who refused to bare their heads while the Star-Spangled Banner was being played at a recruiting meeting of Polish-speaking citizens in Perrier Park Sunday were fined Monday by Justice Stein. The ringleader, who, it is alleged, started a near riot by cursing the flag, was fined $10 or 30 days, even though penitent. The others paid $5 fines.

Document 3.24

New York Times, April 10, 1917.

ALIENS WARNED AGAINST DESECRATING AMERICAN FLAG

Washington, April 9—Warning against desecration of the American flag by aliens was issued today by the Department of Justice. The following notice was sent to Federal attorneys and marshals:

"Any alien enemy tearing down, mutilating, abusing or desecrating the United States flag in any way will be regarded as a danger to the public peace or safety within the meaning of Regulation 12 of the proclamation of the President issued April 6, 1917, and will be subject to summary arrest and confinement."

Document 3.25

Ruling by federal district court upholding a World War I flag desecration conviction.

Source: Ex-Parte Starr, 263 Federal Reporter 145 (1920).

BOURQUIN, District Judge. In this habeas corpus it appears that in February, 1918, the Montana Legislature enacted a statute "defining the crime of sedition," which, in so far as it relates to the flag, is like the federal Espionage Law of May, 1918 [document 2.18]. In August, 1918, an information was filed in the state court, charging that in March, 1918, this petitioner had "committed the crime of sedition," by uttering and publishing contemptuous and slurring language about the flag, and language calculated to bring the flag into contempt and disrepute, as follows:

> What is this thing anyway? Nothing but a piece of cotton with a little paint on it and some other marks in the corner there. I will not kiss that thing. It might be covered with microbes.

Tried and convicted, he was sentenced to the state penitentiary for not less than 10 years nor more than 20 years at hard labor, and to pay a fine of $500 and costs. . . .

His principal contention is that the state law is repugnant to the federal Constitution, in that it assumes powers vested in the United States alone and by it exercised, and hence that he is imprisoned in violation of the Thirteenth and Fourteenth Amendments. That the state may legislate in protection of the flag is settled by *Halter v. Nebraska* [document 3.10]. . . .

In the matter of his offense and sentence, obviously petitioner was more sinned against than sinning. It is clear that he was in the hands of one of those too common mobs, bent upon vindicating its peculiar standard of patriotism and its odd concept of respect for the flag by compelling him to kiss the latter. . . . Its unlawful and disorderly conduct, not his just resistance, nor the trivial and innocuous retort into which they goaded him, was calculated to degrade the sacred banner and to bring it into contempt. Its members, not he, should have been punished. . . .

As for the horrifying sentence itself, . . . so frivolous is the charge that a nominal fine would serve every end of justice. And it, with too many like, goes far to give color, if not justification to the bitter comment of George Bernard Shaw, satirist and cynic, that during the war the courts in France, bleeding under German guns, were very severe; the courts in England, hearing but the echoes of those guns, were grossly unjust; but the court of the United States, knowing naught save censored news of those guns, were stark, staring, raving mad. All this, however, cannot affect habeas corpus. It can appeal to the pardoning power alone.

The state law is valid, petitioner's imprisonment is not repugnant to the federal Constitution, this court cannot relieve him and the writ is denied.

Document 3.26

Ruling by the Kansas Supreme Court upholding a World War I flag desecration conviction.

Source: State v. Shumaker, 175 Pacific Reporter 978 (1918).

MARSHALL, J. The defendant appeals from a judgment of conviction on an information in part reading:

"That on the 12th day of February, 1918, . . . one Frederick Shumaker, Jr., did then and there, unlawfully, publicly defile, defy or cast contempt on the flag . . . by then and there saying in words as follows: 'It is nobody's business.'"

The rest of the language charged to have been used expressed a very vulgar and indecent use of the flag, and the court is of the opinion that the exact language should not find a permanent place in the report of its decisions.

1. The defendant's first contention is that the verdict is contrary to law . . . based on the proposition that the language used was not used in a public place [as required by the Kansas state law]. . . .

The defendant was in a blacksmith shop . . . when he used the language. . . . A "blacksmith shop" is . . . a "public place."

2. The next proposition urged is that the language used did not cast contempt on the flag. In response, it must be said that it is hard to conceive of language that would express greater contempt for the flag. . . . The man who uses such language concerning it, either in jest or in argument, does not have that respect for it that should be found in the breast of every citizen of the United States. . . .

The judgment is confirmed.

Document 3.27

Ruling by Maine Supreme Court overturning a 1940 flag desecration conviction.

Source: State v. Peacock, 25 Atlantic Reporter 491 (1942).

The respondent was indicted for a violation of the [Maine flag desecration law outlawing "publicly" casting contempt upon the American flag "by word or act"]. . . .

The indictment charges that the respondent [violated the act by declaring], " 'What is the flag anyway? It is nothing more than a piece of rag. If I had an American flag here now I would strip it up and trample it under my feet,' and by then and there moving his hands in front of him as though he were tearing an object, and by then and there stamping his feet on the floor as though he were stamping upon an object. . . ."

The respondent on June 30, 1940, called at the home in Plymouth of Herbert J. Tozier to seek his signature to a petition . . . and it was during the course [of this visit] that the jury as indicated by their verdict apparently found that the respondent spoke the words and did the acts attributed to him. . . .

It is apparent that the very essence of this offense is its publicity. The statute is designed to prevent that which would shock the public sense, and . . . would be likely to result in breaches of the peace.

The jury were fully warranted in finding that this respondent by his words and acts showed contempt for the flag of our country which those of us who believe in liberty so dearly love. The question before the jury was, did he speak or act "publicly"?

The rule is not whether the words are spoken or the acts are done in the presence of others in a place where persons have an opportunity to come. Such a test would bring within the statutory prohibition conduct which might take place privately. . . . [The definition of "publicly" given in this case by the judge] to the jury is not in accord with the common understanding of the term as it is used in every-day life and is unsupported by the decision in any decided case.

Exceptions sustained.

Some Dissenting Voices in the Controversy
1897–1928

Although the vast majority of the publicly voiced opinions concerning the flag desecration controversy urged passage of state and/or national legislation, a few opponents of such measures also spoke out. As previously noted, several judges, among others, questioned whether using the flag for advertising purposes was in fact a form of desecration (documents 3.5, 3.6, and 3.7). Similarly, voices were periodically raised suggesting that for political parties to attach slogans or pictures to the flag hardly defamed it, or, at any rate, that so long as the major parties wished to do so, agitating for flag desecration legislation would be a pointless exercise (document 4.1). In Congress, a major barrier to the passage of a federal flag desecration law was the argument that most (and, by 1932, all) of the states already had such statutes and that a federal law was therefore both unnecessary and would usurp states' rights and responsibilities; this position was especially stressed by Rep. Hatton Sumners of Texas, who served for many years as ranking HJC minority member and chairman (document 4.2).

A number of critics suggested that the FPM sought to make a "fetish" of the flag, in which mindless idolatry was substituted for understanding of what the flag truly represented. Thus, the *Independent,* a popular journal, satirically attacked the hyperventilated language of FPM spokesman Charles Kingsbury Miller (documents 2.5, 2.6, and 2.7); attacked groups like the DAR and the SAR, which formed the heart of the FPM, for stressing their heredity over the principles of American democracy; and declared that there was a greater need to support the ideals of "freedom and good government" represented by the flag rather than "superstitious reverence for it," which neglected "reality" in "zeal for the symbol" (document 4.3). Arguments against flag desecration laws on more central free-speech grounds were relatively rare before the Vietnam War, but they were occasionally voiced, usually on the far left of the political spectrum, such as by the anarchists Alexander Berkman and Emma Goldman (documents 4.4 and 4.5), who suggested that such laws revealed the hypocrisies of the United States's claim to be the "land of the free." (As if to prove their point, the federal government deported both of them, solely for their political beliefs, during the 1919 Red Scare.)

Document 4.1

New York Times, June 1, 1898.

The *Springfield* [Massachusetts] *Republican* is troubled by fears that love for the flag turn into mere fetish worship. A bill recently introduced in the Massachusetts Senate punishes with a fine "any person who shall willfully mutilate, deface, alter or falsify the surface of the United States flag [by] causing to be affixed thereon, any label, stamp, advertisement, print, imprint, portrait, printed or painted, or any emblem, mottoes, design, or names." . . . This, in *The Republican*'s opinion—or at least that of its Boston correspondent, will prohibit the use of the flag for campaign purposes, and it asks what more useful purpose the flag can serve in time of peace than as a silent but powerful decoration by each party which uses it to bear the names of its candidates that party is subordinate to country, to see how ridiculously the Senate has slopped over. "It is one thing," it seems [quoting the *Republican*] "to forbid the desecration of the flag for advertising purposes, but to forbid its use as sweepingly as it is prohibited in the above section is making a fetish of it, and removing it from a very effective way of use. The next thing they will be forbidding its use for any decorative purposes whatever. We must expect some excess of zeal in these times, but don't let us be foolish about it."

Document 4.2

Congressional debate on a flag desecration bill, March 19, 1928.

Source: Congressional Record, 1928, 5001–2.

MR. SUMNERS OF TEXAS. . . . .There is some embarrassment, of course, in opposing this bill, a Bill to protect the flag. But why this bill? Since the organization of the Federal Government the flag has been fairly well protected without national legislation on the subject.

To me there is a principle of government involved in this proposed legislation. Gentlemen stand on the floor of this House and decry concentration of power in the Federal Government, and yet every time we are confronted with a proposition to increase power, . . . we vote to give a little more power to the Federal Government. . . .

This is a government created by the people, for the people. In such a system, a system of popular government, if we are to preserve it as a vital, efficient system of government, we must let the smaller units of government do whatever they will do, because in the smaller units of government there is the larger personal interest and responsibility. . . .

Forty-six state legislatures have written prohibitions against the desecration of the American flag. Why do we not leave it there? Nobody claims that the flag is not being protected by the States. . . .

This Government is not made up of capitals, of officials, of laws, or even of written constitutions or yet of flags. It is of the people. This is their flag. It is better for them if they will, and the record shows they will, protect their own flag in their own local governments through their own elected officers than to have an appointed [federal] marshall make the arrest and the trial before an appointed federal judge. They are doing that now. Everybody admits it. . . . I submit that it would be a grander, a more assuring spectacle to see some local constable hail a violator of the flag before a local justice of the peace. . . .

MR. STOBBS. Mr. Speaker, . . . it is perfectly true that the people of the United States express themselves through their State legislature, and they also express themselves through the Congress, here.

This whole legislation is nothing more or less than an expression on the part of the people of the United States through Congress itself of the determination to protect the emblem of our national sovereignty. It is a matter peculiarly within the domain of the National Congress. . . . The function of the Congress of the United States more than any State government is to protect the emblem of national sovereignty, and as the situation is at present, if there is any desecration of the flag within any state and the state does not see fit to prevent it or punish . . . or if there is any desecration of the flag in connection with its use or any article shipped in interstate commerce there is no single law on our statute books by which we can protect our Stars and Stripes. I say that it is a part of the function of the Congress of the United States to protect the emblem of its own sovereignty. . . .

Document 4.3

The Independent, January 15, 1903, 182–83.

THE FLAG AS A FETISH

One of the customs which most astonish and amuse foreigners is our lavish use of the national flag. The American citizen turns to it instinctively whenever he wishes to express exuberant emotion of any kind. On the slightest provocation of patriotic enthusiasm, tiny flags blossom out in his button-hole and hat, even on his necktie and handkerchief. . . . In all this, as in every other manifestation of popular taste, there is much that is irreverent and even ridiculous; but matters of taste are not usually subjects for argument, still less for legislation. On the whole, we prefer the flag to become commonplace rather than to be regarded as in itself sacred, never to be torn down or burned up or handled with other than the purest of patriotic motives.

There are men, in state as in church, who fail to distinguish clearly between a symbol and the idea symbolized, and who take and use metaphors literally. . . . As an example of this kind of thought clothed in rhetoric equally interesting we quote the following [from a pamphlet by Charles K. Miller]:

> Disgraced America, her constitution follows a violated flag and the most brilliant pages of her marvelous history are marred by a blot of shame—the indifference to the honor of the symbol of our sovereignty, unprotected by our national lawmakers from domestic abuses. The scarlet folds of her flag blush like the crimson blossoms of the coral tree, for the perfidy of our national Government in surrendering the emblem of our sacred rights to the vandals of our land to do with it as they will. Our flag has been torn down in the United States, used as a floormat, a footstool cover and carpet to walk upon. . . . [T]he flag itself is apparently neglected by our Government and held in the grasp of avaricious tradesmen and crafty politicians, who turn it into a campaign banner for rival political clubs, a mop for the floors of barrooms and other despicable misuses. These permitted acts of violability to the Stars and Stripes encourage and develop the low ideals of greedy Americans, who deem it their right to walk upon, spit upon, deface and mutilate the flag for personal use in commerce and politics.

. . . From the same source we learn of several shocking events which have occurred in the United States. For instance, a Massachusetts man was caught in the act of burning in his back yard an American flag used for decorative purposes, together with a pile of rubbish which had collected in his store. We hasten to relieve the minds of our readers by adding that the crime was not consummated, for the flag "was rescued tho in a scorched condition by Officer Curtine." This is going nearly as far as the Mohammedans who gather up every scrap of paper lest it should contain the name of Allah and of the ancient Jews who prevented desecration by not writing the name of God at all. The only safe way of avoiding sacrilege is not to have a flag. What can we do now with the flag which we have inadvertently tacked upon our wall since we can neither tear it down nor burn it up? Will not some of the patriotic orders supply a decorous ritual for the disposal of super-annuated flags?

Awful as are the revelations of this pamphlet we know of worse things still. The American flag has actually been sold, openly, for money, on the streets of some of our cities! (In case this is doubted we will furnish names and dates.) Our coins, which bear the national arms, the American eagle and a religious motto, are often in the hands of irreverent and disreputable people, and are sometimes used for the basest purposes. Still more humiliating to a person of sensitive patriotic susceptibilities is the treatment of stamps, not only by individuals, but in post offices. Just as the Buddhists have praying machines, we have the opposite—what might be called "desecrating machines," which at the rate of a thousand a minute deface the portraits of George Washington and other great men, whom on the contrary, we ought to honor and respect. Lately, perhaps through the machinations of the Democratic party, the portrait of the recently assassinated President McKinley has been placed on the postal cards, and every postmaster, under penalty of losing his position, is required to punch the head of our martyred President. . . . .

We have also heard that the "Star Spangled Banner" has been sung in low theaters by actresses whose characters were not above reproach. Let us have legislation to stop this at once, and allow no one to sing our sacred national anthems except those who are inspired with true patriotic motives and have a good moral character.

There is one form of desecration of our national emblems more serious than those mentioned. That is using them in any way as the distinguishing badge of those self-styled "patriotic" societies which base their membership on their ancestry or which find their chief occupation in opposing the influence of "foreigners." If our flag stands for anything, it stands for opposition to hereditary privilege, the spirit of caste and exclusiveness, and all artificial distinctions and eminences; and we confess that of the two, it seems less incongruous and distasteful to see a national emblem used to advertise a railroad, a patent medicine or a sugar-coated ham than to see it used to advertise the wearer as the thirty-second fraction of a Revolutionary hero. . . .

Revolutionary patriots did not fight for a "flag." They fought for freedom and good government, and they fought just as bravely under the sign of a tree or a rattlesnake or no flag at all as under "Old Glory." We hope, in spite of appearances, that their descendants will not neglect the reality in their zeal for the symbol. . . . Whatever legislation may be necessary to protect the flag against intentional insult should not be based on a superstitious reverence for it.

Document 4.4

Mother Earth, anarchist journal edited by Emma Goldman, July 1916, 535; Apr. 1917, 35–36.

[July, 1916] One of the deplorable results of the preparedness craze [prior to American entry into World War I] is the flag mania. Dozens of persons, lecturers, teachers, clerks, workingman, even school boys are denounced, persecuted or sentenced by courts, like Bouck White and some of his followers [document 3.12], for alleged or real disrespect for the flag. The other day a principal of a Public School found it in keeping with his honor to denounce two teachers, who were suspected that they did not salute the flag. An able pedagogue would perhaps think that servility and hypocrisy were rampant enough far and wide in the country and that it really is not necessary to foster them and force them on people. . . .

[April, 1917] It is worth while to observe that a number of judges recently have expressed their regret that the laws in question when they passed sentence on the culprits did not permit them to condemn them to a longer period of imprisonment. This happened also in the case of Bouck White and his friends. The judge gave him the full limit of the law and almost shed tears that he could not do more harm to the defendant, who had nothing else than to express his love for universal brotherhood by a solemn ceremony and symbolic act [of flag-burning]. The sarcasm of it is that at the same time the government of this country is hailed to be the world's guardian of liberty, freedom of conscience, thought and expression. Evidently the meaning of the situation in Russia [where the czar had just been overthrown by a revolution] where the strictest, tyrannical laws reigned supreme has not penetrated the brains of many persons in this country.

Document 4.5

The Blast, anarchist journal edited by Alexander Berkman, July 1, 1916, 5.

THE SACRED RAG

Bouck White . . . is in prison in New York for having circulated a cartoon in which the American flag was represented as stamped with the dollar mark [document 3.12]. When White's term expires he will be tried for having "destroyed and desecrated" an American flag. . . . There may have been a time when the American flag stood for freedom of conscience and political justice, though even that is doubtful. Today the flag stands only for exploitation and militarism. It is the emblem of prostituted justice and greedy capitalism. It waves proudly over the tents of Ludlow, where women and children or striking miners are burned alive [in the "Ludlow Massacre" of 1914, in which 13 women and children were killed when state militia burned down a striking miners' tent colony] by hired gunmen protected by the American flag. . . . The very fact that men are sent to prison for "desecrating" a rag proves that there is no freedom of conscience under that flag. No decent man or woman can respect the symbol of such tyranny.

The Supreme Court and the Flag
1931–1943

After the 1907 *Halter* decision (document 3.10), in which the Supreme Court upheld the constitutionality of state flag desecration laws, at least insofar as they banned the use of the flag for commercial purposes, the Supreme Court never ruled again on flag desecration laws until the Vietnam War era. In 1931 and in 1943, however, the Court ruled in two cases concerning flag usage that were ultimately to provide key legal building blocks leading to its Vietnam-era rulings (documents 8.1–8.3) and later to those of 1989–90 (documents 10.12 and 12.7), the latter of which clearly struck down all flag desecration laws used to prosecute peaceful symbolic political dissent involving the flag, even if such protest involved physical destruction of the emblem.

The 1931 case, *Stromberg v. California* (document 5.1), struck down the so-called red flag laws, passed in thirty-two states during the 1919 post–World War I Red Scare, which outlawed the display of red flags because they were associated with procommunist political views. Although the red flag laws were clearly distinct from flag desecration laws, in that they forbade the display of "opposition" flags rather than the commercial use, verbal criticism, or physical damage of "government" flags, their passage was clearly motivated by the same fear of dissent, and especially of left-wing radicalism, that had motivated the FPM to stress the need to ban dissenting symbolic use of the American flag. Therefore, the Supreme Court's 1931 *Stromberg* ruling, which declared illegal, as a violation of the First Amendment, attempts to ban the peaceful display of opposition symbols, was clearly pregnant with implications for flag desecration laws. In *Stromberg*, the Court for the first time declared that the First Amendment's guarantee of freedom of speech encompassed so-called symbolic speech, such as the display of flags, and in so doing it laid one crucial part of the foundation for its subsequent flag desecration rulings by making clear that the First Amendment protected the right to use flags to express peaceful political opposition.

In fact, had the Court upheld the red flag laws, theoretically Congress and the states could have outlawed the peaceful display of any and all symbols, including the American flag, unless the Court was able to somehow distinguish the national flag from all other symbols. In the 1943 case of *West Virginia Board of Education v. Barnette* (document 5.2), the Court made it clear that it could not and would not do this, by striking down laws that required compulsory flag salutes and recitals of the Pledge of Allegiance in the public schools (in so doing, the Court reversed its own decision of only three years earlier in *Minersville School District v. Gobitis* [310 *United States Reports* 586, 1940], which had upheld such laws as vital to American "national unity," which was held to be the "basis of national security"). In its 1943 *Barnette* ruling, the Court declared that the "case is made difficult not because the principles of its decision are obscure but because the flag involved is our own," and held that "freedom to differ is not limited to things that do not matter much" but extended to "things that touch the heart of the existing order." The Court added that the "fixed star" in the American "constitutional constellation" was that government could not "prescribe what shall be orthodox in politics, nationalism, religion or other matters of opinion."

As will be noted in chapter 8, the Court's subsequent ruling in the 1969 case of *Street v. New York* (document 8.1), outlawing provisions of flag desecration laws that banned verbal criticism of the flag, rested heavily on the *Stromberg* and (especially) *Barnette* precedents to conclude that the freedom to differ even about "things that touch the heart of the existing order" included "the freedom to express publicly one's opinions about our flag, including those opinion which are defiant or contemptuous." After ducking the question of the legality of physical (as opposed to verbal) flag desecration for twenty years following the 1969 *Street* ruling, and thus avoiding extending the *Street* doctrine to its obvious logical conclusion, the Court ruled in the 1989 case of *Texas v. Johnson* (document 10.12), that the same principle applied to peaceful "nonverbal conduct" involving the flag, including "outright destruction" such as burning, "where the nonverbal conduct is expressive." This principle was reaffirmed and made unmistakably clear by the Court in the 1990 case of *U.S. v. Eichman* (document 12.7) to those in Congress and elsewhere who found ambiguity in the 1989 *Johnson* ruling (as is discussed in chapters 10 and 12).

Document 5.1

Supreme Court majority opinion in the 1931 case of *Stromberg v. California*.

Source: 283 United States Reports 259.

The appellant was convicted in the Superior Court of San Bernardino County, California, for Violation of §403-a of the Penal Code of that State. That section provides:

"Any person who displays a red flag, banner or badge or any flag, badge, banner or device of any color or form whatever in any public place or in any meeting place or public assembly, or from or on any house, building or window as a sign, symbol or emblem of opposition to organized government or as an invitation or stimulus to anarchistic action or as an aid to propaganda that is of a seditious character is guilty of a felony."

It appears that the appellant, a young woman of nineteen, a citizen of the United States by birth, was one of the supervisors of a summer camp for children. . . . Appellant led the children in their daily study, teaching them history and economics. "Among other things, the children were taught class consciousness, the solidarity of the workers, and the theory that the workers of the world are of one blood and brothers all." Appellant was a member of the Young Communist League. . . . The charge against her concerned a daily ceremony at the camp, in which the appellant supervised and directed the children in raising a red flag, "a camp-made reproduction of the flag of Soviet Russia, which was also the flag of the Communist Party in the United States." In connection with the flag-raising, there was a ritual at which the children stood at salute and recited a pledge of allegiance "to the worker's red flag, and to the cause for which it stands; one aim throughout our lives, freedom for the working class."

. . . The charge in the information, as to the purposes for which the flag was raised, was laid conjunctively, uniting the three purposes which the statute condemned. . . . As there were three purposes set forth in the statute and the jury were instructed that their verdict might be given with respect to any one of them, independently considered, it is impossible to say under which clause of the statute the conviction was obtained. If any one of these clauses which the state court has held to be separable, was invalid, it cannot be determined upon this record that the appellant was not convicted under that clause. . . .

We are thus brought to the question whether any one of the three clauses, as construed by the state court, is upon its face repugnant to the Federal Constitution so that it could not constitute a lawful foundation for a criminal prosecution. The principles to be applied have been clearly set forth in our former decisions. It has been determined that the conception of liberty under the due process clause of the Fourteenth Amendment embraces the right of free speech. The right is not an absolute one, and the State in the exercise of its police power may punish the abuse of this freedom. There is no question but that the State may thus provide for the punishment of those who indulge in utterance which incite to violence and crime and threaten the overthrow of organized government by unlawful means. . . . We have no reason to doubt the validity of the second and third clauses of the statute as construed by the state court to relate to such incitements to violence.

The question is thus narrowed to that of the validity of the first clause, that is, with respect to the display of the flag "as a sign, symbol or emblem of opposition to organized government," and the construction which the state court has placed upon this clause removes every element of doubt. . . . The court considered that it might be construed as embracing conduct which the State could not constitutionally prohibit. Thus it was said that the clause "might be construed to include the peaceful and orderly opposition to a government as organized and controlled by one political party by those of another political party equally high minded and patriotic, which did not agree with the one in power. It might also be construed to include peaceful and orderly opposition to government by legal means and within constitutional limitations." The maintenance of the opportunity for free political discussion to the end that government may be responsive to the will of the people and that change may be obtained by lawful means, an opportunity essential to the security of the Republic, is a fundamental principle of our constitutional system. A statute which upon its face, and as authoritatively construed, is so vague and indefinite as to permit the punishment of the fair use of this opportunity is repugnant to the guaranty of liberty contained in the Fourteenth Amendment. The first clause of the statute being invalid upon its face, the conviction of the appellant, which so far as the record discloses may have rested upon that clause exclusively, must be set aside.

Document 5.2

Supreme Court majority opinion in the 1943 case of *West Virginia State Board of Education v. Barnette.*

Source: 319 United States Reports 624.

Following the decision by this Court on June 3, 1940, in *Minersville School District v. Gobitis,* the West Virginia legislature amended its statutes to require all schools therein to conduct courses of instruction in history, civics, and in the Constitution of the United States and of the State "for the purpose of teaching, fostering and perpetuating the ideals, principles and spirit of Americanism, and increasing the knowledge of the organization and machinery of the government."

The [West Virginia] Board of Education on January 9, 1942, adopted a resolution . . . ordering that the salute to the flag become "a regular part of the program of activities in the public schools," that all teachers and pupils "shall be required to participate in the salute honoring the Nation represented by the Flag; provided, however, that refusal to salute the Flag be regarded as an act of insubordination and shall be dealt with accordingly." . . . Failure to conform is "insubordination" dealt with by expulsion. . . . Appellees, citizens of the United States and of West Virginia, brought suit in the United States District Court for themselves and others similarly situated asking its injunction to restrain enforcement of these laws and regulations against [the religious organization the] Jehovah's Witnesses [whose] religious beliefs include a literal version of Exodus, Chapter 20, verses 4 and 5, which says: "Thou shalt not make unto thee any graven image . . . ; thou shalt not bow down thyself to them nor serve them." They consider that the flag is an "image" within this command. For this reason they refuse to salute it.

The freedom asserted by these appellees does not bring them into collision with rights asserted by any other individual. . . . Nor is there any question in this case that their behavior is peaceable and orderly. The sole conflict is between authority and rights of the individual. The State asserts power to condition access to public education on making a prescribed sign and profession and at the same time to coerce attendance. . . .

There is no doubt that, in connection with the pledges, the flag salute is a form of utterance. Symbolism is a primitive but effective way of communicating ideas. The use of an emblem or flag to symbolize some system, idea, institution, or personality is a short cut from mind to mind. . . . A person gets from a symbol the meaning he puts into it, and what is one man's comfort and inspiration is another's jest and scorn.

Over a decade ago Chief Justice Hughes led this Court in holding that the display of a red flag as a symbol of opposition by peaceful and legal means to organized government was protected by the free speech guaranties of the Constitution [*Stromberg v. California*, document 5.1]. Here it is the State that employs a flag as a symbol of adherence to government as presently organized. It requires the individual to communicate by word and sign his acceptance of the political ideas it thus bespeaks. . . .

[T]he compulsory flag salute and pledge requires affirmation of a belief and an attitude of mind. . . . It is now a commonplace that censorship or suppression of expression of opinion is tolerated by our Constitution only when the expression presents a clear and present danger of action of a kind the State is empowered to prevent and punish. It would seem that involuntary affirmation could be commanded only on even more immediate and urgent grounds than silence. But here the power of compulsion is invoked without any allegation that remaining passive during a flag salute ritual creates a clear and present danger that would justify an effort even to muffle expression. To sustain the compulsory flag salute we are required to say that a Bill of Rights which guards the individual's right to speak his own mind, left it open to public authorities to compel him to utter what is not in his mind. . . .

The very purpose of a Bill of Rights was to withdraw certain subjects from the vicissitudes of political controversy, to place them beyond the reach of majorities and officials and to establish them as legal principles to be applied by the courts. One's right to life, liberty, and property, to free speech, a free press, freedom of worship and assembly, and other fundamental rights may not be submitted to vote; they depend on the outcome of no elections. . . .

Struggles to coerce uniformity of sentiment in support of some end thought essential to their time and country have been waged by many good as well as by evil men. . . . [The lessons of history such as attempts by the Romans to stamp out Christianity teach us that such efforts are ultimately futile and that t]hose who begin coercive elimination of dissent soon find themselves exterminating dissenters. Compulsory unification of opinion achieves only the unanimity of the graveyard.

It seems trite but necessary to say that the First Amendment to our Constitution was designed to avoid these ends by avoiding these beginnings. There is no mysticism in the American concept of the State or of the nature or origin of its authority. We set up government by consent of the governed, and the Bill of Rights denies those in power any legal opportunity to coerce that consent. Authority here is to be controlled by public opinion, not public opinion by authority.

The case is made difficult not because the principles of its decision are obscure but because the flag involved is our own. Nevertheless, we apply the limitations of the Constitution with no fear that freedom to be intellectually and spiritually diverse or even contrary will disintegrate the social organization. To believe that patriotism will not flourish if patriotic ceremonies are voluntary and spontaneous instead of a compulsory routine is to make an unflattering estimate of the appeal of our institutions to free minds. We can have intellectual individualism and the rich cultural diversities that we owe to exceptional minds only at the price of occasional eccentricity and abnormal attitudes. When they are so harmless to others or to the State as those we deal with here, the price is not too great. But freedom to differ is not limited to things that do not matter much. That would be a mere shadow of freedom. The test of its substance is the right to differ as to things that touch the heart of the existing order.

If there is any fixed star in our constitutional constellation, it is that no official, high or petty, can prescribe what shall be orthodox in politics, nationalism, religion, or other matters of opinion or force citizens to confess by word or act their faith therein. If there are any circumstances which permit an exception, they do not now occur to us.

We think the action of the local authorities in compelling the flag salute and pledge transcends constitutional limitations on their power and invades the sphere of intellect and spirit which it is the purpose of the First Amendment to our Constitution to reserve from all official control.

The [1940] decision of this Court in *Minersville School District v. Gobitis* [holding to the contrary of this ruling is overruled].

The Dispute During the Vietnam War Era

Between World War II and the beginning of wide-scale protest against the Vietnam War during the mid-1960s only a handful of flag desecration prosecutions appear to have occurred, and general interest in the entire subject virtually disappeared. This was especially true with regard to the universal provision of the state flag desecration laws that forbade advertising use of the flag, which had, in fact, gradually fallen into misuse since the Supreme Court's 1907 *Halter* ruling (document 3.10) upholding the constitutionality of such measures. The widespread and usually unpunished use of flags in merchandising was clearly indicated in a 1941 Commerce Department pamphlet that noted that Americans had increasingly wished to display their patriotic feelings amidst the "crescendo of warfare abroad," and that, in response, merchants and manufacturers had "exploited" such feelings with products that featured flags "beyond bounds of good taste and even beyond the limits of the law."[1]

Perhaps the clearest sign of the vanishing interest in commercial use of the flag was that in 1962 the American Law Institute, a private organization of influential judges, lawyers and professors concerned with legal reform, proposed a model state penal code that deleted all references to forbidding such uses (while retaining bans on physical destruction of the flag that could "outrage the sensibilities" of onlookers), because, "Whatever may have been true [previously] it is scarcely realistic today to regard commercial exploitation" of the flag as "a serious affront to popular sensibilities" and, in any case, any such restriction "belongs outside the legal code." Perhaps because instances of symbolic political protest use of the flag had always been as rare as commercial exploitation had become routine, in 1966 the National Conference of Commissioners on Uniform State Laws, which in 1917 had recommended that all the states enact a Uniform Flag Law, based on the American Flag Association's 1900 model law (documents 2.11 and 2.19), withdrew the proposal in its entirety from its list of recommended statutes, on the grounds that it was "obsolete."[2]

In retrospect, there is a rich irony in the fact that popular interest in flag desecration, at least where it was perceived as representing political protest, suddenly and drastically resumed just as the NCCUSL had deemed the entire subject "obsolete." Beginning in about early 1966, antiwar demonstrators started using the flag for symbolic protests in ways that gradually began to arouse congressional, press, and public criticism, with the result that in 1968, for the first time in American history, Congress passed a national flag desecration law (document 6.1). Although a scattering of flag desecration incidents attracted local media attention in 1966, flag desecration became a prominent national issue primarily as the result of a flag burning that occurred on April 15, 1967, in New York City's Central Park, during a massive antiwar demonstration that attracted an estimated two hundred thousand protesters.

The Central Park incident became important primarily because, unlike the earlier scattered incidents, it was photographed, and pictures of it were widely published in the American press. On May 8, 1967, as the result of the congressional furor that was touched off by the Central Park burning, a House Judiciary Committee (HJC) subcommittee began four days of hearings on federal flag desecration legislation that received widespread publicity. By the time the hearings began, more than sixty House members had already proposed virtually identical flag desecration bills, which generally banned a wide variety of acts, such as burning and mutilation as well as words, that "cast contempt" upon the flag. During the hearings, more than five dozen House members appeared before the subcommittee to denounce flag desecrators and demand harsh action against them; not a single Congressman appeared to oppose such action, and only a handful of outside witnesses took such a stance.

Supporters of the legislation made clear that their aim was to suppress a form of dissent that they found especially upsetting and powerful and that they repeatedly claimed would undermine the morale of American soldiers fighting in Vietnam; thus, Pennsylvania Supreme Court Justice Michael Musmanno asked the HJC subcommittee, "How could demonstrations against American policy be more vividly and dramatically manifested than by burning the very flag of the United States?"[3] Typical of the testimony before the subcommittee was that of Rep. James Quillen (R., Tenn.), who was to fight twenty years later for a constitutional amendment outlawing flag desecration in the wake of the 1989 and 1990 Supreme Court rulings that effectively struck down all legislation that outlawed such symbolic political protest, including the 1968 law that emerged as a result of the 1967 House hearings (document 6.2).

On June 5, 1967, the House subcommittee approved a flag desecration bill by a 6–1 vote, and the parent HJC acted likewise by an overwhelming vote on June 6. In response to concerns expressed by Attorney General Ramsay Clark, who made clear his general lack of enthusiasm for federal legislation in a May 8 letter to HJC chairman Emanuel Cellar, which the HJC published in its report (document 6.3), the recommended bill omitted, on grounds of dubious constitutionality, language that would have outlawed purely verbal criticism of the flag, thus foretelling the Supreme Court's 1969 ruling in *Street v. New York* (document 8.1). In recommending a flag desecration bill, the HJC majority bluntly reported that the proposal was "occasioned by a number of recent public flag-burning incidents" and maintained that action was justified because public "destruction and dishonor" of the flag "inflicts an injury on the entire Nation," and that outlawing such conduct imposed "no substantial burden on anyone."

Only three out of the thirty-four HJC members, John Conyers (D., Mich.), Robert Kastenmeier (D., Wis.) and Don Edwards (D., Calif.), dissented from the majority report (document 6.3). They stressed the same kinds of free speech arguments that were to dominate the 1989–90 debate but that had been relatively scarce during prior consideration of flag desecration laws. Thus, Conyers and Edwards argued that the proposal would "do more real harm to the Nation than all the flag burners could possibly" inflict, because it would infringe "one of the most basic freedoms, the freedom to dissent," which they characterized as the "real 'evil'" targeted by the bill.

On June 20, 1967, in an action reported on the front page of the June 21 *New York Times*, the House of Representatives approved a flag desecration bill by a 385–16 vote, after a five-hour debate that was dominated by attacks by more than sixty congressmen on flag burners as "un-American," "traitors," "misfits," "anarchists," "crackpots," "irresponsible louts," "rats," and a wide variety of other well-chosen epithets that may well have exhausted the vocabulary of insults. Only ten congressmen took the floor to oppose the bill, with free speech arguments their dominant theme. The Senate subsequently passed a similar bill on June 24, 1968, and President Johnson placed his signature on the first federal flag desecration law in American history on Independence Day, July 4, 1968.

Document 6.1

The 1968 Federal Flag Desecration Law (18 U.S.C. § 700[b] [1988]).

Be it enacted by the Senate and House of Representatives of the United States of America in Congress assembled, That Chapter 33 of title 18,

United States Code, is amended by inserting immediately preceding section 701 thereof, a new section as follows:

"§ 700. Desecration of the flag of the United States; penalties

"(a) whoever knowingly casts contempt upon any flag of the United States by publicly mutilating, defacing, defiling, burning, or trampling upon it shall be fined not more than $1,000 or imprisoned for not more than one year, or both.

"(b) The term 'flag of the United States' as used in this section shall include any flag, standard, colors, ensign, or any picture representation of either or of any part or parts of either, made of any substance or represented on any substance, of any size evidently purporting to be either of said flag, standard, colors, or ensign of the United States of America, or a picture or a representation of either, upon which shall be shown the colors, the stars and the stripes, in any number of either thereof, or of any part or parts of either, by which the average person seeing the same without deliberation may believe the same to represent the flag, standard, colors, or ensign of the United States of America.

"(c) Nothing in this section shall be construed as indicating an intent on the part of Congress to deprive any State, territory, possession, or the Commonwealth of Puerto Rico of jurisdiction over any offense over which it would have jurisdiction in the absence of this section."

Document 6.2

Congressional testimony by Rep. James Quillen, May 8, 1967.

Source: Hearings Before Subcommittee No. 4 of the Committee on the Judiciary, House of Representatives on H. R. 271 and Similar Proposals to Prohibit Desecration of the Flag, 90th Cong., 1st sess., 1967, 28–45.

. . . We meet to discuss legislation, the need for which shocks us and people throughout this nation.

For all of us and all those like us whose hearts are filled with patriotism and love and respect for all that our flag symbolizes, it is deplorable to think that anyone could be so bold, thankless, and thoughtless as to scar in any way the traditional symbol of our free land.

Yet we need only to pick up a newspaper or see or hear a newscast to be aware that in this country today there are those who would and do, abuse and insult our flag, and even go to such lengths as to publicly burn it in defiance and disgust.

The flag that is being desecrated today is among the oldest of the national standards of the world, the symbol which Oliver Wendell Holmes so movingly described as—

> Washed in the blood of the brave and the blooming,
>   Snatched from the altars of insolent foes,
> Burning with star-fires but never consuming,
>   Flash its broad ribbons of lily rose.
> Vainly the prophets of Baal would rend it,
>   Vainly his worshippers pray for its fall,
> Thousands have died for it, millions defend it,
>   Emblem of justice and mercy to all.

"Emblem of justice" the poet calls our flag; so it is and the symbol of liberty, not just for our own people but for millions of men, women, and children around the globe. . . . Thousands of miles from this committee room, many of our young men are dying at this very minute in Vietnam for the principles and beliefs that we hold most dear and most sacred. But here in the cities torn amidst riots and demonstrations, these same principles and beliefs are ignored, and our flag has become one of the targets at which are hurled insults of all kinds.

But what can the Federal government do to stop such insults to our national standards? We all know that we don't have a [federal flag desecration] law but we should and must have one. In all logic and reasonableness, the Federal Government must be capable of protecting those symbols that embody our Nation's principles. . . . [W]hen flag burnings overshadow and take the headlines from those who would uphold our flag and would die for it, we must take steps to see that these detractors receive the punishment which their actions merit.

If these young rebels [who burn the flag would only] . . . compare our lives to those in communistic and socialistic countries, I am sure they would be much more appreciative of what they have. . . .

[I do not mean to say] that no one can disagree with the policies of those in authority, but there are bounds in which these disagreements are to be manifested. I feel that when anyone goes so far as to desecrate our beloved flag for their own personal satisfaction, he has gone too far.

The proper authority must step in and take the appropriate action. . . .

Let all of us here—this committee and the entire Congress—bring a new surge of patriotism to our Nation by showing our people that we do care what happens to the great symbol of our great Nation. . . .

Mr. Chairman, I would like to read a resolution that was passed by the Tennessee State Legislature on April 20, 1967:

> Whereas, the Daughters of the American Revolution, at the Seventy-Fifth Continental Congress, on June 18–22, 1966, in Washington, D.C. adopted the following Resolution:
> Whereas, the flag of the United States of America is the emblem of the Nation and a symbol of liberty wherever displayed and
> Whereas apathy, indifference and lack of respect for the Flag are

becoming increasingly evident by incidents of desecration and some-times violent destruction; and

Whereas Public Law 829 (Flag Code) does not provide penalties for desecration and misuse of the Flag;

Resolved, That the National Society, Daughters of the American Revolution support legislation which would make desecration of the Flag of the United States of America a Federal offense with penalties of fines and/or imprisonment,

Now, therefore, be it resolved by the House of Representatives of the Eighty-fifth General Assembly of the State of Tennessee, the Senate concurring, that the United States Congress be urged to enact legislation to carry out the objectives of the DAR Resolution. . . .

Mr. Chairman, I would like to insert at this point in my remarks, a resolution that was adopted by the 16th Annual Tennessee Service Officers Conference, Division of Veterans' Affairs, meeting in Nashville, Tenn., on April 20–22, 1967, . . .

Whereas, At the present time there is no federal law on the books against desecration of the United States flag; and

Whereas, There is more need today than in quite some time to respect the United States, with our fighting men dying in Vietnam; and

Whereas, The passage of this bill will serve as a reminder to those persons who would disrespect the United States Flag that they can no longer do this without being punished:

And therefore be it resolved, That the Sixteenth Annual Tennessee Service Officers Conference . . . does hereby request . . . passage by the Congress [of] a bill by Representative James H. Quillen which provides that anyone who "publicly mutilates, defaces, defiles, tramples upon or casts contempt by word or act upon any flag, standard, colors or ensign of the United States," shall be punished by imprisonment of not more than one year and a fine of not more than $1,000. . . .

Just last Tuesday, the new national commander of the Veterans of World War I, William H. Walker, stated in a bulletin:

We stop in our daily tasks and wonder what is happening to our way of life in this great country of ours. In the past month we have seen pictures of the burning of the flag * * * in Central Park in New York. This is enough to make men who have given their lives for Old Glory turn over in their graves. What an insult to our entire Country that we allow such actions to go unpunished. . . .

I have received letters and wires from all over the country expressing support for this legislation.

I will mention here just a few of the many editorials that have appeared in the newspapers in my district strongly supporting my bill. . . . [F]rom the *Kingsport Times*, . . .

> When it comes to silly arguments, about the silliest to come to our attention in a long time is the one that the proposal of a federal law to forbid and punish desecration of the American Flag might "violate the constitutional guarantee of free speech."
>
> Any member of the Congress entertaining such a theory, as ground for legal objection, is fabricating his own gnat to strain at. . . .
>
> Technically, and in the eyes of the law, there is a difference between saying "Let's burn the house down," and setting fire to it.
>
> The Flag has been desecrated time and again in this era of rampant hooliganism and apparently privileged seditious mischief. Subversive characters have spat on it, walked on it, burned it, and torn it to shreds. They thereby were showing contempt not only for Old Glory, but for the thousands of young Americans who are fighting and dying for it.
>
> Yet with a spate of measures before Congress to make that offense a federal crime, there still is no national law against it. The culprits go free! . . .

In earlier times, it was thought better to kill anyone who would harm the American flag rather than let it be mistreated in any way. In an official dispatch to the Treasury Officer in New Orleans in 1861, [Treasury Secretary] John Adams Dix said:

> If anyone attempts to haul down the American flag, shoot him on the spot.

I do not think we need to go that far, but we must not let anyone who would harm our flag go scot free.

We must consider the morale of our people here at home, our fighting forces in Vietnam, as well as world reaction. . . .

Let us not tarry any longer. Let us rally 'round the flag. Let us rededicate ourselves to the principles of freedom. . . .

I really think that we could not have any penalty too strict for the desecration of our flag. . . . To me it is not just a piece of cloth. It represents all the things that these thousands and hundreds of thousands of men have died for, and many hundreds of thousands are going to die in the future to protect it. Anything short of a firing squad, even though it be severe, would be agreeable to me.

Document 6.3

1967 House of Representatives Judiciary Committee report, with majority views in support of a federal flag desecration bill, followed by the text of a letter from Attorney General Ramsay Clark, separate views of Rep. Robert Kastenmeier, and minority views of Reps. John Conyers, Jr., and Don Edwards.

Source: Penalties for Desecration of the Flag, 90th Cong., 1st sess., 1967, H. R. No. 350.

PURPOSE The Purpose of the bill is to prohibit and punish by Federal law certain public acts of desecration of the flag.

STATEMENT The bill is occasioned by a number of recent public flag-burning incidents in various parts of the United States and in foreign countries by American citizens. It is designed to remedy an anomaly in existing law wherein desecration of the flag is proscribed by Federal statute only in the District of Columbia. What is more, although each of the 50 states by statute prohibits certain acts of flag desecration, the penalties imposed by the State statutes vary widely. The committee concludes that the national emblem should be given concurrent Federal protection. . . .

The bill, as amended, will assure Federal investigative and prosecutive jurisdiction over those who would cast contempt by publicly mutilating, defacing, defiling, burning, or trampling upon the flag of the United States. It is intended that State jurisdiction in this matter should not be displaced. . . . The committee is persuaded that it is in the national interest that concurrent jurisdiction be exercised by Federal and State law enforcement agencies over this subject. . . .

The committee believes that the bill which it here reports will successfully withstand all constitutional challenges to which it may be subjected in the courts. The bill does not prohibit speech, the communication of ideas or political dissent or protest. The bill does not prescribe orthodox conduct or require affirmative action. The bill does prohibit public acts of physical dishonor or destruction of the flag of the United States. The language of the bill prohibits intentional, willful, not accidental or inadvertent public physical acts of desecration of the flag. Utterances are not proscribed. Specific examples of prohibited conduct under the bill would include casting contempt upon the flag by burning or tearing it and by spitting upon or otherwise dirtying it. There is nothing vague or uncertain about the terms used in the bill. . . .

Of course, nothing in the bill will prohibit any person from complying with section 176(j), title 36, United States Code, which provides that when the flag "is in such condition that it is no longer a fitting emblem for display (it) should be destroyed in a dignified way, preferably by burning." Compliance with this provision obviously does not cast contempt on the flag. . . .

Public burning, destruction, and dishonor of the national emblem inflicts an injury on the entire nation. Its prohibition imposes no substantial burden on anyone. The committee believes that enactment of this legislation is wholly salutary. . . .

DEPARTMENTAL COMMUNICATION
Attached and made a part of this report is a letter dated May 8, 1967, from the Attorney General of the United States to Hon. Emanuel Celler, chairman of the House Committee on the Judiciary, on the subject of the proposed legislation.
OFFICE OF THE ATTORNEY GENERAL, Washington, D.C., May 8, 1967.
. . . This is in response to a request for the views of the Department of Justice on [a variety of proposed bills] to prohibit desecration of the flag of the United States. . . .

The American people are deeply devoted to their flag. It is in the hearts and minds of our citizens, the symbol of our national ideal: "liberty and justice for all." We are deeply hurt when our flag is dishonored for it represents not only a noble history and the sacrifice and spirit of our fathers, but our aspirations for our children and their fulfillment.

Whether a Federal criminal statute is the proper redress for the injury inflicted on the Nation when the flag is burned and whether it would serve as a needed deterrent against further transgressions is a question for the Congress.

As you address yourselves to this issue, I would urge study of the following considerations:

The real tragedy when the flag is willfully burned is not the loss of the flag, but the fact that there are those among us, however few who have so little love for country or confidence in its purposes, or are otherwise so thoughtless or insensitive, that they want to burn the flag. Today their number is infinitesimal; a handful among 200 million. Should their number ever become substantial, and there is no evidence of any likelihood of this, then their conduct would be a matter of deepest concern, which all history shows a mere statute cannot resolve.

We are a Federal system. Our national strength depends on the strength of State and local governments and their devotion to the union. . . . . Each of the 50 States, like the District of Columbia, has laws prescribing criminal penalties for desecration of the flag. Until this time, a general Federal law has not been found necessary. Ideally, we would look to the States for effective enforcement of their laws against such local conduct. . . .

If the Congress determines that State or local enforcement is for any reason inadequate, or that there are overriding reasons why burning the

Nation's flag should be a Federal offense, the Department of Justice can, and of course will, vigorously prosecute violators. . . .

If Congress decides to enact such legislation, it should be clear that the States will not by such enactment be precluded from prosecuting for desecration of the national flag. . . .

Particular care should be exercised to avoid infringement of free speech. To make it a crime if one "defies" or "casts contempt * * * either by word or act" upon the national flag is to risk invalidation. This broad language may be too vague under standards of constitutional law to constitute the basis of a criminal action. Such language reaches toward conduct which may be protected by first amendment guarantees, and the courts have found vagueness in this area. `

. . . The phrases in question are in fact unnecessary to accomplish the goal of prohibiting direct acts of disrespect or desecration, because the remaining language comprehensively describes such acts. Accordingly, in order to reduce the risk of challenge on vagueness and first amendment grounds, it is recommended that the word "defies" and the phrase "or casts contempt, either by word or act," be deleted as separate acts constituting offenses. To secure further protection against such constitutional challenge, we suggest that the objective acts described in the provision be made criminal only if performed as a means of casting contempt upon the flag. . . .

Sincerely,
RAMSEY CLARK,
Attorney General

SEPARATE VIEWS OF HON. ROBERT W. KASTENMEIER

In my judgment this measure, like the acts of flag desecration it purports to prevent, is a warning sign in the life of our Republic. As the dissenting views of my colleagues, Mr. Conyers and Mr. Edwards, amply and seriously set forth, the measure may be an unconstitutional attack on the free expression of thought so vital to the continued successful operation of a democracy, even though State statutes to the same effect have not been struck down for that reason.

I do consider the measure, however, to be unresponsive to the basic issues of our times, since the people who feel constrained to burn the flag of their country apparently are acting out of despair over its current policies and a particular love of country which they feel is oppressed by these policies. Whether that is true or not, they will certainly find other means, perhaps equally or more abhorrent to conventional behavior standards, to dramatize their opposition to national policy. . . .

This statute, if enacted as it can reasonably be expected to be, will in the final analysis only provide empty rhetorical ammunition for the flag wavers, needless martyrdom for the flag burners and embarrassment for this Congress among serious students and advocates of free speech and the right of dissent. The proposal appears to be grounded in a general climate of war hysteria which is more a comment about the advocates than it is about the protestors they seek to curb. . . . Its real vice is that it feeds irrational demands for conformity.

MINORITY VIEWS OF HON. JOHN CONYERS, JR., AND HON. DON EDWARDS ON H.R. 10480

As the majority report states: "The bill is occasioned by a number of recent public flag burning incidents. . . ." It also states: "Public burning, destruction, and dishonor of the national emblem inflicts an injury on the entire nation." It seems anomalous to us that the legislature of what we hope should be the most highly civilized nation the world has ever known could seriously consider enacting a law based on so primitive a concept. Whatever results flow from the acts of those who burn our flag, they can do no injury to the Nation. . . . [E]nactment of this legislation would do more real harm to the Nation than all the flag burners can possibly do. This legislation would infringe upon what is certainly one of the most basic of freedoms, the freedom to dissent.

Although the bill itself does not use the word "dissent," it was made abundantly clear in the hearings that dissent and particularly opposition to our policies in Vietnam are the real "evil" at which the bill as directed. . . .

[T]his bill, because it is designed to suppress dissent, is unconstitutional as an abridgement of First Amendment guarantees and, in any event, it is unwise because it can only result in making the dissent more widespread, more bitter, and more valid.

H.R. 10480 IS UNCONSTITUTIONAL

The majority would have us believe that because the bill no longer prohibits "words" but only "acts," that there can be no doubt about its constitutionality. Yet, "It has long been beyond doubt that symbolic action may be protected speech." In *Stromberg v. California* [document 5.1] . . . the court held invalid a California statute which prohibited displaying a red flag as a sign of symbol of opposition to organized government. . . .

How is the "dignified" burning, suggested by 36 U.S.C. 176(j) as an appropriate method to dispose of outworn flags, to be distinguished from the burning which "cast contempt" that the bill prohibits? . . . [W]e feel that the courts will have a very difficult, and most unusual task, in determining whether the conduct of particular flag burners does or does not violate this bill. The little weight given to whether these difficulties would make the bill both unconstitutional and unwise public policy makes clear to us that *the real purpose of this bill is to wrap up all the speeches in opposition to the draft and to our position in Vietnam, and characterize and punish them as acts which "cast⟨s⟩ contempt upon the flag" if they are accompanied by a public burning of the flag.*

HR. 10480 IS NOT NECESSARY FOR ANY APPROPRIATE LEGISLATIVE PURPOSE
Lest there be any who might consider this bill a necessary weapon to combat those who interfere with the morale of our men in Vietnam or subvert the operation of the draft law, it should be noted that such statutory weapons [punishing attempts to cause disloyalty within the armed forces or urging drafting evasion] already exist. . . . [Moreover] there are flag desecration statutes in all 50 States. . . . [Would] it not be wiser to wait until the constitutionality of one or another of the State statutes has been tested [in the Supreme Court]?

CONCLUSION: H.R. 10480 IS NOT CONSTITUTIONAL OR WISE
In urging the chairman of the Judiciary Committee that this legislation be not passed, Professor Sutherland [said]:

> I deplore destruction of a national symbol to demonstrate protest against a governmental decision; but I recognize that tolerance of dissent, tolerance even of irrational dissent, tolerance which the first amendment exemplifies, is a sign of our constitutional strength. That tolerance is a convincing demonstration of our confidence in the rightness of our constitutional theory. . . . Prison sentences and fines for the flagburners would not increase respect for the flag; among their adherents such punishments would only increase the effect of the burnings by making martyrs of the burners. And in certain foreign countries we would open ourselves to propaganda that dissent about our present military had become so serious that we had been forced to suppress it by imposing prison sentence on the dissenters. I respectfully urge that this legislation be not passed.

We, too, would respectfully urge that this legislation be not passed. In doing so, we echo not only Professor Sutherland but all those others who, though they deplore destruction of our national symbol, doubt that this statute will accomplish its objective and who believe that, even if it would, suppression of dissent is too high a price to pay to rid us of the flag burners. . . .

Prosecutions in the Lower Courts
During the Vietnam War Era

During the Vietnam War, more flag desecration prosecutions occurred than in all of previous American history. Most of these prosecutions took place under state flag desecration laws, which had generally survived more-or-less unchanged since the 1900–1920 period, rather than under the new 1968 federal flag desecration law (document 6.1). Because most flag desecration prosecutions never got into the appeals courts and therefore were never "reported" in standard legal references, it is impossible to determine precisely how many such prosecutions were effected. However, an undocumented March 15, 1973, estimate in the *Christian Science Monitor* that "some 1,000" flag desecration prosecutions had been initiated by then is almost certainly an underestimate, as the American Civil Liberties Union reported in May 1971 that it was then handling "easily 100 cases."[1]

Although the 1967 Central Park flag burning and a few other scattered flag burnings attracted the most public and press attention, the majority of flag desecration prosecutions did not involve flag burnings. Far more typical were prosecutions for wearing flag patches, often but not always on trouser seats, or for other forms of "wearing" flags or flag depictions, such as on, or as, shirts, jackets, vests, and capes. Also extremely common were prosecutions for displaying "altered" flags, most often for replacing the field of stars with the "peace symbol" (an inverted trident surrounded by a circle). A wide variety of other miscellaneous types of flag desecration prosecutions also occurred, such as for publishing a picture of a burning flag, pouring paint on the flag, and displaying the flag upside down. Although almost all flag burning prosecutions were upheld on appeal, a majority of the other convictions that were appealed were ultimately struck down.

On June 12, 1971, Robert Dietsch, a reporter for the Scripps-Howard Newspaper Alliance, published in the *New Republic* an account that summarized the general trends evident in the Vietnam-era flag desecration prosecutions (document 7.1). Dietsch accurately stressed that flag laws were enforced during the Vietnam War era "unevenly and unfairly," because perceived "dissidents" were almost invariably the targets of such prosecutions, although other violations of the same laws were not prosecuted, apparently because they involved members of the "establishment." Many police, for example, wore flag patches on their shoulders or flag pins in their lapels even as they arrested what Dietsch characterized as "peace demonstrators and young persons with long hair and beards" for symbolically using flags, and massive, clearly illegal, advertising use of the flag was rarely, if ever, prosecuted. Dietsch also correctly pointed out that most flag desecration prosecutions were ultimately unsuccessful (at least those that got into the appeals courts), but that their fundamental constitutionality had not been settled because most courts that overturned convictions handed down decisions based on "narrow grounds" (and, he might have added, because the Supreme Court repeatedly refused to resolve the issue, as explained in chapter 8 below).

Left adrift without any real direction from the Supreme Court, the lower courts during the Vietnam War era created a chaotic and often contradictory legal record concerning flag desecration prosecutions. For example, in the 1971 case of *State v. Liska* (document 7.2), an Ohio appeals court overturned a conviction for displaying a flag decal upon which the "peace symbol" had been superimposed, on the grounds that such a display did not constitute a "contemptuous" act in violation of the state law, yet in another 1971 Ohio case, *State v. Saulino*, a municipal court found that displaying a painted flag in which the face of Mickey Mouse replaced the field of stars did violate the law. Displaying a peace symbol in front of a flag was found permissible in the 1973 case of *State v. Kool* (document 7.3) by the same Iowa Supreme Court that found wearing the flag as a poncho illegal in the 1971 case of *State v. Waterman*, although in both cases the court held that the critical issue was whether such acts were likely to breach the peace and in both cases it found that no actual disturbances had resulted from the displays.

Cases involving wearing flag patches also provoked numerous contradictory lower court decisions. For example, in the 1973 case of *Delorme v. State* (document 7.4), the Texas Court of Criminal Appeals (the highest state court for criminal cases) upheld a conviction arising from wearing a flag patch on a pair of jeans, on the grounds that such conduct was "equally as contemptuous and defiles the flag as much as the act of burning the flag," but in the 1972 case of *State v. Claxton* (document 7.5), a Washington state appeals court threw out a similar conviction, on the grounds that such conduct simply did not violate the state law, which outlawed publicly "mutilating, defacing, defiling or trampling upon" the flag.

In the 1972 Ohio case of *State v. Kasnett,* a state appeals court upheld another conviction for wearing a flag patch, in this case on the back pocket of a pair of jeans, on the grounds that wearing the flag "over the anus" was clearly an act of "defilement" banned by the state flag desecration law, but the Ohio Supreme Court overturned the conviction the following year, holding that the state flag desecration law was unconstitutionally vague. The Ohio Supreme Court also declared that the lower court was "anatomically in error," because a flag patch sown to a pants pocket simply was not located "over the anus." The court added that the emphasis placed by the lower court on the precise location of the patch suggested that a "flag worn by a policeman over his heart, or on his sleeve, or on his helmet" was legal, although the legality of a student wearing the same flag depended upon "which part of his anatomy it is upon or near," thereby making clear that the state law was hopelessly vague, because it failed to contain "such predictable indicia of guilt so as to provide fair nature of what acts are punishable thereunder."

In general, when lower courts upheld flag desecration convictions (as they were more likely to do for flag-burning cases than for other types of alleged violations), they generally pointed to two government interests that were held to justify overriding any free speech rights that might be involved: an interest in preventing breaches of the peace and/or an interest in protecting the flag's symbolic value. Thus, both of these reasons were cited by the Texas Court of Criminal Appeals in upholding what appears to have been the most severe penalty for flag desecration in American history since the World War I–era *Starr* case (document 3.25)—the four-year jail term issued in the 1971 flag-burning case of *Deeds v. State* (document 7.6). These same reasons were also cited in numerous other cases, such as the 1974 Iowa Supreme Court ruling in the flag-burning case of *State v. Farrell* (document 7.7). Almost invariably, when the lower courts upheld flag desecration prosecutions, they cited, and, as in the *Deeds* case, often extensively quoted from, the Supreme Court's 1907 *Halter* ruling (document 3.10) upholding the Nebraska flag desecration law, especially the portion of Halter that declared that insults to the flag were likely to provoke immediate physical reprisals and that state action to protect the flag properly sought to foster patriotic feelings.

In general, when the lower courts overturned flag desecration prosecutions, they tended to focus on narrow technicalities rather than to challenge the fundamental constitutionality of such laws. For example, as noted earlier, in the 1972 case of *State v. Claxton,* involving a flag patch worn on a pair of jeans, a Washington appeals court found that such conduct simply did not amount to a form of "mutilating, defacing, defiling, burning or trampling" upon the flag, which was forbidden by state law, and in the 1971 case of *State v. Liska* an Ohio appeals court declared that displaying a flag decal with a peace symbol superimposed upon the flag was "not a contemptuous act" within the terms of the state law. In the 1971 case of *Parker v. Morgan* (document 7.9), involving prosecutions in North Carolina for wearing a jacket to which a flag with superimposed antiwar material had been sewn and for attaching a flag to a car ceiling in a manner that had slightly torn the fabric, a federal district court declared the state law unconstitutionally vague and overbroad because of its expansive definition of what constituted a flag and because it banned actions that extended beyond physical flag desecration. Although explicitly declaring that forbidding "physical defilement" of flags would not seriously violate the First Amendment, the court held that the state law was flawed because its sweeping definition of the national flag was "simply unbelievable," possibly regulating the usage of anything that was "red, white and blue," and because the conduct it prohibited was so vague and expansive that it appeared to ban even the "expression of attitudes by a gesture or even facial expression," such as turning "thumbs down at the flag" or saluting it "with a clenched fist."

In the 1973 case of *State v. Kool*, involving displaying, in the front window of a private home, a flag upside-down immediately behind, but not touching, a peace symbol, the Iowa Supreme Court cited maintaining the peace as the "important" government interest put forth by the state as justifying the state flag desecration law but declared that the conduct involved simply was not "likely" enough to threaten the peace to uphold the conviction. The court therefore held that the law was constitutional, but that it had been unconstitutionally applied, because although it was theoretically possible that someone viewing the display might have been "so intemperate as to disrupt the peace," the vague fear of such a disturbance was not enough to silence political expression, because "if absolute assurance of tranquility is required, we may as well forget about free speech."

Lower court rulings that rejected outright the government's interest in protecting the symbolic value of the flag as a justification for outlawing flag desecration as a form of political protest were extremely rare during the Vietnam period. One such case was the 1970 decision of a federal district court in *Crosson v. Silver* (document 7.8), striking down Arizona's flag desecration law squarely on First Amendment grounds in a flag-burning case, a decision that was largely circumvented when defendant Sharon Crosson was later successfully prosecuted for the same act under the 1968 federal flag desecration law. The 1970 *Crosson* district court ruling largely prefigured the Supreme Court's 1989–90 flag-burning decisions by forbidding Arizona from prosecuting Crosson on the grounds that the state flag law unconstitutionally interfered with First Amendment rights, first because it was written too broadly to be upheld on maintenance of the peace grounds, and second because the court explicitly rejected the contention that there was any "constitutionally recognized state power to prohibit flag desecration based on an interest in preserving loyalty or patriotism."

Just as courts that upheld flag desecration convictions frequently cited and quoted from the Supreme Court's 1907 *Halter* decision, rulings such as the *Crosson v. Silver* decision, the 1973 Iowa Supreme Court decision in *State v. Kool,* and the 1971 federal district court ruling in *Parker v. Morgan,* which struck down such convictions, frequently cited and quoted the Supreme Court's 1943 *Barnette* decision (document 5.2), which had declared unconstitutional forcing public school students to salute the flag and recite the Pledge of Allegiance. Among the phrases frequently cited from *Barnette* were the declarations that the issue was difficult to decide not because its principles were "obscure, but because the flag involved is our own," and that "the freedom to differ is not limited to things that do not matter much."

Although courts that upheld flag desecration convictions were fond of citing *Halter,* and courts that struck them down often cited *Barnette,* courts on both sides of the question frequently cited and quoted from the Supreme Court's decision in the 1968 case of *U.S. v. O'Brien,* a ruling that was to play a central legal role in the 1989–90 flag desecration debate. In *O'Brien,* the Supreme Court upheld the constitutionality of a 1965 federal law banning draft card burning, declaring that it could not "accept the view that an apparently limitless variety of conduct can be labelled 'speech'" and thus be granted First Amendment protection. Although the congressional debate preceding passage of the 1965 law was filled with references to draft card burners as filthy beatniks, communist stooges, and traitors, the Court upheld it on the grounds that it was designed not to hinder free expression, but rather to administratively foster the effective functioning of the draft, which allegedly would somehow be hampered if individuals burned their draft cards (a suggestion that ignored the obvious fact that the draft administration maintained its own records on individuals). In the key passage of the *O'Brien* ruling, the Court, which had previously provided First Amendment protection for a wide variety of acts of "symbolic speech" (such as peaceful picketing and marching) that went well beyond displaying red flags and refusing to salute the American flag, sought to clarify when conduct that had expressive aspects could be constitutionally regulated. It declared that:

> [W]hen "speech" and "nonspeech" elements are combined in the same course of conduct . . . a government regulation is sufficiently justified if it is within the constitutional power of the Government; if it furthers an important or substantial governmental interest; if the government interest is unrelated to the suppression of free expression; and if the incidental restriction on alleged First Amendment freedoms is no greater than is essential to the furtherance of that interest.

In practice, when the lower courts sought to apply the *O'Brien* guidelines to flag desecration cases, the key point was frequently whether the governmental interests advanced in support of flag desecration laws, namely seeking to preserve the peace and above all the professed purpose of protecting the symbolic value of the flag, were interests "unrelated to the suppression of free expression." Thus, reaching different conclusions on this same point, the federal district court in the 1970 *Crosson* case cited *O'Brien* as the "controlling precedent" upon which it relied to strike down Arizona's flag desecration law, but a federal appeals court in the 1972 case of *U.S. v. Crosson* (document 7.10) relied equally heavily upon *O'Brien* to uphold a conviction, under the 1968 federal flag desecration law, arising from the very same flag-burning incident. Although the 1970 Crosson court flatly rejected the concept that the state could constitutionally "prohibit flag desecration based on an interest in preserving loyalty or patriotism," the 1972 Crosson court found that the 1968 federal flag desecration law had merely forbidden the "physical act of contemptuously burning a flag," and declared that this purpose did not "in any way" seek to "suppress free speech."

Ultimately, the key legal holding in the Supreme Court's 1989–90 rulings striking down statutes that were applied to forbid flag desecration as a form of political dissent was that, under the *O'Brien* test, such laws were not "unrelated to the suppression of free expression," because they had no valid nonsuppressive purpose, unlike the 1965 draft card burning law. Therefore, the Court held, such laws had to meet a more stringent standard than what it termed, in the 1989 *Texas v. Johnson* ruling (document 10.12), the "relatively lenient" O'Brien test requiring only demonstration of an "important or substantial governmental interest" (which the 1965 draft card law passed with its allegedly nonsuppressive purpose). Instead, the Court declared, such laws would have to demonstrate a "compelling state interest" and be subject to the "most exacting scrutiny" to overcome the purely First Amendment interests at stake. It held that they could not do so because the state's interest in preserving the flag's symbolic value could not override what it termed the "bedrock principle underlying the First Amendment," namely that "Government may not prohibit the expression of an idea simply because society finds the idea itself offensive or disagreeable."

Until 1989, however, as discussed in detail in chapter 8, the Supreme Court failed to clarify the application of the *O'Brien* test to the flag desecration issue. Of all of the Vietnam-era court decisions, the opinion that came the closest to forecasting the ultimate approach of the Supreme Court in 1989–90 was a dissent written by Justice Browning in the 1972 *U.S. v. Crosson* flag-burning case (document 7.10). As the Supreme Court would eventually do in 1989–90, after ducking the fundamental issue at stake in political flag desecration cases for twenty years, Browning relied above all upon *Barnette, Street,* (Document 8.1) and *O'Brien* to declare that, just as the government could not compel expressions of respect for the flag, neither could it forbid "the expression of disrespect," and that when the purpose of legislation was designed to suppress "disrespect," it did not matter whether the expression was verbal or nonverbal. As the Supreme Court would also resolve in 1989–90, the key legal determination made by Browning was that what he termed the "less stringent" standards of the *O'Brien* test were simply inapplicable to incidents of political flag desecration because, unlike the government's nonsuppressive interest in facilitating the administration of the draft held to be threatened by draft card burnings, the government's interest in forbidding political flag burnings was solely to punish "the communicative aspect" of such conduct, in particular the "expression of an idea the government found abhorrent."

Browning noted that such punitive intent was especially evident because the 1968 federal flag desecration law (document 6.1) invoked in the case banned only acts that "knowingly" and "publicly" cast "contempt" upon the flag by "various means, including burning," while exempting "flag burning that is not communicative" or that "expresses loyalty and respect," a reference to the fact that the 1942 congressional voluntary flag code actually recommended ceremonial flag burning as the preferred means for disposal of worn flags. Taken together, Browning argued, the 1942 and 1968 congressional enactments made it obvious that in 1968 Congress sought to protect "the flag as a symbol, not as a physical object," for the sole purpose of suppressing the "public display of defiance and contempt for the flag," an interest that was squarely antithetical to the First Amendment.

Document 7.1

Robert W. Dietsch, "Raising the Flag," *New Republic,* June 12, 1971, 18–19. Reprinted by permission of the *New Republic,* copyright 1971, The New Republic, Inc.

. . . Prison penalties for desecrating the flag range from none in New Hampshire to 25 years in Texas. But it wasn't until 1968 that Congress passed a federal flag desecration law [document 6.1], . . . There have been as many "flag desecration" arrests, trials and court appeals in the last six years as in all the proceeding years of our history. . . .

Meanwhile, research is showing that the flag has indeed been put to many uses over the years, almost all of which have gone uncontested. Attorney Bernard L. Segal, who cooperates with the American Civil Liberties Union in handling flag desecration suits, unearthed these illustrations involving (so one might argue) some kind of demeaning of the flag: A canceled (defaced) six cent flag stamp; a bikini designed in red, white and blue and modeled after the flag; a photograph of Roy Rogers and Dale Evans in flag vests; dinnerware with flag designs; a beer serving tray with the flag design on the bottom; a toilet seat with a flag design on top . . . and a photograph of Lincoln and McClellan in a tent, eating from a table covered with a flag.

Recent court cases illustrate that the flag desecration laws have been enforced unevenly and unfairly. Cowboy star Rogers and his wife could appear in public with their flag vests and win cheers, but when Yippie leader Abbie Hoffman wore a shirt that resembled the flag he was arrested by Capitol policemen while waiting to testify before the House Un-American Activities Committee . . . charged with intending to cast contempt upon the flag and sentenced to pay a $100 fine or spend 30 days in jail. Three years later, a U.S. Appeals Court upset the conviction, saying Hoffman was brought to trial not because he had desecrated Old Glory, but "because of his well known public image which is highly controversial." In Happauge, N.Y., a young housewife was arrested for flying her American flag upside down to protest the war in Southeast Asia; but no action was taken when a nearby American Legion post flew its flag upside down to protest the government's "dovish" reaction to North Korea's seizure of the [U.S ship] *Pueblo.* In Nassau County, N.Y., the district attorney threatened to arrest any person displaying the emblem of Women Strike for Peace, an emblem consisting of a peace symbol superimposed on the flag; but no threat was issued to persons displaying an emblem including the flag and the slogan: "America Love It or Leave It." Nor were any arrests made when New York State farm products were advertised in a poster displaying the likeness of Gov. Nelson Rockefeller superimposed on the flag and potatoes in place of the stars. A 16-year-old youth was arrested in Alexandria, Va., for wearing a tricolor vest; the youth was from Boston, and an Alexandria judge handed the youth a mild, but medieval-like sentence: banishment from the city until the age of 21. A few days later, in an Alexandria city parade a man marched unchallenged wearing an Uncle Sam suit with flag symbols. He was escorted past (not into) the court house by city motorcycle policemen.

Uneven enforcement of the flag desecration laws is often intended to harass peace demonstrators and young persons with long hair and beards. A bearded youth was arrested and charged with violating New York's flag desecration law because he was driving a car painted red, white and blue and decorated with a star on the hood. Other kids have been hauled in for sewing a flag on the seat of their pants, using the flag as an auto seat cover and even reporting to an Army induction center dressed in undershorts but with an American flag slung over their shoulders. A spokesman for the

Flag Research Center in Lexington, Mass., says "the commercial misuse of the flag is much more extensive than its misuse by leftists or students. But this is overlooked because the business interests are part of the establishment."

Defenses in flag desecration cases—while winning a majority in numbers—have so far been only nibbling away at the state and federal statutes. Most victories have been on narrow grounds; in Minnesota, for example a man was acquitted for displaying a flag with a peace symbol instead of stars when the judge ruled the flag at issue was not a flag within the meaning of the state law. What lawyers handling flag cases want is Supreme Court resolution of present judicial ambiguity [concerning the constitutionality of laws forbidding the physical desecration of the flag]. Two flag cases have come before the Court: in 1969, it overturned a flag desecration conviction for a man who burned a flag and made a radical speech, but the overturning came because the justices said it was unclear whether the man was convicted for the burning or for the speech [document 8.1]. Early in 1972, the Court divided 4 to 4 and thus let stand the conviction of a New York City art dealer who used the flag in antiwar sculptures. . . .

The attorneys defending the New York art dealer put it as well as anyone: "Under our system of government, it cannot be a crime for a citizen to cast contempt upon any symbol of government. Since casting contempt inevitably involves the communication of an idea, it cannot be made criminal."

Document 7.2

Ruling of the Court of Appeals of Ohio, Cuyahoga County, in the 1971 case of *State v. Liska.*

Source: 291 North Eastern Reporter, 2d series, 498.

This action comes here from the Berea Municipal Court on appeal from the appellant's conviction and fine of One Hundred Dollars ($100) for an alleged violation of R.C. § 2921.05, the so-called "flag desecration" statute. For the reasons stated below, the judgment of the trial court is reversed as being contrary to law.

The appellant, Liska, a student at Baldwin-Wallace College was arrested and charged with unlawfully and willfully exposing a contemptuous representation of the American flag on the rear window of his automobile. The alleged contemptuous representation consisted of a decal composed of thirteen red and white stripes with a peace symbol appearing on a blue field.

There is nothing in the record to indicate that the appellant was in violation of any traffic laws, nor that he was behaving in a disorderly manner when arrested. The appellant described himself at trial as a conscientious objector to the Viet Nam War and a pacifist, and testified that his purpose in displaying the decal in question was to make a political statement of peace. . . .

Under the law it is our duty to avoid constitutional issues if the questions presented can be disposed of on any other basis. . . . [As this is the case here] we do not decide the issues involving claimed violations of due process and the First Amendment or unconstitutional overbreadth for R.C. § 2921.05. . . .

[T]he most this appellant has done is to display a decal [with a flag design] upon which is superimposed a peace symbol. On the evidence in this case that configuration indicates only the appellant's aspiration for peace for his country. We hold that the symbolic indication indicated by the facts of this case, without more, was, as a matter of law, not a contemptuous act within the meaning of R.C. § 2921.05. . . .

Document 7.3

Ruling of the Iowa Supreme Court in the 1973 case of *State v. Kool.*

Source: 212 North Western Reporter, 2d series, 518.

The critical issue in this appeal is whether defendant's manner of displaying the American flag could reasonably be expected to produce a breach of the peace.

Defendant was charged with desecration of the flag in violation of § 32.1 of the Code. The parties stipulated in writing:

(a) That the defendant, on or about Christmas of 1969, hung an eight inch in diameter peace symbol made of cardboard and wrapped with tin foil in the front window of his home.

(b) That the defendant, on or about Flag Day, June 1, 1970, hung an eighteen inch by thirteen inch plastic replica of the United States flag in the front window of his home.

(c) That the defendant hung the above mentioned replica of the United States flag behind the peace symbol, which was still in the front window of his home.

(d) That the said peace symbol was lying against the front of the window, and the replica of the United States flag was about one-half inch to an inch behind the peace symbol. The peace symbol was not touching the plastic flag, nor was it attached to the flag. . . .

(e) That the defendant hung the United States flag in an upside down position as an expression, or to signify a signal of distress, that distress being the involvement of the United States in the Vietnam war. The defendant did not intend to desecrate the United States flag or hold the United States flag up to ridicule. The defendant did not mutilate the United States flag.

(f) There were no riots or violence as a result of the defendant's action. . . .

I. Vagueness. We reject defendant's contention that the statute under which he was convicted is unconstitutionally vague. . . .

II. Desecration in Fact? Defendant's contention that he did not in fact desecrate the flag requires us to consider the language of § 32.1. Section 32.3 of the same chapter defines "flag" broadly to include a replica such as we have here. Section 32.1 itself makes three main activities crimes: first, to place marks upon flags or to expose to view a flag on which a mark has been placed; second, to use a flag on an article for advertising or decoration; and third, publicly to "mutilate, deface, defile or defy, trample upon, cast contempt upon, satirize, deride or burlesque" the flag or to place the flag "upon the ground. . . ."

Most of the proscriptions in § 32.1 are not applicable to the present facts. But the Attorney General claims defendant did "defile" and "cast contempt upon" the flag. . . .

III. Free Speech. . . . Defendant's conduct here constituted symbolic speech. The parties stipulated that defendant did what he did "as an expression, or to signify a signal of distress," . . . Can the statute be constitutionally applied to prohibit the symbolic speech which defendant employed? We think not.

Freedom of expression is a vital right in an open society. We cannot lose sight of that basic constitutional principle although in a given case we have an unconventional display of the flag which disturbs our sensibilities [as Justice Jackson pointed out in the *Barnette* case].

Nevertheless, freedom of symbolic speech is not absolute [as the Supreme Court pointed out in the *O'Brien* draft card burning case of 1968]. . . .

. . . The State insists that § 32.1 of the Code, applied to this case, meets the [*O'Brien*] test. The important or substantial governmental interest here, according to the State, is prevention of a threatened breach of the peace. That interest, if it actually exists, is a sufficient one.

The ultimate issue, therefore, is whether that interest does actually exist here. . . . [I]n order to uphold the conviction, we must say that the display itself of the peace symbol and upside-down flag made violence likely. We cannot say that.

This is not to say we are completely sure that no one would be violent. Someone in Newton [Iowa] might be so intemperate as to disrupt the peace because of this display. But if absolute assurance of tranquility is required, we may as well forget about free speech. . . .

[T]he framers of the constitutional guaranties must have known they were taking some risk when they inserted the free speech clause, for many utterances of unpopular ideas are fraught with the possibility of retaliatory action. . . . [W]e will uphold incursions upon symbolic expression on the basis of probable violence only when we are convinced that violence really is probable.

We hold that likelihood of violence does not sufficiently appear here. The statute is not unconstitutional, but it cannot be constitutionally applied to these facts. . . .

Document 7.4

Ruling of the Texas Court of Criminal Appeals in the 1973 case of *Delorme v. State.*

Source: 488 *South Western Reporter,* 2d series.

The conviction is for the public desecration of the flag of the United States. The jury assessed a punishment of two years imprisonment and the appellant was placed on probation as required by the jury's mandatory recommendation.

The indictment charges that the appellant "did publicly defile and defy by act the flag of the United States, to wit, having it affixed to the seat of his pants and wearing the same in public," in violation of Article 152, Vernon's Ann.P.C., [which makes it illegal and punishable by jail terms of between two and 25 years to "publicly or privately, mutilate, deface, defile, trample upon, or cast contempt" upon the flag or a representation of the flag "either by word or act"]. . . .

The appellant urges this court to declare that Article 152, V.A.P.C., is so vague and overbroad on its face that the entire statute must fall because it violates the First and Fourteenth Amendments to the Constitution of the United States. He also argues in the alternative that Article 152, V.A.P.C., as applied to him in the circumstances of this case, is a violation of his rights protected by the same constitutional provisions.

This court has recently refused to hold the Article 152, V.A.P.C., is so vague and overbroad on its face as to render it in violation of the First and Fourteenth Amendments [in the *Deeds* case, document 7.6].

It is the duty of the court, if it can be done, to construe a statute so that it will remain valid. . . . Article 152, V.A.P.C., insofar as it prohibits acts done in "private" and communication by "words" is undoubtedly in violation of the First Amendment to the Constitution of the United States [under the *Street* doctrine, document 8.1].

In the case at bar, we are not confronted with allegations or proof of acts done in "private" or communication by "words." . . .

By enforcing the statute as if acts done in "private" and communication by "words" had been omitted, it is a valid statute. We so interpret Article 152, V.A.P.C. . . .

When the statute is interpreted in this way, it is neither vague nor overbroad. . . .

Statutes similar to Article 152, V.A.P.C., as we interpret it, have withstood similar constitutional attacks. . . .

The holding in this case is consistent with the results reached by the courts of three states, where convictions have been upheld under facts almost identical to those presented here and where the prosecution was under an identical or similarly worded statute. . . .

In *State v. Van Camp,* the Circuit Court of Connecticut, Appellate Division, upheld the conviction of the defendant for the crime of misuse of the flag in violation of Section 53-255 of the General Statutes where the defendant was arrested while walking along a city street, wearing the flag of the United States on the buttocks portion of his trousers. The Supreme Court of Connecticut refused certification for appeal.

In *State v. Kasnett,* an Ohio Court of Appeals affirmed where it was charged the defendant "unlawfully ⟨and publicly⟩ defile⟨d⟩, deface⟨d⟩ and cast contempt upon the Flag of the United States ⟨for⟩ having said Flag sewn on the seat of his pants," where the prosecution was under a statute providing that "no person shall * * * publicly mutilate, burn, destroy, defile, deface, trample upon, or otherwise cast contempt upon such flag." . . .

The act of wearing in public the United States flag or a representation thereof on the seat of trousers [as here] is equally as contemptuous and defiles the flag as much as the act of burning the flag, which was held to be a violation of this statute in *Deeds v. State.* We find the evidence sufficient to support the conviction.

Document 7.5

Ruling of the Court of Appeals of Washington, Division I, Panel One, in the 1972 case of *State v. Claxton.*

Source: 501 Pacific Reporter, 2d series, 192.

Mr. Claxton appeals from a conviction of the crime of flag desecration. The facts are not in dispute. The appeal questions whether his acts were a violation of RCW 9.86.030. That statute provides:

> No person shall knowingly cast contempt upon any flag, standard, color, ensign or shield, as defined in RCW 9.86.010, by publicly mutilating, defacing, defiling, burning, or trampling upon said flag, standard, color, ensign or shield.

The record establishes that Mr. Claxton, while sitting in an automobile which was parked on a public street, wore a pair of dungarees which had a tear in the area of the left knee. A small American flag had been sewn to the underside of the tear so that a substantial portion of the flag showed through. Mr. Claxton had purchased the flag for the alleged purpose of patching his pants in a "decorative fashion" and had sewn it in place himself.

The flag was made of cloth and identical except for size to the standard American flag. . . . RCW 9.86.010 specifies that any flag "evidently purporting to be ⟨a⟩ flag, * * * of the United States * * *" of any size is included within the flag desecration statute: . . .

The purpose of RCW 9.86.030 and flag desecration statutes in general is to prevent breaches of the peace which might result from a public act of desecration. . . . There is no evidence, either direct or circumstantial, from which it could be inferred that Mr. Claxton publicly mutilated, defaced, defiled, burned or trampled upon the flag. . . . There is no lesser included offense within the crime of flag desecration.

Reversed.

Document 7.6

Ruling of the Texas Court of Criminal Appeals in the 1971 case of *Deeds v. State*.

Source: 474 *South Western Reporter,* 2d series 718.

Appellant was convicted for violating Article 152, Vernon's Ann.P.C which makes it a felony to insult the flag of the United States. Punishment was assessed by a jury at four years.

The constitutionality of Article 152 is challenged on two grounds. First, appellant argues that this state may not punish one who publicly destroys or damages an American flag as a means of protest without contravening rights protected by the First Amendment to the United States Constitution. Second, he contends that Article 152 is impermissibly vague and overbroad.

In order to determine whether appellant's rights under the First Amendment have been denied in the instant case, a decision must first be made as to whether the act of burning a flag of the United States in a public place constitutes an attempt at communication. Such an act does involve a rather crude form of communicating a person's beliefs [citing the *Barnette* decision]. . . .

While recognizing that the act of burning an American flag may be, in part, a form of communication, we find nothing in such act which would merit the protection of the First Amendment.

Certain forms of symbolic conduct have been determined to serve this purpose and have been recognized within the ambit of First Amendment protection [such as] labor picketing, the wearing of black arm bands and political buttons, refusal to salute the United States flag, sit-ins, and street theatre. . . .

However, the degree of protection afforded to communicative acts is not the same as that afforded to pure speech [citing the Supreme Court's *O'Brien* ruling and other decisions].

In the instant case, appellant burned a United States flag, or an imitation of that flag, on a Sunday afternoon in a crowded public park in Dallas. There is nothing in the record to indicate that this act was performed in the context of a political rally and, aside from appellant's later explanation of his actions, nothing to indicate what ideas appellant was attempting to express by such act. The First Amendment protects the communication of ideas, not all communication. Incitement to illegal action, libel, obscenity, and "fighting words," while communicative, do not express ideas and do not merit First Amendment protection. . . .

Even assuming that the act of flag desecration was committed within a factual framework which clearly demonstrated an intent to communicate certain ideas, we hold that a state may validly prohibit such conduct [citing the *Halter* decision].

The flag of the United States is a symbol of the nation and all its people. It represents those who agree with governmental policies and those who dissent. It is a symbol of the unity of purpose of this nation. The act of flag desecration degrades the flag's symbolic value and weakens its unifying effect. The reasoning of the Supreme Court of the United States in *Halter v. Nebraska* is still applicable today [including its statement that] "it has often occurred that insults to a flag have been the cause of war, and indignities put upon it, in the presence of those who revere it, have often been resented and sometimes punished on the spot."

Since the flag symbolizes the entire nation, not just one particular political philosophy, the state may determine that it be kept above the turmoil created by competing ideologies.

The emotions of the people of this nation are so integrally linked to this symbol that its desecration in public is an invitation to violence. . . .

The act of desecrating a flag involves two different aspects: one communicative and one purely physical and non-communicative. It is the non-speech aspect of such conduct which the state has a right to regulate [under the *O'Brien* doctrine of the Supreme Court].

Article 152 is directed toward prohibiting the nonspeech aspect of flag desecration. While it incidentally limits expression, it leaves appellant free to express his views in an alternate forum. Conduct, not speech, is prohibited by the statute, and the prohibition applies equally regardless of the political views of the person engaging in such acts.

The statute being challenged in the instant case is based upon two important governmental interests: (1) the preservation of public order and (2) the preservation of the flag as a symbol of national purpose and unity. These interests far outweigh any communicative value implied by an act of flag desecration, and the furtherance of these interests is within the police power of the state. . . .

Appellant also contends that Article 152 is unconstitutionally vague and overbroad. We find, however, that the vagueness and overbreadth doctrines are inapplicable in a case such as this where appellant's act . . . constitutes the type of hardcore conduct which would be prohibited under any construction which we might give the statute. The record in the instant case does not require this court to determine the vagueness and overbreadth contentions. . . .

Appellant also contends that four years confinement for the offense of flag desecration constitutes cruel and unusual punishment. We find no merit in this contention since the punishment assessed by the jury is within the statutory limits established by the legislature.

There being no reversible error, the judgment is affirmed.

Document 7.7

Ruling of the Iowa Supreme Court in the 1974 case of *State v. Farrell.*

Source: 223 *North Western Reporter,* 2d series, 270.

We here accord further consideration to *State v. Farrell,* vacated opinion 209 N.W.2d 103 (Iowa 1973), pursuant to a directive issued August 6, 1974, by the Supreme Court of the United States.

More particularly, this court is called upon to now reevaluate its position in *Farrell,* supra, in light of *Spence v. State of Washington* [document 8.3].

At the threshold it is to us apparent, for reasons later set forth, *Spence* is inapposite. We again respectfully affirm on defendant's Farrell's appeal to this court.

I. *State v. Farrell* unquestionably involved the mutilation by burning of a United States flag in a public place. . . .

Conversely, *Spence* dealt with the nonmutilative removable taping of a peace symbol on a flag then displayed on defendant's privately occupied premises. This was done, as says *Spence*, "* * * in a way closely analogous to the manner in which flags have always been used to convey ideas."

Furthermore, as noted by Mr. Justice Rehnquist, dissenting in *Spence*, "The Court takes pains to point out that petitioner did not 'permanently disfigure the flag or destroy it' * * *." Significantly, defendant Farrell made no pretense of displaying our national emblem in a manner akin to that historically done to express a personal belief. Rather, she permanently and contumaciously, in a public place, destroyed our symbol of patriotism, of pride in the history of our country and of the service, sacrifice and valor of millions of Americans.

We are again constrained to hold the statute here in question . . . is directed to and regulates the form by which defendant Farrell's message was expressed, not the content thereof, and is sufficiently irrelative to suppression of free expression.

III. It is also to us evident a "risk of breach of the peace" attended Farrell's aforesaid flag desecration in a public place.

[T]his court is persuaded the State of Iowa does have a viable interest in the preservation of peace and order within this jurisdiction. . . .

[Reasonably addressing this interest does] not to us mean a breach of the peace must have occurred or even be imminent. On the contrary, it denotes nothing more than words or conduct creating exposure to a chance, danger, hazard or peril of breach of the peace.

[W]e are persuaded defendant Farrell's conduct created a risk of breach of the peace.

In light of the foregoing we find Code § 32.1 furthers the preservation of peace and order, a substantial State interest, with nothing more than incidental restriction on First Amendment liberties [and was therefore] constitutionally applied to defendant Farrell's conduct.

IV. Moreover, upon the aforesaid mandated reconsideration of the case at bar, we further conclude Code § 32.1, to the extent here involved, serves a viable State interest in preserving the physical integrity of the United States flag as an unalloyed symbol of our country. . . .

Patricia Farrell's incendiary flag mutilating conduct does not approach the degree of tranquility attendant upon that denoted in *Spence*.

On the contrary, Farrell manifested a total disregard for the flag as a symbol of patriotism, and by the same token espoused disunity.

As aforesaid we are persuaded the State of Iowa has a substantial interest in preserving the flag of this Nation, and § 32.1, Code of Iowa, is to us sufficiently justified upon that basis. It furthers an important governmental interest unrelated to free expression and, as applied in the case now before us, any incidental restriction on First Amendment freedoms was no greater than essential to the furtherance of this State's interest in the protection of our national emblem. . . .

Document 7.8

Ruling of the U.S. District Court for Arizona in the 1970 case of *Crosson v. Silver.*

Source: 310 *Federal Supplement* 1084.

Plaintiff brought this action . . . seeking declaratory relief and an injunction restraining defendant from further criminal proceedings against plaintiff under the Arizona flag desecration statute, A.R.S. § 41-793, subsec. C (1956) [which makes guilty of a misdemeanor anyone] "who publicly mutilates, defaces, defiles, tramples upon or by word or act casts contempt upon a flag." . . .

At the trial, defendant intends to prove that . . . plaintiff publicly burned or aided or abetted the public burning of a United States flag . . . with intent to cast contempt upon the flag. . . .

In this court, plaintiff has moved for summary judgment asking that we declare [the statute unconstitutional as] violative of the First and Fourteenth Amendment . . . in that it impermissibly infringes on protected expression and . . . uses terminology so vague that men of common intelligence must necessarily guess at its meaning and differ as to its application. . . .

For the reasons set out below, we find A.R.S. § 41-793, subsec. C unconstitutional.

The controlling precedent on the issues before this court is *United States v. O'Brien.* Plaintiff asserts, and we agree, that her act of publicly burning the flag was symbolic speech. . . . [W]e think it is self-evident that most, if not all, conduct associated with the United States flag is symbolic speech. . . . Further, such conduct is invariably successful in communicating the idea. There is nothing equivocal about a flag-draped casket or a flag flying at half-mast at the death of a dignitary. Nor in this day and time is anyone likely to mistake the nature of the ideas expressed by a young person who desecrates his country's flag at an anti-war gathering. . . . In *O'Brien* the Court noted that when " 'speech' and 'nonspeech' elements are combined in the same course of conduct, a sufficiently important governmental interest in regulating the nonspeech element can justify incidental limitations on First Amendment freedoms." . . .

The only state power this court perceives as a constitutional basis for a penal statute of the type here involved is the police power, We specifically reject the existence of a constitutionally recognized state power to prohibit flag desecration based on an interest in preserving loyalty or patriotism [citing the *Barnette* decision]. . . .

Having decided that flag desecration can be symbolic speech, we must now determine what are the speech and non-speech elements in such conduct in order to decide whether there is an important or substantial governmental interest in regulating the nonspeech element. . . . The nonspeech element . . . is the physical act of desecration. What governmental interest, then, could there be in regulating this element?

When accomplished in public, this nonspeech element of flag desecration has a dual impact. The first impact is on the flag itself: it is mutilated, destroyed, or otherwise desecrated. The second impact is on the viewers: the emotions they experience, approval, disapproval, or even indifference. . . . Since these two "impacts" can fairly be characterized as part and parcel of the nonspeech element of public flag desecration, a statute prohibiting such behavior must be justified by virtue of a finding that there is a substantial or important governmental interest in preventing one or both "impacts." . . .

We find that the State has no property interest in the flag sufficient to support a prohibition against the first "impact"; i.e. physical desecration of the flag. And we read *Street* as holding that the State cannot justify such a prohibition in order to insure that the potential desecrator shows proper respect for the flag.

Insofar as the second "impact" is concerned, we . . . find nothing inherent in the act which stimulates those viewers who sympathize with the aims of the desecrator to engage in unlawful acts, such as rioting. Nor is the protection of the "sensibilities of passersby" the proper concern of the State. On neither score is there a substantial or important governmental interest furthered by a prohibition based on the second "impact." . . .

This court cannot say, however, that the state legislature could not validly find that certain types of public flag desecration are so inherently inflammatory that in and of themselves they are likely to provoke the average person to retaliation and thereby cause a breach of the peace. . . .

It is also clear that [under *O'Brien*] the state interest in preventing breaches of the peace is, in the flag desecration context, unrelated to the suppression of free expression. . . .

[Therefore] we must examine the statute in question here to determine whether its method of prohibiting public flag desecration places no greater burden on protected expression than is necessary to further the state's interest in preventing breaches of the peace [as is required under *O'Brien* to uphold it]. In other words, is A.R.S. § 41-793, subsec. C drawn so as to include within its prohibition only those types of flag desecration which per se are likely to cause breaches of the peace or does it include nonprovocative yet protected symbolic types. . . .

[W]e cannot find that a prohibition of any "act [that] casts contempt" include only acts the doing of which the legislature may validly prohibit. . . . ["Contempt"] would describe such acts as sticking out one's tongue, turning one's thumbs downward, or raising a clenched fist salute. Rather than provoke the average person to retaliate violently, these acts would likely merit no more than a scornful glance. . . .

[T]hese acts, which are clearly symbolic speech, do not affect the only legitimate state interest underlying such a prohibition. Even assuming there are acts of contempt which, when directed toward the flag, are inherently inflammatory, the prohibition against "acts [which] cast contempt" by its terms proscribes substantially more than is necessary to protect the state's interest; and that which is unnecessarily proscribed includes protected symbolic speech. Since we cannot see that any limiting construction short of excision can cure the defect this portion of § 41-793, subsec. C must be struck down. . . .

Document 7.9

Ruling of the U.S. District Court for the Western District of North Carolina in the 1971 case of *Parker v. Morgan.*

Source: 322 Federal Supplement 585.

This is a suit brought to test the constitutionality of one of North Carolina's miscellaneous police regulations, . . . entitled "Desecration of State and National flag." . . .

Enacted in 1917 during a period of national chauvinistic fervor, it is an uncommonly bad statute. Despite our respect, and indeed love, for these symbols of state and nation, we are compelled to hold the statute unconstitutional. . . .

Parker [was arrested in this case in 1970 after he] wore a jacket on the back of which he had sewn an American flag, on which was superimposed the legend "Give peace a chance" and the depiction of a hand with index and middle finger forming a "V" [and was subsequently tried and convicted for flag desecration]. . . .

Plaintiff Berg's confrontation with the statute occurred [because he had, with no intention of expressing any idea,] affixed a United States flag to the ceiling of his automobile and in the course of doing so had torn it about the edges and pierced it with fasteners. . . .

We believe the flags of the United States of America and the State of North Carolina to be sui generis. In our opinion the Congress of the United States is constitutionally empowered to reasonably regulate display of the national emblem, and may constitutionally permit the states also to reasonably regulate such display. . . .

We reject plaintiff's argument that because the national flag is a symbol it is always "saying" something, and because it says something control of its display and usage is outlawed by the freedom of speech clause of the First Amendment. The argument is based on a false premise: that what the flag stands for can be authoritatively stated, i. e., that it represents government and/or official policy. . . . It belongs as much to the defeated political party, presumably opposed to the government, as it does to the victorious one. . . . Always it represents America in all its marvelous diversity.

That the government in the name of all the people may reasonably regulate usage and display of the flag, qua flag, does not mean, we think, that the government may appropriate the colors red, white and blue and the depiction of stars and stripes. Thus we think for a flag control statute to be constitutional it must precisely define a flag and carefully avoid expropriation of color and form other than the defined emblem itself, e. g., it seems to us that red, white and blue trousers with or without stars are trousers and not a flag and that it is beyond the state's competence to dictate color and design of clothing, even bad taste clothing.

The trouble with the North Carolina statute is that it attempts too much and goes much too far and infringes upon the reserved liberties of the people. We think it void both for vagueness and overbreadth.

The definition of a flag in the North Carolina statute is simply unbelievable. It would doubtless embrace display of the Star of David against a red, white and blue background. The statute makes plain that it matters not how many stripes or how many stars. One of each is enough. This is expropriation of color and design—not flag protection. Size is of no consequence and substance of no importance. . . . Read literally, it may be dangerous in North Carolina to possess anything red, white and blue. Such a definition is a manifest absurdity. Since it is not suggested that the state has the slightest interest in singling out from the spectrum certain colors for unique protection, this definition alone is sufficient to void the statute. . . .

It is impossible to tell in the context of this unintelligible statute whether it was the legislative intent to prohibit all marks, figures, etc., [from being placed on the flag] or simply those thought to deface, defile or cast contempt upon the flag. . . .

Aside from the "words" phrase of the statute which clearly invalidates it under *Street*, the North Carolina statute is overly broad with respect to prohibited conduct. Protection of the flag, qua flag, is one thing. To go further and forbid expression of attitudes by a gesture or even facial expression is quite another. . . . The right of protest includes the right to be derisive, disdainful, contemptuous and even defiant of government and what may be thought to be in a given context its symbols of authority. . . .

We do not doubt the right of a citizen, however misguided, to turn thumbs down at the flag, or stick out his tongue, or salute it with a clenched fist, or otherwise express his derision and contempt for what to him it may represent.

We think the line must be drawn at the point of contemptuous physical contact with the clearly defined flag and that physical protection of the flag itself is the outermost limit of the state's legitimate interest. It is absurd to say that one may verbally abuse the flag, but that he may not direct toward it a derisive gesture.

Reading *Barnette* and *Street* together, we venture to derive these rules: no man can be punished for refusal to affirmatively demonstrate respect for the flag, nor can anyone be punished for speaking contemptuously of the flag, whether by word or gesture; but the legislature may constitutionally, whether wisely or foolishly, make it criminal to willfully and knowingly cast contempt upon the flag by public acts of physical contact such as mutilation, defiling, defacing or trampling. . . .

In so concluding we adopt a middle ground and fail to follow *Street* to what the Second Circuit [Federal Court of Appeals] has considered to be its logical conclusion. In *Long Island Vietnam Moratorium Committee v. Cahn*, 437 F.2d 344 (2d Cir. 1970), the plaintiffs were threatened with prosecution under a New York statute virtually identical in language with the North Carolina statute [for distributing] decals and lapel buttons on which appeared a circular representation of the American flag . . . upon which . . . the traditional peace symbol had been superimposed. . . .

The Second Circuit held the statute unconstitutional. . . .

The court concluded its opinion with these words which are equally applicable to the North Carolina statute before us:

> Plaintiffs also argue that § 136(a) is unconstitutional on its face because it fails to provide enforcement officials adequate guidance concerning what is proscribed. We agree. Because of its overbreadth, the statute vests local law enforcement officers with too much arbitrary discretion in determining whether or not a certain emblem is grounds for prosecution. It permits only that expression which local officials will tolerate; for example, it permits local officials to prosecute peace demonstrators but to allow "patriotic" organizations and political candidates to go unprosecuted. . . . This opportunity for discriminatory selective enforcement, which § 136(a) provides, renders the statute unconstitutional. Finally, § 136(a) is unconstitutional because it fails to afford adequate notice to the public of the scope of its proscription and is thus void for vagueness. . . .

[T]he Second Circuit additionally considered whether the prohibition of forbidding verbal disrespect for the flag contained in the *Street* decision also should apply to physical acts expressing similar views and concluded this was the case because [the New York statute]

> in effect requires worship of the flag by compelling a series of taboos concerning flag display. Thus in the absence of any valid state interest in prohibiting them, the many flag uses and flag alterations which [the New York statute] proscribes, are protected by the First Amendment and cannot constitutionally be forbidden.

If this means, as it appears to mean, that the First Amendment prevents even minimal state control of flag display and usage, we think it goes too far—albeit a logical extension of *Street*. Worship is an affirmative concept. To protect the flag, qua flag, from physical defilement does not require dissidents to affirm the wisdom of such legislation or prevent expressions of scorn and derision toward all such legislative taboos. Narrow flag protection does not seem to us to infringe too much on First Amendment freedom where actual speech is not circumscribed. . . . We think the First Amendment is not infringed by reasonable state regulation of usage and display of a carefully defined flag.

Having carefully examined this statute, and after giving due regard to the presumption of its validity, we conclude that there is no possible construction that could remedy its impermissible intrusion into area of free expression protected by the First Amendment, and we hold it to be unconstitutional and void.

Document 7.10

Dissenting opinion (to majority ruling of the Ninth Circuit Federal Court of Appeals upholding a flag-burning conviction under the 1968 federal flag desecration law [document 6.1]) by Judge Browning in the 1972 case of *U.S. v. Crosson*.

Source: 62 Federal Reporter, 2d series, 96.

Most of the First Amendment issues that once might have been raised on the facts of this [flag-burning] case have been settled by the Supreme Court adversely to the government. On the basis of principles announced in the most relevant Supreme Court decisions, it is reasonably clear that appellant's act of protest, ineffectual and offensive as it may have been, cannot be punished by government consistent with the First Amendment. I. A. The Court has held [in *Barnette*] that under the First Amendment, the government has no legitimate interest in compelling an individual to express respect for the flag and what it symbolizes.

B. In *Barnette* the government sought to compel the expression of respect toward the flag; in this case the government seeks to prevent the expression of disrespect. There is no apparent reason why this difference should be significant in applying the Constitution's guaranty against interference with free expression, and *Street v. New York* establishes that it is not.

Street holds that under the First Amendment, there is no legitimate governmental interest in punishing expressions of disrespect for the flag. The reason is the same as that underlying *Barnette*. The individual's right to express disagreement with the government includes the right to express that disagreement in terms of the symbol the government has chosen to represent itself. . . .

The [*Street*] Court expressly relied upon the decision in *Barnette*, thus rejecting any difference, for constitutional purposes, between the "affirmative compulsion" of the flag salute struck down in *Barnette* and the "negative prohibition" of flag desecration statutes. . . .

II A. *Street* differs from the present case [only in that] Street was convicted of having "cast contempt upon [the flag] by words," while Mrs. Crosson was convicted because she "knowingly cast contempt upon a flag of the United States by * * * burning." This difference between words and conduct, it is said [by the majority here], distinguishes the two cases for First Amendment purposes.

As *Barnette* demonstrates, First Amendment limitations upon governmental power to directly regulate the expression of views regarding the flag apply to nonverbal expression as well as to verbal expression. And the Court's reliance upon *Barnette* in *Street* demonstrates that the First Amendment standards applicable to direct governmental regulation of verbal and nonverbal expression are the same. . . .

Barnette and *Street*, together, suggest that direct governmental regulation of nonverbal expression is subject to the same limitations under the First Amendment as direct regulation of verbal expression, as distinguished from the less stringent standards applied under *United States v. O'Brien*, to regulation aimed at controlling conduct which may involve expression only incidentally.

This conclusion is supported by *Stromberg v. California*, [document 5.1, wherein the Supreme Court held a "red flag" statute that] permitted the punishment of peaceful and orderly opposition to government . . . invalid as a denial of the constitutionally guaranteed opportunity for free political discussion.

Stromberg was reexamined in *O'Brien*. While distinguishing *Stromberg*, the Supreme Court in *O'Brien* emphasized its scope and continuing vitality. O'Brien burned his Selective Service registration certificate as a demonstration of protest against the Vietnam conflict. . . .

The Court rejected O'Brien's contention that his conviction violated the First Amendment.

The Court distinguished *Stromberg,* noting that the Selective Service Act simply prohibits the destruction of certificate without regard to circumstances or purpose; it "does not distinguish between public and private destruction, and it does not punish only destruction engaged in for the purpose of expressing views," as did the statute in *Stromberg.*

The Court pointed out that the prohibition against the destruction of a Selective Service certificate served many important government interests wholly unrelated to the suppression of expressions of protest. The certificate provided the government with a ready means of verifying the registration and classification of the individual. . . .

Thus, a statute nominally directed at the regulation of conduct but in substance aimed at suppressing communication must meet the First Amendment standards applied to the suppression of speech itself, and not merely the standards applied in *O'Brien* to the regulation of conduct in its noncommunicative aspect.

B. In the present case, the statute, the charge, and the evidence were all directed at punishing the communicative aspect of Mrs. Crosson's conduct—the expression of an idea, and, more specifically the expression of an idea the government found abhorrent.

18 U.S.C. § 700 does not simply prohibit the burning of a flag. It punishes one who "knowingly casts contempt" upon a flag, by various means, including burning. . . . Flag burning that is not communicative is not prohibited, nor for that matter, is flag burning or other conduct that expresses loyalty and respect. The statute does not prohibit the private destruction of a flag even if done to express contempt. The conduct is punished only if done "publicly." . . . Thus, precisely contrary to the statute upheld in *O'Brien,* 18 U.S.C. § 700 "*does* distinguish between public and private destruction, and *does* * * * punish only destruction engaged in for the purpose of expressing views" (emphasis added).

Section 700 accurately reflects the interest the government seeks to serve. That interest is in the flag as a symbol, not as a physical object. The physical destruction of a flag—the noncommunicative element of the prohibited conduct—affects no governmental interest. The value of the flag as a symbol is not diminished by the physical destruction of one flag or of many. The government is interested only in the suppression of the public display of defiance and contempt for the flag—the communicative element of the prohibited conduct—for it is thought that the value of the flag as a symbol may be adversely affected by the public manifestation of such attitudes. . . .

Accordingly, Mrs. Crosson's conviction can be sustained only if it meets the constitutional standards under which government may punish speech.

III. A. It may be that in some contexts flag desecration to convey a message of protest would create a clear and present danger of breach of the peace or of incitement to crime. The government concedes, however, that neither section 700 nor this prosecution can be supported on these grounds. . . .

B. Nor can Mrs. Crosson's conviction be sustained by balancing the governmental interest served by the prosecution against the adverse impact on free expression. The government relies upon a single interest, namely, "its interest in the preservation of the flag as a symbol of unity on national ideals and purpose." As important as this interest undoubtedly is, it could not be more clear that it cannot justify compelling expression of respect for the flag [citing *Barnette*], or justify suppressing expression of disrespect for the flag [citing *Street*].

Since the national interest in patriotism, loyalty, and unity does not warrant censorship of contemptuous and disrespectful views directed against the government itself, it can hardly justify censorship of such views when directed against the mere symbol of government. . . .

Although it seems clear that the *O'Brien* test is not applicable to the prosecution of Mrs. Crosson under section 700, for the reasons suggested [above] this prosecution would fare no better if the *O'Brien* test were applicable.

The most obvious deficiency is the failure to satisfy the requirement that the governmental interest served by the regulation and punishment of the conduct must be "unrelated to the suppression of free expression." . . .

[T]he sole interest served by the prosecution of Mrs. Crosson is the suppression and punishment of her expression of contempt for the flag and the ideas and institutions it represents. This stands in marked contrast to the neutrality toward expression required under *O'Brien*. . . .

The conviction should be reversed.

The Desecration Issue
in the United States Supreme Court
1969–1974

The United States Supreme Court bears much of the responsibility for the fact that the handling of flag desecration prosecutions by the lower courts (as discussed in the previous chapter) during the Vietnam War period was marked by legal chaos and contradiction, with different courts treating similar legal issues in widely varying manners. Essentially, the Supreme Court, right up until its 1989–90 rulings in *Texas v. Johnson* (document 10.12) and *U.S. v. Eichman* (document 12.7), repeatedly ducked the fundamental issue: whether physical flag destruction used to express political dissent was a form of symbolic speech protected by the First Amendment.

Between 1969 and 1989 about twenty appeals that potentially raised this issue reached the Court, but it refused to hear the vast majority of these cases and issued substantive rulings in only three of the handful of cases it agreed to hear. Furthermore, in each of these three cases, *Street v. New York* (document 8.1), *Smith v. Goguen* (document 8.2), and *Spence v. Washington* (document 8.3), the Court avoided the fundamental free speech issue raised by symbolic flag desecration, an issue that, in the light of modern constitutional law principles, had not been clearly settled by the 1907 *Halter* precedent [document 3.10]. That case had upheld a law used to prosecute commercial, rather than politically expressive, use of the flag, at a time before the Supreme Court had even held that the First Amendment applied to the states and before the Court had begun to interpret substantively the "free speech" clause of the First Amendment.

In the 1969 case of *Street v. New York* (document 8.1), the trial record suggested that the prosecution had arisen solely owing to Sidney Street's 1967 burning of a flag to protest the shooting of civil rights activist James Meredith. However, a slender Court majority avoided ruling on the constitutionality of banning physical flag desecration by seizing upon the fact that the New York flag desecration law had outlawed casting contempt upon the flag "by words or act," and that Street's indictment and the trial testimony had mentioned that he had verbally criticized the flag while burning it. Although the three New York courts that considered the case (and found Street guilty or upheld his conviction) focused entirely upon the flag burning, a 5–4 Supreme Court majority overturned Street's conviction on the strained grounds that it was possible that he was convicted solely for his words and that it was clearly established, especially under the 1943 *Barnette* precedent (document 5.2), that the First Amendment forbade outlawing the expression of views simply because they were "offensive to some of their hearers," including even the expression of "distasteful" or "defiant or contemptuous" views about the flag.

Although the Court majority therefore explicitly declared it unnecessary to face the issue of banning physical flag desecration, the *Street* ruling in fact laid the legal groundwork for the 1989–90 *Johnson* and *Eichman* rulings, especially because it relied so heavily on *Barnette* by extending the latter's logic to find that just as the state could not compel Americans to say positive things about the flag, the state could also not forbid them to say negative things about it. Thus, in a key but widely overlooked part of its 1989 *Johnson* flag-burning ruling, which in general relied heavily upon the *Street* and *Barnette* precedents, the Court declared, with reference to a Texas flag desecration law that banned physical flag destruction but not verbal criticism of the flag, that any attempt to distinguish between "written or spoken words and nonverbal conduct" was of "no moment where the nonverbal conduct is expressive, as it is here, and where the regulation of that conduct is related to expression, as it is here." (Although the Court rebuked Texas for arguing that there could be such a distinction, in fact it was the Court itself that had, until 1989, refused to establish the legal identity between physical and verbal flag desecration for twenty years.)

The Court majority's refusal to face the issue of physical flag desecration in the *Street* case drew four separate, bitter dissents from the minority justices, all of whom suggested that the majority had split hairs to avoid confronting this question and made clear that they felt that Street had been convicted for burning the flag, not for criticizing it, and that New York was constitutionally entitled to forbid such acts. Chief Justice Warren also aptly and presciently suggested that, especially given the "widespread concern" over the use of the flag in protest activities, the Court was ducking its responsibility to inform both protesters and law enforcement officials of the "scope of constitutional protection" related to flag desecration, and complained that its silence "encourages" the further testing of the issue "in the streets." Justice Fortas spelled out in greatest detail a legal argument for forbidding physical flag desecration, citing the Court's 1907 *Halter* decision and declaring that, although flags might be privately owned, their "ownership is subject to special burdens and responsibilities."

In the 1974 cases of *Smith v. Goguen* and *Spence v. Washington,* the Supreme Court, in both cases by 6–3 votes that provoked bitter dissents, again overturned flag desecration convictions, but once more did so in ways that avoided facing the central free speech issue raised by physical flag desecration. The *Goguen* case (document 8.2) originated from the 1970 conviction and six-month jail term given to an apparently apolitical Massachusetts teenager who was prosecuted under a state law that punished anyone who "publicly mutilates, tramples upon, defaces, or treats contemptuously the flag of the United States," for wearing a flag patch on the seat of his jeans. The *Spence* case (document 8.3) involved a Seattle man who was fined and given a suspended jail sentence in 1970 for hanging, from his apartment window, a flag to which he had attached removable black plastic tape in the form of a peace symbol, in order, he testified, to protest the American invasion of Cambodia and the killing of four students during an antiwar protest at Kent State University. He was prosecuted for violating the Washington state flag desecration law that banned attaching any words or markings to flags.

Both the *Goguen* and *Spence* cases had intricate legal histories that reflected the widespread juridical confusion prevailing in the lower courts on the flag desecration issue. Goguen's original conviction had been upheld by the Massachusetts Supreme Judicial Court, which rejected challenges to the state law both on grounds of vagueness and of violation of the First Amendment, but it had been subsequently overturned on appeal by two federal courts that had, in turn, based their rulings on crucially distinct grounds. A federal district court found the "contemptuously" provision of the state law unconstitutionally vague, and suggested that a law limited to banning physical flag destruction would be constitutionally sound; but a federal appeals court not only declared the law unconstitutionally vague but also suggested that all flag desecration laws were in violation of the First Amendment, unless they were narrowly targeted to preventing breaches of the peace, because "it is not within the constitutional power of the state" to punish people "for failure to show proper respect toward our flag by words or acts." Spence's conviction had been reversed by the Washington Court of Appeals on First Amendment grounds, citing the Supreme Court's 1969 *Street* ruling, but the Washington Supreme Court had subsequently reinstated the conviction, citing the Supreme Court's 1907 *Halter* ruling and holding that the flag desecration law had not sought to suppress dissent, but only to preserve the flag as a "symbol of the nation" by keeping it "free of extraneous adornment."

In the *Goguen* case, a five-member Supreme Court majority ruled (with support from a sixth justice on separate grounds) that the "contemptuously" clause of the Massachusetts laws was unconstitutionally vague and that therefore there was "no need" to decide "additional [i.e. First Amendment] issues." Because the ruling simply held that the state law had been inartfully drafted, it provide no guidance on the far more crucial free speech issue at the heart of the flag desecration controversy.

In the *Spence* case, the 6–3 Court majority struck the conviction on grounds that were so confusing and so specifically tied to the details of the case (such as the fact that Spence had used his own flag and displayed it on his own property) that its broader meaning and application were, at best, highly obscure. The Court's ruling seemed ultimately to hinge on the esoteric point that, even if the state had a legitimate interest in "preserving the physical integrity of a privately owned flag" in order to preserve the flag as an "unalloyed symbol of our country," Spence had not "significantly impaired" any such interest because his removable tape did not "permanently disfigure the flag or destroy it" (thus provoking a bitter retort by Justice Rehnquist, who asked, in dissent, if the majority was suggesting that Spence "could be prosecuted if he subsequently tore the flag" in the process of removing the tape). By phrasing its key point in this manner, the Court again avoided confronting the central issue of whether the state in fact had a legitimate interest in banning physical flag desecration that would "permanently disfigure" or "destroy" the flag.

Although the *Goguen* and *Spence* holdings (as in *Street*) thus reversed flag desecration convictions while skirting the fundamental First Amendment issues they raised, the majority opinions nonetheless left the clear impression that the Court majority took a dim view of the language and the enforcement of many state flag desecration laws. Thus, in the *Goguen* case, the Court said that the especial flaw of the Massachusetts law's vagueness was that it provided a "standardless" discretion for "policemen, prosecutors and juries to pursue their personal predilections"; in the *Spence* ruling, the Court, although declaring that there was no need to decide whether the state law as written (as opposed to its application to Spence) was inherently unconstitutional, nonetheless noted that, applied literally, the law had a "nearly limitless sweep" and would even forbid "photographs of war heroes standing in front of the flag" or "newspaper mastheads composed of the national flag with superimposed print."

Although the convoluted nature of the *Spence* ruling deprived it of any immediate clear precedential value, it did contain (in a rather obscure fashion) three key points that were later to become significant in the Court's ultimate determination in 1989–90 that symbolic flag burning was a form of protected First Amendment expression. Therefore, along with the *Barnette* and *Street* rulings, it was one of the three most important legal precursors of the 1989–90 *Johnson* and *Eichman* decisions. First, the Court produced in *Spence* a clear guideline for determining what constituted symbolic conduct potentially protected by the First Amendment, namely when "an intent to convey a particularized message was present, and in the surrounding circumstances the likelihood was great that the message would be understood by those who viewed it" (a test that the Court found Spence easily passed given the close conjunction of his altered flag display with events related to the Vietnam War).

Second, the Court (in a footnote), "summarily" rejected a key rationale for the Washington Supreme Court's upholding of Spence's conviction, namely that Spence allegedly could have expressed his views in "thousands" of other ways without altering a flag, on the grounds that the availability of alternative means of expression could not deprive one of the liberty to express oneself in one's preferred, constitutionally protected, form. Third, in another footnote, the Court made a determination that was to prove absolutely critical to its 1989–90 rulings, namely that even if the state of Washington had a legitimate interest in preserving the flag's symbolic value, this interest was "directly related to expression" and involved "no other government interest unrelated to expression," a finding that implied that the government would face a higher hurdle than the relatively lenient *O'Brien* test in demonstrating that such an interest was more important than the First Amendment's protection of freedom of speech.

As in the *Street* case, the *Spence* and *Goguen* rulings provoked angry dissents from the dissenting justices. In *Goguen*, for example, Justice Blackmun, joined by Chief Justice Burger, argued that the "contemptuously" provision of the Massachusetts law was neither unconstitutionally vague nor aimed at punishing Goguen for expression, but simply and constitutionally punished him for "harming the physical integrity of the flag by wearing it affixed to the seat of his pants," just as it would have constitutionally punished anyone who damaged a flag "regardless of his motive or purpose" (document 8.4). This suggestion that Blackmun would uphold any flag desecration law that was not explicitly aimed at punishing political dissent and that sought to protect the flag's "physical integrity" under all circumstances was later to play a major role in the 1989–90 flag desecration controversy (although Blackmun concurred, without explanation, "in the result," but apparently not the reasoning, of the 1974 *Spence* decision, which overturned a conviction under a Washington law that seemed precisely designed to protect the flag's physical integrity regardless of what motivated anyone to damage it).

In both *Spence* and *Goguen*, Justice Rehnquist penned the most embittered and lengthy dissents, thus foreshadowing his emotional dissent from the 1989 *Johnson* ruling (document 10.14), even down to referring to and quoting (in his *Goguen* dissent, document 8.5) the same patriotic poetry that he would later cite at length in his *Johnson* opinion. As Justice Fortas had maintained in his *Street* dissent, Rehnquist, in his *Goguen* dissent, argued that the government had a "property interest" in even privately owned flags, which enabled it to regulate their usage, because what individuals purchased was not "merely cloth dyed red, white and blue, but also the one visible manifestation of 200 years of nationhood" that represented the "deep emotional feelings" of a "large part of our citizenry," which could not be "fully expressed in the two dimensions of a lawyer's brief or of a judicial opinion." In his *Spence* dissent, Rehnquist cited the 1907 *Halter* ruling to support his position that the government could constitutionally protect the flag "as an important symbol of nationhood and unity," and argued that doing so no more impermissibly burdened First Amendment rights than did laws against perjury, libel, copyright infringement, incitement to riot or "the painting of public buildings." He also poured scorn on the majority's reasoning, arguing that whether Spence used removable tape to attach his peace symbol to the flag was irrelevant, because it was the flag's symbolic value, not its "resale value," and its "character, not the cloth," that was at issue.

Document 8.1

Supreme Court majority ruling written by Justice Harlan in the 1969 case of *Street v. New York*.

Source: 394 United States Reports 576.

Appellant Street has been convicted in the New York courts of violating former § 1425, subd. 1, par. d, of the New York Penal Law, which makes it a misdemeanor "publicly ⟨to⟩ mutilate, deface, defile, or defy, trample upon, or cast contempt upon either by words or act ⟨any flag of the United States⟩." He was given a suspended sentence. We must decide whether, in light of all the circumstances, that conviction denied to him rights of free expression protected by the First Amendment and assured against state infringement by the Fourteenth Amendment. According to evidence given at trial, . . . during the afternoon of June 6, 1966, [Street] . . . heard a news report that civil rights leader James Meredith had been shot by a sniper in Mississippi. . . . [He] took from his drawer a neatly folded, 48-star American flag [and went to a nearby intersection where he] lit the flag with a match. . . .

[A police officer who stopped at the scene] testified that as he approached within 10 or 15 feet of appellant, he heard appellant say, "We don't need no damn flag," and that when he asked appellant whether he had burned the flag appellant replied: "Yes; that is my flag; I burned it. If they let that happen to Meredith we don't need an American flag." . . .

Later the same day, appellant was charged [with] "the crime of Malicious Mischief in that ⟨he⟩ did willfully and unlawfully defile, cast contempt upon and burn an American Flag, in violation of 1425 16-D of the Penal Law, under the following circumstances ⟨he⟩ did willfully and unlawfully set fire to an American Flag and shout, 'If they did that to Meredith, We don't need an American Flag.'"

[Street was subsequently convicted and his conviction was upheld by two New York State appeals courts.] Street argues that his conviction was unconstitutional for three different reasons. *First*, he claims that § 1425, subd. 16, par. d, is overbroad, both on its face and as applied, because the section makes it a crime "publicly ⟨to⟩ defy * * * or cast contempt upon an American flag by *words* * * *." (Emphasis added.) *Second*, he contends that § 1425 subd. 16, par. d, is vague and imprecise because it does not clearly define the conduct which it forbids. Third, he asserts that New York may not constitutionally punish one who publicly destroys or damages an American flag as a means of protest, because such an act constitutes expression protected by the Fourteenth Amendment. We deem it unnecessary to consider the latter two arguments, for we hold that § 1425, subd. 16, par. d, was unconstitutionally applied in appellant's case because it permitted him to be punished merely for speaking defiant or contemptuous words about the American flag. In taking this course, we resist the pulls to decide the constitutional issues involved in this case on a broader base than the record before us imperatively requires. . . .

We turn to considering whether appellant's words could have been the sole cause of his conviction, or whether the conviction could have been based on both his words and his burning of the flag. . . . The State argues that appellant's words were at most used to establish unlawful intent in burning the flag. However, after a careful examination of the comparatively brief trial record, we find ourselves unable to say with certainty that appellant's words were not an independent cause of his conviction . . . [i]n the face of an information explicitly setting forth appellant's words as an element of his alleged crime, and of appellant's subsequent conviction under a statute making it an offense to speak words of that sort. . . .

We come finally to the question whether, in the circumstances of this case, New York may constitutionally inflict criminal punishment upon one who ventures "publicly ⟨to⟩ defy * * * or cast contempt upon ⟨any American flag⟩ by words * * *." . . .

[W]e can think of four governmental interests which might conceivably have been furthered by punishing appellant for his words: (1) an interest in deterring appellant from vocally inciting others to commit unlawful acts; (2) an interest in preventing appellant from uttering words so inflammatory that they would provoke others to retaliate physically against him, thereby causing a breach of the peace; (3) an interest in protecting the sensibilities of passers-by who might be shocked by appellant's words about the American flag; and (4) an interest in assuring that appellant, regardless of the impact of his words upon others, showed proper respect for our national emblem.

In the circumstances of this case, we do not believe that any of these interests may constitutionally justify appellant's conviction . . . for speaking as he did. We begin with the interest in preventing incitement. Appellant's words, taken alone, did not urge anyone to do anything unlawful. . . . It is clear that the Fourteenth Amendment prohibits the States from imposing criminal punishment for public advocacy of peaceful change in our institutions. Even assuming that appellant's words might be found incitive when considered together with his simultaneous burning of the flag, [the statute] does not purport to punish only those defiant or contemptuous words which amount to incitement. . . . Hence, a conviction for words could not be upheld on this basis.

Nor could such a conviction be justified on the second ground mentioned above: the possible tendency of appellant's words to provoke violent retaliation. Though it is conceivable that some listeners might have been moved to retaliate upon hearing appellant's disrespectful words, we cannot say that appellant's remarks were so inherently inflammatory as to come within that small class of "fighting words" which are "likely to provoke the average person to retaliation, and thereby cause a breach of the peace." . . .

Again, such a conviction could not be sustained on the ground that appellant's words were likely to shock passers-by. . . . It is firmly settled that under our Constitution the public expression of ideas may not be prohibited merely because the ideas are themselves offensive to some of their hearers. . . .

Finally, such a conviction could not be supported on the theory that by making the above quoted remarks about the flag appellant failed to show the respect for our national symbol which may properly be demanded of every citizen. In *Board of Educ. v. Barnette* [document 5.2], this Court held that to require unwilling schoolchildren to salute the flag would violate rights of free expression assured by the Fourteenth Amendment. . . . We have no doubt that the constitutionally guaranteed [quoting from *Barnette*] "freedom to be intellectually . . . diverse or even contrary," and the "right to differ as to things that touch the heart of the existing order," encompass the freedom to express publicly one's opinions about our flag, including those opinions which are defiant or contemptuous. . . .

Since appellant could not constitutionally be punished under [the statute] for his speech, and since we have found that he may have been so punished, his conviction cannot be permitted to stand. In so holding, we reiterate that we have no occasion to pass upon the validity of this conviction insofar as it was sustained by the state courts on the basis that Street could be punished for his burning of the flag, even though the burning was an act of protest. . . .

Document 8.2

Supreme Court majority ruling written by Justice Powell in the 1974 case of *Smith v. Goguen.*

Source: 15 *United States Reports* 566.

The sheriff of Worcester County, Massachusetts, appeals from a judgment of the United States Court of Appeals for the First Circuit holding the contempt provision of the Massachusetts flag-misuse statute unconstitutionally vague and overbroad. We affirm on the vagueness ground. We do not reach the correctness of the holding below on overbreadth or other First Amendment grounds.

The slender record in this case reveals little more than that Goguen wore a small cloth version of the United States flag sewn to the seat of his trousers [and was subsequently arrested] under the contempt provision of the Massachusetts flag-misuse statute [penalizing] "whoever publicly mutilates, tramples upon, defaces or treats contemptuously the flag of the United States." . . .

Goguen was not charged with any act of physical desecration [but only that he] "did publicly treat contemptuously the flag of the United States." [After conviction by a jury and being sentenced to six months in jail, Goguen's appeal to the Massachusetts Supreme Court was rejected. However, a federal district court found the flag-contempt portion of the Massachusetts laws impermissibly vague under the Fourteenth Amendment's due process clause and overbroad under the First Amendment, and a federal appeals courts affirmed this decision.]

We agree with the holdings of the District Court and the Court of Appeals on the due process doctrine of vagueness [that] requires legislatures to set reasonably clear guidelines for law enforcement officials and triers of fact in order to prevent "arbitrary and discriminatory enforcement." . . .

Flag wearing in a day of relaxed clothing styles may be simply for adornment or a ploy to attract attention. It and many other current, careless uses of the flag nevertheless constitute unceremonial treatment that many people may view as contemptuous. Yet in a time of widely varying attitudes and tastes for displaying something as ubiquitous as the United States flag or representations of it, it could hardly be the purpose of the Massachusetts Legislature to make criminal every informal use of the flag. The statutory language under which Goguen was charged, however, fails to draw reasonably clear lines between the kinds of nonceremonial treatment that are criminal and those that are not. Due process requires that all "be informed as to what the State commands or forbids," and that "men of common intelligence" not be forced to guess at the meaning of the criminal law. Given today's tendencies to treat the flag unceremoniously, those notice standards are not satisfied here. . . .

Statutory language of such a standardless sweep [as the "treats contemptuously" provision of the Massachusetts law] allows policemen, prosecutor, and juries to pursue their personal predilections. Legislatures may not so abdicate their responsibilities for setting the standard of the criminal law [as is evident from the possible results illustrated in] appellant's candid concession during oral argument before the Court of Appeals regarding state enforcement standards for that portion of the statute under which Goguen was convicted:

> [A]s counsel [for appellant] admitted, a war protestor who, while attending a rally at which it begins to rain, evidences his disrespect for the American flag by contemptuously covering himself with it in order to avoid getting wet, would be prosecuted under the Massachusetts statute. Yet a member of the American Legion who, caught in the same rainstorm while returning from an "America—Love It or Leave It" rally, similarly uses the flag, but does so regrettably and without a contemptuous attitude, would *not* be prosecuted. (emphasis in original).

Where inherently vague statutory language permits such selective law enforcement, there is a denial of due process. . . .

The language at issue is void for vagueness as applied to Goguen because it subjected him to criminal liability under a standard so indefinite that police, court, and jury were free to react to nothing more than their own preferences for treatment of the flag. . . .

[B]ecause display of the flag is so common and takes so many forms, changing from one generation to another and often difficult to distinguish in principle, a legislature should define with some care the flag behavior it intends to outlaw. Certainly nothing prevents a legislature from defining with substantial specificity what constitutes forbidden treatment of United States flags. The statutory language at issue here fails to approach that goal and is void for vagueness. The judgment is affirmed.

It is so ordered.

Document 8.3

Supreme Court per curiam majority ruling in the 1974 case of *Spence v. Washington*.

Source: 418 United States Reports 405.

Appellant displayed a United States flag, which he owned, out of the window of his apartment. Affixed to both surfaces of the flag was a large peace symbol fashioned of removable tape. Appellant was convicted under a Washington statute forbidding the exhibition of a United States flag to which is attached or superimposed figures, symbols, or other extraneous material. The Washington Supreme Court affirmed [rejecting challenges to the statute as unconstitutionally vague and in violation of the First Amendment, which had been upheld by the Washington Court of Appeals]. We reverse on the ground that as applied to appellant's activity the Washington statute impermissibly infringed protected expression. . . .

[During his trial, Spence] testified that he put a peace symbol on the flag and displayed it to public view as a protest against the invasion of Cambodia and the killings at Kent State University. He said his purpose was to associate the American flag with peace instead of war and violence. . . . Appellant further testified that he chose to fashion the peace symbol from tape so that it could be removed without damaging the flag. . . .

A number of factors are important in the instant case. First, this was a privately owned flag . . . not the property of any government. . . .

Secondly, appellant displayed his flag on private property. . . . Third, the record is devoid of proof of any risk of breach of the peace. . . .

Fourth, the State concedes . . . that appellant engaged in a form of communication. . . . [T]he nature of appellant's activity, combined with the factual context and environment in which it was undertaken, lead to the conclusion that he engaged in a form of protected expression.

The court for decades [as in the *Stromberg* and *Barnette* cases, documents 5.1 and 5.2] has recognized the communicative connotations of the use of flags. . . . On this record, there can be little doubt that appellant communicated through the use of symbols. The symbolism included not only the flag but also the superimposed peace symbol.

[In the context of developments in Cambodia and the events at Kent State] it would have been difficult for the great majority of citizens to miss the drift of appellant's point at the time he made it. . . . [T]his was not an act of mindless nihilism. . . . An intent to convey a particularized message was present and in the surrounding circumstances the likelihood was great that the message would be understood by those who viewed it. . . .[4]

[W]e think it appropriate to review briefly the range of various state interests that might be thought to support the challenged conviction, drawing upon the arguments before us, the opinions below, and the Court's opinion in *Street v. New York* [document 8.1]. The first interest at issue is prevention of breach of the peace. In our view, the Washington Supreme Court correctly rejected this notion. It is totally without support in the record.

We are also unable to affirm the judgment below on the ground that the State may have desired to protect the sensibilities of passersby . . . . Nor may appellant be punished for failing to show proper respect for our national emblem [citing *Street* and *Barnette*].

We are brought, then, to the state court's thesis that Washington has an interest in preserving the national flag as an unalloyed symbol of our country. . . .

But we need not decide in this case whether the interest advanced by the court below is valid.[8] We assume, arguendo, that it is. The statute is nonetheless unconstitutional as applied to appellant's activity.[9] There was no risk that appellant's acts would mislead viewers into assuming that the Government endorsed his viewpoint. . . . Appellant [did not] permanently disfigure the flag or destroy it. He displayed it as a flag of his country in a way closely analogous to the manner in which flags have always been used to convey ideas. Moreover, his message was direct, likely to be understood, and within the contours of the First Amendment. Given the protected character of his expression and in light of the fact that no interest the State may have in preserving the physical integrity of a privately owned flag was significantly impaired on these facts, the conviction must be invalidated.

The judgement is reversed.

It is so ordered.

4. A subsidiary ground relied upon by the Washington Supreme Court must be rejected summarily. It found the inhibition on appellant's freedom of expression "miniscule and trifling" because there are "thousands of other means available to ⟨him⟩ for the dissemination of his personal views. * * *" As the [Supreme] Court noted in, e.g. *Schneider v. State,* "one is not to have the exercise of liberty of expression in appropriate places abridged on the plea that it may be exercised in some other place."

8. If this interest is valid, we note that it is directly related to expression in the context of activity like that undertaken by appellant. For that reason and because no other governmental interest unrelated to expression has been advanced or can be supported on this record, the four-step analysis of *United States v. O'Brien* is inapplicable.

9. Because we agree with appellant's as-applied argument, we do not reach the more comprehensive overbreadth contention he also advances.

But it is worth noting the nearly limitless sweep of the Washington [flag desecration] statute. Read literally, it forbids a veteran's group from attaching, e.g., battalion commendations to a United States flag. It proscribes photographs of war heroes standing in front of the flag. It outlaws newspaper mastheads composed of the national flag with superimposed print. Other examples could easily be listed. . . .

Document 8.4

Dissenting opinion by Supreme Court Justice Blackmun (joined by Chief Justice Burger) in the 1974 case of *Smith v. Goguen*.

Source: 418 *United States Reports* 590.

I agree with MR. JUSTICE REHNQUIST [in his dissent, document 8.5] when he concludes that the First Amendment affords no shield to Goguen's conduct [on the ground that the Supreme Judicial Court of Massachusetts had interpreted the state law] to require that "treats contemptuously" entails physical contact with the flag and the protection of its physical integrity. . . . Having rejected the vagueness challenge and concluded that Goguen was not punished for speech, the Massachusetts court, in upholding the conviction, has necessarily limited the scope of the statute to protecting the physical integrity of the flag. The requisite for "treating contemptuously" was found and the court concluded that punishment was not for speech—a communicative element. I therefore, must conclude that Goguen's punishment was constitutionally permissible for harming the physical integrity of the flag by wearing it affixed to the seat of his pants. . . .

Document 8.5

Dissenting opinion by Supreme Court Justice Rehnquist (joined by Chief Justice Burger) in the 1974 case of *Smith v. Goguen*.

Source: 418 *United States Reports* 591.

. . . Massachusetts metes out punishment to anyone who publicly mutilates, tramples, or defaces the flag, regardless of his motive or purpose. It also punishes the display of any "words, figures, advertisements or designs" on the flag. . . .

The variety of these prohibitions demonstrates that Massachusetts has not merely prohibited impairment of the physical integrity of the flag by those who would cast contempt upon it, but equally by those who would seek to take advantage of its favorable image in order to facilitate any commercial purpose, or those who would seek to convey any message at all by imprinting words or designs on the flag. . . . [T]he Massachusetts statute is one essentially designed to preserve the physical integrity of the flag, and not merely to punish those who would infringe that integrity for the purpose of disparaging the flag as a symbol. . . .

[In terms of the 1968 *O'Brien* doctrine], I think the governmental interest in unrelated to the suppression of free expression . . . and that the government interest is sufficient to outweigh whatever collateral suppression of expressive conduct was involved. . . .

From its earliest days, the art and literature of our country have assigned a special place to the flag. . . . No one who lived through the Second World War . . . can forget the impact [of the Iwo Jima flag-raising] photographs. . . .

Ralph Waldo Emerson, writing 50 years after the battles of Lexington and Concord, wrote:

> By the rude bridge that arched the flood
> Their flag to April's breeze unfurled
> Here once the embattled farmers stood
> And fired the shot heard 'round the world. . . .

John Philip Sousa's "Stars and Stripes Forever" and George M. Cohan's "It's a Grand Old Flag" are musical celebrations of the flag familiar to adult and children alike. . . .

The United States flag flies over every federal courthouse. . . . It is the one visible embodiment of the authority of the National Government. . . .

The significance of the flag, and the deep emotional feelings it arouses in a large part of the citizenry, cannot be fully expressed in the two dimensions of a lawyer's brief or a judicial opinion. But if the government may create proprietary interests in written work and in musical and theatrical performances by virtue of copyright laws, I see no reason why it may not . . . create a similar governmental interest in the flag by prohibiting even those who have purchased the physical object from impairing its physical integrity. For what they have purchased is not merely cloth dyed red, white and blue, but also the one visible manifestation of two hundred years of nationhood. . . .

Massachusetts has not prohibited Goguen from wearing a sign sewn to the seat of his pants expressing in words his low opinion of the flag. . . . It has prohibited him from wearing there a particular symbol of extraordinary significance and content, for which . . . Goguen is in no wise responsible. The flag of the United States is not just another "thing," and it is not just another "idea." . . .

[Goguen] was not compelled in any way to salute the flag, pledge allegiance to it, or make any affirmative gesture of support [in violation of the *Barnette* doctrine, document 5.2]. . . . He was simply prohibited from impairing the physical integrity of a unique national symbol which has been given content by generations of his and our forebears, a symbol of which he had acquired a copy. I believe Massachusetts had a right to enact this prohibition.

The Desecration Issue in the Courts
1975–1984

After 1974, as American involvement in Vietnam came to an end, public and political concern with flag desecration virtually disappeared. No doubt one reason for this was that very few incidents of flag desecration were reported in the press during the period, and those that were generally received only localized media attention. Most of the dozen or so flag burnings recorded between 1979 and 1989 involved members of the Revolutionary Communist Party (RCP), a Maoist-oriented fringe group that frequently adopted tactics designed to shock the public and to attract press attention. Following the seizure of American hostages at the American embassy in Iran in late 1979, which was accompanied by well-publicized Iranian burnings of the American flag, the RCP repeatedly applauded such acts and encouraged its members to engage in flag burnings. In three cases involving convictions for RCP flag burnings, the Supreme Court refused to hear appeals between 1981 and 1984, thus continuing its persistent policy, ever since the 1969 *Street* decision (document 8.1), of refusing to hear appeals in flag burning cases (including refusals to hear appeals from convictions in the cases of *U.S v. Crosson,* document 7.10 [409 U.S. 1064, 1972] and of *Farrell v. Iowa,* document 7.7 [421 U.S. 1007, 1975]).

In general, both the RCP flag burnings and the Supreme Court's refusal to hear appeals arising from flag burnings after 1969 attracted little national media attention. However, there was one exception to this rule in 1982. Although the Court refused to hear an appeal resulting from an RCP flag-burning conviction arising under the 1968 federal flag desecration law (document 6.1) in *U.S. v. Kime,* Justice William Brennan wrote an impassioned dissent (document 9.1), an action extremely rare when the issue is simply whether the Court will consider a case (as opposed to an actual decision on a case). Brennan's argument largely echoed Justice Browning's dissent in *U.S. v. Crosson* and largely prefigured his own majority opinions in the 1989–90 flag-burning cases (documents 7.10, 10.12 and 12.7). Citing *Stromberg* (document 5.1), *Barnette* (document 5.2), *Street* (document 8.1), *Spence* (document 8.3) and *O'Brien*, Brennan declared that it was obvious that the defendants had burned the flag to express a political message and that the government's only motivation for outlawing such action was to preserve the flag's symbolic value, as was evident from the fact that only acts that sought to "knowingly" cast "contempt" upon the flag were forbidden by the 1968 law.

Brennan argued that this motivation was clearly related "to the suppression of free expression" and, because flag burning "impaired no non-speech related governmental interest," there was no difference between the type of oral flag criticism held by the Supreme Court to be protected First Amendment expression in *Street* and any other kind of "specific physical medium petitioners chose for their expression." Brennan declared that the particular language of the federal law was especially "odious," as the "contempt" language made it so "narrowly drawn" that "everything it might possibly prohibit is constitutionally protected" and therefore it could not be violated "without espousing unpopular political beliefs," thus amounting to the "very definition of a censorship statute." He made clear, however, that in his view, even without the "contempt" language all flag desecrations laws would still be unconstitutional as motivated by purely suppressive aims in violation of the First Amendment.

In 1984, a three-judge federal appeals court essentially followed Brennan's reasoning in unanimously overturning, in *Monroe v. Fulton County,* a RCP-related flag-burning conviction for violating the Georgia state flag desecration law, thereby reversing prior rulings by the Georgia Supreme Court and a federal district court (document 9.2). Although this decision was not appealed to the Supreme Court, it marked the first time that a federal appeals court had struck down a flagburning conviction squarely on free speech grounds, and thus, along with the federal district court ruling in *Crosson v. Silver* (document 7.8), the Browning dissent in *U.S. v. Crosson,* and the Brennan dissent in *U.S. v. Kime,* further bolstered the legal principles that the Supreme Court would finally endorse in 1989–90. The *Monroe* ruling followed essentially the same legal analysis that had been applied by Brennan in *Kime* and by Judge Browning in his *Crosson* dissent (the latter of whom was cited at length), and it relied heavily, as they had earlier, upon *Barnette, Street, O'Brien,* and *Spence.*

Document 9.1

Dissent by Justice Brennan from refusal of the U.S. Supreme Court to grant certiorari in the 1982 case of *U.S. v. Kime.*

Source: 459 United States Reports 949.

On March 27, 1980, petitioners Teresa Kime and Donald Bonwell participated in a political protest on a public sidewalk in front of the Federal Building in Greensboro, N. C. The stated purposes of the demonstration were to call attention to a planned May Day demonstration and to protest the prosecution of a leader of the political party to which petitioners belonged. During the demonstration, petitioner set fire to a privately owned United States flag [and were subsequently charged] with casting contempt on a United States flag by publicly burning it, in violation of 18 U. S. C. § 700 [document 6.1]. That statute prohibits *"knowingly cast⟨ing⟩ contempt upon any flag of the United States* by publicly mutilating, defacing, defiling, burning, or trampling upon it" (emphasis added).

[Petitioners were convicted by a jury before a U.S. magistrate and sentenced to eight months imprisonment each, and their convictions were subsequently upheld by a federal district and a federal appeals court.] I would grant certiorari . . . because I feel sure the Court would be persuaded . . . that petitioners' convictions violate their First Amendment rights under the principles established in *Spence v. Washington* [document 8.3]; *Schacht v. United States; Street v. New York* [document 8.1]; *United States v. O'Brien;* and *West Virginia State Board of Education v. Barnette* [document 5.2].

It is not seriously contested that petitioners' action in burning a flag was, at a minimum, expressive conduct "sufficiently imbued with elements of communication to fall within the scope of the First . . . Amendmen⟨t⟩," [citing *Spence*]. This Court has repeatedly recognized the communicative connotations of the use of flags, including the United States flag [citing *Spence* and *Stromberg,* document 5.1]. . . . The statute under which petitioners were convicted requires, as an element of the offense, that they "knowingly cast contempt" on the flag by burning it. Thus, if the Government were to contend that petitioners were not engaged in expressive conduct, it would be confessing that petitioners did not commit the crime charged.

Nor can there be any doubt that the subject matter of petitioners' communication is well within the core of the First Amendment's protection. Nearly four decades ago, this Court held that the First Amendment does not permit a legislature to require a person to show his respect for the flag by saluting it [citing *Barnette*]. The same constitutional principle applies when the legislature, instead of compelling respect for the flag, forbids disrespect [citing and quoting from *Street*].

The only difference between this case and *Street* is that petitioners here communicated their contempt for the flag through expressive conduct rather than through spoken or written words (or through both words and conduct, as in *Street*). The First Amendment standard for government regulation of expressive conduct is the now familiar four-part test first announced in *United States v. O'Brien*. . . .

It is the third branch of the *O'Brien* test [requiring that the government interest behind regulating the expressive part of conduct be "unrelated to the suppression of free expression" to pass the relatively lenient test of furthering an "important or substantial governmental interest"] that is dispositive of this case. The Government suggests only one possible "substantial governmental interest" underlying § 700—"preservation of the flag, not as a mere chattel, but as the 'visible embodiment of the Nation.'" In *Spence*, we expressly *rejected* this alleged governmental interest as a basis for meeting the "unrelated to expression" branch of the *O'Brien* test. . . . Even if that interest exists, we held, such an interest is directly related to expression, at least where it is invoked against one who would use the flag to make a political statement. . . . The Government has no esthetic or property interest in protecting a mere aggregation of stripes and stars for its own sake; the only basis for a governmental interest (if any) in protecting the flag is precisely the fact that the flag has substantive meaning as a political symbol. . . . Hence, the one governmental interest suggested as support for this statute, and these convictions, is one clearly foreclosed by both precedent and basic First Amendment principles. . . .

Section 700 is neither an arson statute nor a breach of the peace statute; the Government does not and cannot suggest that the statute's prohibition is directed at any interest other than enforcing respect for the flag.

So far I have analyzed this case simply as one governed by *Spence*. But even if that case were somehow distinguishable (on the basis of burning or otherwise), there is an entirely independent reason why . . . § 700 is flagrantly unconstitutional on its face indeed, a ground much stronger than anything in *Spence*. For § 700 contains an odious feature not shared by the statute in *Spence*. Section 700 makes it a crime *"knowingly ⟨to⟩ cast contempt* upon any flag of the United States by publicly . . . burning . . . it." *Thus, it is an indispensable element of the offense under § 700 that one intend to engage in political expression—and not just any political expression, but only that espousing a particular, unpopular point of view.* This is indeed a narrowly drawn statute; it is drawn so that everything it might possibly prohibit is constitutionally protected expression. This statute is thus different from one that simply outlawed any public burning or mutilation of the flag, regardless of the expressive intent or nonintent of the actor.[7] To put it bluntly, one literally cannot violate § 700 *without* espousing unpopular political views. That is the very definition of a censorship statute. . . .

In short, § 700 constitutes overt content based censorship, pure and simple. Under this statute, one may freely burn, mutilate, or otherwise abuse a flag for any reason in the world, *except* for the purpose of stating a contemptuous political message about the flag and what it stands for. This censorship goes to the heart of what the First Amendment prohibits. Of course, § 700 does not bar petitioners from seeking to express their message by other means; but that is immaterial. It has long been settled that a government may not justify a content-based prohibition by showing that speakers have alternative means of expression. This statute is unconstitutional on its face. . . .

7. I do not mean to be read as suggesting that such a statute would be constitutional. On the contrary, it would be invalid for the reasons stated in my discussion of *Spence*. My present point is that even if we had reached the opposite conclusion in *Spence* from the one we state, there would be an independent fatal flaw in § 700.

Document 9.2

Ruling of the Eleventh Circuit Court of Appeals in the 1984 case of *Monroe v. State Court of Fulton County*.

Source: 739 Federal Reporter, 2d series, 568.

On September 17, 1980, appellant, Diane Monroe, was convicted in State Court of Fulton County for misuse of the national flag [for having burned a flag in Atlanta in 1979 during a protest against American foreign policy sponsored by the Revolutionary Communist Party] in violation of a Georgia statute, Ga. Code Ann. § 26-2803, [which makes it illegal to mutilate, deface or defile the American flag] and was sentenced to twelve months imprisonment. [The Georgia Supreme Court subsequently upheld the conviction and a federal district court denied a petition for a writ of habeas corpus.] Because we hold that the Georgia statute is unconstitutional as applied, we reverse the denial of appellant's petition for writ of habeas corpus. . . . .

To determine whether appellant's conduct is entitled to first amendment protection, "the nature of appellant's activity, combined with the factual context and environment in which it was undertaken" must be considered [citing *Spence,* document 8.3]. If appellant shows "[a]n intent to convey a particularized message . . . and in the surrounding circumstances the likelihood was great that the message would be understood by those who viewed it," the activity falls within the scope of the first and fourteenth amendments. . . .

[I]t is clear that Monroe intended to convey a particularized message: her dissatisfaction with the United States's policies. Because the flag was burned during a larger demonstration that involved picketing and speeches the likelihood that Monroe's message would be understood by those who viewed it was great. . . . Therefore, we conclude that Monroe's burning of the flag constituted speech and symbolic expression within the purview of the first amendment.

Having concluded that Monroe's conduct was a form of speech, however, does not mean that any infringement on her freedom of expression would be unconstitutional. The first amendment ban against the making of laws abridging free speech is not absolute. . . .

[T]he [Supreme] Court in *Spence* adopted a two-step analysis [to determine the standard by which expressive conduct involving the flag should be judged]: first, a determination of whether the conduct is within the protections of the first amendment; and second, whether, upon the record of the given case, the interests advanced by the state are so substantial as to justify infringement of constitutional rights.

To determine whether to apply the [relatively lenient] framework of *O'Brien* [as a test of the government's interests] or [the implication in] *Spence* [that where the government's only interest is suppression of expression a much more stringent test must be applied to justify governmental restrictions], we must examine the state's asserted interests. One of criteria of *O'Brien* is that the governmental interest must be unrelated to the suppression of free speech. Thus, if the state's interests are related to the suppression of free speech, this criterion under *O'Brien* is not met and instead, *Spence* will apply. The state asserts two interests in suppressing Monroe's activity: 1) the protection of the national flag as a symbol; and 2) the prevention of breaches of the peace. We conclude that both interests to the extent that either or both of them were sought to be implemented by the prosecution in the case are related to the suppression of free speech and accordingly that *Spence* applies.

The state's interest in protecting the integrity of the national flag is not unrelated to the suppression of free speech [citing and quoting from Judge Browning's dissent in *U.S. v. Crosson,* document 7.10]. . . .

Nor is the state's interest in preventing a breach of the peace unrelated to the suppression of free speech. As Professor Nimmer has stated [in his article, "The Meaning of Symbolic Speech under the First Amendment," 21 *UCLA Law Review* 29 (1973), 57]:

In the context of flag desecration, it is precisely the particular idea conveyed by the act of desecration that it is feared will lead to a violent or unlawful reaction. Thus, insofar as the governmental objective is the suppression of the communication of an idea in order to avoid resulting violence, it is an anti-speech interest, i.e. an interest in the suppression of speech.

Having adopted the framework of *Spence,* we must determine whether the state's interests are so substantial as to justify infringement of Monroe's constitutional rights.

The first interest advanced by the state to support its position is the protection of the flag as the symbol of the nation. . . . We conclude, however, that the state's interest is not sufficiently substantial as to justify infringement of Monroe's constitutional rights.

The Supreme Court has held that under the first amendment, the government has no legitimate interest in compelling an individual to express respect for the flag and what it symbolizes. In *Barnette* [document 5.2], the Supreme Court held that the flag salute was symbolic speech, and the government could not require an individual to salute the flag in the interest of national unity. As pointed out by Judge Browning in his dissent in *United States v. Crosson,* there is no significant difference between *Barnette,* in which the government sought to compel the expression of respect toward the flag and this case, in which the government seeks to present the expression of disrespect. . . .

A similar notion was conveyed by the Supreme Court in *Street* [document 8.1]. In *Street,* the Court considered the state's interest in assuring that the appellant showed proper respect for the national emblem. The Court, which held that this interest could not support the conviction, noted that the Constitution "encompasses the freedom to express publicly one's opinions about our flag, including those opinions which are defiant or contemptuous."

The only difference between *Street* and this case is that Street was convicted of having "cast contempt upon ⟨the flag⟩ by words," while Monroe was convicted of deliberately mutilating, defacing, or defiling the flag. But direct governmental regulation of nonverbal expression should be subject to the same limitations under the first amendment as direct regulation of verbal expression. Thus, we hold that the state's interest in protecting the flag as a symbol is not so substantial as to permit the state to infringe on Monroe's right to free speech.

The second interest asserted by the state is prevention of breaches of the peace. Clearly, the state has a valid interest in preventing breaches of the peace that might arise from certain acts of flag desecration. Some courts have concluded that acts of flag desecration are, of themselves, always so inherently inflammatory that the state may act to prevent a danger to the public peace. Other courts have concluded that an act of flag dese-cration alone is insufficient provocation to abridge first amendment rights; rather, the state must introduce other objective evidence that demonstrates the imminence of public unrest or a clear and present danger of breach of the peace. We hold that the latter view is required under the Constitution. . . .

Monroe's act of burning the flag, which we have concluded was sym-bolic speech, did not produce a clear and present danger of a serious, substantive evil. There was no evidence demonstrating the likelihood and imminence of public unrest [as required to justify suppression of expres-sion by the Supreme Court's 1969 ruling in *Brandenburg v. Ohio*]. . . .

[Furthermore, no] spectator could reasonably have regarded Monroe's communicative conduct as a direct personal insult [as required by the Su-preme Court to justify suppression of expression under the "fighting words" doctrine of its 1942 ruling in *Chaplinsky v. New Hampshire*]. . . .

Although Monroe's opinions and her means of expressing her ideas are doubtless highly unpopular, her right to express her beliefs is guaran-teed by the Constitution. We hold that Ga. Code Ann. § 26-2803 is uncon-stitutional as applied to Monroe.

Accordingly, the judgment below is REVERSED.

10

Origins of the 1989–1990 Controversy

The immediate origins of the 1989–90 flag desecration controversy date back to a 1984 RCP-influenced flag burning. On August 22, 1984, while the Republican National Convention was meeting in Dallas, Texas, to renominate President Ronald Reagan, an American flag was burned in front of the Dallas city hall to protest this event and other aspects of American politics, as the culmination of a demonstration involving about one hundred people, some of whom were affiliated with the RCP. No disorders occurred during or after the actual flag burning although, according to subsequent, uncontested trial testimony and contemporary journalistic accounts, before the demonstrators reached city hall they had paraded through downtown Dallas, along the way spray-painting the walls of several buildings and committing several other minor acts of vandalism, such as overturning potted plants in a bank lobby and stealing a flag from a bank (according to trial testimony, this was the flag that was later burned). Dallas police officers who observed the entire protest took no action until approximately forty-five minutes after the flag burning, whereupon all of the protesters still present at city hall were arrested on charges of disorderly conduct.

Subsequently, most of those arrested were freed and the charges against them were dropped; however, in the case of Gregory Lee (Joey) Johnson, a member of the RCP's youth group, the Revolutionary Communist Youth Brigade (RCYB), a new charge was substituted, alleging that he had violated Texas Penal Code 42.09 (a) (3) (1989), known as the Venerated Objects Law (documents 10.1 and 10.2). The Texas statute, which had been adopted by the state legislature in 1973, was a modified form of the "desecration of venerated objects" provision endorsed by the American Law Institute in its 1962 Model Penal Code. It replaced Texas's World War I–era flag desecration statute, which had been invoked in 1970 to jail Gary Deeds for four years for a Vietnam-era flag burning in a conviction and sentence that the Texas Court of Criminal Appeals subsequently upheld in 1971 (document 7.6). In addition to replacing the draconian maximum twenty-five-year jail term penalty of the 1917 law with a more typical state flag desecration penalty of one year in jail and a $2,000 fine, the 1973 law discarded all specific restrictions on commercial use of the flag, instead defining the offense as "intentionally or knowingly" desecrating a "national flag," with "desecration" defined as to "deface, damage or otherwise physically mistreat in a way that the actor knows will seriously offend one or more persons likely to observe or discover his action."

Johnson was subsequently convicted on December 13, 1984 (document 10.3) and sentenced to the maximum penalty after a four-day jury trial, which mostly focused on the disorders that had preceded the flag burning and on Johnson's role as an apparent leader of the demonstration, as evidenced by his leading of chants and shouting of political slogans over a megaphone (however, no evidence was produced that indicated that Johnson had been engaged in any of the petty vandalism).[1] Although the protest had been heavily surveilled by Dallas police and filmed by local journalists (whose videotapes were subpoenaed by Dallas prosecutors and introduced at the trial), only one witness, an undercover Dallas police officer, identified Johnson as the flag burner when the prosecution first presented its case, and no videotape or photographs were introduced that depicted the actual flag burning (a Dallas City Hall security guard also identified Johnson as the flag burner during rebuttal testimony, but her evidence about the circumstances of the flag burning contradicted statements made by all other witnesses for both sides).

Johnson himself did not testify during the guilt or innocence phase of the trial (in Texas a separate proceeding is held to determine punishment if a defendant is found guilty, in what is known as a "bifurcated" criminal trial procedure), but he was allowed by presiding Dallas County Criminal Court judge John Hendrik to present a closing argument to the jury, in which he praised the August 22 protest but denied that he had burned the flag; earlier the defense had presented two eyewitnesses who testified that Johnson was not the flag burner. Throughout the trial, Johnson's lawyers argued that, although Johnson had not burned the flag, in any case the Texas Venerated Objects Law violated Johnson's First Amendment right to burn it to make a symbolic political point if he so wished. However, Judge Hendrik repeatedly rejected defense motions to declare the law unconstitutional and halt the trial.

Given the heavy stress that the prosecution placed on the disorderly events that preceded the flag burning, which were graphically depicted in videotapes that were introduced over vigorous defense objections, it seems likely that the jury conviction was heavily influenced by Judge Hendrik's charge, in which he instructed them that, under Texas's so-called law of parties, Johnson could be convicted either for personally breaking the

Texas Venerated Objects Law or for encouraging, directing, or aiding others in committing the offense. In his closing remarks to the jury, Dallas County Assistant District Attorney Michael Gillett said that although the prosecution believed that Johnson had burned the flag, he was, in any case, "guilty as sin as far as the law of parties is concerned," because there was "no question he encouraged it at all." Another factor that probably harmed Johnson was that, throughout the trial, the prosecution heavily stressed the radical political views that had been expressed, sometimes in graphic and obscene terms, by Johnson and other demonstrators during the protest.

Johnson himself seemed quite happy to advertise his views during the trial, for example, wearing to court each day a T-shirt with the RYCB logo on it, which featured a silhouette of a man holding a rifle, and distributing news releases and holding press conferences in the courtroom halls during trials breaks. Following his conviction, Johnson took the stand during the sentencing portion of his bifurcated trial and engaged in an extended dialogue with Gillett, in which Johnson happily expressed his political views at length in response to Gillett's questions (document 10.4). Gillett repeatedly referred to Johnson's T-shirt and asked why, if Johnson didn't "like the way it's [the country is] run, why don't you just leave?" Johnson responded by declaring that the real message of the trial was to tell "anyone who has unpatriotic beliefs to keep them to yourself" and to brand him officially as a "thought criminal." During his closing sentencing argument, Gillett successfully urged the jury to give Johnson the maximum penalty, because he had "offended the nation" and was "creating a lot of danger for a lot of people by what he does and the way he thinks." Gillett added that the jury should "represent each and every" American in delivering a "message" to Johnson and "others like him, 'No more. We won't have it.'"

After his conviction, Johnson was allowed to post an appeal bond and remain out of prison while his lawyers exercised the right guaranteed in Texas to obtain a review of the conviction on appeal. The briefs filed by Johnson and in response by Dallas County prosecutors before the Court of Appeals for the Fifth Texas Supreme Judicial District in mid-1985 set out the basic arguments that were to be pursued for the remaining four years of litigation. Johnson's brief stressed above all that he had been prosecuted in violation of the First Amendment to the U.S. Constitution, as well as the free speech clause of the Texas Constitution, because the Dallas flag burning was expressive under the guidelines of the Supreme Court's 1974 *Spence* decision (document 8.3); his lawyers also pointed especially to the then very recent federal appeals court ruling overturning a flag-burning conviction in the *Monroe* case (document 9.2), which like their brief, had heavily relied, in addition to *Spence,* on *Barnette* and *Street* (documents 5.2 and 8.1). The Dallas reply brief, which relied heavily on rulings by state supreme courts upholding flag desecration laws in the 1971 *Deeds* and the 1974 *Farrell* flag-burning cases (documents 7.6 and 7.7), conceded "for purposes of argument," that the 1984 Dallas flag burning gave "rise to First Amendment protections," but maintained that the state's interests in "prevention of breaches of the peace" and protection of the flag as a "symbol of national unity" outweighed Johnson's free speech rights.

On January 23, 1986, the Court of Appeals unanimously upheld Johnson's conviction (document 10.5). The heart of the ruling, written by Judge John Vance (who had been presiding judge at the original 1970 trial in the *Deeds* case and who would assume the role of Johnson's prosecutor on appeal when he shortly afterwards was elected Dallas County district attorney), was that although the Dallas flag burning theoretically was "constitutionally protected free speech" requiring First Amendment scrutiny under the *Spence* test, Texas had overriding interests "substantial" enough to "justify infringement of Johnson's constitutional rights." Relying heavily on the 1971 *Deeds* ruling of the Texas Court of Criminal Appeals, the appeals court endorsed Dallas's arguments that Johnson's rights had to yield to Texas's "legitimate and substantial interest in protecting the flag as a symbol of national unity" and to the conclusion that "acts of flag desecration are, of themselves, so inherently inflammatory that the State may act to prevent breaches of the public peace" even absent any "objective evidence of imminent public unrest."

Johnson thereupon requested that the Texas Court of Criminal Appeals exercise its discretion to hear a further appeal of his conviction. The Criminal Appeals court agreed to do so and on April 20, 1988, handed down a 5–4 ruling that declared that the Texas Venerated Objects Law had been unconstitutionally applied to Johnson by violating his First Amendment rights to engage in peaceful political protest (document 10.6). Rejecting its own earlier analysis in *Deeds* as inadequate owing to subsequent Supreme Court decisions, including the 1974 *Spence* case, the Criminal Appeals court agreed with the lower appeals court that Johnson had engaged in "symbolic speech," but rejected the claim that Texas had compelling overriding state interests. First, the court held that the Texas law was "too broad for First Amendment purposes" to be used properly to prevent breaches of the peace in the case at hand, because by banning all flag desecration that merely caused "serious offense" it outlawed "protected conduct which has no propensity to result in breaches of the peace." Thus, the court found that trial testimony in the Johnson case indicated that the Dallas flag burning had caused "serious offense" to some onlookers yet had provoked no violence; the court added that a separate state disorderly conduct law was adequate to punish incidents of flag desecration that actually provoked violence.

More centrally, the court held, relying heavily upon the Supreme Court's 1943 *Barnette* ruling outlawing compulsory public school flag salutes, that Texas's professed interest in preserving the flag as a symbol of unity could not justify compromising Johnson's First Amendment rights because the government could not constitutionally "carve out a symbol of unity and prescribe a set of approved messages to be associated with that symbol when it cannot mandate the status or feeling the symbol purports to represent." In any case, the court held, again relying upon *Barnette*, for Texas to legally override Johnson's First Amendment rights in furtherance of promoting national unity it would have to demonstrate that symbolic flag burning posed a "grave and immediate danger" that the flag would lose its ability to "rouse feelings of unity or patriotism" and become devalued "into a meaningless piece of cloth. We do not believe such a danger is present."

On July 26, 1988, Dallas petitioned the United States Supreme Court to grant a writ of certiorari and thus hear its appeal from the decision of the Texas Court of Criminal Appeals. The Dallas petition reiterated the contention that the twin state interests of preserving the peace and protecting the flag's symbolic value justified Johnson's conviction under the Venerated Objects Law. In response, Johnson's lawyers endorsed the Texas high court ruling and maintained that it conformed with the Supreme Court's 1974 *Spence* ruling and post-*Spence* lower court rulings, such as the 1984 *Monroe* decision. On October 17, 1988, the Supreme Court granted certiorari in *Texas v. Johnson,* which was docketed as case No. 88-155.

Although typically Supreme Court decisions simply to hear a case rarely attract significant press attention, the October 17 announcement was widely publicized in the national press (although prior developments in Texas had received no national media attention), primarily because it happened to coincide with a presidential election campaign in which the Republican candidate, Vice President George Bush, had repeatedly criticized the Democratic candidate, Massachusetts governor Michael Dukakis, for vetoing legislation in 1977 that would have required public school teachers to lead daily recitals of the Pledge of Allegiance. Although Dukakis had acted on the advice of the Supreme Judicial Court of Massachusetts and the state attorney general that the law would violate the *Barnette* ruling, Bush suggested that the veto reflected adversely on his opponent's patriotism, asking at one point, "What is it about the American flag that upsets this man so much?"[2] The so-called Pledge of Allegiance issue was massively publicized and, by general consensus, proved to be one of Bush's most effective arguments in his successful presidential campaign.

Shortly before the scheduled March 21, 1989, Supreme Court oral argument in the *Johnson* case, a controversy over an art exhibit in Chicago returned both the flag and the specific issue of flag desecration to the national headlines (document 10.7). The exhibit, part of a February 17–March 18 showing of seventy-two minority student displays at the School of the Art Institute of Chicago (SAIC), was entitled, "What is the Proper Way to Display the American Flag?" It featured a photographic collage of flag burnings and flag-draped coffins displayed on a wall above a ledger placed on a shelf; a flag was draped on the floor directly in front of the ledger, so that patrons seemed to be invited to walk on the flag if they wished to record in the ledger their answer to the question posed by the display.

The exhibit, which was designed by a SAIC student named Scott Tyler (who called himself "Dread Scott"), set off a storm of controversy in Chicago, where veterans' groups organized mass picketing to protest the display, which they said amounted to an ongoing desecration of the flag. As a result of the exhibit, the Chicago City Council and the Illinois legislature passed laws designed specifically to outlaw placing flags on the floor, and the legislature drastically cut state funding both for SAIC and a state arts council that had defended SAIC's right to sponsor the exhibit. On March 16, two days before the exhibit was scheduled to close, the United States Senate joined in the chorus of condemnation by voting 97–0 to amend the federal flag desecration law of 1968 (for the first time since its passage) to outlaw displaying the flag of the United States on the "floor or ground" (document 10.8).

After the Supreme Court agreed to hear Dallas's appeal from the ruling of the Texas Court of Criminal Appeals overturning Johnson's conviction, both sides submitted a new round of briefs to the Court.[3] Early in its brief (document 10.9), Dallas maintained that "flagrant acts of flag desecration" simply did not constitute First Amendment–protected expression. However, the bulk of the brief conceded that flag desecration was subject to First Amendment scrutiny, and argued that the state's legitimate twin interests in protecting both the peace and the flag's ability to "symbolize the unity of one nation of people with many differing philosophies" simply overrode any First Amendment interests that Johnson might have had in burning the flag.

Dallas argued that these two interests aimed at "reaching only the noncommunicative aspects" of flag desecration, because the Texas Venerated Objects Law outlawed all such "overt physical acts," whether the flag was destroyed "out of treason or patriotism, love or hate," thereby qualifying for scrutiny under the Supreme Court's relatively lenient 1968 *O'Brien* guidelines for reviewing laws that regulated potentially First

Amendment–protected expression that was intermixed with conduct possibly subject to valid state restriction. However, according to Dallas, even if the higher standards implied by the Supreme Court's 1974 *Spence* ruling were applied on the supposition that the Supreme Court found that the state law reflected purely suppressive concerns, Texas's interests were so "compelling" that they "supersede any First Amendment rights which an individual might have," an argument that was based in part on the Court's 1907 *Halter* ruling (document 3.10). The brief further argued that the Texas statute was neither unconstitutionally vague nor overbroad, contending that its "serious offense" provision referred "not to the reaction" of observers but rather limited the forbidden conduct to that involving "serious acts of physical abuse" of the flag that were "designed to seriously offend" others and that had a "high potential for creating unrest." Therefore, Dallas maintained, the law did not outlaw the ceremonial reverential public destruction of worn flags as was recommended in the 1942 congressional voluntary flag code.

In response to the Dallas brief, Johnson's lawyers argued that the Texas law was designed purely to suppress unwelcome political expression and therefore squarely violated the First Amendment (document 10.10). The brief argued that the fact that the Texas law only banned flag desecration that caused "serious offense" made this point evident, as did Texas's explicit statements that it sought to protect the flag as a symbol of national unity and that the law would not outlaw the ceremonial burning of worn flags. The brief added that the Dallas claim that flag desecration inherently threatened the peace had been disproved by numerous such incidents in which no disorders had resulted and maintained that banning acts that caused "serious offense" but not actual violence violated Supreme Court rulings that upheld restrictions on political expression only where direct personal insults or other expression likely to incite immediate violence was involved.

During the March 21, 1989, Supreme Court oral arguments, Dallas County Assistant District Attorney Kathi Drew was battered with hostile questions and remarks from two members of the Court's conservative wing, Antonin Scalia and Anthony Kennedy (document 10.11). Thus, in response to Drew's argument that flag burning harmed the flag's symbolic value, Scalia argued that such acts simply did not make the flag "any less a symbol" and in fact "would have been useless unless the flag was a very good symbol." Kennedy suggested that Drew was asking the Court to establish a special "flag exception" to the First Amendment. When Drew argued that the flag was a form of public property in which all Americans had an interest because "it is such an important symbol of national unity," much as Texas could ban people from painting "swastikas on the Alamo," Scalia evoked laughter in the courtroom by declaring, "I never thought that the flag I owned is your flag."

In comparison to Drew's treatment, Johnson's advocate, the well-known civil liberties attorney William Kunstler, drew few hostile questions and even engaged in bantering with the justices. Kunstler maintained that the Supreme Court's 1943 *Barnette* ruling outlawing compulsory school flag salutes had set "to rest" any argument for suppressing expression in the name "of nationhood and national unity." Johnson's prosecution, Kunstler argued, went "to the heart of the First Amendment," which he declared protected the right to "hear things or to see things we hate," because "things we like" had "never needed a First Amendment." Kunstler was seriously challenged only once, when Chief Justice William Rehnquist maintained that *Barnette* was not an apt precedent, because forbidding government to require affirmative statements about the flag involved "quite different" facts than forbidding individuals to commit acts of flag desecration.

On June 11, 1989, the Supreme Court made headline news across the nation by ruling, 5–4 (with Justices Brennan, Blackmun, Marshall, Scalia, and Kennedy in the majority), that the Texas Court of Criminal Appeals had correctly held that the Texas Venerated Objects Law had been unconstitutionally applied to deprive Johnson of his First Amendment rights to engage in peaceful political expression (document 10.12). The Court's ruling, written by Brennan, closely followed the reasoning and pattern of argument advanced earlier by Judge Browning in dissent in the 1970 *U.S. v. Crosson* flag-burning case (document 7.10) and by the Eleventh Circuit Federal Court of Appeals in the 1984 *Monroe* case (document 9.2).

First, the Court found that under the guidelines of its 1974 *Spence* case, the "expressive, overtly political nature" of Johnson's conduct was "both intentional and overwhelmingly apparent," and thus qualified for First Amendment scrutiny. The Court then declared that of the two interests that Texas maintained justified overriding any presumptive First Amendment rights, "the state's interest in maintaining order" was simply "not implicated," because "no disturbance of the peace actually occurred or threatened to occur because of Johnson's burning of the flag" and therefore to sanction suppressing free speech in such circumstances would "eviscerate" past holdings placing a high constitutional value on free expression.

Turning to Texas's second asserted interest, that of "preserving the flag as a symbol of nationhood and national unity," Brennan declared that such an interest could be threatened "only when a person's treatment of the flag communicates some message," which meant that this interest was related "to the suppression of free expression," and therefore the "relatively lenient" 1968 *O'Brien* test was completely inapplicable. Instead, the Court held, because this state interest could not be "justified without reference to the content of the regulated speech," it must be subject to "the most exacting scrutiny." But the Court held that Texas could not meet such a high standard, because its purpose of seeking to prevent citizens from conveying messages that were perceived as "harmful" violated the "bedrock principle underlying the First Amendment," namely "that the Government may not prohibit expression of an idea simply because society finds the idea itself offensive or disagreeable."

Citing its previous holding in *Street* that "a State may not criminally punish a person for uttering words critical of the flag," the Court, after twenty years of evading the subject, flatly declared that any attempt to distinguish between "written or spoken words and nonverbal conduct" was "of no moment where the nonverbal conduct is expressive, as it is here, and where the regulation of that conduct is related to expression, as it is here." The Court declared that "the enduring lesson" of its past decisions, that "the Government may not prohibit expression simply because it disagrees with its message, is not dependent on the particular mode in which one chooses to express an idea" and therefore that the state could not "criminally punish a person for burning a flag as a means of political protest."

Echoing the Texas Court of Criminal Appeals, the Court further rejected the concept that laws could constitutionally mandate that a symbol "could be used to express only one view of its referents" and thus allow the government to "foster its own view of the flag by prohibiting expressive conduct relating to it." Such doctrines, the Court suggested, would open up a legal "territory having no discernible or defensible boundaries," which could subsequently justify banning protests involving other symbols such as copies of the Constitution or the presidential seal. The Court also rejected the creation of a "separate juridical category for the American flag alone," which would exempt the flag from the "joust of principles protected by the First Amendment," noting that other concepts "virtually sacred to our Nation as a whole," such as the principle that racial discrimination was "odious and destructive," was not protected from questioning "in the marketplace of ideas." Declaring that "We do not consecrate the flag by punishing its desecration, for in doing so we dilute the freedom that this cherished emblem represents," the Court suggested that the proper means of preserving the flag's role was "not to punish those who feel differently" but to "persuade them that they are wrong," and that there was "no more appropriate response to burning a flag than waving one's own."

The *Texas v. Johnson* ruling clearly caused considerable agony to the Court. Thus, while Justice Kennedy joined in Brennan's ruling, he also wrote a separate, extraordinary concurring opinion (document 10.13) in which he declared that his decision had taken a "painful" and "personal toll" on him, but that the "hard fact is that sometimes" the Constitution commanded that "we must make decisions we do not like" and that "It is poignant but fundamental that the flag protects those who hold it in contempt." In two separate, anguished dissents, Chief Justice Rehnquist (joined by Justices White and O'Connor) and Justice Stevens argued that ordinary principles of law were inapplicable when the flag was involved, in opinions that overflowed with patriotic oratory but made relatively few references to legal principles. Thus Stevens argued (document 10.15) that the flag was "unique" and not subject to legal doctrines that might apply "to a host of other symbols," and after a lengthy disquisition on the flag's history, which ranged from Patrick Henry to the "soldiers who scaled the bluff at Omaha Beach" during World War II, he concluded that if "liberty and equality" were "worth fighting for," then it could not be true "that the flag that uniquely symbolizes their power is not itself worthy of protection from unnecessary desecration."

Rehnquist similarly maintained (document 10.14) that the flag occupied a "unique position" that "justifies a governmental prohibition against flag burning." His bitter dissent, which had been prefigured in his 1974 dissents in *Goguen* and *Spence* (document 8.5), bluntly rejected the majority's suggestion that the flag could not be exempted from the "marketplace of ideas," instead maintaining that it was "not simply another 'idea' or 'point of view' competing for recognition," because "millions and millions of Americans regard it with an almost mystical reverence" and a "uniquely deep awe and respect." Although most of his dissent consisted of a lengthy civics lesson that quoted patriotic poetry and emphasized the flag's history and symbolic importance, ranging from the fact that the flag appeared "more times than any other symbol" on American stamps to the presence of two flags "prominently placed in our courtroom," Rehnquist denounced the majority ruling for advocating education as a response to flag burning, terming this a "regrettably patronizing civics lecture" that admonished American political leaders "as if they were school children" in a way that had no "place in our system of government."

Rehnquist and Stevens both compared flag burning to defacing the Lincoln Memorial, while Rehnquist suggested that it was a "high purpose" of a democratic society for majorities to legislate against conduct that they regarded as "inherently evil and profoundly offensive," whether such conduct was "murder, embezzlement, pollution or flag burning." Both dissenters maintained that any limit imposed on Johnson's free speech rights by forbidding flag desecration was trivial because, in Rehnquist's words, Johnson could have conveyed his views "just as forcefully in a dozen" other ways, including verbal criticism of the flag or burning government leaders in effigy, thus demonstrating, in Stevens's words, that he was not prosecuted for "disagreeable ideas" but only "because of the method he chose to express his dissatisfaction," which would "tarnish" and "diminish" the "value of an important national asset."

Document 10.1

Text of the Texas Penal Code provision used to prosecute Gregory Lee Johnson for the August 22, 1984, burning of a flag at the Dallas City Hall.

Source: Texas Penal Code § 42.09, Vernon 1974, Desecration of Venerated Object Law.

§ 42.09 Desecration of Venerated Object
   (a) A person commits an offense if he intentionally or knowingly desecrates:
(1) a public monument;
(2) a place of worship or burial; or
(3) a state or national flag.
   (b) For purposes of this section, "desecration" means deface, damage, or otherwise physically mistreat in a way that the actor knows will seriously offend one or more persons likely to observe or discover his action.
   (c) An offense under this section is a Class A misdemeanor [with a maximum sentence of one year in jail and a $2,000 fine].

Document 10.2

Text of the Information charging Gregory Lee Johnson with violation of the Texas Desecration of Venerated Object Law, Dallas, Texas, August 23, 1984.

Source: Joint Appendix, No. 88-155, *Texas v. Johnson,* in the Supreme Court of the United States, Oct. term, 1988, 43.

Defendant: Johnson, Gregory Lee Wm [White Male]/ [date of birth] 10-21-51
Charge: Desecrate Venerated Obj
Address: 615 Blvd. S.E. 6, Atlanta, GA 30312
Location: Jail
Filing Agency: DPD [Dallas Police Department]
Date Filed: 8-23-84
Court: [Dallas County Criminal Court] #7
Complainant: T. E. Stoker [complaint #] MA8446013 H. . . .
                         INFORMATION
In the Name and by the Authority of the State of Texas.

NOW COMES THE CRIMINAL DISTRICT ATTORNEY of Dallas County, State of Texas, and presents in and to the County Criminal Court #7 of Dallas County, State aforesaid, that one GREGORY LEE JOHNSON hereinafter styled Defendant, heretofore, on or about the 22nd day of AUGUST A.D., 1984 in the County of Dallas and State of Texas, did unlawfully on or about August 22, 1984 intentionally and knowingly desecrate a United States of America flag, to-wit: a national flag, in that the said Gregory Lee Johnson did intentionally and knowingly damage and physically mistreat a United States of America flag by burning the said flag in a way that the said Gregory Lee Johnson knew would seriously offend one or more persons likely to observe and discover his action, Against the peace and dignity of the state.

/s/ Henry Wade
Criminal District Attorney of Dallas County, Texas

Document 10.3

Text of jury finding of guilt and assessment of penalty against Gregory Lee Johnson for violation of the Texas Desecration of Venerated Object Law, Dallas, Texas, December 13, 1984.

Source: Joint Appendix, No. 88-155, *Texas v. Johnson,* in the Supreme Court of the United States, Oct. term, 1988, 9–10.

On this day, this case being called for trial, came the Criminal District Attorney for the State of Texas, and came the defendant in person and by his attorney; and the defendant being duly arraigned, pleaded not guilty to the charge contained in the information, to-wit:

DESECRATE VENERATED OBJ, AS CHARGED
IN THE INFORMATION

And both parties announcing ready for trial, a jury of six good men and true was duly selected, impaneled and sworn, who, having heard the information read and the defendant's plea of not guilty thereto, and having heard the evidence submitted, and having been duly charged by the Court, and having heard argument of counsel, retired to consider their verdict, and thereafter returned into the Court in due form of law the following verdict, which was received by the Court, and is here now entered upon the minutes of this Court, to-wit:

"We, the jury, find the Defendant guilty as charged in the information.

/s/ KAREN A. ANDERSON
FOREMAN"

And the defendant having requested the Court that his punishment be assessed by the Court, the jury was discharged, and the Court, having heard further evidence submitted on the issue of punishment, and having heard argument of counsel thereon, assessed the defendant's punishment herein at a fine of $2,000.00 and confinement for 365 DAYS in the county jail.

IT IS THEREFORE CONSIDERED, ORDERED AND ADJUDGED, that the defendant is guilty of
DESECRATE VENERATED OBJ, AS CHARGED
IN THE INFORMATION
as found by the jury in its verdict herein returned, and that he be punished by a fine of $2,000.00 and confinement for 365 days in the Dallas County Jail, and that the State of Texas do have and recover of him all costs in this prosecution expended.

/s/ J. Hendrik
JUDGE

Document 10.4

Testimony by Gregory Lee Johnson during the sentencing portion of his trial, after having been found guilty of violation of the Texas Venerated Object Law, under questioning by Dallas County Assistant District Attorney Michael Gillett, Dallas, Texas, December 13, 1984.

Source: Transcript of trial testimony in Texas v. Johnson, No. MA8446013-H/J, in the County Criminal Court No. 8, Dallas County, Texas, Nov. term, 1984 (unpublished), 764–81.

Q Do you like the American Flag?
A No, I do not. . . . I challenge anyone who upholds the patriotism of that flag to tell me how in the final analysis that doesn't boil down to wanting to maintain a privileged position over the people of the world. . . .
Q Do you think the American flag represents anything good at all?
A We've already been over that.
  If you want me to state repeatedly for the record, "No," and I think it's an honor to be compared to the Iranian people who, in 1953, the United States had put a bloody dictator in power, then people want to know why the Iranian people use the American flag to carry trash in.
  If somebody installed a dictator in your country, what would you do with the flag of the country that—that installed that dictator? . . .
  I'm not going to sit up here and especially at times like these in history when the government is crying out for the allegiance, the blind patriotic allegiance of millions [and] say, "America number one," which is what you want to hear and I think it's disgusting. . . .
  You're going against your so-called First Amendment and the whole

Constitution all that by saying that you can protest just as long as you bow down before the American flag. . . .

It's revealing as to the compulsion that you feel to enforce patriotism, it's a desperation that you feel, the weakness that you feel, and the need to enforce patriotism to demand it from everyone. . . .

Q Mr. Johnson, let me ask you this:

If you don't like the country and you don't like the flag and you don't like the way it's run, why don't you just leave? . . . [I]f you dislike it so much, why you just don't move to Russia?

A Well, . . . I don't consider it [Russia] to be any sort of society that people in the world who are striving for a future without oppression should look to for—for guidance. . . . If anything I think that there are more similarities between the United States and the Soviet Union. They mutually possess over 50,000 nuclear weapons. . . .

I don't know these things aren't as of strong concern to you. What's more of concern is that the people here blindly and obediently follow and look brightly into the mushroom clouds and march off, and I suspect if you were in the Soviet Union, you would be guilty of doing the same thing: blindly following the government of the Soviet Union. . . .

Q All I'm simply asking . . . is if you don't like our country, you don't like our flag, why don't you just move to some other country and leave? . . .

A We have an enormous responsibility to work for a future that is free of the madness . . . as it's concentrated in times like these when the very future of humanity's at stake. . . .

We have a responsibility, so for me to just move, to leave, would be an abdication, I think, of that responsibility.

Q So you just want to stay here and work burning up American flags, huh?

A That's a rather vulgar way of expressing it. . . . And I didn't actually do it. . . .

Q [D]idn't you say it was great to see the American flag go up in flames?

A And reduced to ashes, yes. . . .

Q There's something real dangerous about you, isn't there?

A To you and your society, to your system, not to the people. . . . I'm not a criminal element, if that's what you're trying to erect. . . . I think that . . . eventually the situation will arise where millions of people will be confronted with the alternative of either fighting in a third world war or fighting to overthrow the system that exists. . . .

Q What's—what's the rifle up in the air on your shirt stand for?

A It stands for revolution.

Q Well, why the gun?

A Because it's going to take violence.

Q So you do advocate violence?

A Not individual violence.
Q Oh, just as a group? . . .

Document 10.5

Ruling of the Court of Appeals for the Fifth Supreme Judicial District of Texas in the 1986 case of *Johnson v. State.*

Source: 706 South Western Reporter, 2d series 120.

Gregory Lee Johnson appeals from a jury trial conviction [document 10.3] for desecration of a venerated object. . . .
Johnson contends that: . . . Section 42.09 of the Texas Penal Code [document 10.1] violates the First Amendment to the United States Constitution, Article I, Sec. 8 of the Texas Constitution, and Article 1.16 of the Texas Code of Criminal Procedure as an unconstitutional restraint on Johnson's right to free speech. . . . Because we find no error, we affirm the judgment of the trial court. . . .
Johnson contends that the application of section 42.09 of the Texas Penal Code is unconstitutionally vague, unconstitutionally overbroad, and violative of his first amendment rights. . . .
Johnson claims that the statute is unconstitutionally vague because "desecration" depends upon the sensibilities of persons likely to observe the action. . . . However, due process merely requires that the law give sufficient warning so that people may conduct themselves so as to avoid that which is forbidden. . . . Here, the relevant terms of the offense, "deface," "damage," and physically mistreat" are all well understood terms. The act of burning the United States flag would clearly constitute desecration under the statute.
Johnson also contends that the statute is unconstitutionally overbroad. A statute is overbroad when it prohibits both activity which is protected by the constitution and activity which is not. Johnson's argument is without merit. While the flag burning did occur during a political protest rally, the statute in no way prohibited legitimate protest activities.
Johnson further urges that the statute violates his rights to free speech under the First and Fourteenth Amendments. In *Spence v. Washington* [document 8.3], the Supreme Court adopted a two-part analysis for flag desecration cases: the appellate court must determine, first, whether the conduct is protected under the First Amendment; and second, whether, upon the record of the given case, the interests advanced by the state are so substantial as to justify infringement of appellant's constitutional rights [citing the *Monroe* case, document 9.2].
Thus, we must first determine whether Johnson's act of burning the

flag is constitutionally-protected free speech. . . . [Citing the *Spence* case] we conclude that Johnson's act of burning the flag constituted symbolic speech requiring First Amendment scrutiny.

Next, we must determine . . . whether the interests advanced by the State are so substantial as to justify infringement of Johnson's constitutional rights. The State advances two interests: preventing breaches of the peace and protection of the flag as a symbol of national unity.

The first substantial interest asserted by the State is to prevent breaches of the peace. This is a valid state interest [citing the *Street* case, document 8.1]. Some courts have concluded that an act of flag desecration by itself is insufficient provocation to infringe upon First Amendment rights; they require objective evidence of imminent public unrest [citing the *Monroe* case]. Other courts have held that acts of flag desecration are, of themselves, so inherently inflammatory that the State may act to prevent breaches of the public peace [citing the *Deeds* case, document 7.6]. We choose to follow the Texas Court of Criminal Appeals in [*Deeds* in] preferring the latter view. Thus, the statute is a legitimate and constitutional means of protecting the public peace.

The second substantial interest asserted by the State is the preservation of the flag as a symbol of national unity. . . . While the State has no legitimate interest in compelling respect for the flag [citing *Barnette*, document 5.2], we disagree with the Eleventh Circuit in *Monroe* and hold that the State does have a legitimate and substantial interest in protecting the flag as a symbol of national unity. Thus, we hold that section 42.09 is constitutional. . . .

Because we find no error, we affirm the judgment of the trial court. Affirmed.

Document 10.6

Ruling of the Texas Court of Criminal Appeals in the 1988 case of *Johnson v. State*.

Source: 755 South Western Reporter, 2d series, 92.

Appellant was convicted, after a jury trial, of desecration of a venerated object. . . . We hold that the First Amendment to the Constitution obviates appellant's conviction under section 42.09(a)(3) [document 10.1] and we will remand. . . .

In analyzing a symbolic speech question, the proper methodology requires the reviewing court to first determine whether a defendant's acts fall within the First Amendment [citing *Spence*, document 8.3]. . . . There is no reason for us to reach a different conclusion [than that reached below by the Court of Appeals that the defendant's acts do so qualify]. . . .

Falling within the umbrella of First Amendment protection will not shield speech from all government regulations. . . .

The first interest averred offered by the State [to override Johnson's First Amendment rights] is the prevention of breaches of the peace which would likely be attendant to acts of flag desecration. . . .

[Although this is a valid state interest], section 42.09(a)(3) is so broad that it may be used to punish protected conduct which has no propensity to result in breaches of the peace. "Serious offense" does not always result in a breach of the peace. The protest in this case did not lead to violence. . . . [T]here was no breach of peace nor does the record reflect that the situation was potentially explosive. One cannot equate "serious offense" with incitement to breach the peace. . . .

The second interest asserted by the State is that of preserving the flag as a symbol of unity. In *Barnette* [document 5.2, the Supreme Court held that for the state interest in promoting national unity] to be sufficient to abridge activity protected by the First Amendment, it must be necessary to prevent "grave and immediate danger" to that interest. . . .

Recognizing that the right to differ is the centerpiece of our First Amendment freedoms, a government cannot mandate by fiat a feeling of unity in its citizens. Therefore, that very same government cannot carve out a symbol of unity and prescribe a set of approved messages to be associated with that symbol when it cannot mandate the status or feeling the symbol purports to present.

If the State has a legitimate interest in promoting a State approved symbol of unity, that interest is not so compelling as to essentially license the flag's use for only the promotion of the governmental status quo. . . . [T]he State does not aver why the American flag is in such "grave and immediate danger" of losing its ability to rouse feelings of unity or patriotism such that section 42.09(a)(3) is "essential" to prevent its devaluation into a meaningless piece of cloth. We do not believe such a danger is present [and therefore] must hold that the interest of providing a symbol of unity is inadequate to support 42.09(a)(3).

We hold that section 42.09(a)(3) may not be used to punish acts of flag desecration when such conduct falls within the protections of the First Amendment. We express no view as to whether the State may prosecute acts of flag desecration which do not constitute speech under the First Amendment. . . .

The judgments of the Court of Appeals and the trial court [documents 10.3 and 10.5] are reversed and the cause is remanded to the trial court for dismissal of the information.

Document 10.7

Newspaper article by Marney Rich Keenan, "Stars & Gripes: Chicago Exhibit Attracts Unflagging Criticism."

Source: Detroit News, March 19, 1989. Reprinted by permission of the *Detroit News*, a Gannett newspaper, copyright 1989.

Chicago—Outraged by an art exhibit in which the American flag lies on the floor, protesters have screamed their throats raw in past weeks outside the Chicago School of the Art Institute. But inside, a silent drama turned into an often poignant ritual.

For days, veterans picked the flag up off the floor, folded it in the ceremonial military fashion and placed it on the shelf. Their faces were almost always stoic; one was visibly in tears at the sight of grimy footprints on the flag. Moments later, however, the flag was unfolded by supporters of the art, usually students with indignant faces, who shook out the flag like a bedsheet, and then draped it on the floor.

This procedure, eyed by security guards with intercoms pressed to their lips, occurred at least a dozen times a day.

No less striking were two leather bound ledgers placed on a shelf above the flag where viewers were invited to respond to the title of the artwork: *What is the proper way to display a U.S. flag?*

But the flag-lined pathway to the ledger prompted some to step on the nation's symbol of patriotism, spurring vigilant protest unequaled in recent memory in Chicago.

The once blank pages are now filled with comments ranging from praise to scorn, obscenities notwithstanding. Ironically, the comments and footprints have become part of the "participatory installation" artwork—all at the artist's provocative invitation. A sampling of visitors' impressions:

* "On a pole."
* "Lightly seasoned with high octane new superleaded Shell gasoline and then torched before a televised audience encompassing everyone who's been used and abused by Old Glory."
* "Hang it over the grave of Mad-Dog Quadaffi."
* "Why don't we have a Scott Tyler flag and put it on the floor where dogs can crap on it?" (Tyler is the artist.)
* "I am a U.S. Marine and it kills me to think that I'm protecting a person like you."
* "I saw an 18-wheeler today with the U.S. flag on the mud flaps. What is the difference?"
* "I have seen this flag desecrated in the bodies of young Nicaraguan

civilian women and a 7 month old baby when I cleansed their wounds and picked fragments of U.S. bullets from the bodies."

*"Your (sic) a commie bastard."

The battlelines have been drawn—thankfully not in blood—between the freedom of expression and the freedom to defame. Since Feb. 17, when the exhibit opened, thousands have marched on the steps of the Art Institute—veterans, artists, skinheads, yuppies, Rastafarians, housewives and politicians.

Tyler, the 24-year-old artist who inspired the artwork that represents, in his words, "the outlook and hope and aspirations of the oppressed," has done little to discourage the public anger. He calls himself a "revolutionary" and has issued press releases announcing that he "welcomes these rebellions and the targeting and torching of this symbol."

Whatever one's politics or theology, a large number of people have been provoked and forced to examine just what the right of free speech means to them. In Tyler's case, What is the proper way to display the U.S. flag? has achieved its intended effect—albeit in hoarse and passionate voices.

Last week, a day before the show closed, a few diehard protesters remained on the steps of the Art Institute, chanting "One, two, three, four, get the flag off the floor!"

Frank J. Marsh, a Chicago Vietnam veteran was there, waiting to take his turn to fold up the flag.

"I can't believe they had the gall to put the flag on the floor," he says. "The flag means that I can walk the streets free. That I can call my home my own. That I'm a free man. * * * I fought two wars for it. I fought in Korea and in Vietnam and I'd fight another war if I have to for it." . . .

When a coalition of army veterans filed a suit March 1 in Cook County Circuit Court requesting the exhibit be closed because federal and state law prohibit defiling the flag, Judge Kenneth Gillis lined up on Tyler's side, ruling: "Placing a flag on the floor is not mutilating, defacing or trampling it [the terms of the Illinois state flag desecration law]."

Supporters of the artwork are equally ardent. "It is easy for white people to say this is our flag, protect it," says Alfred Lewis, a construction worker in Chicago who had just viewed the exhibit. "The same flag was there in numerous courtrooms where lynching mobs were set free."

When the uproar began to escalate in late February, Art Institute officials, faced with bomb threats, beefed up security and prayed. More than one official publicly fell on Voltaire's oft quoted refrain, "I do not agree with a word that you say, but I will defend to the death your right to say it."

When Judge Gillis refused to close the exhibit, school officials were given a strong but brief reprieve in the fury. "No matter how hateful the idea, free speech has a (fundamental) role in our society," Gillis said. He added: "It is good to know that the flag has not lost its ability to communicate and motivate as well."

But those were considered moot points to the more than 1,500 demonstrators who marched in front of the Art Institute on Sunday, March 6, reciting the Pledge of Allegiance and singing *God Bless America*. Politicians jumped into the theatrical controversy, calling for boycotts of all companies that contribute to the Art Institute. . . .

Tyler has received threats: "The Flag and the Artist, Hang them Both High!" but he seems to readily dismiss them. "Given that these are the same people that went to Vietnam and kind of sort of enjoy it, I mean, these guys have never fought a war they didn't like," he says. . . .

At the very least, in Chicago, Scott Tyler has prodded the public to face the meaning of their own patriotism and the power of its symbol. In some people's minds, particularly Tyler's, that makes the artwork valid. But an irony remains expressed in the words of a protesting Vietnam veteran, who said, "It is the American flag that gives (Tyler) the freedom to say the things that he is saying."

In a way, Tyler now finds himself protected by the freedoms of the country he so provocatively denounces.

Document 10.8

Senate floor debate leading to adoption of an amendment to the 1968 federal flag desecration law (document 6.1) outlawing "displaying the flag of the United States on the floor or ground," March 16, 1989.

Source: Congressional Record, 1989, S279-94, S2811.

Mr. DOLE. . . . Many have seen on television or read about or seen pictures of a U.S. flag and how it is being displayed in Chicago in the art institute. . . .

Now I do not know much about art, but I do know desecration when I see it. Title 18 of the United States Code is clear on this point. Trampling the U.S. flag is desecration subject to criminal penalties. . . .

In this instance, however, the existing statute might be interpreted to apply to the public [invited to step on the flag in order to write in the ledger] and not to the so-called artist who invited this trampling on the flag. . . .

The amendment I am offering [to the 1968 federal flag desecration law] . . . would simply extend the current statute . . . to include "knowingly displayed on the floor or ground." . . .

The display at the School of Arts Institute in Chicago . . . shows disrespect and contempt for our flag and should be prohibited by law. . . .

Mr. COHEN. . . . I would agree with [Sen. Dole], this is not art. This is an epithet.

We all know that freedom of speech is not without its limitations. . . . This is an incendiary act of sorts because it is shouting fire, I think, in a crowded theater—it is shouting fire in the hearts of millions of men and women in this country who have either sacrificed themselves or . . . lost their loved ones who have tried to defend the integrity and the spirit and the symbolism of that flag. . . .

Mr. BYRD. . . . The so-called art exhibit at the School of the Art Institute of Chicago, in which a young student has placed the U.S. flag on the floor in a way that encourages people to walk on it, is an abomination. . . .

Document 10.9

Brief for Petitioner, the state of Texas, in the case of *Texas v. Johnson,* in the U.S. Supreme Court, October term, 1988.

SUMMARY OF ARGUMENT

This case presents for determination the question of whether an act of flagburning which occurs during the course of a political demonstration is protected under the First Amendment. This important issue of federal law has not been decided by this Court but was reserved in both *Spence v. Washington* [document 8.3] and *Street v. New York* [document 8.1].

The Constitution does not prevent Texas from defining with substantial specificity what constitutes forbidden treatment of a United States flag [citing *Goguen,* document 8.2]. The Texas Legislature has enacted 42.09(a)(3) of the Texas Penal Code [document 10.1] to prohibit desecration of the flag in a way that the actor knows will seriously offend persons likely to observe his act. The statute is specifically designed to reach only flagrant acts of flag desecration carried out in a public context.

The State maintains that an act of flagburning does not constitute "speech" entitled to First Amendment protection because the conduct involved is essential neither to the exposition of any idea or to the peaceful expression of an opinion. The Texas statute is aimed at reaching only the non-communicative aspects of that conduct. The public burning of a United States flag is exactly the type of conduct prohibited by § 42.09(a)(3).

Texas recognizes that certain forms of non-verbal expression have, in the past, been characterized as "symbolic speech" within the ambit of the First Amendment. A determination that burning an American flag constitutes "symbolic speech" does not automatically render the statute inapplicable. The First Amendment is not absolute and expressive conduct demands less constitutional protection than does "pure speech." A state may forbid or regulate expressive conduct if a sufficiently important governmental interest justifies the incidental limitation on the First Amendment [citing O'Brien]. Throughout the history of this case, Texas has asserted two substantial interests that justify the prohibition against flagrant acts of flag desecration carried out in a public context: 1) protection of the flag as an important symbol of nationhood and unity and 2) prevention of a breach of the peace.

As to the first interest, it is fundamental that the flag of the United States is a unique, important symbol of nationhood and unity. An act of flag desecration which occurs in a public context degrades the symbolic value of the flag and weakens its efficacy to serve as a symbol. Texas has a compelling interest in protecting the physical integrity of the flag so that it may serve as the paramount symbol of nationhood and unity. Protection of the flag may extend to regulating conduct which destroys that symbol, even if an incidental limitation on an individual's First Amendment right occurs in the furtherance of that interest.

Texas has also enacted § 42.09(a)(3) as a legitimate means of preventing a breach of the peace. Traditionally, acts of flag desecration, standing alone, are viewed as so inherently inflammatory as to constitute a danger to the public peace. . . . The absence of an actual breach of the peace is not dispositive because the goal of the statute is prevention, not punishment, of a breach of the peace.

Moreover, an act of flagburning should not be cloaked with immunity simply because the act occurred at the culmination of a demonstration with political overtones. Section 42.09 does not provide for, nor should the First Amendment countenance, such a "content-based" exception. Since the act may be prohibited, exceptions should not be made for an act performed as part of a political protest.

Section 42.09 may also be considered valid as a "time, place and manner" restriction since it regulates the manner in which an individual may demonstrate. The statute, which prohibits acts of flag desecration regardless of the message sought to be conveyed, if any, is content neutral. The statute is narrowly tailored to prohibit only flagrant acts of flag desecration, i.e., those involving the most serious form of physical abuse, carried out in a public context. The statute does no more than prohibit one form of conduct by which a demonstrator may express himself; there remain abundant alternative avenues of communication by which the same message, if any, may be conveyed.

Contrary to the holding of the Texas Court of Criminal Appeals [document 10.6], the language of § 42.09(b) is not unconstitutionally overbroad. That court reached this conclusion primarily on the basis of that portion of 42.09(b) which requires that the actor know his act is likely to seriously offend those who observe it. This "serious offense" language is, in fact, a narrowing rather than a broadening of its reach. Section 42.09 is narrowly tailored because it targets and eliminates no more than the exact source of the evil it seeks to remedy. By inclusion of the "serious offense" language, the state criminalizes only those acts which are done in a public context and which are more likely than not to create a breach of the peace. . . . There are no alternative means whereby the State can protect the physical integrity of the flag.

ARGUMENT

. . . In considering Texas' interest in preserving the flag as a symbol of nationhood in the context of its flag desecration statute, any comparison to the principles announced in *Barnette* [document 5.2] is misplaced. *Barnette* held that a state could not compel the expression of respect for the flag by forcing school children to recite the pledge of allegiance. Section 42.09(a)(3) does not compel expressions of respect for the flag. . . .

The terms of 42.09 are not affirmatively coercive; nothing in the statute mandates that Johnson salute the flag, take a pledge or oath to the flag, or make any other expression of respect or belief. Nor does 42.09 prohibit expressions of disrespect. An individual is free to express any thoughts he may have concerning the flag, no matter how contemptuous. . . . Texas exercised its authority only to punish Johnson for wantonly, intentionally and totally destroying the flag in a public context. . . .

Preventing physical destruction of the flag is an interest wholly removed from the prevention of an expression of disrespect. By preserving the flag's physical integrity, so that it may serve as a symbol of nationhood and unity, Texas is not endorsing, protecting, avowing or prohibiting any particular philosophy; rather, Texas is protecting the flag against destruction regardless of the philosophy, political or otherwise, that would motivate such destruction. It is the medium, not the message, which is controlled by 42.09(a)(3). . . .

Document 10.10

Brief for Respondent, Gregory Lee Johnson, in the case of *Texas v. Johnson,* in the U.S. Supreme Court, October term, 1988.

. . . .

SUMMARY OF ARGUMENT

This case presents the question whether, consistent with the First and Fourteenth Amendments to the United States Constitution, a state can criminally convict a person of peacefully burning a flag in an overtly political demonstration, under a statute that hinges punishment on the act's communicative effect on third persons "likely to observe or discover" it.

Mr. Johnson maintains that Tex. Penal Code Ann. § 42.09(a)(3) [document 10.1] is unconstitutional both on its face and as applied to the symbolic speech for which he was convicted. As this Court held forty-six years ago when confronted with another statutory regulation of respect for the flag, the dual principles of freedom of expression and government by the people prohibit the State from mandating respect for its icons by imprisoning those who express disrespect [citing *Barnette*, document 5.2].

a. Section 42.09(a)(3) must be analyzed under the same First Amendment analysis applicable to "pure" speech, because it singles out conduct for punishment solely on the basis of its communicative effect, namely, that which "seriously offends." The less stringent test articulated in *United States v. O'Brien* is inapplicable, because neither the statute nor the State's interests are "unrelated to expression."

b. Section 42.09(a)(3) is facially unconstitutional, first, because it imposes a viewpoint-based restriction on political expression. Texas explicitly asserts that its interest is to promote one view—that the flag is a symbol of nationhood and national unity. The First Amendment, however, mandates viewpoint neutrality, and accordingly Texas may not "prescribe what is orthodox" concerning the flag's symbolic meaning by prohibiting private persons from using private flags to express opposing points of view [citing *Barnette*].

c. However, as in its previous flag misuse and desecration cases, the Court may continue to reserve the question whether a state may proscribe flagburning per se. Because § 42.09(a)(3) singles out conduct that will "seriously offend one or more persons," the statute violates the First Amendment's prohibition on content-based discrimination, and its invalidation is compelled by this Court's recent decision in *Boos v. Barry*. The First Amendment forbids the proscription of expression on the basis of the likely hostile reactions of an audience, and the asserted state interests—to preserve the flag as a symbol of nationhood and to prevent breaches of the peace—do not justify § 42.09(a)(3)'s infringement of First Amendment freedoms.

d. Third, and again whether or not a state may proscribe flagburning per se, § 42.09(a)(3) is unconstitutionally vague and overbroad. It is vague because it requires one who seeks to "physically mistreat" the flag to place himself or herself in the shoes of wholly unidentifiable third persons in order to gauge whether they will be "seriously" offended, an impossible inquiry. And because the First Amendment protects "seriously offen⟨sive⟩" expression, the statute's prohibition casts an impermissibly wide net over clearly protected First Amendment activity.

Even if the Court concludes that § 42.09(a)(3) survives a facial challenge, it must nonetheless affirm the Texas Court of Criminal Appeals' conclusion [document 10.6] that it is unconstitutional as applied to Mr.

Johnson. Mr. Johnson was convicted for peacefully burning a flag in an overtly political demonstration, clearly protected expression. Moreover, it appears that his conviction may have rested in part on his words and associations, and not solely on the flagburning.

The subject matter of this case—desecration of the national flag—stirs strong emotions precisely because of the flag's unique symbolic power. But as this Court recognized in *Barnette,* that fact only underscores the need for constitutional protection of this form of expression: "Freedom to differ is not limited to things that do not matter much. . . . The test of its substance is the right to differ as to things that touch the heart of the existing order."

ARGUMENT

. . . Where, as here, both the statute on its face and the State's interests are expressly directed not to a particular physical act, but to the act's communicative effect, traditional First Amendment scrutiny applies. . . . [T]he statute singles out for prohibition only such conduct as will have a "seriously offen⟨sive⟩" communicative impact on others.

Texas states that its interest in proscribing flag desecration is to promote its view that the flag is a "symbol of nationhood and national unity" deserving of great respect, and to forbid "mistreat⟨ment⟩" of the flag which challenges that view. On the face of the statute and that interest alone, § 42.09(a)(3) is unconstitutional.

The First Amendment requires the government to maintain strict viewpoint-neutrality. "[A]bove all else, the First Amendment means that government has no power to restrict expression because of its message, its ideas, its subject matter, or its content." *Police Department of Chicago v. Mosley.* . . .

Section 42.09(a)(3) impermissibly favors the State's viewpoint that the flag is a "symbol of nationhood and national unity" at the expense of all other views. Persons who believe that the flag symbolizes oppression or imperialism, and therefore deserves disrespect, are forbidden from expressing that viewpoint through physical "mistreat⟨ment⟩ of even privately-owned flags. . . .

Texas's attempt to cast its statute in viewpoint-neutral terms only underscores the extent to which the statute and the State's underlying interests are viewpoint-based. It contends that it is not "prohibiting defiant or contemptuous opinions about the flag," but only protecting "the flag's physical integrity, so that it may serve as a symbol of nationhood and unity." But § 42.09(a)(3) does not neutrally prohibit all destruction of the flag's physical integrity; it singles out only those acts which constitute "mistreat⟨ment⟩" and "will seriously offend one or more persons." Moreover, it makes no sense to assert that an interest in preserving the flag "as a symbol of nationhood and unity" is "not endorsing, protecting, avowing, or prohibiting any particular philosophy." Texas is protecting the philosophy that the flag symbolizes "nationhood and unity," and proscribing persons who seek to burn it or otherwise deface it precisely to question that for which it stands.

This Court's decisions regarding flag regulation make abundantly clear that the requirement of viewpoint-neutrality bars the government from utilizing criminal sanctions to compel respect for the flag. As far back as 1943, the Court held that compulsory flag salutes violate the First Amendment [citing *Barnette*]. . . . The First Amendment was designed to forestall the dangers that result when government abandons viewpoint-neutrality and attempts to coerce respect by forbidding dissent. . . .

[W]hether one is compelled to respect a flag by saluting it or by observing a series of taboos concerning its use or misuse, the compulsion is viewpoint-based, and is presumptively unconstitutional in a society which declares itself dedicated to political toleration.

. . . Section 42.09(a)(3) provides that defacing, damaging, or physically mistreating the flag will be punished only where the communicative content of the action is such that the actor knows will "seriously offend" others. . . .

Both the majority and the principal dissent in *Spence v. State of Washington* [document 8.3] agreed that punishing flag misuse because of its communicative impact on others is invalid.

The Court has held that a state interest in preserving "respect for our national symbol" is insufficient to justify punishing contemptuous words directed at the flag [citing *Street*, document 8.1]. Because § 42.09(a)(3) is directed at communicative impact and therefore must be scrutinized under the same standard as a proscription on "pure" speech, this rationale must be rejected here as well. It is inimical to First Amendment principles to claim that in order to preserve a symbol of "national unity," the government must be permitted to suppress citizens' use of that symbol to express dissent. Commitment to a symbol cannot justify political repression.

Moreover, even if the interest in preserving the flag as a symbol of national unity were a compelling state interest, Texas has made no showing that this interest is actually endangered by flagburning. People choose to burn the flag to express dissent precisely because it is such a powerful symbol. . . . There is simply no showing that flagburning threatens the flag's symbolic meaning. . . .

Document 10.11

Oral argument before the U.S. Supreme Court, March 21, 1989, in the case of *Texas v. Johnson*, Dallas County Assistant District Attorney Kathi

Drew, representing Texas, petitioner, and attorney William Kunstler of the New York Center for Constitutional Rights, representing Gregory Lee Johnson, respondent.

MS. DREW: Throughout the course of the appellate history in this case, Texas has advanced two compelling state interests. . . .

I would like to address first the nationhood interest. We believe that preservation of the flag as a symbol of nationhood and national unity is a compelling and valid state interest. We feel very certain that Congress has the power to both adopt a national symbol and to take steps to prevent the destruction of that symbol, to protect the symbol.

QUESTION: Now, why does the . . . defendant's actions here destroy the symbol? His actions would have been useless unless the flag was a very good symbol for what he intended to show contempt for. His action does not make it any less a symbol.

MS. DREW: Your Honor, we believe that if a symbol over a period of time is ignored or abused that it can, in fact, lose its symbolic effect.

QUESTION: I think not at all. I think when somebody does that to the flag, the flag becomes even more a symbol of the country. I mean, it seems to me you're running quite a different argument—not that he's destroying its symbolic character, but that he is showing disrespect for it, that you not just want a symbol, but you want a venerated symbol, and you don't make that argument because then you're getting into a sort of content preference. But I don't see how you can argue that he's making it any less of a symbol than it was.

MS. DREW: Your Honor, I'm forced to disagree with you. . . . Texas is not suggesting that we can insist on respect. We are suggesting that we have the right to preserve the physical integrity of the flag so that it may serve as a symbol because its symbolic effect is diluted by certain flagrant public acts of flag desecration.

QUESTION: Well, in the sense you're arguing a minimal form of respect for the flag, aren't you? Not that you have to take your hat off or salute when it goes by. Now, the state can't require you but at least can it insist that you not destroy it?

MS. DREW: Yes, Your Honor. . . . [T]o the extent that we are asking for any respect for the flag, we are asking for respect for its physical integrity. Certainly we do not demand that any individual view it with any discernible emotion whatsoever, only that its physical integrity be respected. . . . [R]eally all Texas is suggesting with this is that we have got to preserve the symbol by preserving the flag itself because there really is no other way to do it. . . .

QUESTION: What is the juridical category you're asking us to adopt in order to say we can punish this kind of speech? Just an exception for flags? . . . [T]here's just a flag exception of the First Amendment?

MS. DREW: To a certain extent, we have made that argument in our brief. With respect to the symbolic speech standard, we believe that there are compelling state interests that will in a balancing posture override this individual's symbolic speech rights, and that preserving the flag as a symbol . . . is one of those. . . .

QUESTION: Well, this statute prohibits the desecration of a state flag as well.

MS. DREW. Yes, it does.

QUESTION: Of the Texas state flag?

MS. DREW: Yes.

QUESTION: And I assume if we upheld the statute in every other state, it would have the same right?

MS. DREW: Yes, Your Honor.

QUESTION: So, your category for one flag is now expanded to fifty-one.

MS. DREW: The statute does say a state or national flag. That is correct. And we do believe Texas certainly has a right to protect its own flag. And I think that a similar interest would be for sister states. . . .

QUESTION: Could Texas prohibit the burning of copies of the Constitution, state or federal?

MS. DREW: Not to my knowledge, Your Honor.

QUESTION: Well, how do you pick out what to protect? I mean, you know, if I had to pick between the Constitution and the flag, I might well go with the Constitution. I don't know.

MS. DREW: Your Honor, I think Texas in this area . . . has made a judgment that certain items are entitled to more protection.

QUESTION: I understand that. But we up to now have never allowed such an item to be declared a national symbol and to be usable symbolically only in one direction, which is essentially what you're arguing. You can honor it all you like, but you can't dishonor it as a sign of disrespect for the country. . . .

MS. DREW: Not at all. We are in no way arguing that one cannot dishonor the flag or that one cannot demonstrate disrespect for the flag. Individuals have that right. What we are arguing is that you may not publicly desecrate a flag, regardless of the motivation for your action.

QUESTION: Well, one hardly desecrates it in order to honor it. I mean, you only desecrate it in order to show your disagreement with what it stands for, isn't that right? So, it is sort of a one-way statute. . . .

MS. DREW: Not necessarily.

QUESTION: Will you give me an example where one—somebody desecrates the flag in order to show that he agrees with the policies of the United States. . . . ⟨General Laughter⟩

MS. DREW: I think it is possible . . . that an individual could choose to burn a flag as an honor for all the individuals who died in Vietnam. . . .

QUESTION: Your statute would cover that example that you just gave?

MS. DREW: Yes, it would, Your Honor, because it does not go to the motive of the actor. . . . I'd like to turn very briefly, if I may, to the breach of the peace interest. We do feel that preventing a breach of the peace is a legitimate state interest. . . . [T]he Texas legislature has made a judgment in this area that public desecration is likely to lead to violence. . . . [I]t is our good luck that a breach of the peace did not occur as a result of this particular flag desecration. . . .

And, again, the goal is a prevention of a breach of the peace, not a punishment for a breach of the peace. And in analyzing this particular statute, the Texas court of criminal appeals [document 10.6] utilized a much higher standard than any court has ever used before. They went to an actual breach of the peace and they said well, there was no actual breach of the peace. That's true. . . . I believe that the court of criminal appeals suggestions in this regard are a bit too narrow; that if you have to show an actual breach of the peace, your purpose in a flag desecration statute is obviated. Some other statute would serve that interest, but not a flag desecration standard because its purpose is prevention.

QUESTION: I suppose . . . if that theory alone is enough to support the statute . . . you could have such statutes for Stars of David and crosses and maybe—I don't know Salman Rushdie's book or whatever might incite people—you can prevent such desecration.

MS. DREW: Your Honor, again, there are other sections of this statute where other items are protected, specifically public monuments, places of burial and worship. I don't believe that anyone could suggest that one may paint swastikas on the Alamo in San Antonio. . . .

QUESTION: [B]ut that's because it's public property . . . and unless you want to say that the flag is somehow public property of us all and ignore traditional distinctions of property, then your example just doesn't work.

MS. DREW: . . . I believe it does.

I think the flag is this nation's cherished property, that every individual has a certain interest. The government may maintain a residual interest, but so do the people. And you protect the flag because it is such an important symbol of national unity.

QUESTION: If we say so, it becomes so. But it certainly isn't self-evident. . . . I never thought that the flag I owned is your flag. . . . ⟨General Laughter⟩

MR. KUNSTLER: . . .[T]his particular act that we're concerned with here, this 42.09(a)(3) of the Texas statute [document 10.1], singles out communicative impact for punishment. . . .

With reference to the nationhood and national unity, which Ms. Drew raised . . . I thought *Barnette* [document 5.2] set that to rest. I thought that when Justice Jackson said that if there is any fixed star in our constitutional constellation, it is that no official, high or petty, can prescribe what shall be orthodox in politics, nationalism—

QUESTION: Well, the facts of *West Virginia v. Barnette* were quite different from this. There the students were required to salute the flag.

MR. KUNSTLER: And here . . . people are required not to do something. . . . And I think that's a comparable situation. We can't order you to salute the flag, we can't order you to do all these obeisances with relation to the flag. Can we order you not to do something to show something about the flag?

QUESTION: Well, to me they're quite different. . . . [I]t seems to me one could quite easily say, you can't do one but you can do the other. . . .

MR. KUNSTLER: I guess I have too much of a First Amendment consciousness, I guess, in my makeup.

With reference to breach of the peace, . . . none of the flag cases that you have . . . ever had before you have involved a breach of the peace. . . .

If you're going to [forbid flag desecration, the threat of violence] has to be so imminent that it really reaches clear and present danger proportions. . . . The statute here is not limited to an imminent breach, by the way. It doesn't say imminent breach of the peace at all. It just says "likely" or "might" or "The actor could reasonably believe that someone might be seriously offended by it."

The Texas Court of [Criminal] Appeals, . . . in its opinion . . . said "This statute is so broad that it may be used to punish protected conduct which has no propensity to result in breaches of the peace." Serious offense does not always result in a breach of the peace. The protest in this case did not lead to violence. . . . Serious offense [according to trial testimony] occurred, but there was no breach of the peace, nor does the record reflect that the situation was potentially explosive. One cannot equate serious offense with incitement to breach the peace. And I think that any breach of the peace argument here falls on its face. . . .

On vagueness and overbreadth, I think the vagueness is apparent. . . . What does "serious offense" mean? What is "unserious offense" as against "serious offense"? . . .

You don't even know what physical mistreatment means in the statute. Does physical mistreatment mean wearing it, twisting it, burning it? It's just an undefinable statute. . . .

I think this is a fundamental First Amendment case, . . . Justice Jackson said in *Barnette*. "Those who begin coercive elimination of dissent soon find themselves eliminating dissenters. Compulsory unification of opinion achieves only the unanimity of the graveyard. The First Amendment was designed to avoid these ends by avoiding these beginnings." . . .

[I]n just a recent article in the *New York Times* called "In Chicago a Holy War over the Flag" by J. Anthony Lukas . . . he said, "Whatever pain freedom of expression may inflict, it is a principle on which we can give no ground.". . . . I think it's a most important case. I sense that it goes to the heart of the First Amendment, to hear things or to see things that we hate test the First Amendment more than seeing or hearing things that we like. It wasn't designed for things we like. They never needed a First Amendment.

Document 10.12

Majority ruling by the U.S. Supreme Court, written by Justice Brennan, in the 1989 case of *Texas v . Johnson.*

Source: 491 *United States Reports* 397.

After publicly burning an American flag as a means of political protest, Gregory Lee Johnson was convicted of desecrating a flag in violation of Texas law. This case presents the question whether his conviction is consistent with the First Amendment. We hold that it is not. . . .

Johnson was convicted of flag desecration for burning the flag rather than for uttering insulting words[2]. . . . We must first determine whether Johnson's burning of the flag constituted expressive conduct, permitting him to invoke the First Amendment in challenging his conviction [citing *Spence,* document 8.3]. If his conduct was expressive, we next decide whether the State's regulation is related to the suppression of free expression [citing *O'Brien* and *Spence*]. If the State's regulation is not related to expression, then the less stringent standard we announced in *United States v. O'Brien* for regulations of noncommunicative conduct controls. If it is, then we are outside of *O'Brien's* test, and we must ask whether this interest justifies Johnson's conviction under a more demanding standard.[3] A third possibility is that the State's asserted interest is simply not implicated on these facts, and in that event the interest drops out of the picture.

The First Amendment literally forbids the abridgement only of "speech," but we have long recognized that its protection does not end at the spoken or written word. While we have rejected [citing *O'Brien*] "the view that an apparently limitless variety of conduct can be labeled 'speech' whenever the person engaging in the conduct intends thereby to express an idea," we have acknowledged [citing *Spence*] that conduct may be "sufficiently imbued with elements of communication to fall within the scope of the First and Fourteenth Amendments."

In deciding whether particular conduct possesses sufficient communicative elements to bring the First Amendment into play, we have asked [citing *Spence*] whether "⟨a⟩n intent to convey a particularized message was present, and ⟨whether⟩ the likelihood was great that the message would be understood by those who viewed it." . . .

Especially pertinent to this case are our decisions recognizing the communicative nature of conduct relating to flags. Attaching a peace sign to the flag [citing *Spence*], refusing to salute the flag [citing *Barnette*, document 5.2] and displaying a red flag [citing *Stromberg*, document 5.1] we have held, all may find shelter under the First Amendment. . . . That we have had little difficulty identifying an expressive element in conduct relating to flags should not be surprising. The very purpose of a national flag is to serve as a symbol of our country. . . .

We have not automatically concluded, however, that any action taken with respect to our flag is expressive. Instead, in characterizing such action for First Amendment purposes, we have considered the context in which it occurred [citing *Spence*]. . . . Johnson burned an American flag as part— indeed, as the culmination—of a political demonstration that coincided with the convening of the Republican Party and its renomination of Ronald Reagan for President. The expressive, overtly political nature of this conduct was both intentional and overwhelmingly apparent. . . . Johnson's burning of the flag was conduct "sufficiently imbued with elements of communication," [citing *Spence*] to implicate the First Amendment.

The government generally has a freer hand in restricting expressive conduct than it has in restricting the written or spoken word [citing *O'Brien*]. It may not, however, proscribe particular conduct because it has expressive elements. . . . It is, in short, not simply the verbal or nonverbal nature of the expression, but the governmental interest at stake, that helps to determine whether a restriction on that expression is valid.

Thus, [citing *O'Brien*] although we have recognized that where " 'speech' and 'nonspeech' elements are combined in the same course of conduct, a sufficiently important governmental interest in regulating the nonspeech element can justify incidental limitations on First Amendment freedoms," we have limited the applicability of *O'Brien*'s relatively lenient standard to those cases in which "the governmental interest is unrelated to the suppression of free expression." . . .

In order to decide whether *O'Brien*'s test applies here, therefore, we must decide whether Texas has asserted an interest in support of Johnson's conviction that is unrelated to the suppression of expression. If we find that an interest asserted by the State is simply not implicated on the facts before us, we need not ask whether *O'Brien*'s test applies [citing *Spence*]. The State offers two separate interests to justify this conviction: preventing breaches of the peace and preserving the flag as a symbol of nationhood and national unity. We hold that the first interest is not implicated on this record and that the second is related to the suppression of expression.

Texas claims that its interest in preventing breaches of the peace justifies Johnson's conviction for flag desecration. However, no disturbance of the peace actually occurred or threatened to occur because of Johnson's burning of the flag. . . . The only evidence offered by the State at trial to show the reaction to Johnson's actions was the testimony of several persons who had been seriously offended by the flag burning.

The State's position, therefore, amounts to a claim that an audience that takes serious offense at particular expression is necessarily likely to disturb the peace and that the expression may be prohibited on this basis. Our precedents do not countenance such a presumption. . . .

Thus, we have not permitted the government to assume that every expression of a provocative idea will incite a riot, but have instead required careful consideration of the actual circumstances surrounding such expression, asking whether the expression "is directed to inciting or producing imminent lawless action and is likely to incite or produce such action." *Brandenburg v. Ohio.* To accept Texas' arguments that it need only demonstrate "the potential for a breach of the peace," and that every flag burning necessarily possesses that potential, would be to eviscerate our holding in *Brandenburg.* This we decline to do.

Nor does Johnson's expressive conduct fall within that small class of "fighting words" that are "likely to provoke the average person to retaliation, and thereby cause a breach of the peace." *Chaplinsky v. New Hampshire.* No reasonable onlooker would have regarded Johnson's generalized expression of dissatisfaction with the policies of the Federal Government as a direct personal insult or an invitation to exchange fisticuffs.

We thus conclude that the State interest in maintaining order is not implicated on these facts. . . . The State also asserts an interest in preserving the flag as a symbol of nationhood and national unity. In *Spence,* we acknowledged that the government's interest in preserving the flag's special symbolic value "is directly related to expression in the context of activity" such as affixing a peace symbol to a flag. We are equally persuaded that this interest is related to expression in the case of Johnson's burning of the flag. The State, apparently, is concerned that such conduct will lead people to believe either that the flag does not stand for nationhood and national unity, but instead reflects other, less positive concepts, or that the concepts reflected in the flag do not in fact exist, that is, that we do not enjoy unity as a Nation. These concerns blossom only when a person's treatment of the flag communicates some message, and thus are related "to the suppression of free expression" within the meaning of *O'Brien.* We are thus outside of *O'Brien*'s test altogether.

It remains to consider whether the State's interest in preserving the flag as a symbol of nationhood and national unity justifies Johnson's conviction.

As in *Spence,* "⟨w⟩e are confronted with a case of prosecution for the expression of an idea through activity," and "⟨a⟩ccordingly, we must examine with particular care the interests advanced by ⟨petitioner⟩ to support its prosecution." Johnson was not, we add, prosecuted for the expression of just any idea; he was prosecuted for his expression of dissatisfaction with the policies of this country, expression situated at the core of our First Amendment values.

Moreover, Johnson was prosecuted because he knew that his politically charged expression would cause "serious offense." If he had burned the flag as a means of disposing of it because it was dirty or torn, he would not have been convicted of flag desecration under this Texas law; federal law designates burning as the preferred means of disposing of a flag "when it is in such condition that it is no longer a fitting emblem for display," 36 U. S. C. § 176(k), and Texas has no quarrel with this means of disposal. The Texas law is thus not aimed at protecting the physical integrity of the flag in all circumstances, but is designed instead to protect it only against impairments that would cause serious offense to others. . . .[6]

Whether Johnson's treatment of the flag violated Texas law thus depended on the likely communicative impact of his expressive conduct. Our decision in *Boos v. Barry* tells us that this restriction on Johnson's expression is content based. In *Boos,* we considered the constitutionality of a law prohibiting "the display of any sign within 500 feet of a foreign embassy if that sign tends to bring that foreign government into 'public odium' or 'public disrepute.'" Rejecting the argument that the law was content neutral because it was justified by "our international law obligation to shield diplomats from speech that offends their dignity," we held that "⟨t⟩he emotive impact of speech on its audience is not a 'secondary effect'" unrelated to the content of the expression itself.

According to the principles announced in *Boos,* Johnson's political expression was restricted because of the content of the message he conveyed. We must therefore subject the state's asserted interest in preserving the special symbolic character of the flag to "the most exacting scrutiny."

Texas argues that its interest in preserving the flag as a symbol of nationhood and national unity survives this close analysis. . . . According to Texas, if one physically treats the flag in a way that would tend to cast doubt on either the idea that nationhood and national unity are the flag's referents or that national unity actually exists, the message conveyed thereby is a harmful one and therefore may be prohibited.

If there is a bedrock principle underlying the First Amendment, it is that the government may not prohibit the expression of an idea simply because society finds the idea itself offensive or disagreeable.

We have not recognized an exception to this principle even where our flag has been involved. In *Street v. New York* [document 8.1], we held that a State may not criminally punish a person for uttering words critical of the flag [and] concluded that "the constitutionally guaranteed 'freedom to be intellectually * * * diverse or even contrary,' and the 'right to differ as to things that touch the heart of the existing order,' encompass the freedom to express publicly one's opinions about our flag, including those opinions which are defiant or contemptuous." Nor may the government, we have held, compel conduct that would evince respect for the flag [citing *Barnette*].

In holding in *Barnette* that the Constitution did not leave this course open to the government, Justice Jackson described one of our society's defining principles in words deserving of their eloquent repetition: "If there is any fixed star in our constitutional constellation, it is that no official, high or petty, can prescribe what shall be orthodox in politics, nationalism, religion, or other matters of opinion or force citizens to confess by word or act their faith therein." In *Spence*, we held that the same interest asserted by Texas here was insufficient to support a criminal connection under a flag-misuse statute for the taping of a peace sign to an American flag. . . .

In short, nothing in our precedents suggests that a State may foster its own view of the flag by prohibiting expressive conduct relating to it. To bring its argument outside our precedents, Texas attempts to convince us that even if its interest in preserving the flag's symbolic role does not allow it to prohibit words or some expressive conduct critical of the flag, it does permit it to forbid the outright destruction of the flag. The State's argument cannot depend here on the distinction between written or spoken words and nonverbal conduct. That distinction, we have shown, is of no moment where the nonverbal conduct is expressive, as it is here, and where the regulation of that conduct is related to expression as it is here. In addition, both *Barnette* and *Spence* involved expressive conduct, not only verbal communication, and both found that conduct protected.

Texas' focus on the precise nature of Johnson's expression, moreover, misses the point of our prior decisions: their enduring lesson, that the government may not prohibit expression simply because it disagrees with its message, is not dependent on the particular mode in which one chooses to express an idea. If we were to hold that a State may forbid flag burning wherever it is likely to endanger the flag's symbolic role, but allow it wherever burning a flag promotes that role—as where, for example, a person ceremoniously burns a dirty flag—we would be saying that when it comes to impairing the flag's physical integrity, the flag itself may be used as a symbol . . . only in one direction. We would be permitting a State to "prescribe what shall be orthodox" by saying that one may burn the flag to convey one's attitude toward it and its referents only if one does not endanger the flag's representation of nationhood and national unity.

We never before have held that the Government may ensure that a symbol be used to express only one view of that symbol or its referents. Indeed, in *Schacht v. United States*, we invalidated a federal statute permitting an actor portraying a member of one of our armed forces to " 'wear the uniform of that armed force if the portrayal does not tend to discredit that armed force.'" This proviso, we held, "which leaves Americans free to praise the war in Vietnam but can send persons like Schacht to prison for opposing it, cannot survive in a country which has the First Amendment."

We perceive no basis on which to hold that the principle underlying our decision in *Schacht* does not apply to this case. To conclude that the government may permit designated symbols to be used to communicate only a limited set of messages would be to enter territory having no discernible or defensible boundaries. Could the government, on this theory, prohibit the burning of state flags? Of copies of the Presidential seal? Of the Constitution? In evaluating these choices under the First Amendment, how would we decide which symbols were sufficiently special to warrant this unique status? To do so, we would be forced to consult our own political preferences, and impose them on the citizenry in the very way that the First Amendment forbids us to do.

There is, moreover, no indication—either in the text of the Constitution or in our cases interpreting it—that a separate juridical category exists for the American flag alone. . . . The First Amendment does not guarantee that other concepts virtually sacred to our Nation as a whole—such as the principle that discrimination on the basis of race is odious and destructive—will go unquestioned in the marketplace of ideas. We decline, therefore, to create for the flag an exception to the joust of principles protected by the First Amendment.

It is not the State's ends, but its means, to which we object. It cannot be gainsaid that there is a special place reserved for the flag in this Nation, and thus we do not doubt that the government has a legitimate interest in making efforts to [citing *Spence*] "preserv⟨e⟩ the national flag as an unalloyed symbol of our country." . . . To say that the government has an interest in encouraging proper treatment of the flag, however, is not to say that it may criminally punish a person for burning a flag as a means of political protest. . . .

We are fortified in today's conclusion by our conviction that forbidding criminal punishment for conduct such as Johnson's will not endanger the special role played by our flag or the feelings it inspires. To paraphrase Justice Holmes, we submit that nobody can suppose that this one gesture of an unknown man will change our Nation's attitude towards its flag. . . .

We are tempted to say, in fact, that the flag's deservedly cherished place in our community will be strengthened, not weakened, by our holding today. Our decision is a reaffirmation of the principles of freedom and inclusiveness that the flag best reflects, and of the conviction that our toleration of criticism such as Johnson's is a sign and source of our strength. . . . It is the Nation's resilience, not its rigidity, that Texas sees reflected in the flag—and it is that resilience that we reassert today.

The way to preserve the flag's special role is not to punish those who feel differently about these matters. It is to persuade them that they are wrong. . . . We can imagine no more appropriate response to burning a flag than waving one's own, no better way to counter a flag burner's message than by saluting the flag that burns, no surer means of preserving the dignity even of the flag that burned than by . . . according its remains a respectful burial. We do not consecrate the flag by punishing its desecration, for in doing so we dilute the freedom that this cherished emblem represents.

Johnson was convicted for engaging in expressive conduct. The State's interest in preventing breaches of the peace does not support his conviction because Johnson's conduct did not threaten to disturb the peace. Nor does the State's interest in preserving the flag as a symbol of nationhood and national unity justify his criminal conviction for engaging in political expression. The judgment of the Texas Court of Criminal Appeals [document 10.6] is therefore

Affirmed.

2. Because the prosecutor's closing argument observed that Johnson had led the protesters in chants denouncing the flag while it burned, Johnson suggests [in his brief] that he may have been convicted for uttering critical words rather than for burning the flag [in violation of the Supreme Court's prior holding in *Street*]. . . . [W]e find it too unlikely that the jury convicted Johnson on the basis of this alternative theory to consider reversing his conviction on this ground.

3. Although Johnson has raised a facial challenge to Texas' flag-desecration statute, we chose to resolve this case on the basis of his claim that the statute as applied to him violated the First Amendment. . . . Because the prosecution of a person who had not engaged in expressive conduct [under the Texas law at issue here] would pose a different case, and because this case may be disposed of on narrower grounds, we address only Johnson's claim that § 42.09 as applied to political expression like his violates the First Amendment.

6. Cf. *Smith v. Goguen,* (Blackmun, J., dissenting [document 8.4]) (emphasizing that lower court appeared to have construed state statute so as to protect physical integrity of the flag in all circumstances). . . .

Document 10.13

Concurring opinion by U.S. Supreme Court Justice Kennedy in the 1989 case of *Texas v. Johnson.*

Source: 91 *United States Reports* 20.

I write not to qualify the words JUSTICE BRENNAN chooses so well, for he says with power all that is necessary to explain our ruling. I join his opinion without reservation, but with a keen sense that this case, like others before us from time to time, exacts its personal toll. . . .

The hard fact is that sometimes we must make decisions we do not like. We make them because they are right, right in the sense that the law and the Constitution, as we see them, compel the result. And so great is our commitment to the process that, except in the rare case, we do not pause to express distaste for the result, perhaps for fear of undermining a valued principle that dictates the decision. This is one of those rare cases. . . .

Though symbols often are what we ourselves make of them, the flag is constant in expressing beliefs Americans share, beliefs in law and peace and that freedom which sustains the human spirit. The case here today forces recognition of the costs to which those beliefs commit us. It is poignant but fundamental that the flag protects those who hold it in contempt. . . .

[W]hether or not [Johnson] could appreciate the enormity of the offense he gave, the fact remains that his acts were speech, in both the technical and the fundamental meaning of the Constitution. So I agree with the Court that he must go free.

Document 10.14

Dissenting opinion by U.S. Supreme Court Chief Justice Rehnquist (joined by Justices White and O'Connor) in the 1989 case of *Texas v. Johnson*.

Source: 91 United States Reports 436.

. . . For more than 200 years, the American flag has occupied a unique position as the symbol of our Nation, a uniqueness that justifies a governmental prohibition against flag burning in the way respondent Johnson did here. . . .

One of the great stories of the Civil War is told in John Greenleaf Whittier's poem, "Barbara Frietchie" . . .

> Up rose old Barbara Frietchie then,
> Bowed with her fourscore years and ten;
> Bravest of all in Frederick town,
> She took up the flag the men hauled down;
> In her attic window the staff she set,
> To show that one heart was loyal yet.
> Up the street came the rebel tread,
> Stonewall Jackson riding ahead.
> Under his slouched hat left and right
> He glanced: the old flag met his sight.
> 'Halt!'—the dustbrown ranks stood fast.

'Fire!'—out blazed the rifleblast. . . .
Dame Barbara snatched the silken scarf;
She leaned far out on the window-sill,
And shook it forth with a royal will.
'Shoot, if you must, this old gray head,
But spare your country's flag,' she said. . . .

No other American symbol has been as universally honored as the flag. In 1931, Congress declared "The Star Spangled Banner" to be our national anthem. In 1949, Congress declared June 14th to be Flag Day. In 1987, John Philip Sousa's "The Stars and Stripes Forever" was designated as the national march. Congress has also established "The Pledge of Allegiance to the Flag" and the manner of its deliverance. The flag has appeared as the principal symbol on approximately 33 United States postal stamps and in the design of at least 43 more, more times than any other symbol. . . .

The flag is not simply another "idea" or "point of view" competing for recognition in the marketplace of ideas. Millions and millions of Americans regard it with an almost mystical reverence regardless of what sort of social, political, or philosophical beliefs they may have. I cannot agree that the First Amendment invalidates the Act of Congress, and the laws of 48 of the 50 States, which make criminal the public burning of the flag. . . .

But the Court insists that the Texas statute prohibiting the public burning of the American flag infringes on respondent Johnson's freedom of expression. Such freedom, of course, is not absolute. In *Chaplinsky v. New Hampshire* a unanimous Court said:

> Allowing the broadest scope to the language and purpose of the Fourteenth Amendment, it is well understood that the right of free speech is not absolute at all times and under all circumstances. There are certain well-defined and narrowly limited classes of speech, the prevention and punishment of which have never been thought to raise any Constitutional problem. These include the lewd and obscene, the profane, the libelous, and the insulting or "fighting" words—those which by their very utterance inflict injury or tend to incite an immediate breach of the peace. It has been well observed that such utterances are no essential part of any exposition of ideas, and are of such slight social value as a step to truth that any benefit that may be derived from them is clearly outweighed by the social interest in order and morality. . . .

Here it may equally well be said that the public burning of the American flag by Johnson was no essential part of any exposition of ideas, and at the same time it had a tendency to incite a breach of the peace. Johnson was free to make any verbal denunciation of the flag that he wished; indeed, he was free to burn the flag in private. He could publicly burn other symbols of the Government or effigies of political leaders. . . .

[Johnson's act] conveyed nothing that could not have been conveyed and was not conveyed just as forcefully in a dozen different ways. . . . The highest courts of several States have upheld state statutes prohibiting the public burning of the flag on the grounds that it is so inherently inflammatory that it may cause a breach of public order.

The result of the Texas statute is obviously to deny one in Johnson's frame of mind one of many means of "symbolic speech." Far from being a case of "one picture being worth a thousand words," flag burning is the equivalent of an inarticulate grunt or roar that, it seems fair to say, is most likely to be indulged in not to express any particular idea, but to antagonize others. . . . The Texas statute deprived Johnson of only one rather inarticulate symbolic form of protest—a form of protest that was profoundly offensive to many—and left him with a full panoply of other symbols and every conceivable form of verbal expression to express his deep disapproval of national policy. Thus, in no way can it be said that Texas is punishing him because his hearers—or any other group of people—were profoundly opposed to the message that he sought to convey. Such opposition is no proper basis for restricting speech or expression under the First Amendment. It was Johnson's use of this particular symbol, and not the idea that he sought to convey by it or by his many other expressions, for which he was punished. . . .

But the Court today will have none of this. The uniquely deep awe and respect for our flag felt by virtually all of us are bundled off under the rubric of "designated symbols," that the First Amendment prohibits the government from "establishing." But the government has not "established" this feeling; 200 years of history have done that. The government is simply recognizing as a fact the profound regard for the American flag created by that history when it enacts statutes prohibiting the disrespectful public burning of the flag.

The Court concludes its opinion with a regrettably patronizing civics lecture . . . : "The way to preserve the flag's special role is not to punish those who feel differently about these matters. It is to persuade them that they are wrong." The Court's role as the final expositor of the Constitution is well established, but its role as a platonic guardian admonishing those responsible to public opinion as if they were truant schoolchildren has no similar place in our system of government. . . . Surely one of the high purposes of a democratic society is to legislate against conduct that is regarded as evil and profoundly offensive to the majority of people— whether it be murder, embezzlement, pollution, or flag burning.

Our Constitution wisely places limits on powers of legislative majorities to act, but . . . uncritical extension of constitutional protection to the burning of the flag risks the frustration of the very purpose for which organized governments are instituted. The Court decides that the American flag is just another symbol, about which not only must opinions pro and con be tolerated, but for which the most minimal public respect may not be enjoined. The government may conscript men into the Armed Forces where they must fight and perhaps die for the flag, but the government may not prohibit the public burning of the banner under which they fight. I would uphold the Texas statute as applied in this case.

Document 10.15

Dissenting opinion by U.S. Supreme Court Justice Stevens in the 1989 case of *Texas v. Johnson*.

Source: 91 United States Reports 21.

. . . In my judgment rules that apply to a host of other symbols, such as state flags, armbands, or various privately promoted emblems of political or commercial identity are not necessarily controlling [because of the unique nature of the flag]. Even if flag burning could be considered just another species of symbolic speech under the logical application of the rules that the Court has developed in its interpretation of the First Amendment in other contexts, this case has an intangible dimension that makes those rules inapplicable. . . .

The value of the flag as a symbol cannot be measured. Even so, I have no doubt that the interest in preserving that value for the future is both significant and legitimate. . . . [I]n my considered judgment, sanctioning the public desecration of the flag will tarnish its value—both for those who cherish the ideas for which it waves and for those who desire to don the robes of martyrdom by burning it. That tarnish is not justified by the trivial burden on free expression occasioned by requiring that an available, alternative mode of expression—including uttering words critical of the flag [citing *Street*, document 8.1] be employed. . . .

The Court is . . . quite wrong in blandly asserting that respondent "was prosecuted for his expression of dissatisfaction with the policies of this country, expression situated at the core of our First Amendment values." Respondent was prosecuted because of the method he chose to express his dissatisfaction with those policies. Had he chosen to spraypaint . . . his message of dissatisfaction on the facade of the Lincoln Memorial, there would be no question about the power of the Government to prohibit his means of expression. The prohibition would be supported by the legitimate interest in preserving the quality of an important national asset. Though the asset at stake in this case is intangible, given its unique value, the same interest supports a prohibition on the desecration of the American flag.

The ideas of liberty and equality have been an irresistible force in motivating leaders like Patrick Henry, Susan B. Anthony, and Abraham Lincoln, schoolteachers like Nathan Hale and Booker T. Washington, the Philippine Scouts who fought at Bataan, and the soldiers who scaled the bluff at Omaha Beach. If those ideas are worth fighting for—and our history demonstrates that they are—it cannot be true that the flag that uniquely symbolizes their power is not itself worthy of protection from unnecessary desecration.

I respectfully dissent.

Public and Political Response
to *Texas v. Johnson*
1989

The *Johnson* ruling touched off what *Newsweek* termed "stunned outrage" across the United States. According to Sen. Strom Thurmond (R., S.C.), the ruling "opened an emotional hydrant across our country demanding immediate action to overturn it." Thurmond captured the overwhelmingly emotional nature of the immediate reaction to the ruling when he proclaimed to the Senate, "We must stand up for America. The flag, the flag. America, America. For us!" A typical national poll, published in the July 3 *Newsweek,* indicated that 65 percent of Americans disagreed with the ruling and that 71 percent favored a constitutional amendment to overturn it.[1]

The thrust of the clear majority of public and political elite opinion in immediate response to the ruling boiled down to the proposition that the flag, as the most well-known symbol of "freedom" and the nation, was "unique" and "special," that dissent was a legitimate and critical part of the democratic process, but that desecrating the flag went "too far." Critics of the ruling argued that this was especially so because American soldiers, as Justice Rehnquist claimed in his dissent, had "died for the flag," and that, in any case, flag burning was "conduct" and not "speech" and thus should not receive First Amendment protection. Scores of congressmen bitterly denounced the *Johnson* decision (document 11.1) and rushed to introduce constitutional amendments to overturn it; by July 1, 172 representatives and 43 senators had sponsored thirty-nine separate resolutions calling for an amendment to outlaw flag desecration.

On June 22, the Senate voted 97–3 to express its "profound disappointment" with the ruling (document 11.2), and the House followed up with an 411–15 vote on June 27 that voiced "profound concern" about it (document 11.3). On the night of June 28, the House held a highly unusual all-night session devoted to speeches denouncing both flag burners and the Supreme Court. By mid-July, one or both of the legislative chambers of most of the twenty or so state legislatures still in session at the time of the *Johnson* ruling passed resolutions denouncing the decision and/or demanding constitutional or legislative action to overturn it (document 11.4).

Much, although by no means all, of the criticism of the *Johnson* decision, especially in the immediate period after June 21, was couched in highly vitriolic terms. Thus, Rep. Ron Marlenee termed the decision "treasonous" and, referring to the six marines depicted in the Iwo Jima Memorial, declared, "These six brave soldiers were symbolically shot in the back by five men in black robes." The chairman of the South Carolina Joint Veterans Council called on Americans to write to their elected officials to demand that "this crap" be stopped, while conservative columnist Pat Buchanan termed the decision an "atrocity" and the court a "renegade tribunal" to which the American people should respond by putting "a fist in their face." The *New York Daily News* termed the *Johnson* decision "dumb" and declared that it put the court in "naked contempt" of the American people and displayed "pompous insensitivity to the most beloved symbol of the most benevolent form of government ever to appear on this Earth." Flag burners came in for even more bitter criticism than did the five majority justices, with many comments along the lines of Sen. Dole's remark that "if they don't like our flag, they ought to go find one they do like."[2]

In his first response to the *Johnson* ruling, on June 22, President Bush seemed far more restrained. Although he voiced what he termed his "personal, emotional response" that the flag was "very, very special" and that burning it was "dead wrong," he not only gave no hint that he would seek to overturn the ruling, but even added, "I understand the legal basis for that decision, and I respect the Supreme Court" and "as President of the United States, I will see that the law of the land is fully supported."[3] However, at a hastily called press conference on the morning of June 27, just as coverage of the flag-burning controversy was disappearing from the news media, Bush told reporters that he had decided to sponsor a constitutional amendment to overturn the *Johnson* ruling (document 11.5). He declared that although he would "uphold our precious right to dissent," burning "the unique symbol of America" went "too far" and that his legal advisers had indicated that ordinary legislation could not "correct" the decision, which he maintained had legalized an "egregious offense" that he felt "viscerally about."

On June 30, Bush formally announced the text of his proposed amendment (document 11.6), which authorized both Congress and the states to "prohibit the physical desecration of the flag of the United

States," in a highly publicized speech that he delivered at the Iwo Jima Memorial in Arlington, Virginia, surrounded by flags and accompanied by the Marine Band and congressional sponsors from both parties (document 11.7). In his speech, Bush declared that the flag was "one of our most powerful ideas," as the symbol of "freedom" that represents and reflects "the fabric of our nation"; that to "dishonor it is simply wrong"; and that "like all powerful ideas, if it is not defended, it is defamed." According to Bush, "What that flag embodies is too sacred to be abused."

In the view of many observers, had President Bush not endorsed a constitutional amendment, the entire flag desecration controversy might have dissipated, but his action almost guaranteed that Congress would formally seek to circumvent the *Johnson* ruling. This was especially so because the Bush amendment was rapidly endorsed by the entire Republican congressional leadership, while the Democratic congressional leadership was clearly wary of seeking to limit formally First Amendment freedoms but was equally alarmed about being depicted as "anti-flag," as Bush had succeeded in tagging 1988 Democratic presidential candidate Dukakis amidst the campaign Pledge of Allegiance controversy. In an attempt to delay congressional voting on attempts to overturn the *Johnson* ruling until passions had died down, and simultaneously to block the Bush amendment while still positioning themselves as "pro-flag," immediately after Bush endorsed an amendment the Democratic congressional leadership announced hearings on the *Johnson* decision and declared their support for overturning it by ordinary statute rather than by constitutional amendment. As reporters for the *New York Times* and the *Washington Post* noted in late June, "many Democrats swore they would never be outflagged again" and they "kept up a fusillade of proflag rhetoric," matching "the Republicans word for word" and talking "barroom tough, essentially saying no Republican had better call them soft on the flag."[4]

With most Republicans committed to a constitutional amendment and most Democrats committed to a legislative attempt to overturn the *Johnson* ruling along the lines of the eventually passed Flag Protection Act (FPA) of 1989 (document 11.8), the political possibility that Congress would take no action at all in response to the Court's decision effectively disappeared by the time of President Bush's June 30 Iwo Jima speech. Although the public uproar and massive media attention focused on the flag desecration issue died down considerably after July 4, the only real debate in Washington quickly became centered upon whether it would be possible to circumvent *Johnson* by law or whether a constitutional amendment would be required.

Thus, when the House and Senate judiciary committees held summer hearings on possible responses to the *Johnson* ruling (thereby postponing any voting until the fall), SJC chairman Joseph Biden, a leading FPA proponent, told his colleagues that the only debate was about "the best way" to achieve the "purpose" of determining exactly how to "protect the flag," and Assistant Attorney General William Barr, the Bush administration's chief witness, accurately said that the only question was "not whether to provide protection for the Flag, but how to provide that protection." Many members of Congress who privately apparently believed that neither legislation nor an amendment was really desirable also apparently felt compelled for political reasons to support at least one of these approaches. When Harvard law professor and former Reagan administration solicitor general Charles Fried advocated what became known as the "bravely do nothing" option (document 11.9), HJC subcommittee chairman and FPA cosponsor Don Edwards, who had vigorously opposed the 1968 federal flag desecration law (document 6.3), said, "Your point of view is the correct point of view, but it's such a [political] loser," and Congresswoman Pat Schroeder said, "We're not talking about a purist world. We're talking about a very political world."[5]

The legal argument for the constitutionality of the FPA, advanced by Democratic majorities on the judiciary committees (documents 11.10 and 11.13) and several prominent law professors with liberal reputations, most notably Harvard law professor Laurence Tribe (document 11.11), was based on the theory that the *Johnson* ruling had not banned all flag desecration laws, only those that clearly targeted dissent and that were not designed to protect "neutrally" the flag's "physical integrity" against all assaults, no matter what the motivation or intended message (or lack of one, such as simple vandalism). Although the overwhelming thrust of the *Johnson* ruling seemed to contradict this theory—for example it declared that the state could not "criminally punish a person for burning a flag as a means of political protest" and that government could not "foster its own view of the flag by prohibiting expressive conduct relating to it"—proponents of the legislative approach pointed to several phrases in the ruling as bolstering their approach. For example, they noted that the *Johnson* majority had stated at one point that the ruling was "bounded by the particular facts of this case and by the statute under which Johnson was convicted"; that in a footnote it declared that the prosecution of a flag desecrator who "had not engaged in expressive conduct," such as dragging a flag in the mud because he was tired, would pose different issues; and above all, that Justice Brennan had declared in the opinion that the Texas law at issue in *Johnson* (document 10.1) clearly and unconstitutionally discriminated against expression on the basis of content because it was "not aimed at protecting the physical integrity under all circumstances, but is designed instead to protect it only against impairments that would cause serious offense to others."

FPA proponents especially stressed that this latter comment was accompanied by a footnote reference to Justice Blackmun's 1974 *Goguen* dissent (document 8.4), in which he had maintained that a Massachusetts law found to be unconstitutionally vague by the Supreme Court majority was in fact constitutional because it outlawed all acts that "harmed the physical integrity of the flag" and was therefore not targeted at any "communicative element." In the view of FPA backers, because Blackmun was part of the slender 5–4 *Johnson* majority, this footnote was intended to signal that Blackmun would switch sides and create a majority in support of a flag desecration law that, unlike the Texas statute and the 1968 federal flag law (document 6.1), omitted any reference to casting "contempt" or causing "serious offense," but simply outlawed all conduct that impaired the flag's "physical integrity."

Ultimately, the position of FPA proponents was heavily tied to the argument that such a "content neutral" flag desecration law would be upheld by the Supreme Court because it would be viewed as not having been designed to suppress expression and therefore would be legally subject only to the relatively lenient "important or substantial governmental interest" standard of the 1968 *O'Brien* ruling, which had upheld a law forbidding draft card burning, rather than by the virtually insurmountable "most exacting scrutiny" standard of the *Johnson* ruling, which the Court held applicable when statutes were motivated by suppressive intent. The critical importance of this point was made clear by a Congressional Research Service report about the prospects of an FPA before the Supreme Court (document 11.12). According to Tribe and other promoters of the FPA, the government's interest in protecting the "physical integrity" of all flags was not related to "suppression" of free expression, but rather had the purely nonsuppressive purpose of seeking to honor and protect the flag as a particularly valued object against all physical threats of any nature, just as outlawing the killing of bald eagles or the defacing of gravesites or government buildings sought to protect them against all physical assaults, regardless of their motive, as opposed to seeking to suppress the particular views of someone who might harm them. Thus the HJC majority endorsed the FPA as reflecting the government's power to honor the "diverse and deeply held feelings of the vast majority of citizens for the flag" through the "protection of a venerated object in the same manner that protection is afforded to gravesites or historic buildings."

The key arguments for the constitutional amendment put forth by Assistant Attorney General Barr (document 11.14), Republican minorities on the judiciary committees (document 11.15) and others included the following points: (1) that the Supreme Court had made clear in the *Johnson* ruling that any flag desecration law that sought to forbid symbolic protest would be unconstitutionally aimed at suppressing dissent and unable to meet the applicable standard of "most exacting" First Amendment scrutiny, even if its facial language outlawed all physical damage to flags regardless of its motivation or intended message; (2) that any such so-called content neutral flag desecration law would have to outlaw patriotic conduct, such as the ceremonial burning of worn flags or the pinning of war medals to flags, to which the government and the American public did not object, in order to ban symbolic protests using the flag that were the real targets of the proposed law, although a constitutional amendment could authorize discriminating between similar acts that had different motivations and that the public interpreted differently; and (3) that because any flag desecration law would be struck down eventually by the Supreme Court, passage of such a measure would only postpone the need to adopt the only remedy that could effectively overturn the *Johnson* ruling, namely the enactment of a constitutional amendment. In response to comparisons made by FPA proponents between "neutrally" protecting the flag and "neutrally" protecting bald eagles, gravesites and buildings, Assistant Attorney General Barr termed such arguments "false analogies," because the latter were "inherently rare and irreplaceable," thus having a value and therefore a reason to protect them that went beyond their symbolism; in contrast, he argued, the only reason to protect the flag, an "inherently reproducible" object, was its symbolic value, but this interest was "inherently related to expression" and thus bound to fail the "most exacting scrutiny" test, which the Supreme Court would surely apply.[6]

Backers of the FPA maintained that burning worn flags in order to retire them ceremonially would not violate a "content neutral" ban on physically damaging flags, because such worn objects were no longer truly "flags"; this exemption was written into the final text of the FPA in response to arguments that otherwise the law would threaten veterans' groups, which had long ceremonially burned worn flags, with jail. In response to the argument that the FPA would eventually be struck down by the courts after years of litigation and that therefore only a constitutional amendment could quickly and surely protect the flag, a clause was also included in the FPA to provide for mandatory, expedited review of the law by the Supreme Court.

Many of the leading FPA proponents, including SJC chairman Biden and HJC chairman Jack Brooks, promised that they would support a constitutional amendment if the statutory approach failed; their fundamental point was, as the SJC majority put it (document 11.13), that "the amendment process should be invoked as a last, not as a first resort." According to many FPA supporters, the law would not only constitutionally and effectively ban flag burning, but it could be enacted much more quickly than an amendment and would also avoid "tinkering" with the Constitution, thereby avoiding greasing a "slippery slope" for subsequent infringement of the First Amendment (to which amendment backers responded that the flag was so unique that no precedent for further changes to the Constitution would be created, but that the FPA might open an easy path for overturning unpopular Supreme Court decisions by simple legislation).

Opponents of the Bush amendment, including the SJC majority, also argued that its the text was deeply flawed, especially as it would authorize legislation that would explicitly criminalize conduct solely on the basis of the point of view that it expressed, for example criminalizing physical damage to flags inflicted to express protest, although exempting similar damage inflicted for patriotic reasons (such as pinning medals to a flag). Supporters of the amendment rejected the argument that their language was defective and argued that the unique nature of the flag and the deeply emotional feeling of the American public about it justified giving the flag special protection against acts that were viewed as offensive.

Most political pundits predicted easy passage of a constitutional amendment after President Bush endorsed it in late June 1989, but on October 19, 1989, the Bush amendment was killed when the Senate voted for it by only a 51–48 margin, well short of the two-thirds majority needed to endorse a constitutional amendment. Shortly before the Senate killed the amendment, however, both houses of Congress passed the FPA, which became law on October 28 without Bush's signature and which, like the amendment, was designed to circumvent the *Johnson* ruling. Bush announced his decision to neither approve nor veto the FPA, and thus let it become law without his signature, at an October 13 press conference, at which he said the measure was not "enough," and in a formal statement issued on October 26, which expressed "serious doubts that [the FPA] can withstand Supreme Court review" (documents 11.16 and 11.17). At the press conference, Bush denied that he was afraid to veto the FPA for fear that he would be accused of being "soft" on the flag, just as he had suggested was true of 1988 Democratic presidential candidate Dukakis because of the latter's veto of a bill that would have required daily school recitals of the Pledge of Allegiance. In his October 28 statement, Bush said that he had decided to let the FPA become law without his signature because it was "intended to achieve our mutual goal of protecting our Nation's greatest symbol, and its constitutionality must ultimately be decided by the courts."

There are a number of reasons that explain why the Bush amendment failed to pass the Senate (it was not voted on in the House in 1989) in October although only a few months earlier there had been widespread and generally accepted predictions that it would easily pass both houses of Congress. First, by scheduling hearings on responses to the *Johnson* ruling, the Democratic congressional leadership successfully insured a "cooling off" period in which the intense public and political emotions of the immediate post-*Johnson* period eased considerably (document 11.18). This easing was unquestionably facilitated by the fact that, during the four months of congressional hearings and offstage consideration of the issue between late June and October, the entire controversy dropped out of the news media and thus out of the public eye. For example, between June 27 (when Bush first endorsed an amendment) and July 4, the three major television networks provided massive coverage of the issue, leading the evening news with the story on nine out of twenty-four broadcasts and providing some coverage on another seven broadcasts, but after July 4, the controversy faded from network evening news. The three networks collectively carried only one story on it during the evening news in August and devoted a combined total of less than one minute to House passage of the FPA on September 12, which was the first day since July 4 that all three network evening newscasts even mentioned the issue on the same day.[7]

Aside from the lengthy "cooling off" period provided by the post-June congressional hearings and consideration and by the decline in media coverage, the Democratic sponsorship of an alternative to an amendment via the FPA unquestionably was another major factor in the defeat of the amendment. In short, the availability of the FPA provided political "cover," especially for Democrats (but also for a few Republicans) who were reluctant to support an amendment to the Bill of Rights or who personally were not exercised about the *Johnson* ruling, but who feared being portrayed as "soft" on the flag. Thus, although forty-eight senators voted against the amendment on October 19, the FPA was approved by the Senate by a 91–9 vote on October 5; only six senators voted against both alternatives. In the House, the FPA was approved by a 380–38 vote on September 12, but in 1990, after the Supreme Court had struck down the FPA in its *Eichman* ruling (document 12.7), only 254 representatives supported an amendment; only twenty voted against both the amendment and the FPA. In both the House and the Senate, massive majorities among the Democrats voted for the FPA but against the amendment, while massive Republican majorities voted for both alternatives.

In addition to the "cooling off period" and the availability in 1989 of a politically "safe" cover for opposing the amendment in the form of the FPA, another explanation for the declining support for the amendment after June may have been the outspoken opposition to the amendment by broad segments of the press, including many conservative newspapers, and also the strong attacks that were launched on the amendment by two prominent heroes of the Vietnam War, developments that provided additional "cover" for those who wanted to vote against the amendment but feared the possible political consequences. Opposition to the amendment was extremely widespread in the press and among political columnists, extending far beyond liberal and moderate publications such as the *New Republic* (document 11.19), the *Seattle Times* (document 11.20) and the *Philadelphia Inquirer* (document 11.21) to encompass very conservative outlets such as the *Detroit News* (document 11.22) and the most prominent conservative political columnists, including James Kilpatrick (document 11.23), George Will, and William Safire. Aside from the widespread press opposition to the amendment from all sides of the political spectrum, additional influential opposition was voiced by Democratic senator Robert Kerrey of Nebraska, a winner of the Congressional Medal of Honor, who had lost part of a leg in Vietnam (document 11.24), and by James Warner, a former Vietnam prisoner of war and former Reagan administration official, who recounted in a widely quoted *Washington Post* article (document 11.25) that he had humiliated a North Vietnamese captor by pointing to antiwar flag burnings as a sign of the strength of American democracy (although in fact such acts were then illegal). Warner's article was again widely quoted by amendment opponents when the amendment was revived in 1995 after being defeated in Congress in 1989 and 1990.

Although these amendment opponents in 1989 also explicitly or implicitly opposed the FPA, because the political "choice" in Washington had been effectively defined as one or the other of these two alternatives, and because most supporters of former Solicitor General Fried's "bravely do nothing" approach viewed the amendment as the worse alternative, in practice such expressions especially harmed the case for the amendment. Especially prominent themes in such viewpoints were that President Bush was acting primarily out of political motives in an attempt to place civil liberties–oriented Democrats in an embarrassing position; that flag burners posed no real threat to anything, but consideration of the amendment was diverting time and energy away from facing the real problems of the nation; and, especially, that freedom of speech, the capstone of American democracy, was especially designed to protect the right of highly unpopular expression such as flag burning, and that opponents of the *Johnson* ruling were therefore hopelessly confusing the symbolism of the flag with the substance of the freedom that it was supposed to represent, thus destroying the reality of freedom while seeking to defend mere cloth.

Document 11.1

Congressional reaction in the House of Representatives in the immediate wake of the June 21, 1989, Supreme Court ruling in the case of *Texas v. Johnson*.

Source: Congressional Record, June 22, 1989, H3002-04.

Mr. BURTON of Indiana. Mr. Speaker, George M. Cohan wrote:

> You're a grand old flag,
> You're a high flying flag.
> And forever in peace may you wave.

You're the emblem of the land I love
The home of the free and the brave.
Every heart beats true
Under red, white and blue
Where there's never a boast or a brag
But should old acquaintance be forgot
Keep your eyes on the grand old flag.

Mr. Speaker, Mr. Cohan must be turning in his grave.

Americans have fought and died for that flag all over the world. Many have given their lives just because they did not want it to touch the ground, if you can believe that, during combat.

Yesterday the Supreme Court ruled on a case that involved a Communist, Gregory "Joey" Johnson a member of the Revolutionary Communist Youth Brigade. . . . The Supreme Court said, and I quote, "that neither the States nor the Federal Government may criminalize flag desecration intended as a political statement even if it offends onlookers."

What are we coming to in this country? . . .

Mr. Speaker, the Judiciary in this country has gone too far. Shame . . . on these judges [who voted for the majority], Justice William Brennan, Justice Harry Blackmun, Justice Anthony Kennedy, Justice Thurgood Marshall, and Justice Antonin Scalia; shame on you, shame on you.

Mr. GOSS. Mr. Speaker, yesterday the Supreme Court said burning the American flag is an acceptable form of free expression.

That unbelievable decision sent an ominous message to every American citizen, particularly our Nation's veterans and our children—a message that says "the American flag, and everything it represents, does not deserve a special place in our society."

The U.S. flag is the symbol for everything this country holds dear—including our Constitution and the individual liberties our Constitution protects. . . .

What are we saying to our children when we tell them it is OK to burn the flag in protest? What are we saying to our Nation's veterans who were willing to give their lives to protect the flag? . . .

Mr. APPLEGATE. Mr. Speaker, I am mad as heck. We have witnessed the greatest travesty in the annals of jurisprudence when the U.S. Supreme Court allowed the destruction of our greatest of American symbols. What in God's name is going on?

One and a quarter million of our American veterans fought and died throughout our history to defend this flag and what it stands for.

The flag right here in this Chamber that we pledge to, we can take it down, throw it on the floor, step on it, defecate on it, do anything we want, burn it, as long as we have a message, and the Court is going to say it is all right. . . .

Are there any limitations? Are they going to allow fornication in Times Square at high noon? If one has a political and social message to make, why not go ahead and do it? I am sure the Supreme Court will probably uphold it.

If we change the Court, we change the decision. What we need is a constitutional amendment.

Document 11.2

Resolution adopted by the U.S. Senate, June 22, 1989, by a 97–3 vote, in response to the June 21, 1989, Supreme Court ruling in *Texas v. Johnson*.

Source: Congressional Record, June 22, 1989, S7189.

S. Res. 151

Whereas the first amendment to the United States Constitution lies at the core of our Nation's concept of ordered liberty;

Whereas the flag of the United States is the most profound symbol of our ideals, aspirations, and indeed our identity as a nation;

Whereas the flag stands for our very being, including our commitments to freedom, justice, equal opportunity, and peace;

Whereas Americans have always displayed the flag as a living symbol of our Nation and the values for which it stands;

Whereas the burning of the American flag is an affront to our American heritage and an affront to the American people;

Whereas millions of Americans have fought valiantly, and many thousands have died, to protect this sacred symbol of nationhood, from the beginning of the Republic through the two World Wars, the Korean conflict, the Vietnam conflict, to the present, and that those who risked and gave their lives for our country are profoundly offended by the desecration of this sacred emblem;

Whereas the Congress and forty eight States have enacted laws to protect against desecration of the flag;

Whereas the Senate expressed its respect for the flag as recently as March 16, 1989, when on a vote of 97–0, it passed S. 607, prohibiting the displaying of the flag on the floor or ground [document 10.8];

Whereas throughout the history of our Nation, the Supreme Court has properly defended and protected the first amendment rights of our Nation's citizens;

Whereas the United States Supreme Court yesterday rendered a decision in the case of *Texas v. Johnson,* No. 88-155, finding unconstitutional a Texas statute prohibiting the desecration of the flag, determining that this conduct is an act of "symbolic speech" protected by the first amendment;

Whereas the Congress has believed that the act of desecrating the flag is clearly not "speech" as protected by the first amendment; and that analogous acts, such as desecrating a public monument such as the Lincoln Memorial, would never be tolerated as speech;

Whereas it appears that yesterday's decision may invalidate the Federal and State laws prohibiting desecration of the flag: Therefore, be it

Resolved, That the Senate hereby—

(1) expresses its profound disappointment that the Texas statute prohibiting the desecration of the flag was found to be unconstitutional;

(2) expresses its continued commitment to preserving the honor and integrity of the flag as a living symbol of our Nation and its aspirations and ideals;

(3) intends to make an immediate study of the impact of yesterday's Supreme Court decision on Federal and state laws prohibiting the desecration of the flag, and to seek ways to restore sanctions against such reprehensible conduct; and

(4) urges the American people to continue to display proudly the American flag as a symbol of our Nation and the values for which it stands.

Document 11.3

Resolution adopted by the U.S. House of Representatives, June 27, 1989, by a 411–15 vote, in response to the June 21, 1989, Supreme Court ruling in *Texas v. Johnson*.

Source: Congressional Record, June 27, 1989, H3228.

Whereas for more than 2 centuries the flag of the United States has stood as the paramount symbol of unity for the Nation by transcending political and geographical divisions;

Whereas millions of men and women have served under the flag of the United States in the Armed Forces since the beginning of the Republic, through 2 world wars and in Korea and Vietnam, and many thousands sacrificed their lives in defense of freedom;

Whereas the Congress has commemorated the unique status of the flag through the enactment of detailed legislation prescribing its proper display and treatment;

Whereas desecration of the flag is an act so offensive to individuals in the United States that it may be considered an incitement to violence; . . .

Whereas the decision of the Court [in *Johnson*] calls into question the validity of section 700(a) of title 18, United States Code [document 6.1], prescribing criminal penalties for desecration of the flag, as well as statutes enacted by 48 of the 50 States prohibiting the burning of the flag: Now, therefore, be it

Resolved, That the House of Representatives hereby—

(1) expresses its profound concern over the Supreme Court's decision in *Texas v. Johnson;*

(2) expresses its continued commitment to preserving the honor and integrity of the flag as a living symbol of our Nation and its aspirations and ideas;

(3) condemns all actions intended to desecrate the American flag; and

(4) urges the American people to continue to display proudly the flag of the United States as a symbol of our Nation and the values for which it stands.

Document 11.4

Resolutions adopted by the state legislatures of Colorado and Texas in response to the June 21, 1989, Supreme Court ruling in *Texas v. Johnson.*

Source: *Congressional Record,* 1989, S8487, S10825.

"[Colorado] Senate Joint Resolution 2

"Whereas, the United States Supreme Court, in the case of *Texas v. Johnson,* . . . held that the burning of an American flag as a means of political protest was expressive conduct protected by the first amendment freedoms;

"Whereas . . . the net practical effect of the message communicated to the people of the United States is that desecration of the American flag is acceptable conduct; and

"Whereas the American flag is a visible symbol embodying 200 years of nationhood and national unity, and respecting, cherishing, and honoring the flag is instilled in our children to promote patriotism; and

"Whereas because our nation has honored the flag as a symbol of American values, there should be a right to prohibit desecration of the flag; and

"Whereas prohibiting the desecration of the flag does not prevent expressions of ideas or opinions;

"Whereas the American flag holds a place of honor and esteem in the hearts of our countrymen who have carried it proudly and courageously into battle;

"Whereas the reverence regarded for the American flag by Americans as a whole should transcend individual social, political, and philosophical beliefs; and

"Whereas Colorado, as well as forty-seven other states and the Congress of the United States, has enacted legislation prohibiting the burning of the American flag; and . . .

"Whereas the American flag, the symbol to which we pledge allegiance to the ideals on which America was founded, is a unique symbol deserving of unique national protection.

"Be It Resolved by the Senate of the Fifty-seventh General Assembly of the State of Colorado, the House of Representatives concurring herein:

"(1) That the Supreme Court is urged to reconsider the issue of freedom of speech manifested by the desecration of the American flag and to overturn its holding in *Texas v. Johnson.*

"(2) That the Congress of the United States is memorialized to enact legislation proposing an amendment to the Constitution of the United States which would distinguish the American flag as a unique symbol deserving the highest protection, including protection from conduct which would otherwise be shielded by the first amendment. . . ."

"[Texas] House Concurrent Resolution No. 18

"Whereas the United States flag belongs to all Americans and ought not be desecrated by any one individual, even under principles of free expression, any more than we would allow desecration of the Declaration of Independence, Statue of Liberty, Lincoln Memorial, Yellowstone National Park, or any other common inheritance that the people of the land hold dear;

"Whereas the United States Supreme Court, in contravention of this postulate, has by a narrow decision held to be a First Amendment freedom the license to destroy in protest this cherished symbol of our national heritage;

"Whereas whatever legal arguments may be offered to support this contention, the incineration or other mutilation of the flag . . . is repugnant to all those who have saluted it, paraded beneath in on the Fourth of July, been saluted by its half-mast configuration, or raised it inspirationally in remote corners of the globe where they have defended the ideals of which it is representative; and

"Whereas the members of the Legislature of the State of Texas, while respectful of dissenting political views, themselves dissent forcefully from the court decision echoing the beliefs of all patriotic Americans that this flag is our flag, and not a private property subject to a private prerogative to maim or despoil in the passion of individual protest; and

"Whereas as stated by Chief Justice William Rehnquist [in his dissent, document 10.14] . . . , 'Surely one of the high purposes of a democratic society is to legislate against conduct that is regarded as evil and profoundly offensive to the majority of people—whether it be murder, embezzlement, pollution or flag burning'; and

"Whereas this legislature concurs with the court minority that the

Stars and Stripes is deserving of a unique sanctity, free to wave in perpetuity over the spacious skies where our bald eagles fly, the fruited plain above which our mountain majesties soar, and the venerable heights to which our melting pot of peoples and their posterity aspire; now, therefore, be it

"Resolved, That the 71st Legislature of the State of Texas . . . hereby petition the Congress . . . to propose to the states an amendment to the United States Constitution, protecting the American flag and 50 state flags from willful desecration and exempting such desecration from constitutional construction as a First Amendment right. . . ."

Document 11.5

President Bush's press conference of June 27, 1989, announcing his decision to sponsor a constitutional amendment to authorize outlawing flag desecration, in response to the June 21, 1989, Supreme Court ruling in *Texas v. Johnson*.

Source: Weekly Compilation of Presidential Documents 25, no. 26 (July 3, 1989): 982–91.

The President. I have a brief opening statement, and then I'd be glad to take questions.

On Wednesday morning, the Supreme Court issued a decision which held that a person could not be convicted for desecration of our flag, the American flag, because to do so would infringe upon the right to political protest. Now, we've got to be very careful in our society to preserve the right to protest government action. However, I believe that the flag of the United States should never be the object of desecration. Flag-burning is wrong. Protection of the flag, a unique national symbol, will in no way limit the opportunity nor the breadth of protest available in the exercise of free speech rights.

And I have the greatest respect for the Supreme Court and, indeed, for the Justices who interpreted the Constitution, as they saw fit. But I believe the importance of this issue compels me to call for a constitutional amendment. Support for the first amendment need not extend to desecration of the American flag. . . . [A]s President, I will uphold our precious right to dissent. But burning the flag goes too far, and I want to see that matter remedied. . . .

Q. Mr. President, in light of your renewed concern about the display of proper reverence for the flag, I wonder if you think it helps the situation, sir, for you and other political figures of both parties to make the flag the kind of instrument of partisan politics that it was in your campaign last fall with a visit to Flag City and the tour of flag factories and flags at all the conventions and so on?

The President. I don't view that as partisanship. I think respect for the flag transcends political party. And I think what I've said here is American. It isn't Republican or Democrat; it isn't liberal or conservative. And I just feel very, very strongly about it, and perhaps I haven't been quite as emotional as I feel about it. But I want to take this opportunity to say protest should not extend to desecration of the unique symbol of America, and that is our flag. . . .

Q. You wouldn't dispute, would you, sir, that your visit to Flag City, U.S.A., and your visit to the flag factory last year were for the purpose of advancing your political campaign?

The President. Everything I did last year was for the purpose of advancing . . . my election. And of course I'm not going to say that. But I didn't put it on the basis that Republicans are for the flag and Democrats are not. . . .

Q. Why do you give such a high priority to the issue of flag-burning, . . . ?

The President. I've got to confess, I do feel viscerally about burning the American flag. And therefore, I express it. . . . [T]his decision just came down, and it is one that causes, I think, the American people, and certainly this President, great concern. And I think it can be remedied without doing violence to a person's right to protest. . . .

Q. You didn't explain why you went the constitutional route instead of legislative on flag-burning.

The President. Because I am told that legislation cannot correct the, in my view, egregious offense: burning the American flag.

Document 11.6

Complete text (including preamble) of constitutional amendment sponsored by President Bush to authorize forbidding flag desecration in response to the June 21, 1989 Supreme Court ruling in *Texas v. Johnson*.

Source: Senate Joint Resolution 180, 1989.

JOINT RESOLUTION
Proposing an amendment to the Constitution of the United States authorizing the Congress and the States to prohibit the physical desecration of the flag of the United States.

Whereas the flag of the United States of America is a national symbol of such stature that it must be kept inviolate;

Whereas the physical desecration of the flag should not be considered constitutionally protected speech; and

Whereas physical desecration may include, but is not limited to, such acts as burning, mutilating, defacing, defiling or trampling on the flag, or displaying the flag in a contemptuous manner: Now, therefore, be it

Resolved by the Senate and the House of Representative of the United States of America in Congress assembled (two-thirds of each House concurring therein), That the following article is proposed as an amendment to the Constitution of the United States, which shall be valid to all intents and purposes as part of the Constitution when ratified by the legislatures of three-fourths of the several States within seven years after the date of its submission for ratification:

ARTICLE—
"The Congress and the States shall have power to prohibit the physical desecration of the flag of the United States."

Document 11.7

President's Bush's speech of June 30, 1989, at the Iwo Jima Memorial in Arlington, Virginia, formally introducing his proposed constitutional amendment to authorize forbidding flag desecration.

Source: Weekly Compilation of Presidential Documents 25, no. 26 (July 3, 1989): 1006–8.

. . . .[W]e stand today before a symbol of hope and of triumph. All across America—above farmhouses and statehouses, schools and courts and capitols—our flag is borne on the breeze of freedom. And it reminds Americans how much they've been given and how much they have to give. Our flag represents freedom and the unity of our nation. And our flag flies in peace, thanks to the sacrifices of so many Americans.

A woman in Florida recently shared with me a letter written by her cousin, a young soldier named Wayne Thomas. On December 16, 1966, he wrote, "Every time we go out on patrol, it gets a little scarier. The only thing that gives us a sense of security is when we walk back into camp and our flag is still flying high." She told me that Wayne stepped on a landmine 11 days later and was killed. He was 18 years old. He understood this banner of freedom and ultimately gave his life for the flag to give others the freedom that it represents.

You know, she also pointed out to me, parenthetically, that she was a registered Democrat. And to me that simply states that patriotism is not a partisan issue; it's not a political issue: Our purpose today transcends politics and partisanship.

And we feel in our hearts, and we know from our experience, that the surest way to preserve liberty is to protect the spirit that sustains it. And this flag sustains that spirit. And it's one of our most powerful ideas. And like all powerful ideas, if it is not defended, it is defamed. To the touch, this flag is merely fabric. But to the heart, the flag represents and reflects the fabric of our nation—our dreams, our destiny—our very fiber as a people.

And when we consider the importance of the colors to this nation, we do not question the right of men to speak freely. For it is this very symbol, with its stripes and stars, that has guaranteed and nurtured those precious rights, for those who've championed the cause of civil rights here at home, to those who fought for democracy abroad.

Free speech is a right that is dear and close to all. It is in defense of that right, and the others enshrined in our Constitution, that so many have sacrificed. But before we accept dishonor to our flag, we must ask ourselves how many have died following the order to "Save the Colors!" We must ask how many have fought for the ideals it represents. And we must honor those who have been handed the folded flag from the casket at Arlington.

If the debate here is about liberty, then we cannot turn our backs on those who fought to win it for us. We can't forget the importance of the flag to the ideals of liberty and honor and freedom. To burn the flag, to dishonor it, is simply wrong. . . .

And what that flag embodies is too sacred to be abused. . . .

This amendment [document 11.6] preserves the widest conceivable range of options for free expression. It applies only to the flag, the unique symbol of our nation. . . .

I've seen predictions that [enacting] this [amendment] will take a long time. It need not. It is simple, to the point, direct; and it addresses itself to only one thing: Our flag will not be desecrated. . . . For the sake of the fallen, for the men behind the guns, for every American, we will defend the flag of the United States of America.

Thank you. God bless this flag. And God bless the United States of America.

Document 11.8

Text of the Flag Protection Act of 1989.

Source: Public Law No. 101-131, U.S. Code 103 Stat. 777 (amending 18 U.S.C. § 700 [document 6.1]).

Be it enacted by the Senate and House of Representatives of the United States of America in Congress assembled,

SECTION 1. SHORT TITLE

This Act may be cited as the "Flag Protection Act of 1989".

SEC. 2. CRIMINAL PENALITES WITH RESPECT TO THE PHYSICAL INTEGRITY OF THE UNITED STATES FLAG

(a) IN GENERAL.—Subsection (a) of section 700 of title 18, United States Code, is amended to read as follows:

"(a)(1) Whoever knowingly mutilates, defaces, physically defiles, burns, maintains on the floor or ground, or tramples upon any flag of the United States shall be fined under this title or imprisoned for not more than one year, or both.

"(2) This subsection does not prohibit any conduct consisting of the disposal of a flag when it has become worn or soiled."

(b) DEFINITION—Section 700(b) of title 18, United State Code, is amended to read as follows:

"(b) As used in this section, the term 'flag of the United States' means any flag of the United States, or any part thereof, made of any substance, of any size, in a form that is commonly displayed."

SEC. 3. EXPEDITED REVIEW OF CONSTITUTIONAL ISSUES

Section 700 of title 18, United States Code, is amended by adding at the end the following:

"(d)(1) An appeal may be taken directly to the Supreme Court of the United States from any interlocutory or final judgment, decree, or order issued by a United States district court ruling upon the constitutionality of subsection (a).

"(2) The Supreme Court shall, if it has not previously ruled on the question, accept jurisdiction over the appeal and advance on the docket and expedite to the greatest extent possible."

Document 11.9

Congressional testimony by Harvard law professor and former solicitor general Charles Fried, urging that no action be taken to seek to override the Supreme Court ruling in *Texas v. Johnson.*

Source: Statutory and Constitutional Responses to the Supreme Court Decision in Texas v. Johnson, *Hearings Before the Subcommittee on Civil and Constitutional Rights of the House Committee on the Judiciary,* 101st Cong., 1st sess., 1989, serial no. 24, 222–60.

Gregory Lee Johnson's burning of the American flag was a vile and distressing act. I do not like coming here to urge you to leave alone the laws and Constitution that say he may not be punished for that act. . . .

I came here from Czechoslovakia, a country with a deep and humane tradition of democratic values, crushed first by the Nazis and then by the

Soviets and their disgusting little puppets. To the Czechs, at least from the days when Woodrow Wilson befriended the nation's first President Thomas Masaryk—America was a model and ideal. So America, its traditions and values and its flag are important to me. Foremost among those values is the principle that no one shall be punished for his political expressions—no matter how offensive or bizarre. That commitment to liberty is our first and greatest contribution to the history of mankind. I would not tamper with it. Though I do not often agree with Justice Brennan, I agree with him entirely that our disdainful tolerance of the likes of Gregory Johnson only honors the flag he sought so ineffectively to dishonor.

Remember how rare and glorious that national commitment of ours is. . . . [J]ust when the French were consolidating their revolution in the bloodbath of the Terror, this new nation chose to affirm itself by adopting the Bill of Rights and the First Amendment. The totalitarian ideas and vocabulary of the Terror have persisted and been invoked by tyrants ever since. Ours is a different tradition. It has brought to this country refugees from two hundred years of tyrannies, tyrannies which have killed and imprisoned people in the name of the honor and dignity of the nation.

I beg you not to tamper with our tradition. [Others] have testified that a statute might be drawn that would pass constitutional muster. . . . I very much hope that no such statute will be passed. I agree with the judgment that whatever the technicalities, the evident purpose of such a statute would still be to punish acts of expression, acts that do no harm except as they express political convictions—mistaken and sordid as those convictions are. . . . But I hope and pray that we will not act—that no statute be passed and of course that the Constitution not be amended. In short, I believe the *Johnson* case is right not just as a matter of present constitutional law. It is right in principle. . . . As for the likes of Gregory Lee Johnson, let us simply turn our backs on him.

Document 11.10

Majority report of the House Judiciary Committee urging passage of legislation rather than a constitutional amendment to overturn the Supreme Court ruling in *Texas v. Johnson.*

Source: U.S. House of Representatives, *Flag Protection Act of 1989,* 101st Cong. 1st sess., Sept. 7, 1989, H. Rept. 101–231, 1–14.

. . . The purpose of H.R. 2978 [the FPA], as amended, is to protect the physical integrity of American flags against burning, mutilation, defacing or trampling upon. The bill responds to the Supreme Court decision in *Texas v. Johnson* by amending the current Federal flag statute to make it content-neutral: that is, the amended statute focuses exclusively on the conduct of the actor, irrespective of any expressive message he or she might be intending to convey. The bill serves the national interest in protecting the physical integrity of all American flags in all circumstances. This interest is "unrelated to the suppression of free expression" [citing *O'Brien*]. . . .

Symbolic speech, or conduct symbolizing a specific message, has received constitutional protection for over half a century [citing *Stromberg*, document 5.1].

However, the Supreme Court has not always struck down government regulation of conduct whenever expressive content was involved. It has separated the regulation of "pure speech" from situations in which the government might have an interest in regulating the conduct apart from the suppression of speech. [In the *O'Brien* case], the Court articulated a test to be applied whenever "speech" and "nonspeech" elements were involved in particular conduct. A government regulation would be upheld only if "⟨1⟩ it is within the constitutional power of the Government, ⟨2⟩ it furthers an important or substantial governmental interest, ⟨3⟩ the governmental interest is unrelated to the suppression of free expression, and ⟨4⟩ the incidental restriction on alleged First Amendment freedoms is no greater than is essential to the furtherance of that interest." The Court found that the prohibition involved furthered the governmental interest, unrelated to expression, of the smooth functioning of the draft, and it therefore upheld the conviction and the applicable regulation. . . .

The Supreme Court's symbolic speech cases therefore stand for the proposition that the government can regulate conduct with speech elements, as long as that regulation is "content-neutral," i.e., the government's purpose was not suppression of free expression. . . .

Texas v. Johnson is the fourth Supreme Court decision since 1969 holding that a flag desecration or misuse statute, as drafted or as applied, infringed on expression. . . . In all of these cases, the Court indicated that it would look differently on a content-neutral statute that would protect the physical integrity of the flag in all circumstances, one that focused solely on conduct and did not turn on the message being conveyed by the flag burner. The purpose of the Flag Protection Act is to conform federal law to these decisions by removing from the existing federal statute, 18 U.S.C. § 700 [document 6.1], any language that is content-specific or that focuses on communication. The purpose of the bill is to protect the physical integrity of American flags in all circumstances, regardless of the motive or political message of any flag burner.

The Supreme Court's decision in *Texas v. Johnson* was a very specific one. The Court held that it is impermissible for a statute to target those people who desecrate a flag in a manner that would give offense to others.

The Court's central concern was that the State of Texas had focused on what Johnson intended to express and how he wanted people to feel upon seeing him do it. . . .

Nothing in *Texas v. Johnson,* or in any other . . . Supreme Court [ruling], renders unconstitutional universal, content-neutral protection for the flag. To the contrary, the Court has indicated that a statute aimed solely at protecting the physical integrity of the flag would pass constitutional muster.

In reaching its conclusion in *Johnson* that the Texas law was aimed at suppressing expression, the Supreme Court stated, "The Texas law [document 10.1] is thus not aimed at protecting the physical integrity of the flag in all circumstances, but is designed instead to protect it only against impairments that would cause serious offense to others." As a footnote to this sentence, the Court favorably cited Justice Blackmun's dissenting opinion in *Smith v. Goguen* [document 8.4], in which Justice Blackmun voted to uphold a conviction for flag desecration because the [Massachusetts] Supreme Court, interpreting the statute, "limited the scope of the statute to protecting the physical integrity of the flag." Justice Blackmun joined the majority in *Texas v. Johnson.* . . .

In response to these cases, the bill amends current federal law to delete the language "casts contempt upon" and the words "publicly" and "defiling." Thus, any conduct resulting in physical harm or damage to the flag, regardless of the actor's intent, is prohibited. With the exception of disposal of worn or soiled flags, the amended statute will prohibit all burning of American flags.

The flag is worthy of protection not because it represents any one idea, and the bill does not seek to protect the flag as the embodiment of any one idea . . . [or] elevate any one view of what the flag represents. Rather, it recognizes the diverse and deeply held feelings of the vast majority of citizens for the flag, and reflects the government's power to honor those sentiments through the protection of a venerated object in the same manner that protection is afforded to gravesites or historic buildings.

The bill includes a specific exception for disposal of worn or soiled flags [because when the flag] is no longer a fitting emblem for display, the governmental interest in protecting its physical integrity no longer applies [and several witnesses expressed concern that without such an exemption the bill would, in the words of one expert] "have the odd result of prosecuting veterans who destroy the flag [in a ceremonial manner] whom we really don't want to prosecute." . . .

The disposal provision [reflects the fact that] flags are ordinarily made of materials that wear out [and thus] a strict prohibition against their destruction would require the maintenance of all flags in perpetuity. . . .

In order to achieve prompt Supreme Court review of the constitutionality of the revised federal flag protection law, the bill includes a provision for expedited review. . . .

This section responds to the reservations expressed by a number of witnesses over the delay and uncertainty that might result from extended litigation to determine the constitutionality of the statute. . . .

The current federal flag protection statute includes a definition of "flag" so broad it covers many things that most people would not think of as a flag. For example, under the current definition, a disposable paper cup or napkin with a flag printed on it is itself a flag. The bill corrects this problem, and the potential for overbreadth, by making it clear that a flag does not include depictions such as photographs of flags on magazine covers or products with flags printed on them. The bill further limits the definition of flag by limiting it to those things that are commonly displayed as flags, excluding, for example, a cake in the shape of a flag. . . .

[B]ecause such decorative representations of flags [including clothing or napkins and paper plates with flag designs] are not actual flags in that they are not commonly displayed as flags and have other uses, the government has no interest in protecting their physical integrity. The revised federal flag protection statute thus avoids the definitions problems of the constitutional amendment, as well as any infirmities of vagueness or overbreadth. . . .

Document 11.11

Congressional testimony of Harvard law professor Laurence Tribe arguing that a statute designed to overturn the Supreme Court ruling in *Texas v. Johnson* would be upheld by the U.S. Supreme Court and therefore a constitutional amendment would be unnecessary.

Source: Statutory and Constitutional Responses to the Supreme Court Decision in Texas v. Johnson, *Hearings Before the Subcommittee on Civil and Constitutional Rights of the House Committee on the Judiciary,* 101st Cong., 1st sess., 1989, serial no. 24, 107–24.

When most Americans gaze at our flag we see not only stars and stripes, we see America itself; we see our unyielding optimism, our unbending patriotism and our undying love of freedom.

When we wish to celebrate our national independence, it is the flag we honor; when we win the race to the moon, it is the flag we raise; when we suffer a great loss as a nation, it is the flag we lower; and when brave American men and women lose their lives fighting for our freedom, it is the American flag with which we drape their coffins—and give to their grieving families. . . .

But I also hope we will remember that there are some patriotic Americans who believe that the toughest but best way to show respect for the flag—to show why we are so different from those who massacre protesters in Beijing—is to protect even the freedom of those so misguided as to desecrate this symbol of our freedom. No American should ever question in any way the love for the flag [of] the five Supreme Court Justices who made up the majority in *Texas v. Johnson.* . . . No American should doubt the patriotism of their fellow Americans who may defend the most absolute protection of freedom of expression. . . .

Today, I have been asked by your Committee to speak on a single matter: is there a way that we can move to protect the American flag without taking the monumental step of amending the Constitution? . . . I have come to believe that we can do so—through a properly drawn national statute. . . .

I hope I can succeed in dispelling what I believe are serious misconceptions about the options available today to Congress and the States—statutory options that may be pursued quickly and effectively, without the delay and difficulty that would inevitably be encountered if Congress were to propose an amendment to the Bill of Rights to deal with flag desecration. . . .

What *Texas v. Johnson* Actually Held

A careful reading of the Supreme Court's opinion in *Texas v. Johnson* makes clear that the Court's holding was a very specific one. By a five-to-four vote, the Court held that it is impermissible for a state prosecution to target those people who desecrate a flag in a manner that would give offense to others.

The Court's central point was that the State of Texas . . . had focused on what Johnson intended to express and how he wanted people to feel upon seeing him do it. It was precisely because the prosecution targeted the message being communicated by Johnson's act of flag desecration that the Free Speech Clause of the First Amendment came into play.

Nothing in *Texas v. Johnson,* or in any other majority opinion of the United States Supreme Court, casts doubt on the constitutionality of blanket protection for the flag. If a law is passed banning certain conduct, no one may violate that law simply to express some opinion, political or otherwise. For example, someone who destroys an historic landmark or a piece of government property may be prosecuted for that conduct, even if it is done as part of some political protest. So if the government simply banned all flag destruction, the ruling in *Texas v. Johnson* would not apply, and the flag destroyer could be punished because the prosecution under such a law would not take aim at the flag destroyer's message. . . .

Once one understands the decision correctly, it becomes clear that there are at least three options that exist under current law for prosecuting conduct of the very kind involved in *Texas v. Johnson.* . . .

Option One: State Breach-of-the-Peace Laws

Every state already has power to punish breaches of the peace, including those that are incited by symbolic or even verbal protest and demonstration. . . . [W]hen flag-desecration is such an incitement, it may be prosecuted as such. . . .

Option Two: Special Laws Against Flag-Desecration in Situations Likely to Provoke Violence

Every state already has authority to enact a criminal statute directed specifically against those assaults upon the flag that are likely to cause an immediate and serious physical disturbance among onlookers. The Supreme Court in *Texas v. Johnson* strongly suggested that it would have upheld such a flag-desecration statute—one "drawn narrowly enough to encompass only those flag-burnings that ⟨are⟩ likely to result in a serious disturbance of the peace." . . .

Option Three: Laws Protecting the Physical Integrity of All American Flags

Finally, and probably most important, both Congress and the States may choose to focus not on the likely reaction of an audience to perceiving an act of flag desecration, or on the expressive motive of the actor who attacks the flag, but on the physical integrity of the flag itself.

This focus would sharply distinguish any such law from the Texas law [document 10.1] whose application the Supreme Court struck down in *Texas v. Johnson.* . . . [T]he Supreme Court emphasized that the Texas law at issue in that case was not aimed at "protecting the physical integrity of the flag in all circumstances" but was designed to protect the flag "only against impairments that would cause serious offense to others." Thus, Texas went astray by punishing Gregory Lee Johnson for the views he publicly expressed in burning the flag, and for the offense that people likely to be present would take at his expression of those views, instead of punishing him for the bare fact that he chose, for whatever reason, . . . to burn that flag—an object that government might decide to protect from violent assault in all circumstances. . . .

There is nothing in the least dubious or questionable, either as a matter of tradition or as a matter of constitutional law, about a governmental decision to protect special places or objects by making their physical mutilation or destruction a crime. . . . It is typically a crime, for example, to desecrate a gravesite. Landmark preservation laws prevent many people from defacing even buildings that they themselves own. . . . Such laws are justifiable not because there is a scarcity of gravesites or of historic landmarks, but because the people, acting through the democratic process, have the right to designate particularly significant things or places as off-limits to physical assault. . . . [S]uch laws are justifiable because a duly elected majority may choose, for its own avowedly emotional reasons, to protect every instance of a particularly valued thing—a thing valued for what it represents and embodies.

The Problem of Disposal

. . . It would seem quite sensible that any statute barring the wanton destruction of particular physical objects would not cover the routine and respectful disposition of those objects when they are no longer usable. Certainly laws against the desecration of corpses do not apply to ordinary burial or cremation, or to medically appropriate forms of autopsy. The same rationale would seem to apply to a law designed to protect the physical integrity of the flag, allowing a flag too worn for use to be disposed of in an orderly way rather than rotting in disrepair. . . .

The presence of exceptions such as these would not suggest that the statute is aimed at the expressive impact, or the implicit message, of the acts it forbids. Such an exception would not represent a government endorsement of any message that the routine or ceremonial disposal of a worn-out flag might convey. The exception would be there simply because the statute's purposes do not require protection of a worn-out flag, any more than the purposes of a law against defacing an historic landmark require protection of the landmark after it has been all but flattened in a hurricane, or any more than the purposes of the law against defiling corpses require banning their ceremonial burial.

The Intangible Values That a Flag Protection Law Could Properly Defend

Nothing in the Constitution says or suggests that the only values we may protect by law are tangible ones. Laws protecting wilderness are justifiable not only because paving the world with cement would choke our species but because every tree may nourish the human spirit. . . . Nothing ever written by the Supreme Court . . . prevents government from showing its concern for matters of the spirit by passing laws to protect the physical integrity of those things that a majority of the people regard as the highest embodiments of that spirit.

Once a law has designated all American flags as objects of this sort, enforcement of that law need raise no First Amendment problem as long as those who are punished are not singled out because of any message they might intend to convey, or their audience might happen to receive, by their destruction or mutilation of an American flag. An exception to First Amendment principles [via a constitutional amendment] is needed only if government wishes to arm itself with the quite extraordinary and entirely distinct power to target for special punishment those flag desecrators whose message is deemed most hateful.

What a Constitutional Amendment Would Add to Existing Authority

. . . It is hard to see what could be a better way of protecting the flag than to pass a simple statute making it a crime to destroy a flag or mutilate it in any way. . . .

The amendment proposed by the Bush Administration [document 11.6], it seems, would add only one thing: the ability to target specifically those people who might destroy or mutilate a flag in public with an intent to cast contempt on it. . . .

Attorney General [Richard] Thornburgh has confirmed this emphasis in [a statement made on July 2, 1989, in which he] made clear that the amendment the Administration seeks is meant to enable Congress and the States to do something quite different from simply protecting the physical integrity of all flags. When [reporter] Sam Donaldson asked the Attorney General whether wearing the flag would count as a form of physical desecration, Mr. Thornburgh replied that it depends "how it's worn, where it's worn, under what circumstances, what the intent is." When [columnist] George Will emphasized that this answer would make a flag-wearer's guilt or innocence depend upon his or her intent, the Attorney General responded without hesitation: "Surely. That's why the constitutional amendment is necessary."

I fail to see the usefulness of all this. Certainly such an approach does not protect the flag as much as the statutory approach . . . which would protect all flags from being wantonly and willfully destroyed wherever they are destroyed and regardless of why. . . . An amendment would indeed be necessary if we wanted to arm the government with a power of censorship over particular messages conveyed by those whose assault upon the flag is perceived to express anti-American sentiment. But I submit that what America stands for would itself be defiled by empowering government to pick and choose among messages in this way. And I stress that no such power is needed if all we want to do is protect all American flags from deliberate destruction . . . regardless of any message that might be intended or conveyed by the act of destruction. . . .

Conclusion

Whatever other views we may hold, surely all can agree that the great effort and risk entailed in amending the Constitution should not be undertaken unless the amendment would make a decisive and constructive difference. We can all agree that the Constitution is too vital to be tampered with unnecessarily, and that respect for the Constitution, no less than for the flag, means that its alteration should always be a last, and never a first, resort. . . .

Why pursue a path that would inevitably take months when one is available that would take only days?

On its 200th birthday, the Bill of Rights deserves a better present than a needless amendment.

Document 11.12

Congressional Research Service report for Congress concerning the FPA.

Source: George Costello, *Statutory Protection of the Flag: Constitutional Issues Raised by HR. 2978* [the proposed FPA, document 11.8], Congressional Research Service rept. 89-480A, Aug. 15, 1989, 15–16.

H.R. 2978, which would impose criminal penalties upon anyone who "knowingly mutilates, defaces, burns, or tramples upon the flag of the United States," differs in significant respects from the Texas flagburning statute [document 10.1] at issue in *Texas v. Johnson.* The Court overturned Johnson's conviction because it was based on application of a statute that openly discriminated against controversial views. By contrast, H.R. 2978 is facially neutral as to expression; it applies regardless of what if any message the defendant was trying to convey by his act of flag destruction.

Dictum in *Johnson* suggests that such a facially neutral statute "aimed at protecting the physical integrity of the flag in all circumstances" might be upheld. . . . Justice Blackmun, who voted with the [5–4] majority in *Johnson,* has previously asserted that "physical integrity" flag laws are constitutional [document 8.4]. . . .

The Court applies a two-track approach in reviewing laws for impermissible curbs on expression. Laws that discriminate on the basis of the content or viewpoint of expression must pass strict or "exacting" scrutiny: they must be "narrowly tailored" to achieve a "compelling" governmental interest. The Texas statute, as applied in the context of Johnson's public demonstration, failed under this test. Content-neutral regulation that has only "incidental" effects upon expression is judged by a less rigorous standard announced in the 1968 draft card burning case, *United States v. O'Brien.* It seems likely, given *Johnson,* that a flag protection statute would be struck down if subjected to strict scrutiny. If, on the other hand, *O'Brien*'s 4-part test can be met, the law could be upheld.

O'Brien's first inquiry is whether there is constitutional authority to

enact the regulation. There is no express constitutional authority to legislate to protect the flag, but the Court in various opinions has assumed the
existence of such a power, and Justice White has explained its possible
sources. More difficult hurdles are posed by *O'Brien*'s second and third
inquiries: whether the regulation furthers an important or substantial governmental interest, and whether that interest is "unrelated to the suppression of free expression." These inquiries place a premium on definition of
the governmental interest. Case law indicates that the Court will disregard
a congressional purpose to suppress expression if there is an alternative
interest (legitimate but not necessarily compelling) that can justify the regulation, and if the regulation applies evenhandedly regardless of expressive
context. However, there is language in *Johnson* concluding that Texas' asserted interest in protecting the flag as a "symbol of nationhood and national unity" was necessarily tied to suppression of expression. Whether
the Court would distinguish *Johnson*, perhaps by defining the interest as
merely protecting the physical integrity of the flag, or perhaps by defining
the interest in terms of protecting the integrity of a government-created
symbol, is unclear. If these tests are met, however, the fourth and final
O'Brien inquiry poses less hindrance. As it has evolved, this test merely
requires that the means employed are appropriately narrow to accomplish
the governmental objective.

Document 11.13

Majority report of the Senate Judiciary Committee opposing enactment of
a constitutional amendment, as opposed to legislation, in an attempt to
override the Supreme Court ruling in *Texas v. Johnson*.

Source: U.S. Senate, *S.J. Res. 180,* 101 Cong., 1st sess., Oct. 6, 1989, S. Rept. 101–
62, 1–19.

. . . In a government of checks and balances, the principal check in the
process of amending the Constitution is the United States Congress. Of the
33 amendments proposed by Congress, 26 have been ratified by the States.
And once an amendment is submitted to the States, it is unalterable: The
States cannot amend, revise, soften, or substitute for a proposed constitutional amendment—they can only vote to ratify or reject it. Two hundred
years of history counsel that in order to satisfy its weighty constitutional
responsibility under article V, Congress must ensure that at least three conditions have been met before it approves an amendment to the Constitution. First, it must ensure that the proposed amendment is necessary.
Second, it must ensure that the meaning of the proposed amendment has
been clearly stated by its proponents and is clearly understood. Third, it
must ensure that the proposed amendment does not suffer from any serious flaws. The extensive hearings before the Judiciary Committee dem-

onstrated that S.J. Res. 180 fails each of these tests. It should not be adopted.

Our Constitution has endured the test of time because, to a large degree, we have marked only its great outlines and have reserved the process of amendment for, in James Madison's words, only "great and extraordinary occasions." . . . In contrast, S.J. Res. 180 asks the Congress to turn to the amendment process as a first—not as a last—resort. This amendment is premature and is not necessary at this time because the physical integrity of the American flag can be protected through legislation. . . . Congress [should] not amend the Constitution in advance of the necessity of amending it. . . .

Even if there were a need to amend the Constitution at this time, S.J. Res. 180 would not be the appropriate vehicle. Four days of extensive hearings demonstrated that the meaning of S.J. Res. 180 is entirely uncertain. . . . There simply is no way of knowing with any degree of certainty whether this proposed amendment creates an exception to one, some, none or all of the Bill of Rights.

Finally, even if S.J. Res. 180 were necessary and even if its meaning were clear, it is so seriously and fundamentally flawed that it would undermine the spirit and structure of the Constitution. Based on the testimony of some of its proponents, this amendment, if adopted, would for the first time in our history give Congress and each State legislature the power and discretion to criminalize conduct if that conduct contains an idea or a message of which the legislature does not approve. The power to censor, in other words, would have constitutional sanction. Furthermore, Congress and the States would have nearly unbounded authority to define "physical desecration." . . .

A. THE CONSTITUTION SHOULD BE AMENDED ONLY AS A LAST RESORT

1. The Constitution should be amended out of necessity, not convenience

Amending the Constitution of the United States is an extraordinarily rare and solemn act. . . .

2. There is no need to proceed with S.J. Res. 180 at this time because a statutory alternative is clearly available

The principle that the amendment process should be invoked as the last—not as the first—resort is perhaps most compelling where, as here, legislation is available to address the matter at hand. . . . [T]here is no need to amend the Constitution at this time. Because the physical integrity of the American flag can be protected through legislation, the legislative route should and must be tried first. . . .

As summarized by Senator [Herbert] Kohl:

> All of us agree that flag burning is reprehensible. We know that flag burners are irresponsible, infantile and irrelevant to the real political discourse of our nation. The question is, how should we respond to this offense? As a citizen, I will continue to denounce those who de-

file the symbol of our collective aspirations. But as a lawmaker, I am reluctant to tamper with the document that has served us so well for 200 years. As long as we have a legislative solution at hand, I cannot endorse an exception to the Bill of Rights.

3. S.J. Res. 180 carries a particularly heavy burden of necessity because it would qualify the liberties embodied in the first amendment

There is great risk that S.J. Res. 180 would qualify in some measure the freedoms embodied in the first amendment. . . .

Senator [Edward] Kennedy, for example, succinctly stated that "⟨t⟩he concept of free and open debate, at the heart of our democracy, will be an empty promise if the Government can censor those who criticize it." . . .

B. THE CONSTITUTION SHOULD NOT BE AMENDED WHEN THE MEANING OF THE PROPOSED AMENDMENT IS ENTIRELY UNCERTAIN

Throughout the . . . hearings before the Judiciary Committee, one theme emerged from the testimony of supporters and opponents of a constitutional amendment: The meaning of S.J. Res. 180 is entirely uncertain, and its text leaves entirely unanswered the critical question of which, if any, of the Bill of Rights it will override. As currently worded, the proposed amendment is so ambiguous that either it adds nothing to the Constitution and, in the words of one supporter of a constitutional amendment, "would do nothing to alter the constitutional landscape carved out by the Court" in *Texas v. Johnson,* or it trumps the entire Constitution and confers an unprecedented degree of legislative power and authority. As summarized by Professor [Walter] Dellinger, S.J. Res. 180 "would create an entirely undefined exception to either one, some, none or all of the Bill of Rights."

1. S.J. Res. 180 might do nothing to reverse *Texas v. Johnson*

According to a witness who testified in support of a constitutional amendment, as well as witnesses who testified against it, S.J. Res. 180 will not reverse *Texas v. Johnson* and thus will not accomplish what its proponents say it will accomplish. The text of S.J. Res. 180 simply makes explicit the power of Congress and the states to legislate with respect to the flag—a power that has always been assumed to exist and does not in any way exempt the exercise of that power from the first amendment. Thus, any legislation enacted pursuant to the proposed amendment would still have to satisfy the first amendment and the principles of law articulated by the Court in *Texas v. Johnson.* . . .

2. S.J. Res. 180 might override the entire Constitution

Thus, unless S.J. Res. 180 is understood to override the first amendment, it adds nothing to the Constitution. If it is understood to override the first amendment, however, it might also be understood to override other provisions of the Bill of Rights. After all, nothing in the text of this particular proposed amendment draws any distinction between the application of the first amendment and the application of other provisions in the Constitution.

The implications of such an open-ended and ambiguous amendment are entirely unknown. Professor Dellinger put it well when he said:

> [I]f it does override provisions of the Bill of Rights, which provisions does it override? * * * Could a state, for example, in some time of great strife in the twenty-first century, punish flag desecration without having to meet the standards of the Cruel and Unusual Punishments Clause? Could a state, in a future not yet clear to us, dispense with jury trials for flag desecrators? Could a particularly zealous local government ignore the Fourth Amendment and conduct general house-to-house warrantless searches looking for evidence of desecration?

The scope of the power that this proposed amendment confers upon Congress and the states simply cannot be ascertained—all that can be said with confidence is that it is power of uncertain scope. To submit such an amendment to the states would be an abdication of congressional responsibility.

3. An amendment of such uncertain scope would generate and stimulate litigation

Some might argue that the proposed amendment would be construed as occupying a middle position between having no impact on the Constitution and trumping the Constitution in its entirety. . . . Even if read in that fashion, however, that middle ground is yet another unknown commodity and could be identified only by a series of lawsuits and years of litigation. Thus, even putting the best interpretive light on S.J. Res. 180, it remains seriously flawed because it would stimulate a generation of litigation. . . .

C. S.J. RES. 180 IS SERIOUSLY AND FUNDAMENTALLY FLAWED

. . . [T]here is no need to proceed with S.J. Res. 180 at this time because a statutory alternative is clearly available. Furthermore, the meaning of S.J. Res. 180 is entirely uncertain. Even if a showing of need could be demonstrated and even if the meaning of S.J. Res. 180 were clear, however, there are serious and fundamental problems with the proposed amendment that warrant opposition to its adoption. . . .

The testimony throughout the 4 days of hearings demonstrated that, in the end, S.J. Res. 180 is "little more than a blank check authorizing unspecified withdrawals and withdrawals of an unspecified amount from America's most precious heritage, the Bill of Rights." (Testimony of Laurence H. Tribe)

1. S.J. Res. 180 would give legislatures broad power and discretion to censor conduct judged to be offensive

The proposed constitutional amendment would give Congress and each State legislature the power and discretion to criminalize conduct if that conduct contains an idea or a message that the legislature, in the words of Assistant Attorney General Barr, finds "really offensive." It would mean, as concisely summarized by Senator Kennedy, that "⟨f⟩or the first time in 200 years, an amendment would be enacted that creates an exception to the guarantee of freedom of speech protected by the Constitution."

There is little doubt that S.J. Res. 180 would cede broad latitude and discretion to legislative bodies. Indeed, the proponents of the proposed amendment concede as much and argue that this latitude and discretion to define "offensive" conduct are among the proposed amendment's most appealing features.

For example, Assistant Attorney General Barr testified that Congress and the states would have "wide latitude to prohibit that conduct toward the flag that they believe deserved proscription." . . . To Assistant Attorney General Barr, "offering legislatures the option of prohibiting only intentionally contemptuous physical desecration" is a "significant advantage of the amendment over the statute." . . .

What emerged from the testimony of Assistant Attorney General Barr and other proponents of S.J. Res. 180 is that neither a "neutral" statute nor a "neutral" amendment is desirable or sufficient. In their view, a statute or an amendment that prohibits destruction of the flag in all circumstances and does not give legislatures the power and discretion to define what they consider to be "contemptuous" and, in Assistant Attorney General Barr's words, what they determine to be "really offensive" simply does not go far enough. . . .

We should not celebrate the 200th anniversary of the adoption of the Bill of Rights with an amendment to the Constitution that would, for the first time in our history, qualify the freedoms embodied in the first amendment.

2. S.J. Res. 180 would give legislatures nearly unbounded authority to define "physical desecration"

. . . [I]t is clear that legislatures would have nearly unbounded authority to decide what constitutes "physical desecration." In addition, the scope of what constitutes "physical desecration" would likely vary widely from state to state.

The problems with using the term "physical desecration" are perhaps no better illustrated than by the preamble of S.J. Res. 180, which states:

> Whereas physical description may include, *but is not limited to,* such acts as burning, mutilating, defacing, defiling or trampling on the Flag, or *displaying the Flag in a contemptuous manner* * * * (Emphasis added). . . .

Assistant Attorney General Barr said [document 11.14] that "⟨s⟩ome contact with the Flag, some physical touching of the Flag, whether by the person himself or caused by the person would be essential" [but he also] said that "legislatures could constitutionally prohibit the display of the Flag in a *manner* that they deemed inappropriate. * * * Thus, they could prohibit, for example, the display of the Flag on the floor or the upside-down display of the Flag" (emphasis in original)—situations that might not involve some "physical touching."

Thus, the proposed amendment would grant every legislature nearly unlimited authority to decide what, in the particular legislature's view, constituted "physical desecration."

Former [s]enator Mathias was troubled as well by the term "physical desecration," as he noted that "you could end up with a patchwork of State laws which as you cross State lines, you would have different criminal liabilities for particular acts with relation to the flag.". . . More specifically, Professor Dellinger commented that S.J. Res. 180

> creates the possibility that there will be a wide array of different legislative interpretations of what constitutes "physical desecration," * * * Some States may assume that placing a flag on a pair of boots, similar to those the President gave to a leader of China, constitutes "physical desecration," of the flag. * * * Some may assume that an artist's rendering of "the flag" in green, white and orange constitutes "physical desecration;" others may conclude to the contrary. . . .

Document 11.14

Congressional testimony by Bush administration assistant attorney general William Barr urging passage of a constitutional amendment to overturn the Supreme Court ruling in *Texas v. Johnson.*

Source: Statutory and Constitutional Responses to the Supreme Court Decision in Texas v. Johnson, *Hearings Before the Subcommittee on Civil and Constitutional Rights of the House Committee on the Judiciary,* 101st Cong., 1st sess., 1989, serial no. 24, 172–91.

. . . [A] constitutional amendment is the only way to protect the Flag in the wake of the Court's expansive decision. An amendment is the only way to adequately respond to the overwhelming—and understandable—sentiment of the American people that the Flag must be protected. . . . As the symbol of our Nation, the Flag is the embodiment of our commitment to freedom. It stands in sacred honor of those who have sacrificed their lives in defense of that freedom. It holds in sacred trust the spirit of the American people.

Given the deserved reverence accorded the Flag, it is not at all surprising that the American people reacted with outrage when they were told that this Flag can be burned, shredded and spat upon with impunity. . . .

The President shares the profound sense of personal violation felt by the American people. He firmly believes that we have an obligation to the people to act swiftly and decisively to protect the Flag from those who would break our spirit through desecration of this one symbol that unites us. . . .

I INTRODUCTION

The issue that has occupied the lion's share of the Subcommittee's time thus far is not whether to provide protection for the Flag, but how to provide that protection. . . . You have my assurance that the President and the Attorney General would be the first to support a statute if they thought a statute could survive constitutional challenge and protect the Flag from desecration. Unfortunately, we are convinced that, in light of the expansive decision of the Court, a statute simply would not suffice. . . .

The reason that a statute purporting to protect the Flag would be unconstitutional is simple. In *Texas v. Johnson,* the Court held that whenever someone burns the Flag for expressive purposes, that conduct is protected by the First Amendment; that to prohibit such conduct, the Government must have a compelling reason that is unrelated to expression; that the Government's reason for protecting the Flag (to preserve it as a symbol of national unity) is inherently and necessarily related to expression; and that the Government interest in protecting the symbol of our national unity can never be sufficiently compelling to overcome an individual's First Amendment interest in burning the Flag for communicative purposes. This reasoning plainly would extend to any Flag desecration statute enacted to protect the Flag as a symbol of our Nation.

II ANALYSIS OF *TEXAS v. JOHNSON*

. . . The Court has repeatedly held that the First Amendment extends to symbolic speech where the conduct was intended to convey a message and the likelihood was great that the message conveyed would be understood [citing *Spence*, document 8.3]. Where the Government attempts to prohibit, punish or otherwise burden communicative conduct, the Court carefully analyzes the Government's interest in imposing the burden. If the Government's interest is unrelated to suppression of expression, the regulation is subjected to the comparatively more lenient standard set forth in the Court's opinion in *United States v. O'Brien.* Under that standard, the Government's interest must only be important or substantial to justify the regulation. If, on the other hand, the Government's interest is related to suppression of expression, the regulation is subjected to the most exacting scrutiny [citing *Johnson*]. Under this standard, the Government's interest must be compelling. . . .

[In *Johnson*] the Court held that the government can never assume that Flag burning will cause a breach of the peace. Moreover, said the Court, Johnson's burning of the Flag as a "generalized expression of dissatisfaction with the policies of the Federal Government" was not the equivalent of "fighting words" that could cause a breach of the peace because "⟨n⟩o reasonable onlooker" would regard it as insult or an invitation to exchange fisticuffs."

The Court held that Texas' interest in preserving the Flag as a symbol of our Nation and national unity could not justify its prohibition on Flag burning. . . . Any attempt to preserve the Flag as a symbol offends the "bedrock principle" that "the Government may not prohibit the expression of an idea simply because society finds the idea itself offensive or disagreeable." Finally, the Court explicitly refused the Flag any special constitutional significance, finding "no indication—either in the text of the Constitution or in ⟨its⟩ cases interpreting it that a separate juridical category exists for the American flag alone."

III. CONSTITUTIONALITY OF FLAG DESECRATION STATUTES AFTER *TEXAS v. JOHNSON*

We think it is plain under this reasoning that any statute prohibiting desecration of the Flag for communicative purposes would be unconstitutional. The Flag is by nature communicative. . . . Thus, the Government's interest in preserving the Flag as a symbol is inherently related to expression. It is precisely because the Flag is the symbol of this Nation that the Government wants it protected against conduct that will undermine its communicative force. . . . Accordingly, any Flag desecration statute will be subject to the most exacting scrutiny.

The Court has held that under this exacting scrutiny the Government's interest in preserving the symbolic value of the Flag can never be sufficiently compelling to stop an individual from desecrating the Flag whenever the desecration is done for communicative purposes.

An asserted interest in preventing breaches of the peace would not save the statute because the Court also held that the Government may never assume that Flag burning or other Flag desecration will cause a breach of the peace. . . . The Court's categorical rejection on these grounds of the only two conceivable interests for prohibiting the desecration of the Flag renders it certain that the Court would strike down any such statute.

It has been argued that the Court would uphold a statute if it prohibited all Flag desecration, whether in public or private, and whether done with contempt or not. This argument is demonstrably wrong because it assumes that the Government's reason for enacting a facially neutral prohibition (that is, a statute neutral as to the particular viewpoint expressed) would be unrelated to expression. It would not be. The Government's reason for passing a viewpoint neutral prohibition would be the same as its reason for passing a prohibition on contemptuous desecration only: protection of the symbolic value of the Flag. The Supreme Court has held in two successive cases, *Spence v. Washington* and *Texas v. Johnson,* that it is the Government's reason for the prohibition, not the scope of the prohibition, that determines the level of scrutiny. Because the Government's reason for protecting the Flag is necessarily related to expression, the prohibition would always be subjected to exacting scrutiny, and therefore would never prevail over an individual's First Amendment interest in expressive conduct. . . .

The Supreme Court in *Texas v. Johnson* has now held that the Government's interest in protecting the Flag as a national symbol is, by definition, related to the suppression of free expression. Thus, it simply could never be successfully maintained that such a statute was content neutral. . . . .

Because any statute would necessarily relate to expression, the more relaxed standard of *O'Brien* would never apply, and the statute would always be subject to the "most exacting scrutiny." The Supreme Court . . . has now unequivocally held, however, that the government's interest in protection of the symbolic value of the Flag will never support a prohibition on the communicative desecration of the Flag under this heightened standard.

In the face of the Court's holdings in *Texas v. Johnson* and *Spence v. Washington,* and especially given the sweeping reasoning in those cases, it cannot be seriously maintained that a statute aimed at protecting the Flag would be constitutional. . . .

IV PROPOSED CONSTITUTIONAL AMENDMENT

. . . The first, and perhaps most important, point to be made is that the amendment [supported by President Bush, document 11.6] does not itself prohibit Flag desecration. The amendment merely empowers Congress and the states to prohibit legislatively the physical desecration of the Flag. . . .

If Congress and the States chose to legislate, as we anticipate they would, they would . . . have to determine how they wished to define Flag and physical desecration of the Flag. . . .

There would be any number of options that would be permissible under the amendment. . . .

[One option would be to] define Flag as it is defined in the existing federal Flag desecration statute [document 6.1, which] definition includes any Flag, portion of a Flag, or any picture or representation of a Flag. It would allow the legislatures to protect depictions of the Flag, such as posters, murals, pictures, buttons, and any other representation of the Flag. This definition would be consistent with the Government's interest in preserving the Flag's symbolic value because it recognizes that the desecra-

tion of representations of the Flag damage that interest as much as desecration of the Flag itself. I would note that even the legislative proposals
proffered to redress the Court's decision would retain this definition of
Flag. . . .

We believe the phrase "physical desecration," too, would provide
some latitude to Congress and the States, although the amendment . . .
would not permit Congress or the states to punish or penalize any non-
physical desecration of the Flag. Some contact with the Flag, some physical
touching . . . would be essential. The legislatures thus could not punish or
penalize mere words or gestures directed at the Flag, regardless of their
offensiveness. . . .

But obviously, the legislatures could clearly prohibit the burning,
shredding and similar defilement of the Flag.

I would note, however, that we do not understand that the legislatures
could ever prohibit the proper display of the Flag merely because they
believe the particular surroundings of the display are unfitting for the
Flag. . . . Of course, the legislatures could constitutionally prohibit the
display of the Flag in a *manner* that they deemed inappropriate because
such proscriptions would not require value judgments about who could
display the Flag or where it could be displayed. Thus, they could prohibit,
for example, the display of the Flag on the floor or the upside down display of the Flag. . . .

The third area in which Congress and the States will have to draw
lines relates to the actor's state of mind. The amendment only authorizes
prohibition of voluntary actions; involuntary acts such as accidents could
not be punished. The more difficult issue is whether the actor must intend
to be contemptuous toward the Flag. We believe Congress and the States
are, and should be, free to decide whether to require intent. We suspect
that they will choose to require that the actor intend to cast contempt.
Because the overwhelming number of physical acts that are of concern to
us are intended to express contempt for the Flag, we would not be especially troubled were they to choose to require intent. . . .

We think offering legislatures the option of prohibiting only intentionally contemptuous, physical desecration represents a significant advantage of the amendment over the proposed statute. Presumably to convince
the court that its proscriptions are unrelated to expression, the proposed
statute [document 11.8] would require that the Government prohibit acts
without regard to whether they cast contempt. Thus, a child who inno-
cently steps on a Flag, a person who crumbles a Fourth of July Flag-deco-
rated paper cup, or a veteran who burns an old Flag out of reverence and
respect would all presumably be prosecutable under the proposed statute.
[W]e do not believe that most people want to prohibit [such] actions, [and]
we believe that Congress and the States should be free to make that deter-

mination as they see fit, to create the exceptions that logic and reason compel. . . .

The proposed statute not only prohibits much conduct that no one wishes to prohibit; ultimately it would not constitutionally prohibit the very acts that we wish to prohibit. . . .

Document 11.15

Supplemental views of eight Republican members of the House Judiciary Committee, urging passage of a constitutional amendment to overturn the Supreme Court ruling in *Texas v. Johnson.*

Source: Flag Protection Act of 1989, 101st Cong., 1st sess., Sept. 7, 1989, H. Rept. 101–231, 21–23.

. . . The [HJC] Subcommittee [on Civil and Constitutional Rights] held four days of hearings (July 13, 18, 19, and 20, 1989) at which a majority of those who testified agreed that no statute could be drafted which would be sufficient to overturn *Texas v. Johnson.* . . .

Our vote in favor of H.R. 2978 [the FPA, document 11.8] was simply a vote to protect the flag. By supporting the Chairman's effort to push what is undoubtedly an unconstitutional attempt to overturn *Texas v. Johnson* by statute, we look forward to soon having an opportunity to vote on a constitutional amendment which will prevent future desecration of the flag. . . .

[T]here are several serious defects in the bill. By removing the words "cast contempt upon", "publicly" and "defiling" [from the 1968 federal Flag Desecration Law, document 6.1], the current bill has been gutted of its whole purpose. All express reference to "desecrate" has been removed. To be truly neutral as to viewpoint, the statute has to prohibit even patriotic acts. For example, a movie producer who made a glorious movie about this nation that included scenes from military battles in which the flag was hit by musket fire would be subject to criminal prosecution. A mother, who mourns the loss of her son in battle and pins on the flag the medals he had earned, would also be subject to criminal prosecution.

The exception from prosecution for any conduct consisting of the disposal of a soiled and worn flag allows any flag protestor to, first, dirty the flag in whatever manner it sees fit and, then, burn or mutilate the flag in protest against the United States. This "dirty flag defense" is an absolute defense for any political protestor who feels the need to torch "Old Glory". In an attempt to protect those who reverently dispose of the flag, such as veterans groups, the unfortunate result is that we are, in fact, protecting those acts which we most particularly want to prohibit, i.e., burning or destroying the flag in disrespect.

Narrowing the definition of the flag to forms commonly displayed, this bill would not prohibit such contemptuous conduct as painting a wall-sized mural or billboard of the flag with a swastika superimposed on it. Such conduct certainly impairs the symbolic value of the flag as much as destruction of the flag itself. Finally, the addition of the expedited review process suggests that someone once again desecrate a flag so we can once again ask the Supreme Court whether it's acceptable to burn the flag in protest, just to hear the Supreme Court say it has already answered the question. To encourage the same activity we seek to outlaw is indeed an absurd result. It is far better to undertake a procedure we are confident will succeed than to attempt to place a bandaid on something when amputation is the answer.

Why are we so reluctant to amend the Constitution to demand that flag desecration be prohibited? Is it too much to ask that those who consider themselves Americans be required to have respect for the flag? In this day and age, when it seem that perversion is accepted and morality a taboo religion, perhaps this small mandate for freedom is not asking too much! . . .

Document 11.16

President Bush's press conference, October 13, 1989, announcing his intention to let the Flag Protection Act (document 11.8) become law without his signature.

Source: Weekly Compilation of Presidential Documents 5, no. 41 (Oct. 16, 1989): 1539, 1543.

I believe that the American flag is a unique and special symbol of our nation and it should be protected from desecration. And our administration has proposed a constitutional amendment to protect the flag [document 11.6] because we believe that is the most lasting and legally correct means of protection—a constitutional amendment. And yesterday the House of Representatives agreed to a Senate bill providing statutory protection for the flag. And when this measure comes to the House, I will allow the bill to become law, but without my signature. And I'm withholding that signature to signal our belief that a constitutional amendment is the best way to provide lasting protection for the flag.

Now, we will continue to work for such an amendment. And I can understand the rationale of those who voted for this legislation. But in my view, it is not the ultimate answer, and therefore, I will not put my signature on the legislation. . . .

Q. Mr. President, during the campaign, Michael Dukakis was ridiculed partly by members of your campaign for vetoing a bill mandating teachers say the Pledge of Allegiance during school classes.

The President. Yes, I remember it.

Q. Are you politically afraid, sir, to veto the flag statute if you truly believe it's the wrong way to go?

The President. No. I think it's an overwhelming expression on the part of the Congress to do something about the protection of the flag. So, I'm not going to veto it. But I don't think it's enough. So, I'm saying I'm not going to sign it. And that's a symbol that I don't think it's enough. But I don't want to set the clock way back and rule out the legislation, even though I don't think it's enough. I don't see a parallel [to the Pledge of Allegiance issue] at all. Although I read an argument that was thrown out there on that. I don't agree with it.

Document 11.17

White House statement by President Bush, October 26, 1989, explaining his decision to let the Flag Protection Act [document 11.8] become law without his signature.

Source: Weekly Compilation of Presidential Documents 2, no. 42, Oct. 30, 1989, 1619.

On June 21, 1989, the Supreme Court in *Texas v. Johnson* held unconstitutional a Texas statute prohibiting flag desecration. The Court reasoned that, under the principles of the First Amendment, a State could punish a person who desecrates the flag to communicate a message only if the State had a compelling reason to do so. The Court held that the Government's interest in preserving the symbolic value of the flag is not compelling.

After a careful study of the Court's opinion, the Department of Justice concluded that the only way to ensure protection of the flag is through a constitutional amendment. Pursuant to that advice, I urged the adoption of such an amendment [document 11.6].

After several months of debate about how best to protect the flag from desecration, the Congress has forwarded to me H.R. 2978. The bill provides for a prison term of up to 1 year for anyone who "knowingly mutilates, defaces, physically defiles, burns, maintains on the floor or ground, or tramples upon" any United States flag.

While I commend the intentions of those who voted for this bill, I have serious doubts that it can withstand Supreme Court review. The Supreme Court has held that the Government's interest in preserving the flag as a symbol can never be compelling enough to justify prohibiting flag desecration that is intended to express a message. Since that is precisely the target of this bill's prohibition, I suspect that any subsequent court challenge will reach a similar conclusion.

Nevertheless, because this bill is intended to achieve our mutual goal of protecting our Nation's greatest symbol, and its constitutionality must ultimately be decided by the courts, I have decided to allow it to become law without my signature. I remain convinced, however, that a constitutional amendment is the only way to ensure that our flag is protected from desecration.

Document 11.18

Article by Helen Dewar and Tom Kenworthy, "Support Lags for Amendment to Prohibit Flag Burning," *Washington Post,* July 25, 1989. Reprinted by permission of the *Washington Post,* (copyright 1989, The Washington Post.

In the first few days after the Supreme Court threw out a Texas law prohibiting flag burning, Sen. Nancy Landon Kassebaum (R., Kan.) received 224 pages of petitions from Kansas calling for a constitutional amendment to reverse the court ruling.

But now 60 percent of her mail is running against amending the Constitution, and Kassebaum, who supports a flag amendment, is taking heat for her stand. Much of the pressure is coming from young people, including her four children. Students have asked why the United States should tamper with its Bill of Rights when young people in China are risking their live for those same freedoms, she said.

Rep. Ben Jones (D., Ga.) has found a similar shift in opinion over the past month among his constituents. "Immediately after the decision there was a lot of heat and anger," he said. "Now it's shifted, the issue has cooled and people are more thoughtful * * * People are becoming more reflective about whether they want to alter the Constitution in response to this kind of stupidity."

While pressure is still strong in Congress to amend the Constitution to allow the states and federal government to pass laws outlawing desecration of the American flag, more lawmakers report second thoughts among their constituents about the wisdom of an amendment. . . .

Some say support for an amendment is still strong in their states or districts. . . . But most of nearly 20 lawmakers and congressional aides interviewed on the issue said their constituents want the flag protected but do not differentiate between an amendment, which Bush supports, and a law, which is being pushed as an alternative by most Democratic congressional leaders. Many also said that flag-related calls and letters are trailing off and support for an amendment is dwindling.

From conservative Oklahoma, Democratic Sen. David L. Boren has gotten no more than 500 letters and calls on the flag issue, a fraction of the 10,000 communications he received on the congressional pay raise issue earlier this year, according to Boren's office. Initial demands for impeachment of the justices who voted against the Texas law have given way to reservations about an amendment, a Boren aide said.

Sen. Bob Kerrey (D., Neb.), the Congressional Medal of Honor winner who spoke out last week against a flag amendment [document 11.24], got a positive response from back home even though early polls there showed strong support for an amendment. "It looks like a hot political issue, but it isn't," he said.

In part because of fear of political repercussions, members of Congress "got out ahead of the people" on this issue, said Senate Judiciary Committee Chairman Joseph R Biden Jr. (D., Del.).

"People are conservative about the Constitution," Biden added. "They don't like mucking around with it. People are a lot more reluctant to tamper with the Constitution than Congress is."

In a survey conducted July 14–16 by KRC Communication Research and published last week in the *Boston Globe* and several other newspapers, Americans said by a margin of 51-to-31 percent that they would rather seek to protect the flag through legislation than a constitutional amendment.

The preference for a law was expressed by Republicans as well as Democrats and by people from all regions of the country, including the Midwest and South, where the flag is generally believed to have particularly strong political resonance. . . .

But Senate Minority Leader Robert J. Dole (R., Kan.), who is spearheading the push for an amendment in the Senate, discounts suggestions that it is a 24 hour issue, that emotions have now cooled.

And, regardless of the mixed signals from voters now, the angst level is high among Democrats who are still smarting over the way Bush capitalized successfully on the veto of a Pledge of Allegiance bill by Massachusetts Gov. Michael S. Dukakis to raise questions about Dukakis's priories and patriotism in last year's presidential campaign.

With Bush and congressional Republican leaders backing a flag amendment, many Democrats expect their GOP opponents in the next election to pounce on a vote against the amendment as a sign of a lack of patriotism. They see themselves as "potential victims of political demagoguery," said one Democratic senator who has said he will probably vote for both the legislation and the constitutional amendment. . . .

Document 11.19

Hendrik Hertzberg column, "Flagellation," and "Bushwaterism" editorial, 4–5, from the July 17, 1989, *New Republic*. Reprinted by permission of *The New Republic,* copyright 1989, The New Republic Inc.

Flagellation

Many a bum show has been saved by the flag. George M. Cohan

Amid the current hysteria an important ontological point has been overlooked: you can't burn the flag. It can't be done. A flag, yes. The flag, no. The flag, the American flag, is an abstraction—a certain arrangement of stars, stripes, and colors that exists (a) in the realm of Platonic ideals and (b) in the minds and hearts of people. . . . A flag, any particular flag, is merely a copy. You can no more destroy the flag by burning a flag than you can destroy the Constitution by burning a copy of the Constitution.

The flag, as long as it exists in human hearts, is fireproof. The Constitution, however, is more vulnerable. It can be desecrated quite effectively by amending it in ways foreign to its spirit and hostile to its purposes. Members of Congress rushed to do just that in the wake of *Texas v. Johnson*. George Bush, in the first truly sickening act of demagoguery of his young presidency, has now put the impetus of his support behind them.

Have you read the actual Texas statute the Supreme Court ruled on [document 10.1]? . . . What's surprising is not that this bit of legislative flotsam was struck down, but that four of the nine justices deemed it consistent with the First Amendment.

All the opinions in this case are notable for their passion. The dissenters' passion is reserved mostly for the flag, the majority's mostly for the Constitution. The dissenters venerate the symbol; the majority venerates the thing symbolized. Both have emotion on their sides, but the majority has logic, too.

Chief Justice Rehnquist [documents 10.14] devotes many pages to explicating the special meaning of the flag. His dissent is studded with verse: four lines of Emerson's "Concord Hymn," the opening stanza of "The Star Spangled Banner," two full pages of "Barbara Frietchie." He succeeds beautifully in making the point that the flag is a powerful symbol of a particular set of sentiments and ideas. . . . If flying the flag is symbolic speech, so is burning one; and speech, in this country, is supposed to be free.

Rehnquist argues that we outlaw "conduct that is regarded as evil and profoundly offensive to the majority of people whether it be murder, embezzlement, pollution, or flag burning." We don't, however, outlaw murder, embezzlement, and pollution because they're offensive. We outlaw them because they inflict palpable harm on actual people. Flag burning merely offends, and it offends by what it says.

When the decision came down, I allowed myself to hope it would be the occasion for nothing worse than a harmless festival of hokum calculated to bring pleasure to the shades of Mencken and Sinclair Lewis. And that's how it was, the first day.

The inimitable [Senate Republican leader] Bob Dole rushed a wild, all-caps statement up to the Senate press gallery [which declared]:

PEOPLE [WHO] HATE THE FLAG . . . OUGHT TO LEAVE THE COUNTRY. . . . IF THEY DON'T LIKE OUR FLAG, GO FIND ONE YOU DO LIKE.

. . . The show got ugly the next day, when the texts of proposed amendments started filling the hoppers. . . .

President Bush's role in all this is unusually contemptible. His first reaction was to say that while he regards flag burning as "dead wrong," he could understand why the Court decided as it did. That was the reasonable, moderate fellow one stupidly keeps hoping is the "real Bush." After a day's reflection—and lunch with [Republican national chairman] Lee Atwater—Bush decided that "the importance of this issue compels me to call for a constitutional amendment."

If Bush has his way, the Bill of Rights will be amended for the first time in American history and for what? Because of what danger? Flag burning is extremely rare, and, though offensive, essentially harmless. It has no "importance." . . . So what's going on?

The mystery vanishes when one recalls Bush's use last fall of the Pledge of Allegiance "issue." Now, if he has his way, the same cynical manipulation of patriotic symbols, as perfected by political consultants, is to be enshrined in the Constitution. Negative campaigning is to be raised to the level of a civic sacrament. The desecration of the flag, which is not a problem, is to be made the pretext for the desecration of what the flag represents. For George Bush, nice guy, the defilement of the Bill of Rights itself is just another tactic for narrow partisan gain. And it's hard to see, at this point, who's going to stop him.

BUSHWATERISM

What would it take to shame Lee Atwater into a few consecutive weeks of decency? . . . On June 26 President Bush had lunch with Atwater. Within hours the White House announced that Bush would try to "circumvent" the Supreme Court's recent ruling that burning the American flag is protected as an exercise of free speech. The next day the weapon of choice was announced: a constitutional amendment to ban flag burning. The intent is obviously to turn up the heat under any Democrats in Congress who have an expansive conception of civil liberties, to make them squirm, to show the voters that they're not patriots.

Are we reading too much into this? Is it possible that Atwater didn't strongly advocate this tack? (He claims he didn't.) . . . But even if Atwater were entirely uninvolved in this latest hijacking of the flag, it would still be his legacy. He more than anyone else except Bush himself was responsible for turning patriotism into a partisan issue during the presidential campaign; he is the one who recommended that Bush get optimal mileage out of Michael Dukakis's veto of a state law making the Pledge of Allegiance mandatory in public schools.

The parallels between that case and the present one are exact: some Democrats have taken a principled constitutional stand that may strike coarse minds as unpatriotic, and Bush and Atwater are trying to paint them as traitors. . . .

[W]e can call [these tactics] "Atwaterism" and define it as McCarthyism minus the outright lies. Or, better yet: "Bushwaterism." After all, the buck stops with Bush. . . .

We have Bushwaterism to thank for the Senate's cowardly 97–3 expression of "profound disappointment" [document 11.2] in the Supreme Court's insistence that the Constitution protects even the most offensive forms of political expression. . . .

[W]ith every Chinese who is shot for having briefly reveled in freedom, we are all the more proud to live in a nation where the most vehement imaginable denunciation of the government cannot lead to a single day in prison. (Speaking of China: it is worth noting that some of the conservative commentators who lately have been insisting that only verbal utterances qualify as "speech" were only weeks ago embracing the Goddess of Democracy erected in Tiananmen Square as a symbol that speaks volumes about the aspirations of the Chinese people.) The same legislators who now profess to want an amendment banning flag burning are meanwhile insisting (correctly, we believe) on tougher sanction against China— an example of the grotesque contradictions that Bushwaterism fosters. Give Bush credit, at least, for consistency: at the same time that he is playing footsie with a repressive regime in China, he is trying to make America a bit less free.

Document 11.20

Editorials in the *Seattle Times*, June 28, 1989, and October 14, 1989. Reprinted with permission of the *Seattle Times*.

[June 28, 1989] President Bush is at it again, wearing patriotism on his sleeve in a way that provokes a Capitol Hill flagwaving contest to see who among our political leaders loves the country more. The performance evokes memories of last year's campaign when candidate Bush visited a flag factory to recite the Pledge of Allegiance and question Gov. Michael Dukakis' patriotism. . . . House Democrats, fearful of attacks on their patriotism, have lined up in support of a resolution proclaiming the sacredness of Old Glory. Then Bush outdid everybody by advocating a constitutional amendment to undo the court decision. . . . For 200 years, the First Amendment has weathered all attacks by, among others, cynical politicians and survived with glory. May it continue to do so.

[October 14, 1989] Into a nation plagued by inadequate housing, rampant drug abuse, a mammoth federal budget deficit and the growing specter of AIDS, those wonderful folks in Washington, D.C. have introduced a flag law [the FPA, document 11.8]. . . . President Bush will allow the measure to become law without his signature . . . because he would prefer a constitutional amendment against being mean to flags. No one will be fed or housed because of this law. Nothing will be done to clean the environment, force better government or address even one of the pressing national concerns that truly affect people's lives. The flag is an important symbol. But it's important only in the hearts and minds of those who believe in what the flag symbolizes. That belief can't be harmed by someone who disrespects the painted cloth that symbolizes American democracy. And jail time and fines won't make flag-muggers any more patriotic or respectful. The real desecration of democracy occurs when people don't have places to live or work or adequate health insurance. . . . Those kind of issues don't seem to play well in the nation's capital. Maybe it's because they require real statecraft and that's in a lot shorter supply than the hype and rhetoric that's been conjured up around a non-issue like flag burning.

Document 11.21

Editorial in the *Philadelphia Inquirer,* July 21, 1989. Reprinted with permission of the *Philadelphia Inquirer.*

So the U.S. Senate has embarked on a cynical game of capture the flag [commenting upon introduction of the Bush constitutional amendment]. The worthies saw how Michael S. Dukakis missed the boat on the Pledge of Allegiance. . . . It was President Bush who called for [the amendment], even stumped for it at the Iwo Jima flag-raising memorial while dutiful cameras whirred [document 11.7]. Then he jetted off to hail the blossoming of freedom in the Eastern [European Soviet] bloc, applauding the liberalizing of regimes that had censored and repressed and otherwise stifled the free expression of their peoples. . . . Let Messrs. Bush and [Senate Republican leader and amendment sponsor Robert] Dole persist then, if they must. But they should not be surprised if, come October, their flag gambit is losing steam. Americans won't love the flag any less when the frost is on the pumpkin. They may just decide they like the Constitution the way it is. And don't want anyone messing with it simply to put [political] points on the board.

Document 11.22

Three 1989 editorials in the *Detroit News*. Reprinted with permission of the *Detroit News*, a Gannett newspaper, copyright 1989.

The Flag-Burning Case

[June 23, 1989] Gregory L. Johnson's act of burning the American flag in 1984 was despicable. But the act was in the context of expressing opposition to U.S. government policies. So the U.S. Supreme Court found that the act was protected by the First Amendment's guarantee of freedom of expression. It was a necessary ruling.

Certainly, burning the flag is an assault on the sensibilities of most citizens. . . .

But Justice Anthony Kennedy, in his concurring opinion, correctly noted that "the flag is constant in expressing beliefs Americans share, beliefs in law and peace and that freedom which sustains the human spirit. The case here today forces recognition of the costs to which those beliefs commit us. It is poignant but fundamental that the flag protects those who hold it in contempt.* * * *"

The right of free expression cannot be limited by the sensibilities of those who hold differing views. The sacrifices made by those in the military were to preserve the rights that the flag symbolizes. . . .

Freedom of expression is a right that belongs to everyone. That is ultimately the message of this case. . . .

During the Vietnam War . . . a worldview took hold in some quarters that always sees the United States as the archvillain in world affairs. . . . It always believes that the newest and latest communist dictatorship will be the one that will finally get Marxism right and refrain from opening up gulags.

The American people know better than that; The America blamers and flagburners, have become an isolated and repeatedly defeated political minority. If there is any comfort to be drawn from this ruling, it is from the strength of the ideal of freedom of expression, and the knowledge that the Gregory L. Johnsons are doomed to perpetual irrelevance.

No Flag Amendment

[June 29, 1989] President Bush has announced his support for an amendment to the U.S. Constitution that would make flagburning even in the context of a political gesture a crime. The president and others who advocate a constitutional amendment on this issue are aiming a cannon at a fly. . . .

Flagburning is a studied insult. The appropriate way to deal with such insults is to turn one's back to them. We suspect that the calls for an amendment are really about something else—political posturing. . . .

The flag will endure the occasional insults of the witless Gregory L. Johnsons. Too much more time spent on this issue will be a victory for Johnson. He doesn't deserve that much satisfaction.

Burning the Constitution

[July 29,1989] Democrats in Congress are working to head off President Bush's call for a constitutional amendment that would prohibit flagburning. The Democrats instead are pushing a statute that would do the same thing. Flagburning is despicable, but if there has to be a congressional reaction, a statute is preferable to a constitutional amendment. The best result, however, would be for all parties to just leave the subject alone.

[A constitutional] amendment would carve out an exception to the Bill of Rights. As such, it is extremely dangerous to the concept of free speech. This nation's devotion to freedom of speech is one of the most distinctive things about it. . . . It is one of the things that defines us and makes us unique in the history of the world. President Bush's willingness to jeopardize this heritage by proposing a constitutional amendment on the essentially minor issue of flagburning is possibly the least admirable thing he has done since taking office.

The response of the Democratic Party in Congress has been a tactical one: Pass a statute. Limit the damage. And don't be caught on the wrong side of the flag issue again. . . . The principled response would be for them to say that this country is big enough and great enough to tolerate the occasionally obnoxious actions of the Gregory L. Johnsons. A statute would do less damage to our constitutional freedoms than an amendment. To protect the flag, Mr. Bush is willing to burn the Constitution. The Democrats just want to singe it around the edges. But the best response would be for Congress to simply drop the issue and move on.

Document 11.23

Column by James Kilpatrick, "The Flag Will Survive: No Amendment Is Needed, Mr. President," *Washington Post*, June 28, 1989. Copyright 1989 Universal Press Syndicate, reprinted with permission, all rights reserved.

President Bush is dead wrong in calling for a constitutional amendment to overturn the Supreme Court's ruling last week in the flagburning case. Given the disputed facts, the Texas law and the high court precedents, that case was properly decided. The defendant, one Gregory Lee Johnson, was engaged in a form of political "speech" that clearly merits protection under the First Amendment—and that precious amendment ought to be left alone. . . .

In affirming the Texas court [of Criminal Appeals ruling overturning Johnson's original conviction], five members of the U.S. Supreme Court deliberately faced a constitutional challenge the court twice had avoided in the past.

Back in 1966, Brooklyn police arrested Sidney Street for publicly burning a flag as a protest against the riotous harassment of James Meredith at the University of Mississippi [*sic*]. He was convicted of mutilating a flag, but the high court reversed in 1974 [*sic*] on the grounds that the conviction rested in part upon spoken words [document 8.1]. . . .

In 1970, Massachusetts police arrested Valerie Goguen for walking around with a small American flag sewn to the seat of his trousers. The charge was that he had treated the flag "contemptuously." The Supreme Court in 1974 reversed the conviction on the grounds that the law was impermissibly vague [document 8.2].

Only once before had the court directly faced the issue of defacing a flag as a form of political expression. In 1970, Seattle police arrested Harold Spence for "improper use" of the flag. Spence had affixed a large peace symbol to the flag, and then hung the flag upside down outside the window of his apartment. His purpose was to protest the invasion of Cambodia and the killing of students at Kent State University. The court found the state law unconstitutional in the context of political protest [document 8.3].

In related cases the high court repeatedly has upheld the protected value of "symbolic" speech. In a 1969 case, the court upheld the right of students in Des Moines, Iowa, to wear black armbands as a protest against the war in Vietnam. Much earlier, in 1931, the court voided the conviction of a young Communist for flying a red flag in defiance of a law against "anarchistic" banners [document 5.1]. . . .

There are limits. When such expression takes the form of vandalism, as in spraypainting a swastika upon a Jewish temple, the First Amendment accords no protection. If Johnson's flag burning stunt in Dallas had set off a riot, the old exception for "fighting words" might have sufficed to earn his conviction. But on the record, there was no such disturbance.

It comes down to this: in the context of political protest, flag burning is the expression of an idea. . . .

I am consoled by the thought that the flag itself, and the American ideals for which it stands, will survive the puny assaults of such contemptible maggots as Gregory Lee Johnson. In the wake of the court's opinion, presumably we will see more flag burnings, but these too will pass. If the press will ignore such odious demonstrations, their point will be lost. Meanwhile our most cherished ideal—the ideal of freedom—will be maintained.

Documents 11.24

Remarks delivered to the U.S. Senate by Sen. Robert Kerrey, July 18, 1989.

Source: Congressional Record, 1989, S8102–3.

. . . At first I, like most Americans, was outraged by the [Supreme Court] decision [in *Texas v. Johnson*]. It seemed ridiculous to me that flag burning could be a protected act. . . .

I joined with 96 other Senators expressing our disagreement with the decision [document 11.2]. As I prepared to head home for the fourth of July recess, I declared my disbelief at our apparent impotence in protecting this symbol of American freedom.

Then, during the recess, I read the decision [and] was surprised to discover that I agreed with the majority [and] found the majority argument to be reasonable, understandable, and consistent with those values which I believe make America so wonderful.

Further, I was surprised to discover that after reading this decision my anger was not directed at [the majority justices but rather] it was the language of the dissent which angered me, particularly that of Chief Justice Rehnquist [document 10.14] whose argument appears to stand not on 200 years of case law which has supported greater and greater freedom of speech for Americans, but on a sentimental nationalism which seems to impose a functional litmus test of loyalty before expression is permitted.

Today, I declare that I do not support any of the constitutional amendments which are being offered by my colleagues and friends. . . .

Today I am even skeptical about the need to pass anti-flag burning laws at the state or the federal level. . . . Today, I am disappointed that the strength of leadership shown by President Bush in his travels to Poland and Hungary was not shown here at home. President Bush did not stand before the angry and distressed mob to stop us in our tracks before we had done something we would regret. He did not offer words that calmed us and gave us assurance that the Nation was not endangered. Instead of leading us, President Bush joined us.

The polls showed support for a constitutional amendment and so the President yielded to his political advisers. . . . [T]he President chose the path of least resistance and greatest political gain. . . .

[T]here is simply no line of Americans outside this building or in this

Nation queuing up to burn our flag. On the face of the evidence at hand it seems to me that there is no need for us to do anything. . . .

[A] complete reading of the [*Johnson*] decision will yield the very strong impression that the court broke no new ground. Nor did it create any new rights, protections or guarantees. Rather, it applied longstanding and settled principles of law to this specific case. . .

America is the beacon of hope for the people of the world who yearn for freedom from the despotism of repressive government. This hope is diluted when we advise others that we are frightened by flag burning. . . .

Chief Justice Rehnquist, in his disappointing dissent, asserts that men and women fought for our flag in Vietnam. In my case I do not remember feeling this way.

I remember that my first impulse to fight was the result of a feeling that it was my duty. My Nation called and I went. In the short time that I was there, I do not remember giving the safety of our flag anywhere near the thought that I gave the safety of my men. . . .

America—the home of the free and the brave—is my home, and I give thanks to God that it is. America—the home of the free and the brave— does not need our Government to protect us from those who burn a flag.

I yield the floor.

Document 11.25

"When They Burned the Flag Back Home," by James Warner, former prisoner of war in Vietnam and former Reagan administration White House aide, *Washington Post*, July 11, 1989. Reprinted by permission of the *Washington Post*, copyright 1989, The Washington Post.

In March of 1973, when we were released from a prisoner of war camp in North Vietnam, we were flown to Clark Air Force base in the Philippines. As I stepped out of the aircraft I looked up and saw the flag. I caught my breath, then, as tears fed my eyes, I saluted it. I never loved my country more than at that moment. . . .

Because the mere sight of the flag meant so much to me when I saw it for the first time after $5\frac{1}{2}$ years, it hurts me to see other Americans willfully desecrate it. But I have been in a Communist prison where I looked into the pit of hell. I cannot compromise on freedom. It hurts to see the flag burned, but I part company with those who want to punish the flag burners. Let me explain myself.

Early in the imprisonment the Communists told us that we did not have to stay there. If we would only admit we were wrong, if we would only apologize, we could be released early. If we did not, we would be punished. A handful accepted, most did not. In our minds, early release under those conditions would amount to a betrayal, of our comrades, of our country and of our flag.

Because we would not say the words they wanted us to say, they made our lives wretched. Most of us were tortured, and some of my comrades died. I was tortured for most of the summer of 1969. I developed beriberi from malnutrition. I had long bouts of dysentery. I was infested with intestinal parasites. I spent 13 months in solitary confinement. Was our cause worth all of this? Yes, it was worth all this and more. . . .

[Our captors] tried to "re-educate" us. If we could show them that we would not abandon our belief in fundamental principles, then we could prove the falseness of their doctrine. We could subvert them by teaching them about freedom through our example. We could show them the power of ideas.

I did not appreciate this power before I was a prisoner of war. I remember one interrogation where I was shown a photograph of some Americans protesting the war by burning a flag. "There," the officer said. "People in your country protest against your cause. That proves that you are wrong."

"No," I said. "That proves that I am right. In my country we are not afraid of freedom, even if it means that people disagree with us." The officer was on his feet in an instant, his face purple with rage. He smashed his fist onto the table and screamed at me to shut up. While he was ranting I was astonished to see pain, compounded by fear, in his eyes. I have never forgotten that look, nor have I forgotten the satisfaction I felt at using his tool, the picture of the burning flag, against him. . . .

We don't need to amend the Constitution in order to punish those who burn our flag. They burn the flag because they hate America and they are afraid of freedom. What better way to hurt them than with the subversive idea of freedom? . . . Don't be afraid of freedom, it is the best weapon we have.

12

Testing the Flag Protection Act
in the Courts
1989–1990

The Flag Protection Act [document 11.8], which took effect on the morning of October 28, 1989, touched off a wave of flag burnings designed both to defy and to test it. Although more than a dozen flag-burning incidents were reported (generally only in local media) during October and November 1989, the Justice Department decided to bring test cases only in the two sole flag burnings that received extensive national media coverage, the burning of a post office flag in Seattle during the early morning of October 28, and the burning of several flags on the steps of the Capitol in Washington, D.C., on October 30, 1989 (documents 12.1 and 12.2).

Four defendants were eventually prosecuted in the Seattle case, which became known as *U.S. v. Haggerty,* and three prosecutions were brought in the Washington case, including one against "Dread Scott" Tyler of the Chicago "flag on the floor" exhibit fame [document 10.7], in what became known as *U.S. v. Eichman.* Gregory Lee Johnson, the namesake of the 1989 Supreme Court ruling, also participated in the Capitol incident, but federal officials declined to prosecute him on the grounds that he had failed to ignite his flag, thereby provoking charges of "selective non-prosecution" from Johnson that were an ironic counterpoint to his declarations that he had been prosecuted in Dallas in 1984 for a flag burning which he had not committed.

In identical briefs filed in federal district courts in Seattle and Washington, D.C., in early 1990, the Justice Department took a schizophrenic legal position that reflected the fact that, on the one hand, its duty was to enforce the law, and, on the other hand, its official position, as articulated by Assistant Attorney General Barr before Congress six months earlier [document 11.14], was that any flag desecration legislation would be unconstitutional under the *Johnson* ruling. The department attempted to square this circle by simultaneously telling the district courts that: (1) its own position continued to be that the FPA was unconstitutional under the *Johnson* precedent and that the congressional claim that the FPA was constitutional under the *O'Brien* guidelines as a "content neutral" statute was not only incorrect but could have "serious adverse consequences" that might provide justifying precedent for "virtually any restriction on symbolic speech;" but that (2) the courts should nonetheless uphold the FPA on the grounds that the presidential endorsement of a constitutional amendment and congressional passage of the FPA demonstrated that the government's "only conceivable interest" behind the FPA, namely to protect "the symbolic value of the flag," was a "compelling" interest that met the *Johnson* standard of "most exacting scrutiny" under the First Amendment and therefore could overcome the admittedly purely suppressive purpose of the law.[1]

At least partly because the Justice Department brief was so weak—amounting to asking the district courts to perform the constitutionally impossible by overruling a six-month-old Supreme Court ruling that purely suppressive government interests in protecting the flag's symbolic value could *not* override the First Amendment interest involved—both the Senate and the House filed amicus briefs that took radically different stances. In effect, both argued that Congress had valid nonsuppressive interests in passing the FPA, which qualified it for scrutiny under the relatively lenient "important or substantial" government interest standard set forth in *O'Brien* rather than under the far more stringent "compelling" government interest *Johnson* standard. However, the Senate and House amicus briefs focused on entirely different allegedly nonsuppressive interests as justifying the FPA. The Senate brief argued that the FPA sought to protect the flag's "physical integrity," admittedly because of its symbolic value, against all assaults, regardless of their motive, in a content-neutral manner that allegedly satisfied the *Johnson* ruling (an analysis of the FPA flatly rejected by the Justice Department, which conceded that the statute was not content-neutral); the House introduced the novel argument that the FPA was justified by seeking to protect the flag as an "incident of sovereignty," for example its ability to demarcate American borders and ships on the high sea, and maintained that therefore it reflected no intent to suppress dissenting symbolic speech.

In response to these different arguments from representatives of the federal government, Center for Constitutional Rights attorneys William Kunstler and David Cole, who represented both the *Haggerty* and the *Eichman* defendants, argued that all three government briefs effectively conceded that the FPA was designed to protect the flag's symbolic value (as even its role as a designator of sovereignty was symbolic) and that the Supreme Court had made clear that such a purpose was not compelling enough to meet the "exacting scrutiny" test of the *Johnson* ruling. They also rejected outright claims that the FPA was in any way "content neutral," arguing that it outlawed only those uses of the flag historically associated with opposition to the government, such as flag burning, but did not ban uses such as flying flags in bad weather that could damage the flag but were not typically associated with dissent.

In two parallel rulings issued in February and March 1990, both district courts essentially rejected all of the arguments of the three government briefs, while endorsing the key arguments of the defense; therefore both held the FPA unconstitutional under the *Johnson* precedent insofar as it was used to prosecute symbolic political dissent. The first ruling, handed down on February 21 by Seattle district court judge Barbara Rothstein in the *Haggerty* case (document 12.3] set the pattern for Washington federal district court Judge June Green's March 5 decision in the *Eichman* case.[2] Both courts found that the *Johnson* precedent was controlling because the defendants had engaged in expressive conduct requiring First Amendment scrutiny, and because, as Judge Rothstein declared, the underlying government interest was "in protecting the symbolic value of the flag" and could not "survive the exacting scrutiny which this court must apply," thus rejecting the Justice Department's central argument. Judge Rothstein declared that "in order for the flag to endure as a symbol of freedom, we must protect with equal vigor the right to wave it and the right to destroy it" and that while tolerating flag burning did not jeopardize American freedoms, "What would threaten our liberty is allowing the government to encroach on our right to political protest." Similarly, Judge Green declared, "However compelling the government may see its interests, they cannot justify restrictions on speech which shake the very cornerstone of the First Amendment."

The two courts also rejected the key arguments of the congressional briefs. Thus, Judge Rothstein declared that the Senate contention that the FPA was content neutral was incorrect because it forbade only conduct "generally associated with disrespect for the flag," yet allowed conduct that threatened the flag's physical integrity but did not "communicate a negative or disrespectful message," such as "flying the flag in inclement weather or carrying it into battle." She similarly rejected the House argument concerning allegedly nonsuppressive governmental "sovereignty" interests in protecting the flag, on the triple grounds that this interest was intertwined with protecting the flag as a symbol, that this position had never been advanced in the legislative debate on the FPA, and that the House had never explained "how the governmental interest in preserving the flag as an incident of sovereignty would be harmed by defendants' act of flagburning."

Utilizing the expedited, mandatory Supreme Court review procedures included in the FPA, which quite extraordinarily both required the Supreme Court to hear the cases on appeal in the quickest time "possible" and mandated skipping the normal intermediate consideration by a federal circuit court of appeals, Solicitor General Kenneth Starr asked the Supreme Court in mid-March to consolidate the two district court cases and to hear the government's appeal from the twin decisions. On March 30, the Supreme Court agreed to review the rulings and set oral argument for the consolidated cases, now known as *U.S. v. Eichman,* for May 14, with the usual time allowed lawyers for both sides to file briefs chopped in half (Starr had asked that it be reduced by two-thirds, while the flag burners' lawyers had asked for a normal briefing schedule).

Starr's brief (document 12.4) differed only marginally from the Justice Department district court briefs. He essentially called for the court to overturn its own nine-month-old *Johnson* decision, conceding that the arguments he was advancing were "in tension" with *Johnson.* Echoing the government's position in the district courts, Starr maintained that the Court should reconsider its *Johnson* finding that the government's interest were not compelling enough to overcome flag burners' First Amendment rights in light of the "representative consensus articulated by the Congress and the President in connection with the enactment" of the FPA, a consensus that he declared identified a "substantial potential harm posed by physical damage and mistreatment of the American flag," namely "the assault upon and injury to the shared values that bind our national community." In addition, Starr argued that the Court should find that "physical destruction" of the flag was so uniquely "anathema to the Nation's values" that it constituted a "physical, violent assault on the most deeply shared experiences of the American people" and thus, in clear contradiction to the *Johnson* holding, should be exempted from First Amendment protection, much as the Court had previously excluded other marginal forms of expression such as obscenity, child pornography, defamation, and incitement to violence. As in the Justice Department district court briefs, Starr completely rejected the "content neutrality" argument, instead endorsing in a footnote the district courts' conclusion that the FPA was "based on a view that the flag stands for something valuable, and should be safeguarded because of that value."

Starr's defense of the FPA was supported by five amicus briefs, all of which advanced positions that disagreed with his to varying degrees. The House again reiterated its "sovereignty" argument, while the Senate largely abandoned its earlier "content neutrality" position in favor of a history of flag desecration legislation that stressed its origins as aimed at commercial and partisan political misuse of the flag [see chap. 2] rather than designed to suppress political dissent, with the implication that the FPA was similarly motivated by nonsuppressive purposes. Apparently because none of the three government briefs advanced the "content neu-trality" argument that had been at the heart of the congressional defense of the FPA several months earlier, SJC chairman Biden filed a personal amicus brief advancing that position.

In response to Starr and the pro-FPA amicus briefs, the flag burners' brief, which was largely written by David Cole, essentially reiterated the successful arguments earlier advanced at the district court level (document 12.5). In short, Cole's brief stated that the district court rulings had correctly held that, just as with the Texas law struck down in *Johnson,* the FPA was motivated by the suppressive purpose of seeking to protect the flag's symbolic value and that such a purpose could not withstand the searching scrutiny required by the *Johnson* precedent. To accept Starr's arguments that the flag should be protected because government officials felt strongly about it and that flag desecration should be deprived of First Amendment protection because it violated deeply felt national values, Cole argued, would allow government to forbid any political expression that was deemed highly offensive and would violate the whole purpose of the Constitution and the courts, by denuding minorities of "legal protection from the political inclinations of the majority when they trample upon the freedoms" of dissidents. Cole also again rejected the claim that the FPA was in any sense content-neutral. He argued, for example, that the very act of singling out the flag for special protection was itself "content based," as would be evident if the statute had forbidden desecrating the "emblem of the Democratic Party" instead of the flag, and that the FPA banned "vir-tually all conduct associated with dissent," even acts that would not harm the flag, such as maintaining a flag on the floor under a glass cover.

In oral argument before the Supreme Court on May 14, 1990, Starr changed the emphasis of his argument considerably from that expressed in his brief (document 12.6). Whereas earlier he had dismissed the "content neutrality" argument, in oral argument Starr maintained that Congress had carefully followed the *Johnson* guidelines to create in the FPA a law free of "content-laden language" that protected the physical integrity of the flag without "singling out" any particular viewpoints for disfavored treatment. Thereby, he argued, Congress had successfully fashioned a law that admittedly protected the flag "because of its symbolic value," but "not from criticism but from physical destruction or mutilation," much as governments could protect "houses of worship" or "the bald eagle" against destruction, regardless of what motivated such action. For exam-ple, Starr argued, under the law, one could be prosecuted for "patri-otically" desecrating the flag, such as emblazoning it with the message, "I love the Supreme Court." Starr also introduced an entirely new position in oral argument, arguing that flag burning failed to meet the 1974 *Spence* test [document 8.3] of "expression," which required the delivering of a "particularized message," instead leaving a "major message gap" and resembling an "overload loudspeaker" or even the "mindless nihilism" that the *Spence* court suggested was undeserving of First Amendment protection.[3]

The response of the justices at oral argument suggested, correctly, it would soon turn out, that Starr did not change any minds from the Court's *Johnson* lineup. Although Starr suggested that flag burning did not convey a particularized message, Justice Kennedy termed such conduct an "internationally recognized form of protest," and Justice Scalia said the message clearly was, "I am in opposition to this country." In response to the claim that the FPA was "content neutral," Scalia harshly critiqued the text of the law, declaring, "If I get a spot on my tie, I don't say, gee I've defiled my tie . . . or if I tear my jacket I don't say, my, I've mutilated my jacket. These are words of—cast contempt upon."

Defense lawyer William Kunstler responded to Starr at oral argument by reiterating the main points in the defense brief and by rejecting Starr's arguments about "content neutrality" and lack of a particularized message. With regard to the former point, Kunstler declared that in fact the FPA allowed "patriotic" conduct that physically imperiled the flag, such as flying it in a storm or in battle, while protecting the flag only from "those who would hurt it or cast it in a bad light"; with regard to the latter argument, he told the Court that stripping vague forms of expression of First Amendment protection would relegate all "non-verbal expression to the scrap heap." Responding to Starr's analogizing of flag desecration with child pornography or defamation as not warranting full First Amendment protection, Kunstler declared, "In the area of political speech, the government cannot make judgments of what is overly offensive or unimportant." In effect, Kunstler concluded, the government was seeking to turn the flag into a "golden image" that must be worshipped, but "once people are compelled to respect a political symbol, then they are no longer free and their respect for the flag is quite meaningless. To criminalize flag burning is to deny what the First Amendment stands for."

On June 11, 1990, the Supreme Court, acting with extraordinary speed, handed down a 5–4 decision in the *Eichman* case that upheld the twin district court rulings that the FPA could not be constitutionally used to prosecute those who used the flag to express symbolic political dissent (document 12.7). The ruling, written by Brennan and reflecting the identical division within the Court as in the *Johnson* decision, which he also authored, essentially followed the outlines of the 1989 ruling and the district court opinions. Brennan declared that the "most exacting scrutiny" standard must be applied to the FPA because the government's interest in protecting the flag's "status as a symbol of our Nation and certain national ideals" was related "to the suppression of free expression"; he concluded that this interest could not justify "infringement on First Amendment rights." The court specifically declined to "reconsider our rejection in *Johnson* of the claim that flag burning as a mode of expression, like obscenity or 'fighting words' does not enjoy the full protection of the First Amendment" as well as refusing Starr's "invitation" to reconsider the *Johnson* holding that the government's interest in upholding the symbolic value of the flag would not infringe First Amendment rights in view of "Congress' recent recognition of a purported national consensus favoring a prohibition against flag burning." Rejecting the latter argument, the Court bluntly declared that "any suggestion that the Government's interest in suppressing speech becomes more weighty as popular opposition to that speech grows is foreign to the First Amendment."

Although conceding that the new law, unlike the Texas statute at issue in *Johnson* (document 10.1), "contains no explicit content-based limitation on the scope of prohibited conduct," the court held that the FPA nonetheless still suffered from "the same fundamental flaw" as the Texas law, as it could not be "justified without reference to the content of the regulated speech." The Court held that this was clear not only from the government's asserted interest in protecting the flag's symbolic value, but also from the "precise language" of the law, which outlawed conduct that "connotes disrespectful treatment of the flag," even while exempting forms of disposing of worn flags that are "traditionally associated with patriotic respect for the flag" as well as allowing the flying of flags in storms and "other conduct that threatens the physical integrity of the flag, albeit in an indirect manner unlikely to communicate disrespect." The Court declared that it recognized that flag desecration is "deeply offensive to many," but pointed out that the same could be said about other forms of protected speech, such as "virulent ethnic and religious epithets" and "scurrilous caricatures." It concluded by quoting its own *Johnson* statement that the First Amendment's "bedrock principle" was that government could not "prohibit expression of an idea simply because society finds the idea itself offensive," adding that, "Punishing desecration of the flag dilutes the very freedom that makes this emblem so revered, and worth revering."

The four-member dissent (document 12.8), penned by Justice Stevens, was considerably more tempered than the *Johnson* dissents (documents 10.14 and 10.15), but otherwise made the same claim that the unique importance of the flag, such as its role in symbolizing "the ideas of liberty, equality and tolerance," justified infringing upon political expression to protect its "symbolic value," especially when there was no "interference with the speaker's freedom to express his or her ideas by other means." Aside from the lack of any quoted patriotic poetry, the far calmer tone of this dissent was very marked, including, for example, Stevens's remark that the case came down to "a question of judgment" and that "reasonable judges may differ" about it. Furthermore, although in their *Johnson* dissents Justice Stevens had compared flag desecration to placing "graffiti on the Washington Monument" and Justice Rehnquist had lumped flag burning together with murder and embezzlement, in his *Eichman* dissent (which Rehnquist joined, without writing a separate dissent) Stevens clearly repudiated such analogies by declaring that burning a privately owned flag "is not, of course, equivalent to burning a public building," as it "causes no physical harm to other persons or to their property," and its impact is "purely symbolic." Additionally, in what was widely interpreted as a slap at the Bush administration by its own ideological friends on the Court, Stevens rebuked "those leaders" who had "compromised" the "integrity" of the flag by seeming to "advocate compulsory worship" of it "even by individuals whom it offends" or by seeming to "manipulate the symbol of national purpose into a pretext for partisan disputes about meaner ends."

Document 12.1

Statement issued by flag burners arrested at the Capitol steps in Washington, D.C., on October 30, 1989.

Source: Joint Appendix, *U.S. v. Eichman* and *U.S. v. Haggerty,* Nos. 89-1433 and 89-1444, in the Supreme Court of the United States, Oct. term, 1989, 55–57.

STATEMENT BY THOSE CHALLENGING THE "FLAG PROTECTION ACT OF 1989"
October 30, 1989—12 Noon, Steps of the U.S. Capitol
At midnight this past Friday, October 27, the new national flag statute went into effect, outlawing desecration of the U.S. flag. . . . These dangerous moves to shut people up and shut people down in the name of the red, white and blue are not in the interest of the majority. Today, they try to suppress political expression in the name of the flag, tomorrow what next will become forbidden. We need only look at Nazi Germany to see an answer to that.
At midnight this past Friday, the flag law went into effect. At one minute past midnight hundreds of people across the country delivered their judgment on that law, . . . Over 1,000 U.S. flags were barbecued, napalmed, torched, set ablaze and properly displayed [referring to a demonstration in New York City and especially to one in Seattle in the early morning of October 28, during which hundreds of small flags were burned along with a large government-owned post office Flag]. . . . [E]specially in a political climate marked by increasing racism, assaults on womens' rights, calls for an enforced oppressive moral code, censorship, intervention in other countries and overall escalating attacks on the people, all

[flag burners] deeply felt the need to defy a law that would make the flag a religious icon and its worship mandatory. . . .

We are among those who acted that night [in New York City], and we intend to continue that protest here today. . . . To the government that has made flag desecration illegal, we defy your law. And we challenge you. Arrest us. Test your statute. Take it back to your Supreme Court and try once again to claim it is consistent with your constitutional standards of free speech. . . . As you editorialize on the sanctity of free speech, denouncing the suppression of dissent in other countries you will be silencing it here, provoking questions when you need obedience, opposition when you expect compliance, and millions upon millions more will come to understand what is really going down, that this effort to ban flag desecration is not really about adding some legal asbestos to a piece of cloth, but rather the forceful suppression of political dissent as part of a much larger and vicious agenda. And the people will oppose you. . . .

The battle lines are drawn. On one side stands the government and all those in favor of compulsory patriotism and enforced reverence to the flag. On the other side are all those opposed to this. . . . This flag means one thing to the powers that be and something else to all of us. Everything bad this system has done and continues to do to people all over the world has been done under this flag. No law, no amendment will change it, cover it up, or stifle that truth. So to you we say, Express yourself! Burn this flag. It's quick, it's easy, it may not be the law, but it's the right thing to do.

FIGHT THE FASCIST FLAG LAW
NO FLAG AMENDMENT
NO MANDATORY PATRIOTISM

Dave Blalock, Vietnam Veterans Against the War (Anti-Imperialist)
Shawn Eichman, Coalition Opposed to Censorship in the Arts
Joey Johnson, Revolutionary Communist Youth Brigade
Dread Scott, Revolutionary Artist

Document 12.2

Affidavit filed before federal district court in Seattle, January 8, 1990, by Carlos Garza, one of four defendants prosecuted there in the *Haggerty* case under the 1989 Flag Protection Act

Source: Joint Appendix, *U.S. v. Eichman* and *U.S. v. Haggerty,* Nos. 89-1433 and 89-1444, in the Supreme Court of the United States, Oct. term, 1989, 82–88.

Carlos Garza being first duty sworn on oath, swears and affirms the following:

1. I burned an American flag on October 28, 1989. . . .

2. I am a 32 year old, Mexican-American who was born in Billings, Montana. . . .

3. My formal education consists of having completed the eighth grade in the Los Angeles public school system.

4. I believe 40 to 60 percent of those with whom I attended grammar school are now either dead or in prison. My own brother was killed as a result of gang violence.

5. I spent most of my working hours on jobs in factories or as a gardener. It is almost impossible for Hispanics in America to earn a livable wage.

6. Hispanics in America are very mistreated. Hispanics in America are essentially struggling to survive on a daily basis.

7. America is a beautiful and rich country. There should not be any homeless people on the streets of America.

8. I blame the United States government for the problems of homelessness, hunger and unemployment in our country. I blame the United States government for the fact that 40 to 60 percent of those people I went to grammar school with are either dead or in prison.

9. I burned an American flag to speak out on the problems caused by our government in America. The American flag symbolizes the problems of our country. The American flag was with the United States troops that took the land that belonged to native Americans. While the American flag symbolizes good, it also symbolizes the misdeeds in which our government has participated.

10. The American flag represents the system and the government for which it stands. I love and respect America. I love and respect the American people. I do not love and respect the way Hispanic Americans are treated by the United States government.

11. I burned an American flag to express my outrage over the mistreatment of Hispanic Americans by our government.

12. America is a great country. In America we have the right to freedom of speech and freedom of expression. The day these rights are taken away from us, will be a dark day in American history. When the right to burn a symbol is taken away from American citizens, democracy itself is on the brink of collapse.

13. In an effort to protect and preserve freedom of speech and freedom of expression, I respectfully request this court to declare the "The Flag Protection Act of 1989" a violation of the First Amendment to Our United States Constitution.

I declare under penalty of perjury that the foregoing is true and correct. . . .

Document 12.3

1990 District Court ruling by Judge Barbara Rothstein declaring the Flag Protection Act of 1989 unconstitutional as applied to those who burned the flag in Seattle on October 28, 1989.

Source: U.S. v. Haggerty, 731 Federal Supplement 425.

. . . Early on the morning of October 28, 1989, defendants burned a United States flag belonging to the United States Postal Service. The flag-burning occurred during a political demonstration convened in front of a post office in Seattle, Washington to protest the enactment of the Flag Protection Act of 1989, 18 U.S.C. § 700. That statute, which prohibits flagburning, had taken effect only minutes before defendants' actions against the flag. . . .

Defendants now move to dismiss the flagburning charge on the grounds that the statute forbidding that activity is unconstitutional under the First Amendment to the United States Constitution both on its face and as applied to their conduct. . . .

Defendants contend that, as applied to their flagburning activities, the Act is unconstitutional because it prohibits expressive conduct which is protected by the First Amendment. Defendants insist that this result is required by a very recent decision, *Texas v. Johnson* [document 10.12], in which the United States Supreme Court struck down as unconstitutional a Texas statute forbidding the desecration of venerated objects including the United States flag. . . .

A. Expressive Conduct

The threshold question addressed by the *Johnson* Court in its analysis of the constitutionality of the Texas law as applied to Johnson's conduct was whether his burning of the flag constituted expressive conduct arguably protected by the First Amendment. Although the First Amendment literally protects only freedom of "speech," the Supreme Court has long recognized that "expressive conduct," i. e., conduct through which the actor intends to convey an idea, also falls within its ambit [citing *Stromberg,* document 5.1 and *Spence,* document 8.3].

Based on this well-established precedent, the Court had no difficulty in finding that Johnson could invoke the First Amendment. . . . [T]he Court concluded that the conduct was clearly intended to communicate a political message and that the message was apparent to the audience.

Likewise, this court must determine if defendants flagburning in this case was " 'sufficiently imbued with elements of communication * * * ' to implicate the First Amendment." [quoting from *Johnson*]. No one disputes that their conduct took place during a political demonstration protesting the newly effective Flag Protection Act. Like the *Johnson* Court, this court readily concludes that "⟨t⟩he expressive, overtly political nature of ⟨defendants'⟩ conduct was both intentional and overwhelmingly apparent." Defendants' flagburning was unquestionably expressive conduct intended to convey a political message and thus implicates the First Amendment.

B. Governmental Interest

1. Applicable Standard

If, as this court has found, defendants' conduct was expressive, the next step in the *Johnson* analysis is to determine whether the government's interest in regulating that conduct is related to the suppression of free expression. If it is not, the government need only justify defendants' prosecution under the less stringent standard set forth by the Supreme Court in *United States v. O'Brien,* for regulation of noncommunicative conduct. That standard requires the government to establish an important or substantial interest in regulating the nonexpressive element of the conduct.

If, on the other hand, the government's interest is related to the suppression of free expression, a more demanding standard is applicable [citing *Johnson* and *Spence*]. Under those circumstances, the court must subject the government's asserted interest to "the most exacting scrutiny." In order to survive this strict scrutiny, the government must establish a compelling interest justifying the regulation of expressive conduct.

2. Government Interest in *Texas v. Johnson*

In *Johnson,* the State of Texas asserted an interest in prohibiting flag desecration to preserve the flag as a symbol of nationhood and national unity. The Supreme Court held that this interest in protecting the symbolism of the flag was inextricably tied to the suppression of free expression. . . . Because the State's interest was related to the suppression of free expression, the Court concluded that the more lenient standard of review set forth in *O'Brien* was not pertinent.

Defendants in this case argue that the same reasoning and result apply here. Defendants assert that, although the superficial rationale for the legislation at issue is to protect the physical integrity of the flag, the only underlying governmental interest is the protection of the flag as a political symbol, and that this interest is, by definition, related to the suppression of expression because the government's interest in the flag as a symbol can only be threatened by an act communicating a message which undermines the flag's symbolic value. . . . [D]efendants argue that this court, like the Court in *Johnson,* must apply a standard of strict scrutiny in assessing the constitutionality of the legislation. . . .

3. Department of Justice Position

The Department of Justice agrees with defendants that the Court's ruling in *Johnson* controls this court's decision on the applicable standard.

Pursuant to *Johnson,* the Department of Justice concedes that the government's only conceivable interest in protecting the physical integrity of the flag is to promote its value as a political symbol, that this interest is inherently related to the suppression of free expression and that, therefore, legislation prohibiting flagburning, including the law at issue here, is subject to strict scrutiny.

4. United States Senate Position

The United States Senate agrees that the underlying purpose of the Flag Protection Act of 1989 is to protect the flag as a political symbol. But the Senate insists that *Johnson* is not dispositive of which standard of scrutiny to apply in this case because of significant differences between the Texas statute and the legislation at issue here.

As the Senate points out, a necessary element of an offense under the Texas law was knowledge that the conduct in question would "seriously offend one or more persons likely to observe or discover ⟨the⟩ action." . . . The Senate argues that the Flag Protection Act of 1989 is, by contrast, content-neutral in that it protects the physical integrity of the flag by proscribing certain destructive conduct regardless of the actor's intent to convey a message or the communicative impact on the audience [and that therefore] the Act is not related to the suppression of expression and is accordingly reviewable under the more lenient *O'Brien* standard of scrutiny.

Unfortunately, the Senate's definition of what constitutes content-neutrality is incorrect, thus dooming its entire argument. The United States Supreme Court recently addressed this question in *Boos v. Barry,* [and stated] that content-neutral restrictions on speech are "those that 'are *justified* without reference to the content of the regulated speech'" (emphasis added). Thus, it is the reason for the legislation and not its scope which determines content-neutrality. If the justification for protecting the flag is related to the suppression of expression, it is not content-neutral even though the Act on its face is applicable to anyone who engages in certain conduct regardless of the actor's intent or the impact of the conduct.

Johnson succinctly addresses this point in the context of flag-burning legislation. As this court explained earlier, *Johnson* held that the governmental interest in preserving the flag's symbolic value under the Texas law was directly related to the suppression of free expression in the case of Johnson's burning of the flag. Since the Senate admits that the government's reason for enacting the Flag Protection Act of 1989 was exactly the same, i.e., singling out the flag for protection as a political symbol, it must follow that the Act too is directly related to the suppression of expression in the case of the defendants before this court and cannot be considered content-neutral. Therefore, the less stringent *O'Brien* standard is inapplicable. . . .

5. United States House of Representatives Position

Unlike the Department of Justice and the Senate, the United States House of Representatives does not agree with defendants that the government's sole interest in protecting the physical integrity of the flag arises out of its symbolic value. Instead the House argues that Congress enacted the Flag Protection Act because it wished to shield the flag from harm as an incident of sovereignty with a specific legal significance apart from its symbolic value. It is the House's contention that flying the flag to claim sovereignty has a concrete legal purpose and that protecting the flag protects that sovereignty interest. . . .

However, the use of the flag as a means of indicating sovereignty is itself a symbolic use. The government's only possible interest in protecting the physical integrity of the flag as an incident of sovereignty is to prevent or punish acts of disrespect amounting to a rejection of United States sovereignty, i.e., expressive conduct. Thus, even if Congress does seek to prevent harm to the flag as an incident of sovereignty, that interest relates to the suppression of expression and is subject to strict scrutiny.

C. Strict Scrutiny of Government Interest

The final step in the analysis of the constitutionality of the Flag Protection Act is to determine whether the government's interest in enacting the statute can survive the applicable strict scrutiny standard. The court begins with the observation that, as in *Johnson*, this case involves the prosecution of defendants for expressing political ideas, "expression situated at the core of our First Amendment values." However, the court is also cognizant that an act of Congress carries with it a strong presumption of constitutionality.

After carefully considering the provisions of the Flag Protection Act, the court concludes that the legislation is unconstitutional as applied to the facts of this case. It is clear that, pursuant to the decision in *Johnson*, the asserted governmental interest in protecting the symbolic value of the flag cannot survive the exacting scrutiny which this court must apply. . . .

Indeed, both the House and the Senate in effect concede this point. By arguing so strenuously that the constitutionality of the Flag Protection Act should be decided under the more lenient *O'Brien* standard, they implicitly recognize that the Act cannot survive the more stringent standard applied in *Johnson*.

The Department of Justice, however, urges the court to find that the government does have a sufficiently compelling interest in preserving the flag as a political symbol to survive strict scrutiny. Acknowledging that *Johnson* ruled to the contrary and recognizing that this court cannot overrule the United States Supreme Court, the Department of Justice nevertheless contends that this court can rely on the recent governmental affirmations of a compelling national interest in protecting the flag as evidenced by the congressional enactment of the Flag Protection Act and the presidential call for a constitutional amendment.

Again, *Johnson* precludes such a result. The Court in *Johnson* forcefully rejected the notion that the government can restrict the use of a symbol to reflect only one view of that symbol . . . [and] reaffirmed that the core purpose of the First Amendment is to protect political dissent, and that to suppress such criticism in one instance so as to protect the sensibilities of the majority does not strengthen the nation. On the contrary, it erodes the basis of our political freedom. . . .

III. CONCLUSION

For the above reasons, this court GRANTS defendants' motion [and declares] that the Flag Protection Act is unconstitutional as applied to their conduct in burning a United States flag. . . .

The court is well aware of the reverence with which many people who have sacrificed much for this country regard the United States flag. But in order for the flag to endure as a symbol of freedom in this nation, we must protect with equal vigor the right to wave it and the right to destroy it. . . .

This is an inspiring time for those of us who treasure freedom. Countries all over the world are striving to adopt democratic principles derived from our Constitution as part of their forms of government. The freedom of speech enshrined in our First Amendment is the crucial foundation without which other democratic values cannot flourish. It is a tribute to the strength of our nation and to our faith in democratic government that even a means of protest which is profoundly painful and offensive to many people is protected.

Burning the flag as an expression of political dissent, while repellent to many Americans, does not jeopardize the freedom which we hold dear. What would threaten our liberty is allowing the government to encroach on our right to political protest. It is with the firm belief that this decision strengthens what our flag stands for that this court finds the Flag Protection Act unconstitutional as applied to defendants' conduct in burning the flag.

Given this result, the court need not address defendants' other argument that the Flag Protection Act is unconstitutional on its face.

Document 12.4

Brief for the United States in the consolidated case of *U.S. v. Eichman* and *U.S. v. Haggerty*, Nos. 89-1433 and 89-1434, in the Supreme Court of the United States, October term, 1989.

. . . In separate decisions issued in February and March 1990, the district courts in *Eichman* and *Haggerty* granted appellees' motions to dismiss the flag-burning charges, holding that the Flag Protection Act of 1989, as applied to appellees' conduct, violated the First Amendment [because their conduct was determined to be expressive conduct of an overtly political nature and the government purpose the courts held to be behind the law, that of preserving the symbolic interest of the flag, could not survive the strict scrutiny held to be mandated by the *Johnson* decision, as a result of the Supreme Court finding in *Johnson* that such a government interest was insufficient to survive such scrutiny].

SUMMARY OF ARGUMENT

I. In *Texas v. Johnson*, the Court held that a Texas statute outlawing desecration of venerated objects [document 10.1], as applied to the burning of an American flag, violated the First Amendment. By contrast these cases involve the Flag Protection Act of 1989, a federal statute enacted in response to *Texas v. Johnson*, under circumstances in which Congress was mindful of the First Amendment's express strictures. The Court has long acknowledged "⟨t⟩he customary deference accorded judgments of Congress," particularly where, as here, "Congress specifically considered the question of the Act's constitutionality." In light of that established principle—and Congress's determination of the harm inflicted by burning of the flag—the courts below misconstrued *Texas v. Johnson* as essentially foreclosing the constitutionality of the Flag Protection Act.

The pertinent constitutional analysis should focus on the sort of expressive conduct at issue here . . . and then take into account the national consensus underlying the statute—that physical destruction of the American flag, the unique symbol of the Nation, constitutes a violent assault on the shared values that bind our national community. When viewed from the proper constitutional perspective, the Flag Protection Act fully comports with the First Amendment.

II. The United States does not dispute that appellees' flag burning constitutes expressive conduct. Nor does the United States dispute that Congress enacted the Flag Protection Act in order to protect the physical integrity of the flag under all circumstances and thus necessarily to encompass within its prohibition that narrow category of "symbolic speech." . . . But this does not doom Congress's considered judgment in passing this measure. The First Amendment does not prohibit Congress, as it provided in the Flag Protection Act, from removing the American flag as a prop available to those who seek to express their own views by destroying it.

This court has never assumed that all speech, including expressive conduct, is entitled to full First Amendment protection; to the contrary, the Court over the years has identified a variety of categories of expression as beyond the pale of "the freedom of speech." . . .

These constraining principles of First Amendment analysis apply to appellees' burning of a flag of the United States. Congress and the President—the Nation's elected representatives—have now spoken with one voice: the physical integrity of the flag of the United States, as the unique symbol of the Nation, merits protection not accorded other national emblems. The reason is this: Flag burning is, by its nature, a physical, violent assault on the most deeply shared experiences of the American people, including the sacrifices of our fellow citizens in defense of the Nation and the preservation of liberty. It is the physical assault and accompanying violation of the flag's physical integrity—not robust and uninhibited debate—that occasion the injury that our society should not be called upon to bear.

For these reasons, the Court should treat the conduct at issue—physical destruction of a flag of the United States—as it has other narrowly defined categories of expressive conduct that have not merited full protection under the First Amendment. Flag burning, like obscene materials, defamatory statements and a variety of other "speech" or expressive conduct, presents substantial "evils" incompatible with "the very purpose for which organized governments are instituted" [quoting from Chief Justice Rehnquist's dissent in *Johnson*, document 10.14]. In view of the inherently destructive nature of flag burning, the system of free expression ordained by the First Amendment is not compromised by a highly specific, narrowly tailored prohibition on physical attacks upon the flag.

These cases therefore call for the Court to reconsider the assumption in *Texas v. Johnson* that flag burning is a form of expressive conduct meriting full First Amendment protection. Reconsideration of that premise is particularly appropriate where as here, the people's elected representatives have made the considered decision that (save for a specific and well-recognized exception [the disposal of worn or soiled flag]) the physical destruction of the flag is—uniquely—anathema to the Nation's values. . . .

III. Our submission is, we recognize, in tension with certain doctrinal underpinnings of the Court's recent decision in *Texas v. Johnson*. The Court there, of course, had no occasion to address, much less weigh for constitutional proposes, the sort of Congressional determination regarding the need to protect the American flag that led to enactment of the Flag Protection Act. Moreover, the Court was faced with a statute, unlike the federal measure (as now amended), that prohibited acts that the "actor knows will seriously offend one or more persons * * * ." To the extent that *Johnson* accorded flag burning, as expressive conduct, full First Amendment protection—as the courts below construed that decision and as appellees urge before this Court—*Texas v. Johnson* should be reconsidered and, upon reconsideration, appropriately limited.

ARGUMENT

. . . Absent from the backdrop of *Texas v. Johnson* was the testament to the depth of the national interest in protecting the flag that is embodied in the Flag Protection Act, and the considered judgment of Congress—as opposed to that of a single state legislature—that it was critically important to vindicate that interest in the wake of this Court's decision with respect to the Texas statute. . . . [T]he courts below [in these cases] overvalued, for purposes of the First Amendment, the narrow category of expressive conduct at stake, and undervalued the compelling governmental interest expressly—identified by both the Congress and the President—that lies at the core of the statute: the preservation of the flag as the unique symbol of our Nation. . . .

The Court has often set its face against various forms of expression that have marginal utility in our system of free expression and which occasion (or threaten) cognizable harm [and as a result] has excepted from the ambit of constitutional protection a variety of categories of speech and expressive conduct. . . .

[T]he Court should treat the conduct at issue—physical destruction of a flag of the United States—as it has such other narrowly defined categories of expressive conduct that have not merited full protection under the First Amendment [such as] obscene materials, speech proposing an illegal activity, perjury, and defamatory statements. . . .

This is especially true since the system of free expression ordained by the First Amendment is not compromised by a highly specific, narrowly tailored prohibition of physical attacks upon and destruction of the flag.

These cases call for the Court to reconsider the *Johnson*-created assumption that flag burning is a form of expressive conduct meriting full First Amendment protection. Reconsideration of that premise is particularly appropriate where, as here, the people's elected representatives—the Congress and the President—have made the considered decision that the physical destruction of the flag is—uniquely—anathema to the nation's values. . . .

Regardless of whether the Court regards flag burning as presenting such serious dangers, the Article III branch [the Supreme Court] should, we believe, defer to the considered judgment of the elected branches on the question of how important it is to the Nation to protect the flag from physical attack and destruction. . . .

[T]hrough passage of the Flag Protection Act, the people's elected representatives have now made clear that the physical integrity of the flag of the United States, as the unique symbol of the Nation, merits protection not accorded other national emblems. . . . Upon reflection, therefore, the assumption so newly and narrowly embraced in *Johnson* should not now obliterate Congress's considered and limited legislative determination of the compelling need to protect the physical integrity of the American flag. . . .

Document 12.5

Brief for Appellees in the consolidated case of *U.S. v. Eichman* and *U.S. v. Haggerty,* Nos. 89-1433 and 89-1434, in the Supreme Court of the United States, October term, 1989.

. . . The United States seeks to do in these cases precisely what this Court barred the State of Texas from doing in *Texas v. Johnson:* "criminally punish a person for burning a flag as a means of political protest." The criminal statute invoked is worded differently, but the governing legal principle is the same: the government may persuade and encourage people to respect the flag, but it may not compel the appearance of respect by penalizing flagburning.

The lesson of *Johnson* is so clear that before these cases the United States conceded the point. The Administration testified [in the person of Assistant Attorney General Barr] in Congress [document 11.14] that "⟨i⟩n the face of the Court's holdings in *Texas v. Johnson* and *Spence v. Washington,* and especially given the sweeping reasoning in those cases, it cannot be seriously maintained that a statute aimed at protecting the Flag would be constitutional." To permit the government to incarcerate individuals merely for expressing opposition to its most political symbol would have grave consequences for the meaning of freedom of expression. This Court should reaffirm the principles articulated so recently in *Johnson,* and affirm the district courts' judgments. . . .

SUMMARY OF ARGUMENT

The United States flag was born of a "desecration." When George Washington took command of the Continental Army at Cambridge, Massachusetts in 1776, he defaced a British flag by ordering sewn upon it thirteen red and white stripes. . . . The question before this Court is whether the United States government may incarcerate its citizens for engaging in similar politically expressive flag desecration.

I. The Court answered this question last term in *Texas v. Johnson. Johnson* established that the government may not criminalize flagburning to preserve the flag's symbolic value. A law so designed provokes stringent First Amendment scrutiny because it is necessarily directed at the communicative content of the proscribed flag conduct. And the government's interest in the symbolic value of the flag is insufficiently compelling to justify criminal punishment of politically expressive conduct. *Johnson* reaffirmed what this Court held forty-seven years ago in *West Virginia Board of Education v. Barnette* [document 5.2]: the dual principles of freedom of expression and government by the people prohibit the State from mandating respect for its icons by imprisoning those who express disrespect. These principles compel dismissal of the prosecutions at issue here.

Congressional amici argue that the Flag Protection Act of 1989 is designed to "protect the physical integrity of the flag in all circumstances," and therefore should be treated differently from the Texas statute [document 10.1]. But the Act is not so designed: it permits conduct that would imperil the flag's physical integrity, such as flying it in a storm, and it proscribes conduct that will have no effect on a flag's physical integrity, such as maintaining it on the floor or temporarily attaching a peace symbol to it.

More fundamentally, because "the flag" is not a physical object but an infinitely reproducible symbol, the only conceivable interest for protecting the flag's "physical integrity" is to preserve its symbolic value. And that interest, the Court has already held, cannot justify criminally punishing flagburning.

Nor can the Act be upheld as a restriction on the "manner" of expression, because it is content- and viewpoint-based. It singles out a particular politically charged symbol for "protection"; it proscribes only that flag conduct traditionally associated with dissent; it prohibits "physically defil⟨ing⟩" flags, an inherently viewpoint-based term; and while forbidding most "burning," it permits the burning of flags for disposal, the only flag-burning deemed respectful under the Flag Code.

II. The United States explicitly asks the Court to "reconsider" *Johnson*, but it implicitly asks the Court to reconsider the core principle of the First Amendment: that government may not prohibit political expression merely because it finds it offensive. The United States would have the Court rule that flagburning is unprotected expression because the government finds it an offensive and unimportant form of expression. But the First Amendment is needed precisely for expression that offends the government. The United States' proposed "exception" would swallow the rule of freedom of expression.

III. Finally, the Act is unconstitutional on its face. In addition to being content- and viewpoint-based, it is vague and substantially overbroad. It is impossible to discern which "flags" are covered by its proscriptions, or when a flag has become sufficiently "worn or soiled" to be open to desecration. And it forbids virtually all flag conduct associated with dissent.

ARGUMENT

I. THE FLAG PROTECTION ACT IS UNCONSTITUTIONAL AS APPLIED TO DEFENDANTS' POLITICALLY EXPRESSIVE CONDUCT

The United States and congressional amici assert three interests to justify the Act: (1) preserving the flag's symbolic value; (2) preserving the flag's "physical integrity"; and (3) preserving the flag's function as an "incident of sovereignty." None of these interests is sufficiently compelling to justify incarcerating an individual for burning a flag in political protest.

1. Preserving The Flag's Symbolic Value

In *Johnson*, this Court held that the government's interest in preserving the flag as a national symbol is insufficiently compelling to justify a prosecution for political flagburning.

The United States argues that notwithstanding *Johnson*, this interest should now be found sufficient, because Congress has made a "considered legislative judgment" that it is compelling. . . . The First Amendment was designed precisely to ensure that the majority not impose its notions of "consensus" on those who disagree [citing and quoting from *Barnette*]. The United States' view would leave the Bill of Rights to the whims of legislators. . . .

[I]f Congress wants people to respect the flag, that goal is undermined, not furthered, by a law punishing acts of disrespect. True respect requires the freedom to choose whether to pay respect. Finally, the flag is an infinitely reproducible symbol, and there is no showing that burning, temporarily defiling, or laying on the floor one or more of its representations harms its continuing function as a symbol. . . .

2. Preserving The "Physical Integrity" Of Flags

. . . First, the Act is not "aimed at protecting the physical integrity of the flag in all circumstances," for the same reason that this Court found that the Texas statute in *Johnson* was not so aimed: it contains an exception for the burning and physical destruction of worn or soiled flags.

The Act is both underinclusive and overinclusive with respect to a flag's "physical integrity." One may not lay the flag on the floor even under a glass covering that will preserve it from all physical harm whatsoever. Yet one may wave the flag where its physical integrity will be greatly endangered, as in bad weather or battle.

Second, and more fundamentally, there is an inherent flaw in the "physical integrity" logic: there is no reason for protecting the "physical integrity" of reproductions of the flag other than preserving the flag's symbolic value. "The flag" is not a physical thing, but a symbol, and therefore the only interest the government has in "protecting" it is symbolic.

3. Preserving an "Incident of Sovereignty"

. . . [T]he House Leadership asserts another governmental interest: protecting the flag as an "incident of sovereignty." . . .

Even if this interest actually supported the Act, it would not alter the legal analysis. First, House counsel never explains how flagburning or the other proscribed conduct undermines the flag's value as an "incident of sovereignty." Does the fact that Gregory Johnson burned a flag in 1984, that defendants burned flags on the steps of Congress, or that Scott Tyler placed a flag on the floor in an art exhibit [document 10.7], mean that the flag no longer serves its function in demarcating geographical boundaries and identifying ships? . . .

Second, even if this interest were threatened by flagburning, it is no more compelling than the government's interest in the flag's symbolic value. The government's interest in having a symbol to mark ships cannot justify jailing its citizens for burning reproductions of that symbol as a means of political protest.

The Act's Application Cannot Be Upheld as a Content-Neutral Time, Place or Manner Restriction

Any attempt to single out a particular non-material symbol for "protection" is inherently content-based. . . . Senator Biden and the House Leadership [in their amici briefs] argue that the fact that the Act does not use phrases like "cast contempt" or "seriously offend" renders it content-neutral. But if that were the case, Congress could constitutionally criminalize "⟨w⟩hoever knowingly mutilates, defaces, physically defiles, burns, maintains on the floor or ground, or tramples upon any [emblem of the Democratic party]."

While the American flag may encompass a wider spectrum of political views than the symbol of the Democratic Party, it is no less politically charged. . . . By singling out one symbol and one set of messages for "protection," the Act discriminates on the basis of content. . . .

The Act is viewpoint-based in the scope of flag use that it permits and proscribes. It prohibits those uses of the flag traditionally associated with opposition to the government, while permitting those uses of the flag associated with support of the government. People are free to wave the flag, no matter how dangerous the circumstances, but are not permitted to lay it on the ground, no matter how secure the resting place. . . .

That Congress chose the prohibited forms of conduct because of their historical use in expressing dissent is perhaps best exemplified by the genesis of the clause prohibiting "maintaining the flag on the floor or ground." Congress added this clause in direct response to defendant Scott Tyler's exhibit at the School of the Art Institute of Chicago. . . .

The exception for disposing of "worn or soiled" flags also reveals the statute's viewpoint bias, for it renders the same conduct—burning a flag—permissible for some reasons and not for others. . . .

II. THE COURT SHOULD NOT RECONSIDER *TEXAS V. JOHNSON*, WHICH RE-FLECTS A FUNDAMENTAL AND LONG-STANDING PRINCIPLE OF FIRST AMEND-MENT JURISPRUDENCE: THAT GOVERNMENT MAY NOT PROHIBIT POLITICAL EXPRESSION MERELY BECAUSE IT FINDS IT OFFENSIVE

Straining for some consistency with its congressional testimony, the United States in district court conceded that flagburning was expressive conduct and that any attempt to criminalize it must be justified by First Amendment scrutiny. Now it advances the opposite view, namely that flag desecration should be treated like child pornography, defamation, and "fighting words," and accorded no First Amendment protection whatsoever.

This Court flatly rejected a similar argument from Texas that flag-burning should be likened to "fighting words." The other examples the United States provides are unprotected for reasons inapplicable here: child pornography is unprotected because of the government's compelling interest in protecting children; defamation, like fighting words, harms a particular individual and, where it involves a matter of public concern, must be by definition both false and malicious; and obscenity, also by definition, has no serious political value.

To create an "exception" for overtly political communication such as flagburning would require reversing not only *Johnson,* but the "bedrock principle" upon which it rested: "the Government may not prohibit the expression of an idea simply because society finds the idea itself offensive or disagreeable" [citing *Johnson*].

Were the government permitted to proscribe what it deems offensive in political expression, freedom of expression would be imperiled across the board [with] "no discernible or defensible boundaries" [quoting *Johnson*].

The United States admits that its argument is "in tension" with the Court's analysis in *Johnson.* This is akin to saying that "separate but equal" is "in tension" with [the Supreme Court's 1954] *Brown v. Board of Education* [ruling declaring segrated schools unconstitutional as inherently unequal]. . . .

Texas v. Johnson merely confirms the principles that governed each of the Court's prior First Amendment decisions on flag regulation. It recognizes (1) that expression critical of government policies is at the core of First Amendment values; (2) that patriotism may be encouraged but not compelled; (3) that these principles apply equally to speech and conduct toward the United States flag; and (4) that compulsion is constitutionally forbidden whether it is effected by affirmative flag salute requirements or by criminal prohibitions on flag "mis-use." . . .

III. THE ACT IS UNCONSTITUTIONAL ON ITS FACE

The Act is also unconstitutional on its face, because it is content-based, overbroad and vague.

The Act gives no guidance as to which representations of "the flag" are covered by its prohibitions. . . . It encompasses flags of any substance and any size, with the only limitation being that they must be "in a form that is commonly displayed." Some of the most commonly displayed flags are those drawn by school-children in grade schools. Does the Act prohibit a child from defacing the flag she just drew? . . . .

Similarly, the distinction between a soiled and an unsoiled flag, or a worn and an unworn flag, is wholly evanescent. Every flag that has been removed from its box will be soiled in one sense, simply by contact with human hands. Certainly any flag that has ever been exposed to the elements in Washington, DC, Seattle, Washington, or any other urban area, is soiled. . . . It is impossible to determine when a flag has become sufficiently soiled or worn to permit its burning.

The Act is also substantially overbroad, for it prohibits all of the traditional means of using a flag to express opposition to it. A vast number of the acts prohibited, moreover, would have no conceivable effect on the flag's symbolic value. For example, the Act prohibits maintaining a flag on the floor of a private closet, "defacing" a flag with a veteran's medal or an adhesive peace symbol, "mutilating" a flag at a flag factory, or ceremoniously burning a flag before it is "worn or soiled."

CONCLUSION

The Court's decision in *Texas v. Johnson* provoked a "visceral" response from the President, and a political response from Congress. That is their prerogative. But the Bill of Rights is designed to provide legal protection from the political inclinations of the majority when they trample upon the freedoms of those whose views are in the minority. And the courts are assigned to enforce those constitutional protections. . . . The outcome is again at this Court's door, because the majoritarian branches have been unwilling to protect the rights of an outspoken minority. The decisions below should be affirmed.

Document 12.6

Oral arguments before the U.S. Supreme Court, May 4, 1990, in the consolidated case of *U.S. v. Eichman* and *U.S. v. Haggerty,* Nos. 89-1433 and 89-1434, Solicitor General Kenneth Starr for the United States, petitioner, attorney William Kunstler for the respondents.

MR. STARR: . . . There are four reasons that argue powerfully in support of the constitutionality of this statute.

First, Congress acted carefully and with great respect for this Court's decisions concerning flag protection statutes. It took seriously the Court's expressed statement in Texas against Johnson that the inquiry there was bounded not only by the facts of the case, but by the state's statute there in question.

In relying on this Court's various writings and decisions, Congress amended the Federal statute in response to Texas against Johnson to eliminate the prior, clearly content-laden language of Section 700 [the 1968 federal Flag Desecration Law, document 6.1], the language, "cast contempt" upon and "publicly."

Second, Congress acted very narrowly. . . . Congress carved out a narrowly crafted set of protections as to certain conduct, while permitting robust and uninhibited speech to continue unabated.

There was no prohibition on Congress' part against the publication or the dissemination of ideas.

Third and relatedly, as I will seek to show in the context of the facts of these two cases, flag burning leaves a major message gap, a gap that needs to be filled in with words, either written or spoken, as happened in both the District of Columbia and Seattle demonstrations. It is, in our judgment, the equivalent of shouting or screaming or using a loudspeaker at full blast to arrest the audience's attention. This is not in our judgment an especially weighty value on the First Amendment scales.

Fourth, on the other side of those scales are interests of the highest order in the national community. Those interests are intangible, to be sure, just as the concept of human dignity is intangible. But those interests are no less real, rooted as they are in the Nation's history and experience. . . .

Now a passerby happening on these acts of flag burning would, in our judgment, likely and reasonably conclude that the actor is in a state of profound disagreement. But it does not tell us with what. That message, the what, comes, if at all, from the speech that is incident or tied to the conduct. . . .

QUESTION: General Starr, I don't understand this line of argument. Is . . . it that you're saying that somehow the expression "I hate the United States" is entitled to less constitutional protection than "I disagree with our policy in Eastern Europe"? Is that the point that . . . if it's a political expression, it's too generic, too generalized, it's not entitled to the same degree of protection?

MR. STARR: The message itself enjoys the same protection. The question is what message is being conveyed. . . .

QUESTION: Well, what you convey by burning the flag is, "I hate the United States." . . . What do you think it conveys if it does not convey the notion that, for whatever particular reason it may be, "I am in opposition to this country"?

MR. STARR: I think that assumes too much, with all respect. When Mr. Street burned the flag at issue in Street against New York [document 8.1], his stated concerns were with the failure to provide protection to James Meredith. . . .

QUESTION: Are you saying that this is an invalid form of protest?

MR. STARR: In our judgment, it is conduct, and conduct gives much greater latitude to Congress as long as Congress does not do as the State of

Texas did in Texas against Johnson, and that is, pass a statute that was not viewpoint neutral. . . . That is not so here.

An individual runs afoul of this statute regardless of what message, if any, that individual is seeking to convey. . . . It is because this symbol is important to us as a nation. And Congress in fact protects [things] that are important to the Nation in a variety of ways, by virtue, at times, of its symbolic importance.

But what we have learned from Texas against Johnson and other decisions is that those protections, those prohibitions, cannot be tied to the specific viewpoint.

In the legislative history it was quite clear that Congress had presented to it by eminent scholars examples of exactly this kind of protection. The statutes in force with respect to prohibitions of desecration of houses of worship, additional protections . . . for the bald eagle. . . .

If it is protecting it not from criticism but from physical destruction or mutilation . . . one can protect those things that are special to us as a people.

QUESTION: We don't like, Mr. Starr, to compare our flag with any other flag, but would you be concerned if in Eastern Europe or some foreign country a government punished demonstrators for marching with a defaced flag in support of the demonstrators' cause for freedom?

MR. STARR: I think those are considerations . . . that are very important for Congress to weigh in the balance. . . .

QUESTION: Well, but isn't the point that this is a[n] . . . internationally recognized form of protest?

MR. STARR: It certainly, at this particular stage in our history, is affiliated or associated with forms of protest. . . .

One cannot punish a flag protestor because he or she is expressing outrage about policies to the country. . . . [W]e read Texas against Johnson [to say] that Congress does and should have power to protect the physical integrity of the flag as long as it is not saying we single out certain viewpoints for disfavored treatment. That is the critical point that Congress was responding to in reading Texas against Johnson and the prior flag cases.

QUESTION: But in fact there is only one viewpoint: that you do not mutilate, deface, defile or trample upon the flag in order to show your love for the country. . . . You started by pointing out to us that Congress had taken out of the original Section 700(a) the phrase "casts contempt" upon the flag, but do you really think that in fact there is any difference so long as the words that they describe to protect the physical integrity of the flag are "mutilate, deface, defile, burn or trample"—I guess burn is pretty neutral, but if I get a spot on my tie I don't say, gee, I've defiled my tie. (Laughter.) Or if I tear my jacket I don't say, my, I've mutilated my jacket. These are words of—cast contempt upon. . . .

MR. STARR: The term defaces would in fact encompass activity, conduct. . . . An individual may deface the flag by virtue of emblazoning the words onto that flag, "I love the Supreme Court." That constitutes defacement.

QUESTION: Well, General, I thought at the outset you suggested that burning this flag really didn't have any message of its own anyway in this case, . . . that it was just . . . a flag burning to call attention to some other messages that had nothing to do with the flag. It was just like . . . you burned anything else at the site.

MR. STARR: Exactly right. In fact . . . during the course of the demonstration [in Seattle] there was also burned the McDonald's Golden Arches flag from a nearby restaurant. (Laughter.)

Now, I think this is what this Court was getting at when it spoke of, in Spence against Washington [document 8.3], acts of mindless nihilism as opposed to the acts that this Court has focused on in *Spence* and in other cases where it has found what the Court called an intent to deliver a particularized message. There is no particularized message being delivered by these individuals here.

QUESTION: This is like just an over-loud loudspeaker?

MR. STARR: That, I think, is the most apt analogy. . . . Congress created this flag, and it is seeking in a neutral way, without regard to the message, to protect the physical integrity of that flag without . . . in any way interrupting the flow of free ideas in the marketplace. . . .

MR. KUNSTLER: . . . We think the question before the Court is can the government criminally prohibit flag burning, a form of political expression deeply critical of the government and anathema to its officials?

We hold, one, that *Texas v. Johnson* controls these two cases. Number two, that the Flag Protection Act can simply not be upheld as an attempt to protect the physical integrity of the flag in all circumstances. And three, that there is no basis whatsoever to accept the government's invitation to overturn *Johnson.*

On the first point, that *Texas v. Johnson* controls, all parties have conceded [in the federal district court proceedings] that the defendant's conduct below was expressive enough to raise First Amendment concerns. . . .

Number two, all parties conceded as well that the congressional intent behind this statute was to protect the flag as a national symbol, and by definition the governmental interest was only harmed by conduct expressing some message of disrespect or dissent. . . . In other words, the interest was related to the suppression of free expression. Ergo, the strict scrutiny rule applies.

Then lastly, that the government interest in preserving this symbolic value is not a compelling interest to justify a criminal penal statute and jail flag-burners. That is what *Johnson* held.

Now, the government is now arguing, apparently, that there's now a compelling interest that they have in the flag because . . . a new act was enacted and became effective on October 28th of last year.

If the Court were to accept that argument that the mere adoption of a new act would mean that you would reverse yourself in *Texas v. Johnson,* then I think it would require reversing Marbury against Madison [giving the Supreme Court the power of judicial review]. But that's not a sufficient reason, merely because Congress says that it is now enacting a new act. . . . [T]hey cannot change what is obviously the Court's duty in this case merely by passing legislation.

Secondly, with reference to the question of the physical integrity in all circumstances that are now claimed by General Starr, . . . it's obviously that is not true on the face of the statute itself.

First of all, it is not content neutral. It is content and viewpoint based. It singles out a political symbol . . . and in our brief we indicated what if that political symbol had been instead of the flag the Democratic Party flag. . . . It singles out one particular political symbol, just as in *Stromberg* [document 5.1] the red flag was singled out as one particular political symbol.

And it is viewpoint-based because it proscribes conduct which was associated with dissent, irrespective of the effect on the physical integrity of the flag. It permits, as the Court knows, conduct which shows respect, and that is the ceremonial burning of the flag, which was put in there in order not to penalize patriotic groups. . . .

And then the language of the statute itself is just to pick up all disrespect examples, all dissenting examples—maintained on the floor or ground [in response to act in which] Dread Scott Tyler, one of the Appellees before this Court, had placed a flag on the ground in that rather well-known Chicago Art Institute exhibit [document 10.7].

And the word "defile" has a dictionary meaning of dishonor. And yet it permits conduct . . . dangerous to the flag such as . . . flying in a hurricane. . . . And, therefore, it is totally viewpoint based.

[T]hese terms protect the flag only from those who would hurt it or cast it in a bad light.

And any statute, I submit to this Court, even one designed to protect physical integrity, in all circumstances would be content based because Congress' interest is—ultimately indistinguishable from the flag's symbolic value. . . .

QUESTION: But this case is a case involving a special message, as I understand it. And what was that message?

MR. KUNSTLER: Well, there were a number of messages. . . .

QUESTION: But how—if I just see the flag burning, how do I know which one it is, or is that irrelevant?

MR. KUNSTLER: It's only irrelevant in the sense there are documents being handed out, flyers, declarations. . . . [Observers] will know initially that the burning exhibited a dissatisfaction. . . . And then it's broken down.

QUESTION: Call this . . . number and we'll tell you why we burned the flag. . . .

MR. KUNSTLER : . . . [T]hey did give the messages out, why they burnt the flag. But the burning of the flag itself, I think, even without a message, would convey a message.

You see, General Starr says, essentially, that the burning of a flag by itself carries no message. . . . [H]is argument could prevail in any non-verbal demonstration. How do you know why anybody is doing anything with a non-verbal expression? What if they drew a picture of Uncle Sam being hanged, for example, a caricature? . . . [Y]ou can't relegate non-verbal expression to the scrap heap.

QUESTION: . . . [E]ven with verbal expression, you don't have to be precise in order to be protected, do you? . . .

MR. KUNSTLER: As far as my last point, the invitation to overrule *Texas v. Johnson,* this is a last resort argument, I think. It's an argument based on a recognition that *Texas v. Johnson* applies here. There have been all sorts of methods here to try to get around *Texas v. Johnson.*

They're trying to say that flag burning is not protected. We should put it aside with child pornography and defamation and libel and slander, and excise it from the First Amendment. . . . [I]n the area of political speech, a government cannot make judgments of what is overly offensive or unimportant speech. That simply cannot be done.

The First Amendment was designed to forestall the majority, forestall their inclination to suppress what the government deems offensive at any one time or another. . . .

I would just like to close with the fact that, number one, that respect for the flag must be voluntary. . . . [O]nce people are compelled to respect a political symbol, then they are no longer free and their respect for the flag is quite meaningless.

To criminalize flag burning is to deny what the First Amendment stands for [and to] make the American flag, a political symbol, cherished as it is by many people, into a golden image. . . .

Document 12.7

Majority ruling of the U.S. Supreme Court, authored by Justice Brennan, in the 1990 case of *U.S. v. Eichman.*

Source: 496 United States Reports 310.

In these consolidated appeals, we consider whether appellees' prosecution for burning a United States flag in violation of the Flag Protection Act of 1989 is consistent with the First Amendment. Applying our recent decision in *Texas v. Johnson,* the District Courts held that the Act cannot constitutionally be applied to appellees. We affirm.

I

In No. 89-1433, the United States prosecuted certain appellees for violating the Flag Protection Act of 1989, by knowingly setting fire to several United States flags on the steps of the United States Capitol while protesting various aspects of the Government's domestic and foreign policy. In No. 89-1434, the United States prosecuted other appellees for violating the Act by knowingly setting fire to a United States flag in Seattle while protesting the Act's passage. In each case, the respective appellees moved to dismiss the flagburning charge on the ground that the Act, both on its face and as applied, violates the First Amendment. Both the United States District Court for the Western District of Washington [document 12.3] and the United States District Court for the District of Columbia, following *Johnson* [document 10.12], held the Act unconstitutional as applied to appellees and dismissed the charges. The United States appealed both decisions directly to this Court. . . .

II

Last Term in *Johnson,* we held that a Texas statute criminalizing the desecration of venerated objects, including the United States flag, was unconstitutional as applied to an individual who had set such a flag on fire during a political demonstration. . . . We first held that Johnson's flag burning was "conduct 'sufficiently imbued with elements of communication' to implicate the First Amendment." We next considered and rejected the State's contention that, under *United States v. O'Brien,* we ought to apply the deferential standard with which we have reviewed Government regulations of conduct containing both speech and nonspeech elements where "the governmental interest is unrelated to the suppression of free expression." We reasoned that the State's asserted interest "in preserving the flag as a symbol of nationhood and national unity," was an interest "related 'to the suppression of free expression' within the meaning of *O'Brien*" because the State's concern with protecting the flag's symbolic meaning is implicated "only when a person's treatment of the flag communicates some message." We therefore subjected the statute to "'the most exacting scrutiny,'" and we concluded that the State's asserted interests could not justify the infringement on the demonstrator's First Amendment rights.

After our decision in *Johnson,* Congress passed the Flag Protection Act of 1989. . . .

The Government concedes in this case, as it must, that appellees' flag burning constituted expressive conduct, but invites us to reconsider our rejection in *Johnson* of the claim that flag burning as a mode of expression, like obscenity or "fighting words," does not enjoy the full protection of the First Amendment. This we decline to do. The only remaining question is whether the Flag Protection Act is sufficiently distinct from the Texas statute [examined in *Johnson,* document 10.1] that it may constitutionally be applied to proscribe appellees' expressive conduct.

The Government contends that the Flag Protection Act is constitutional because, unlike the statute addressed in *Johnson,* the Act does not target expressive conduct on the basis of the content of its message. The Government asserts an interest in "protect⟨ing⟩ the physical integrity of the flag under all circumstances" in order to safeguard the flag's identity " 'as the unique and unalloyed symbol of the Nation.' " The Act proscribes conduct (other than disposal) that damages or mistreats a flag, without regard to the actor's motive, his intended message, or the likely effects of his conduct on onlookers. By contrast, the Texas statute expressly prohibited only those acts of physical flag desecration "that the actor knows will seriously offend" onlookers, and the former federal statute [document 6.1] prohibited only those acts of desecration that "cas⟨t⟩ contempt upon" the flag.

Although the Flag Protection Act contains no explicit content-based limitation on the scope of prohibited conduct, it is nevertheless clear that the Government's asserted interest is "related 'to the suppression of free expression,' " and concerned with the content of such expression. The Government's interest in protecting the "physical integrity" of a privately owned flag rests upon a perceived need to preserve the flag's status as a symbol of our nation and certain national ideals. But the mere destruction or disfigurement of a particular physical manifestation of the symbol, without more, does not diminish or otherwise affect the symbol itself in any way. . . .[6]

Moreover, the precise language of the Act's prohibitions confirms Congress' interest in the communicative impact of flag destruction. The Act criminalizes the conduct of anyone who "knowingly mutilates, defaces, physically defiles, burns, maintains on the floor or ground, or tramples upon any flag." Each of the specified terms—with the possible exception of "burns"—unmistakably connotes disrespectful treatment of the flag and suggests a focus on those acts likely to damage the flag's symbolic value. And the explicit exemption in [the Act] for disposal of "worn or soiled" flags protects certain acts traditionally associated with patriotic respect for the flag.[8]

As we explained in *Johnson,* "⟨I⟩f we were to hold that a State may forbid flag burning wherever it is likely to endanger the flag's symbolic role, but allow it wherever burning a flag promotes that role—as where, for example, a person ceremoniously burns a dirty flag—we would be * * * permitting a State to 'prescribe what shall be orthodox' by saying that one may burn the flag to convey one's attitude toward it and its referents only if one does not endanger the flag's representation of nationhood and national unity." Although Congress cast the Flag Protection Act of 1989 in somewhat broader terms than the Texas statute at issue in *Johnson,* the Act still suffers from the same fundamental flaw: It suppresses expression out of concern for its likely communicative impact. Despite the Act's wider scope, its restriction on expression cannot be " 'justified without reference to the content of the regulated speech.' " The Act therefore must be subjected to "the most exacting scrutiny," and for the reasons stated in *Johnson,* the Government's interest cannot justify its infringement on First Amendment rights. We decline the Government's invitation to reassess this conclusion in light of Congress' recent recognition of a purported "national consensus" favoring a prohibition on flag burning. Even assuming such a consensus exists, any suggestion that the Government's interest in suppressing speech becomes more weighty as popular opposition to that speech grows is foreign to the First Amendment.

III

. . . Government may create national symbols, promote them, and encourage their respectful treatment. But the Flag Protection Act of 1989 goes well beyond this by criminally proscribing expressive conduct because of its likely communicative impact.

We are aware that desecration of the flag is deeply offensive to many. But the same might be said, for example, of virulent ethnic and religious epithets, vulgar repudiations of the draft, and scurrilous caricatures [all of which had been previously held protected by the First Amendment in decisions cited by the Court]. "If there is a bedrock principle underlying the First Amendment, it is that the Government may not prohibit the expression of an idea simply because society finds the idea itself offensive or disagreeable" [quoting from *Johnson*]. Punishing desecration of the flag dilutes the very freedom that makes this emblem so revered, and worth revering.

The judgments of the District Courts are
Affirmed.

6. Aside from the flag's association with particular ideals, at some irreducible level the flag is emblematic of the Nation as a sovereign entity. . . . We concede [as the House of Representatives argues in its brief] that the Government has a legitimate interest in preserving the flag's function as an "incident of sovereignty," though we need not address today the extent to which this interest may justify any laws regulating conduct that would

thwart this core function. . . . Amici do not, and cannot, explain how a statute that penalizes anyone who knowingly burns, mutilates or defiles any American flag is designed to advance this asserted interest in maintaining the association between the flag and the Nation. Burning a flag does not threaten to interfere with this association in any way; indeed, the flag burner's message depends in part on the viewer's ability to make this very association.

8. The Act also does not prohibit flying a flag in a storm or other conduct that threatens the physical integrity of the flag, albeit in an indirect manner unlikely to communicate disrespect.

Document 12.8

Dissenting opinion of four justices of the U.S. Supreme Court, authored by Justice Stevens, in the 1990 case of *U.S. v. Eichman.*

Source: 496 United States Reports 319.

The Court's opinion ends where proper analysis of the issue should begin. Of course "the Government may not prohibit the expression of an idea simply because society finds the idea itself offensive or disagreeable." . . . But it is equally well settled that certain methods of expression may be prohibited if (a) the prohibition is supported by a legitimate societal interest that is unrelated to suppression of the ideas the speaker desires to express; (b) the prohibition does not entail any interference with the speaker's freedom to express those ideas by other means; and (c) the interest in allowing the speaker complete freedom of choice among alternative methods of expression is less important than the societal interest supporting the prohibition. . . .

The first question the Court should consider is whether the interest in preserving the value of that symbol is unrelated to suppression of the ideas that flag burners are trying to express. In my judgment the answer depends, at least in part, on what those ideas are. A flag burner might intend various messages. . . .

The idea expressed by a particular act of flag burning is necessarily dependent on the temporal and political context in which it occurs. . . .

The Government's legitimate interest in preserving the symbolic value of the flag is, however, essentially the same regardless of which of many different ideas may have motivated a particular act of flag burning. . . .

[T]he Government may—indeed, it should—protect the symbolic value of the flag without regard to the specific content of the flag burners' speech. . . . It is, moreover, equally clear that the prohibition does not entail any interference with the speaker's freedom to express his or her ideas by other means. It may well be true that other means of expression may be less effective in drawing attention to those ideas, but that is not itself a sufficient reason for immunizing flag burning. Presumably a gigantic fireworks display or a parade of nude models in a public park might draw even more attention to a controversial message, but such methods of expression are nevertheless subject to regulation.

This case therefore comes down to a question of judgment. Does the admittedly important interest in allowing every speaker to choose the method of expressing his or her ideas that he or she deems most effective and appropriate outweigh the societal interest in preserving the symbolic value of the flag? . . .The opinions in *Texas v. Johnson* demonstrate that reasonable judges may differ with respect to each of these judgments. . . .

The freedom of expression protected by the First Amendment embraces not only the freedom to communicate particular ideas, but also the right to communicate them effectively. That right, however, is not absolute—the communicative value of a well-placed bomb in the Capitol does not entitle it to the protection of the First Amendment.

Burning a flag is not, of course, equivalent to burning a public building. Assuming that the protester is burning his own flag, it causes no physical harm to other persons or to their property. The impact is purely symbolic, and it is apparent that some thoughtful persons believe that impact, far from depreciating the value of the symbol, will actually enhance its meaning. I most respectfully disagree. Indeed, what makes this case particularly difficult for me is what I regard as the damage to the symbol that has already occurred as a result of this Court's decision to place its stamp of approval on the act of flag burning. . . .

The symbolic value of the American flag is not the same today as it was yesterday. Events during the last three decades have altered the country's image in the eyes of numerous Americans, and some now have difficulty understanding the message that the flag conveyed to their parents and grandparents. . . . Moreover, the integrity of the symbol has been compromised by those leaders who seem to advocate compulsory worship of the flag even by individuals whom it offends, or who seem to manipulate the symbol of national purpose into a pretext for partisan disputes about meaner ends. And, as I have suggested, the residual value of the symbol after this Court's decision in *Texas v. Johnson* is surely not the same as it was a year ago.

Given all these considerations, plus the fact that the Court today is really doing nothing more than reconfirming what it has already decided, it might be appropriate to defer to the judgment of the majority and merely apply the doctrine of *stare decisis* [precedent] to the case at hand. That action, however, would not honestly reflect my considered judgment concerning the relative importance of the conflicting interests that are at stake. . . .

13

Second Defeat of the
Constitutional Amendment
1990

The June 11, 1990, *Eichman* decision sparked an immediate renewal of calls by President Bush and others for a constitutional amendment to prohibit flag desecration. Bush told reporters on June 12, "The law books are full of restrictions on free speech, and we ought to have this be one of them" (document 13.1). During Senate Judiciary Committee hearings on possible responses to the *Eichman* ruling on June 21, acting assistant attorney general J. Michael Luttig renewed the administration's pleas for an amendment (document 13.2) as necessary to protect "the single symbol of our shared commitment to freedom."

As had been the case right after the *Johnson* ruling, in the immediate aftermath of *Eichman* many predicted that a constitutional amendment would pass handily and rapidly. On June 11, amendment sponsor and Republican House minority leader Robert Michel predicted easy congressional passage, asking rhetorically, "Who wants to be against the flag, mother and apple pie?" However, although public opinion polls indicated that majorities of 60 percent or more of the public favored passage of a constitutional amendment, the intensity of public interest appears to have been far weaker in mid-1990 than it had been a year earlier. For example, Democratic representative Dennis Eckart of Ohio, an amendment supporter, was quoted in the June 18 *Washington Post* as declaring, "There is nowhere near the [mail] volume as there was . . . a year ago," and an anonymous high-level Republican operative was quoted in the same article as lamenting, "This is an issue whose time has come and gone."[1]

Probably at least partly as a result of this perceived lack of intense public demand for a flag amendment—which paralleled the more moderate tone of the Supreme Court dissent in *Eichman* as compared to *Johnson*, as well as a considerably lower profile by President Bush compared to the previous year—almost all of the congressmen who indicated that they were undecided about an amendment in the immediate post-*Eichman* period ultimately voted against it. An Associated Press survey published June 20, 1990, and completed two days previously, reported 255 representatives and 58 senators for or leaning toward the amendment, 114 apparent opponents in the House and 24 in the Senate, and 65 representatives and 18 senators undecided. However, during the climactic June 21 House vote, 177 representatives voted against the amendment, and 42 senators cast negative votes during the June 26 Senate vote, suggesting a massive swing against the amendment in the final days before the vote. These last-minute votes proved crucial in the amendment's demise, as it fell far short of the two-thirds majority required, although still obtaining simple majorities in both houses (254–177 in the House and 58–42 in the Senate).

The defeat of the amendment in 1990 resulted from the interaction of a variety of factors. First, it seems likely that the public simply lost interest in an issue that had dragged on for over a year and ultimately was entirely symbolic, especially because most people never witnessed anyone burn a flag and were not, in any case, concretely affected by flag burnings. By mid-1990, the flag desecration controversy had, in short, become a summer "rerun," a formula notorious for killing public interest.

Republican proponents of the amendment in 1990 also appear to have hurt their cause with frequently voiced comments, particularly by Republican Senate leader and amendment sponsor Robert Dole, that suggested that Democrats who voted against the amendment would suffer political consequences, especially in the form of so-called thirty-second negative television spots, which the Bush administration had used with great skill to attack Dukakis in the 1988 presidential campaign. Such comments were made far more often and more publicly by Republicans in 1990 than had been the case in 1989, when speculation about the political significance of the flag desecration controversy had been voiced mostly in Capitol cloakrooms and in press speculation; the evident result was that the cause of the amendment was discredited in 1990 as simply a matter of partisan politics in the minds of considerable segments of public, and especially of press opinion, which was even more massively and vehemently opposed to the amendment in 1990 than during the previous year. Even friends of the Bush administration such as the *Detroit News* denounced the amendment as primarily an effort to "gain momentary popular support," a motive that was termed "almost as revolting as flag-burning itself" (document 13.3).

An additional key factor that probably influenced the vote outcome in 1990 was that the entire controversy was "framed" for public and congressional consumption far differently than it had been the previous year, in a manner that made the case for not doing anything far more intellectually and politically appealing. In 1989, the issue had been effectively "framed" by both Republican and Democratic leaders as whether the *Johnson* ruling should be overturned by Congress by law or by constitutional amendment, a structuring of the debate that defined "doing nothing" as not even a serious option. However, following the *Eichman* ruling, which effectively eliminated the legislative option, leaving only the possibility of "doing nothing" or amending the Constitution, the Democratic congressional leadership "reframed" the issue as a battle between two icons—the flag versus the Bill of Rights—and adopted the position that the flag was only a symbol of freedom, while the Bill of Rights guaranteed the substance of that freedom and was therefore far more important to protect. Thus, Senate Democratic majority leader George Mitchell, who had largely deferred in 1989 to pro-FPA SJC chairman Joseph Biden, declared in a lengthy Senate speech on June 19, 1990, that, while flag burning was "offensive and obnoxious" and the Supreme Court had erred in its decision, the Bill of Rights was the most eloquent and effective statement of democratic rights in "the whole sweep of human history," and should not face "the unwise action of changing [it] for the first time in American history" (document 13.4).

This theme was repeatedly used in June 1990 by amendment opponents in the press and in Congress. For example, Democratic representative Tim Valentine of North Carolina, who had been an early amendment sponsor, told the House of Representatives during the debate preceding the climactic June 21 vote, that "over the rhetoric of the past few days I have finally heard the voice of my own conscience" and had changed his position, because "after much soul searching, I have concluded that we should not depart from two centuries of constitutional history by placing, for the first time, limitations on the Bill of Rights," as "in the final analysis" the flag was "a piece of fabric," while the "Constitution is the fabric of our nation" (document 13.5). During the June 21 SJC hearing, Duke University law professor Walter Dellinger, who had told Congress in 1989 that the Supreme Court would likely uphold an FPA, similarly blasted the amendment (as he also had in 1989), declaring that it would "compromise the moral legitimacy of the First Amendment" by introducing into the Constitution the principle that "expression that is offensive to the majority may be suppressed," thus leaving the United States "a little less free, and a little less brave" (document 13.6).

The fate of the amendment was sealed in the House on June 21 after a dramatic debate that lasted for an extraordinary eight hours, in which about two hundred representatives spoke. Two of the most powerful speeches were the final orations delivered by Republican representative Henry Hyde of Illinois for the amendment and by Democratic Speaker Tom Foley of Washington against it. Hyde termed the flag "in a class by itself," rising above "the political swamps that we live and work in" to symbolize "as nothing else does" the unity of a deeply heterogeneous nation. He urged his colleagues to "take the flag out of the gutter where the counterculture has dragged it," "to catch the falling flag and raise it up" and to thereby elevate "us all to being worthy of the great country we live in" (document 13.7). Foley, who in keeping with the traditional role played by House Speakers, spoke on the floor only on the rarest and most significant occasions, declared that the debate was about "one of the most important issues and votes" that would perhaps be cast "for many Congresses to come." He termed the flag above all a "symbol of the liberty and freedom that has distinguished this country as a beacon for hundreds of millions of people around the world for two centuries," and urged his colleagues not to begin, amidst "pressure from transitory forces, influences or emotions," the process of "idly or casually" weakening the First Amendment, which he termed "the repository of all the hopes and ambitions of our Founding Fathers to protect individual liberties." Foley closed his remarks by reiterating the main theme of amendment opponents, declaring, "Defeat this amendment. Protect the Bill of Rights" (document 13.8).

Document 13.1

Remarks by President Bush and answers to reporters' questions at a White House ceremony at which he received a replica of the Iwo Jima Memorial, June 12, 1990.

Source: Weekly Compilation of Presidential Documents 26, no. 24 (June 18, 1990): 938–39.

. . . This memorial embodies self-expression and opportunity and democracy for all. And, well, so does another symbol that I'd like to talk about here today: concern for the American flag and what it represents. . . .

What that flag encapsules is too sacred to be abused. You all know yesterday's Supreme Court decision [in the *Eichman* case, document 12.7]. It wasn't surprising. One year ago this month, many of us deeply concerned about protecting the American flag from willful desecration predicted that any congressional legislation would be declared unconstitutional. I take no joy that this prediction has been upheld. Accordingly, I want to take the chance today to renew my commitment to the surest, safest way to guarantee that, while speech remains free, flag desecration is unacceptable and must carry a price, and, yes, a constitutional amendment to protect the truly unique symbol of all that we are and that we believe. Our constitutional amendment will preserve the widest conceivable range of options for free expression. It applies only to the flag [document 11.6]. . . .

Amending the Constitution to protect the flag is not a matter of partisan politics. It's not a Democrat nor a Republican issue. I don't see it as either liberal or conservative. It's an American issue. And so, I call on the Congress to act by July 4th, this nation's birthday. I know that honest and patriotic Americans may differ on this question, but I am absolutely convinced that this is the proper course for our country. . . . Through a constitutional amendment, let us honor the greatest symbol of this great country. . . .

Q. Mr. President, what do you say to those who say every country has a flag, but only we have the Bill of Rights. It's never been amended; why should we amend it today?

The President. I say that the forefathers provided for amendment of the Constitution, including the Bill of Rights, and that the flag is a unique symbol. I can't speak for the other countries, but I can speak for how strongly I feel about this being the unique symbol of the United States. And it should be protected. . . . When [the FPA] was knocked down by the Court [in *Eichman*], I feel there's no other way to go but this constitutional amendment, which was provided for. So, that's what I say; I keep emphasizing the word "unique" symbol of the United States of America.

Q. But isn't burning it free speech, sir? . . .

The President. No, . . . because the Court has determined that there are excesses to free speech. And I would like to see one of these excesses be the burning of the American flag. So, yes, I am all for free speech, but I am for protecting the flag against desecration. The law books are full of restrictions on free speech, and we ought to have this be one of them. Shouting "fire" in a crowded theater is a good one for you.

Q. Mr. President, but that endangers people. Does burning the flag endanger people?

The President. Yes. It endangers the fabric of our country, and I think it ought to be outlawed.

Q. If it's not a matter of partisan politics, Mr. President, why are members of your party already gearing up to put together 30-second campaign commercials dealing with their opponents' votes?

The President. I know nothing about those campaign commercials. . . . And I'm putting it in what I think is best for the United States. I feel strongly about it. . . .

Q. Will you be commenting on this during the election?

The President. You're darn right. I want this done now. I hope it will be out of the way by the time of the election.

Document 13.2

Statement by acting assistant attorney general J. Michael Luttig before the Senate Judiciary Committee, June 21, 1990.

Source: Measures to Protect the American Flag, Hearing before the Senate Judiciary Committee, 101st Cong., 1st sess, 1990, serial no. J-101-77, 43–65.

At the outset, let me assure the Committee and the Congress that the Administration does not believe that we should blithely propose amendments to our basic charter of governance. . . . [Constitutional amendments] should be undertaken only rarely, and then only with the greatest care. We must not lose sight of the fact, however, that the most fundamental right of a free people is to define their freedoms and their system of governance through their Constitution. . . .

The will of the American people is that their Flag, the single symbol of our shared commitment to freedom, be protected from desecration and defilement. The President firmly believes that the people should be permitted to work that will. The American people are the most jealous guardians of their freedoms. . . . The President believes not only that we can, but that we must place trust in the people. . . . It is the people's Flag. It is their Constitution. . . .

In Congress, [last year in the wake of the *Johnson* ruling, document 10.12] there also was a broad consensus that the Flag must be protected. . . .

The only dispute was over the means necessary to protect the Flag. The Administration would have supported a statute had it believed that a statute could have withstood judicial scrutiny. The Department of Justice determined, however, that the Court's decision in *Johnson* could not be legislatively corrected [document 11.14]. Accordingly, the President called for a constitutional amendment. Many members of Congress, on the other hand, believed that a statute might well be upheld by the Court, and that this means should be explored before an amendment was proposed. [However, in response to congressional passage last year of the Flag Protection Act, in the recent *Eichman* ruling, the] same five Justices who comprised the majority in *Johnson* rejected the arguments that the new federal statute was content-neutral and that the government has a compelling interest in the protection of the Flag. The Court has now spoken definitively. If the American people and their representatives wish to protect the Flag, they must do so by constitutional amendment.

The Administration believes that the Flag is worthy of constitutional protection and that a constitutional provision protecting the Flag will not diminish our freedom of speech. The vast majority of Americans, and the Congress as well, share this belief. . . .

Symbols, such as the Flag, often are the shorthand for all that we hold dear, and desecration of a symbol can break the spirit and thus cripple the cause in the name of which the symbol was raised. This is true of the Flag, and the American people recognize this. They know that acquiescence in the desecration of this symbol of liberty is, in the long run, a threat to our spirit, and thereby to our social and political fabric. The American people understandably want this precious symbol protected and believe it is deserving of the fullest protection that we are able to provide. They understand that it can be protected without any threat to free expression. . . . [A] Flag protection amendment would not have any measurable impact on free speech and the values underlying that guarantee. The President would not support an amendment if it were otherwise.

As an initial matter, it is debatable whether Flag burning or physically defiling the Flag should be considered speech at all. . . .

But even assuming that Flag burning or a similar act of desecration is speech, it is manifestly speech of little value. As a people, we have chosen to prohibit similar, discrete and clearly defined categories of speech completely. For example, the First Amendment does not protect obscenity because we believe that it has little, if any, value to society. The proposed Flag amendment no more infringes on free speech than our refusal to accord First Amendment protection to obscenity. . . .

To the veteran, to the family who has sacrificed a daughter or a son in defense of this Nation, and to the average Americans in cities and towns across this Country, desecration of our National symbol has as little to do with free speech as does obscenity or child pornography.

We have almost a century of experience that confirms that Flag desecration prohibitions do not come at the expense of free speech. No one suggests that there was a lack of robust debate or vigorous political disagreement during this history. . . .

The overwhelming vote in favor of passage of the Flag Protection Act of 1989 reflects that the Congress itself believes that protection for the Flag is fully consistent with free political debate, and that the Constitution should permit Congress to protect the Flag. . . .

Some argue that the Bill of Rights, and especially the First Amendment, should never be amended for any purpose, no matter how noble. . . . However, we should not lose sight of the fact that the Bill of Rights itself is a set of amendments. . . . Had we closed our minds as a Nation to any amendment of the original document in 1789, many of our most cherished liberties would not be enshrined in the text of the Constitution today. . . .

Second, it is argued that a Flag amendment itself would trivialize the Constitution. . . . I would be most hesitant to call "trivial" a proposal that some three-quarters of the American people and an overwhelming majority of the Senate of the United States and the House of Representatives believe is worthy of proposal as part of our Constitution.

Finally, it is argued that amending the Constitution to protect the American Flag would open the floodgates to numerous amendments. [But] the Flag is unique. There is simply no danger that this amendment will prompt a multiplicity of claims for constitutional protection for other similar symbols. . . .

[S]ome contend that the Dole-Michel amendment [supported by President Bush, document 11.6] might not succeed in overruling the Flag-burning cases, *Johnson* and *Eichman,* and thus would fail to authorize Congress and the States to protect the Flag. . . . The historical context in which this amendment is being considered will itself evidence that the sole purpose of the amendment is to provide to Congress and the States the power to protect the Flag that the Court held they lacked in *Johnson* and *Eichman.* . . .

Second, some contend that the amendment will create an exception to other provisions of the Constitution, so that, for example, Congress could punish Flag desecration by bill of attainder. Again, both the context of the amendment's adoption and common sense refute this contention. . . . Accordingly, the Dole-Michel amendment should be read as only affecting the First Amendment as currently interpreted by the Court. . . .

Third, it has been suggested that because the amendment authorizes both Congress and the States to protect the Flag, the result will be a confusing patchwork of different Flag protection statutes. It is entirely appropriate that the Dole-Michel amendment empowers both the federal government and the States to protect the Flag from desecration. The Flag represents the entire Nation—a Union of States—and both the federal government and the States have an interest in its protection. This shared power will not lead to a patchwork of conflicting laws. . . . [T]hroughout our history, both Congress and the States have exercised this power without any hint of confusion or conflict. . . .

Finally, some argue that the concept of physical desecration of the Flag is so vague that greater power would be conferred upon Congress and the States than is contemplated or desired. . . .

The argument is meritless in any event. Even at its widest possible scope, the concept of physical desecration of the Flag encompasses only a negligible portion of the means of expression and eliminates no messages at all. Disrespectful speech or speech of condemnation, for example, could not possibly be considered physical desecration, even if the speaker displays the Flag and denounces it by name. . . . [P]hysical desecration entails actual contact with the Flag, including the manner in which it is positioned. Hanging a Flag in a traditional manner in an undesirable place, however, could not reasonably be considered physical desecration.

Finally, it would be necessary to decide on the requisite state of mind for liability. While Congress or a State might go as far as the Flag Protection Act of 1989 and punish all intentional acts, whatever their communicative intent (if any), we think it much more likely that desecration would be defined only to include actions that were intended to convey contempt. Under such a statute, if an individual did something to a Flag in order to honor it, he could not be punished even though someone else was offended. . . .

These are the kinds of definitional questions that Congress and the States . . . had successfully undertaken for many years before *Johnson.* Throughout that period, no one claimed that the statute books were filled with vague or tyrannical Flag protection laws. . . .

We had decades of experience with Flag protection laws before *Johnson,* during which no one suggested that speech was any less free or that America was a crazy-quilt of varying and incomprehensible Flag laws. There is no reason to believe that there will be any difference in the wake of the Dole-Michel amendment. . . .

The people should be permitted to decide for themselves whether they want their Constitution to protect desecration of their Flag. . . .

Document 13.3

Editorial in the *Detroit News,* June 17, 1990. Reprinted with permission of the *Detroit News,* a Gannett newspaper, copyright 1990.

FLAG BURNING: BEYOND SYMBOLISM

The U.S. Supreme Court last week struck down a federal law making flag burning illegal. The court's majority said the ban violated the First Amendment's guarantee of free speech. Immediately, some congressmen and President Bush began pushing for a constitutional amendment to ban flag burning.

Such a move would seem to have tremendous public support. When a sample of citizens was asked by the *New York Times*/CBS poll last week if flag burning should be against the law, 83 percent said it should. Senate GOP leader Robert Dole threatened to make a series of 30-second ads with which to pummel opponents of the idea.

. . . No American with any respect for the most minimal decencies would fail to be repulsed at seeing the flag desecrated. But a constitutional amendment is irresponsible. The idea of tampering with the Bill of Rights to gain momentary popular support in an election year is almost as revolting as flag-burning itself. . . .

And that's what's at stake. . . . A constitutional flag-burning ban, no matter how carefully drafted, would introduce into the Constitution the idea that Congress or the courts can abridge freedom of speech. . . .

And for what? To outlaw an occurrence that happens a few times a year at most? To grant politicians a fleeting advantage in an off-year election? More than preserving a symbol is at stake here. The Bill of Rights is too precious to be squandered for such minor or even ignoble ends.

Document 13.4

Remarks by Democratic Senate majority leader George Mitchell, June 19, 1990.

Source: Congressional Record, 1990, S8211–12.

Mr. President, last year, I supported and voted for a law to protect the flag [document 11.8]. I believed then and believe now that this was the appropriate response to a flag burning that occurred in 1984.

Last week, by the narrow one-vote margin of 5 to 4, the Supreme Court [in *Eichman,* document 12.7] ruled that the law violates the freedom of speech provision of the first amendment to the Constitution.

I disagree with the five Justices who formed the majority in this case. . . .

The question now is whether we should override the Court's decision by amending the Constitution.

I oppose and condemn the burning of the flag. I find it offensive and obnoxious. I am proud to be an American, proud of our flag. But I do not support changing the Constitution. We can support the American flag without changing the American Constitution. . . .

Across the whole sweep of human history, there is no better, clearer, more concise, more eloquent or effective statement of the right of citizens to be free of the dictates of Government than the American Bill of Rights.

For 200 years it has protected the liberties of generations of Americans. During that time, the Bill of Rights has never been changed or amended. Not once. Ever. The Bill of Rights stands today, word for word, exactly as it did when adopted 200 years ago.

Of the 10 amendments which make up the Bill of Rights, none is more important than the first. In this debate, its relevant words are few, direct, and clear.

Congress shall make no law * * * abridging the freedom of speech. . . .

Never in 200 years has the first amendment been changed or amended. . . .

We have personal freedom in America because we reject any government-dictated patriotism. We believe each American will freely discover in his or her own heart the love of country and pride in our Nation that has made so many Americans willing to defend it at the cost of blood and life itself for two centuries. . . .

For 200 years, the Bill of Rights has protected the liberties of Americans through economic turmoil, civil war, political strife, social upheaval, and international tension. Despite the worst that fate and our enemies have hurled at us, we have never found it necessary to change the fundamental principles on which our Government was founded and by which our freedom is secured.

Principles which have stood that test of time should not be discarded or tampered with.

It will be a sad, tragic irony if a few obnoxious publicity seekers, who appear to hate America, achieve their victory by stampeding those who love America to take the unwise action of changing the Bill of Rights for the first time in American history. I love America and the American flag and the American Bill of Rights too much to let that happen without a fight.

Document 13.5

Remarks by Rep. Tim Valentine in the House of Representatives, June 21, 1990.

Source: Congressional Record, 1990, H4016.

Mr. Speaker, much of the rhetoric that the Nation has heard in recent days might lead one to the conclusion that this is a debate about who loves the flag, about who thinks this symbol of our nation deserves respect, about who is the most patriotic, or even about who supports or opposes flag burning.

It is about none of those questions. The only question we need consider is whether we will abridge a document that has served our Nation for 200 years because of a few despicable acts by a few despicable people.

I have nothing but contempt for those who cannot express their views without attempting to debase a national symbol that nearly every American loves and cherishes. The flag is not debased by such actions, the flag burners are.

Mr. Speaker, our flag deserves protection, and I want to protect it. In fact, like many Americans in the immediate aftermath of the Supreme Court decision last year, my first instinct was to support a constitutional amendment if that is what it takes to prevent flag burning.

But after much soul searching and reflection, I have concluded that we should not depart from two centuries of constitutional history by placing, for the first time, limitations on the Bill of Rights. . . .

I do not think it is possible to craft a concise amendment to prohibit flag desecration without spawning a slew of new laws and new court cases and new judicial interpretations and reinterpretations.

More important, in this rush to depart from our heritage we would set a dangerous precedent that should send a cold chill down the spine of every American who loves the Constitution. If flag burning requires a constitutional amendment, where do we stop? What other kind of abhorrent behavior will demand that we revise our basic principles?

Our Nation has faced much greater threats to our security than the misguided action of a few people who burn the flag. Yet we have never limited the Bill of Rights.

We have always tolerated dissent, even when the actions of individual dissenters seemed intolerable. And our Nation is stronger for having done so.

Flag burners are only a threat to our Nation if we allow them to dictate the content of our Constitution. . . .

Our Constitution is not only the fundamental law of the United States; it is a symbol of liberty, equality, and freedom to people around the world who yearn for the rights that the constitution protects for Americans.

Let us remember that the flag, in the final analysis, is a piece of fabric. The Constitution is the fabric of our Nation.

Let us not tear that national fabric asunder by surrendering our Constitution to flag burners. . . .

[U]ntil about 24 hours ago I spoke as those Members on the other side did. I cosponsored House Joint Resolution 350 [document 11.6, the constitutional amendment sponsored by the Bush administration], and I ask unanimous consent to have my name stricken as a cosponsor. Over the rhetoric of the past few days I have finally heard the voice of my own conscience. I urge Members to vote against this constitutional amendment proposal and vote for the Bill of Rights.

Document 13.6

Statement by Duke University law professor Walter Dellinger before the Senate Judiciary Committee, June 21, 1990.

Source: Measures to Protect the American Flag, Hearing before the Senate Judiciary Committee, 101st Cong., 1st sess., 1990, serial no. J-101-77, 121–31.

. . . This potentially dangerous amendment [document 11.6] would create legislative power of uncertain dimension to override the First

Amendment; it would confer that power on all future Congresses, fifty state legislatures, and as many as 14,000 local governments; it would set an undesirable precedent for quick resort to constitutional amendments to curtail the rights of the unpopular; and it would compromise the moral legitimacy of the First Amendment by suggesting that expression that is offensive to the majority may be suppressed, while expression offensive to others must be tolerated. . . .

Because the President's beguilingly simple proposal fails to state explicitly that it overrides the First Amendment, it leaves entirely unclear how much of the Bill of Rights it would trump. . . .

We know, of course, that the sponsors do mean to restrict the First Amendment in order to overrule the Supreme Court's recent flag decisions. But because the drafters of the amendment avoid stating in the text their intent that their proposal override the First Amendment, they leave entirely uncertain the extent of the amendment's displacement of the protection enshrined in the Bill of Rights. . . .

The text does not reveal, for example, whether a defendant's spoken or written anti-patriotic statements could be used as the critical evidence to prove that his physical act involving the flag was intended to be a "desecration." . . . This is not a problem at the margin of the amendment: physical acts involving a cloth flag, or a picture or representation of a flag can be deemed desecrations only by the reference to the message conveyed. . . .

Congress should reject not only the President's proposal but any misguided efforts to construct a "better" draft. Resort to the amendment process to make criminals out of a handful of unpopular dissidents is a dangerous step, no matter how carefully this amendment itself is drafted. Any flag burning constitutional amendment proposed by Congress will lower the threshold for frequent use of the Amendment process, particularly for the curtailment of the right of unpopular groups. . . .

When the only governmental interest in suppressing an activity is opposition to the political message being conveyed, core First Amendment values are at stake. . . .

Constitutional protection of symbolic messages is not some recent gloss invented by the current Supreme Court [citing *Stromberg*, document 5.1]. . . . [Former Reagan administration] Attorney General [Edwin] Meese's argument that only spoken words and printed letters are protected by the First Amendment would lead to a wholly intolerable conclusion: THAT THERE IS NO FIRST AMENDMENT RIGHT TO WAVE THE FLAG.

The argument that one who burns a flag could express the same message by making a verbal statement denigrates the particular expressive power of the flag. When I fly the red, white and blue American flag from the porch of my Chapel Hill home, I am communicating a message different and far more powerful than any I could express by simply posting a placard stating that "We respect the flag as a symbol of national unity."

It would be foolhardy, moreover, to assume that the damage done to the system of freedom of expression by the proposed constitutional amendment could be limited to the narrow category of messages communicated by flag burning. Although the proposed Amendment deals specifically only with the flag, its underlying theory is that it is permissible for government to restrict some forms of political statement because of strong distaste for the message being conveyed. . . .

Any flag amendment, moreover, would undermine the moral legitimacy of the First Amendment. For two hundred years we have told groups of Americans who are deeply and understandably offended by certain kinds of speech activities that they must tolerate offensive messages to serve the higher goal of allowing expression that is free, robust and uninhibited. . . .

What would this proposed act of constitutional revision do to the moral legitimacy of the Constitutional principle that protects expression that many find as offensive as others find flag burning [such as Nazis marching through Jewish communities, displays of the Confederate flag and sexualized, but not constitutionally obscene depictions of women]? Once we have swiftly moved to amend the Constitution to get rid of a form of expression that the majority finds offensive, what enduring principle of our constitutional tradition will remain unimpaired that will legitimately trump the claims of those deeply wounded by other kinds of expression? . . .

[M]any have characterized this issue as a contest between the Flag and the Bill of Rights. But those two great icons are not on opposite sides of this issue, for the proposed constitutional amendment would harm both the Bill of Right and the Flag. Americans are free today to fly the flag proudly, to ignore the flag, or to use it as an expression of protest or reproach. . . . [T]he individual choice of millions of Americans to respect the flag would be far less meaningful if it were the only choice one could take to avoid being imprisoned by the government. . . .

In a world that is bursting forth with new democracies, there is a newly awakened admiration for the Constitution of the United States. Amending our Constitution so that we can punish these few dissidents would make our President seem just a little silly, and make our country—the land of the free, and the home of the brave—seem a little less free, and a little less brave. This amendment is unworthy of the United States.

Document 13.7

Remarks by Rep. Henry Hyde in the House of Representatives, June 21, 1990.

Source: Congressional Record, 1990, 4085–86.

My friends, I do not know which side deserves the credit for courage. I do not know if it takes more courage to vote against this amendment and incur the slings and arrows of some outraged veterans' organizations, or whether it takes more courage on our side to endure the slings and arrows of the media which has relentlessly condemned us as cultural lags, and yahoos, and political pygmies, and all of the rest for our weakness in caving in to the populist patriotic notions of our people. . . .

When the Supreme Court makes a mistake, it is the responsibility of the people's body to propose a correction, and that is all we are doing, we are proposing a correction. Congress has reversed an errant Supreme Court four times by amendment in our history, and certainly when I have heard repeatedly, repeatedly that we have never amended the Bill of Rights before, I must reply that the 13th amendment and the 14th amendment in 1865 and 1867, amended a 1857 decision of the Supreme Court, Dred Scott, which was based on a deplorable interpretation of the fifth amendment, so at least decisions on the Bill of Rights have been reversed by constitutional amendment. . . .

Should we protect the flag? What is so special about this flag?

It is unique, sui generis, in a class by itself, nothing else like it. It is transcendent. It rises above the political swamps that we live and work in and serves as a symbol of our unity and our community as a country. It symbolizes as nothing else does. The uniqueness of this flag is why we want to treat it differently from everything else. . . .

Can we not get a symbol and elevate it and say that it unites us as a country, one Nation, indivisible with liberty and justice for all. I think so, and that is why it is different. . . .

Now, the ghost of Jefferson and the ghost of Madison have been summoned here to oppose this amendment, but I wish whoever has the power to summon ghosts would summon them from [the cemeteries] in Flanders Field [in Europe where American soldiers killed in wartime are buried] and have them come here and tell Members what they mean when they say "We will not sleep if you don't keep faith with us." . . . We owe them keeping faith with their sacrifice.

It is little enough to have the symbol of what they died for, the values they died for, special and protected. Let Members take the flag out of the gutter where the counterculture has dragged it. This is an opportunity not to get even with some creeps, but to say there are transcendent values that are important to every American, that unify Americans, that brings Americans together as a community, one Nation under God, indivisible. Is that not important? It is important, and we have to watch a falling flag and pick it up. That does not interfere or demean or shoot a hole in the Bill of Rights. It exalts the Bill of Rights. . . .

We have 10 amendments that guarantee citizens all kinds of rights. How about one amendment that says we have a duty not to respect the flag or love the flag but just not to destroy it, not to demean it, not to defile it? Is that too much to ask, one duty? . . .

I do not say that the flag is a sacred symbol in the spiritual or religious sense, but I say it is a unique symbol, and too many people have paid for it with their blood. Too many have marched behind it, too many have slept in a box under it, too many kids and parents and widows have accepted this triangle as the last remembrance of their most precious son, father and husband. Too many to have this ever demeaned. That is not punching a hole in the first amendment. We are amending a decision of the Court that distorted the meaning of free speech and said expressive conduct of a particularly demeaning sort is protected, but if obscenity is not protected, if perjury is not protected, if copyright laws protect certain language and punish others, if we cannot burn a $10 bill, can we not protect the transcendent symbol of all that is good in our country?

Listen, the flag is falling. I ask Members to catch the falling flag and raise it up. In my judgment that does not demean the Constitution. It elevates us all to being worthy of the great country we live in.

Document 13.8

Remarks by House Speaker Tom Foley in the House of Representatives, June 21, 1990.

Source: Congressional Record, 1990, 4086–87.

Mr. Speaker, it will be rare indeed for me to take the well [to address the House] during the time I have the honor to serve as Speaker. I take the well today not as Speaker but as a Representative of my own district. I speak on an issue which is, as has been said many times, one of the most important issues and votes that we will cast certainly in this Congress, perhaps for many Congresses to come. . . .

When we say the Pledge of Allegiance in this Chamber we pledge allegiance to the flag, yes, but more importantly to the Republic for which it stands, one Nation under God, indivisible, with liberty and justice for all. The flag is a symbol of our national life and values. It is a symbol of the liberty and freedom that has distinguished this country as a beacon for hundreds of millions of people around the world for two centuries.

In recent months we have seen our ideals championed from Wenceslas Square [in Prague] to Tiananmen Square [in Beijing], by people struggling to achieve democracy and freedom for themselves. The Bill of Rights, Madison wrote to Jefferson, was necessary to counteract against the impulses of interest and passion.

It is an understandable passion to want to punish those who burn the flag. But it would be a strange irony if we let those few people who burn or disrespect the flag push us, force us, into amending for the first time the first amendment to the Constitution, the Bill of Rights. . . .

I hope we will not do so. I hope we do not do so just to reach the acts of the scattered and few disrespectful flag burners. I fear that if we amend the first 10 amendments, the Bill of Rights, that sacred depository of freedom of speech and religion and assembly, we will lower the threshold of resistance to other amendments. Indeed there are other symbols of national religious life which, if burned or desecrated, would create great anger and bring about a demand for other constitutional amendments to further amend the first amendment to prevent such desecration.

I believe we would not wish it recorded that this House began the process of weakening the first amendment to the Constitution, which is the repository of all the hopes and ambitions of our Founding Fathers to protect individual liberties. . . .

I would appeal to conservatives in this House that if there is one underlying principle of conservatism, as I understand it, it is to preserve the basic institutions of liberty and not to change them idly or casually in the face of and pressure from transitory forces, influences or emotions. If it is not conservative to protect the Bill of Rights, I do not know what conservatism means today. If it does not respect the sacrifice of the millions who have served and the hundreds of thousands who have died in the long history of our Nation to say, "Yes, we respect the flag, we honor it, we salute it, as we salute your service and sacrifice itself, but we will not allow these few to force us to defile the institution of liberty that that flag represents every day it flies over this body and in this Chamber," what does?

Above the flag [flying in the House chamber] is a statement that was made by Daniel Webster when he dedicated a monument at Bunker Hill commemorating those who sacrificed selflessly and with a vision to make this democracy possible. . . . [I]t says . . . :

> Let us develop the resources of our land, call forth its powers, build
> up its institutions, promote its great interests and see whether we also
> in our day and generation may not perform something worthy to be
> remembered.

I suggest to the Members that the greatest resource of our country is the Constitution, that it is the means by which the people of this country devolve and distribute their powers. It is the platform upon which our institutions are built, and it is the great promoter of all of our national interests.

Let us, by preserving and protecting that institution today, show that we, too, in our day and generation may perform something worthy to be remembered.

Defeat this amendment. Protect the Bill of Rights.

14

The Revival and Defeat of the Constitutional Amendment 1995

After the June 1990 (second) defeat of the proposed constitutional amendment to ban flag desecration, many of the amendment's proponents (often implicitly seconded by media accounts) suggested that the defeat was bound to lead to the following developments: (1) the flag desecration controversy and, in particular, the dispute over the wisdom of an amendment would remain a continuous "burning issue" for months and possibly years to follow and would become a central issue in the 1990 congressional elections, with amendment opponents likely to suffer severe retribution at the polls; (2) until and unless an amendment was passed, Americans' love for the flag would be imperiled as they were forced to witness legally unfettered physical assaults upon the flag; and (3) such assaults would increase because, as they would now bear no legal penalty, anyone who wished to desecrate the flag would feel free to do so without incurring any reprisals. Each of these intertwined predictions proved false during the four years following the defeat of the amendment, but in 1995, spurred by 1994 Republican electoral victories that gave the GOP control of both houses of Congress for the first time in more than forty years, amendment backers reintroduced the proposal in Congress. Although they succeeded in easily obtaining the required two-thirds majority in the House of Representatives in June 1995, in a cliffhanger December Senate vote the amendment fell three votes short of the needed two-thirds support. Amendment proponents promised to make the flag desecration controversy an issue in the 1996 elections and to bring it back again before Congress no later than 1997.

Until its revival in 1995, the flag desecration issue had faded away from media coverage and thus from public view after June 1990 with stunning completeness and rapidity. Nonetheless, the fervor of flag-waving that accompanied the Persian Gulf war of 1991 and a new burst of popular flag-based fashions in 1990–91 demonstrated that Americans' love for the flag was completely undiminished by the legalization of flag desecration. Moreover, compared to the 1989–90 period when the FPA (document 11.8) temporarily made flag desecration illegal, flag desecration markedly decreased after the 1990 Supreme Court *Eichman* ruling [document 12.7) again legalized such conduct. However, and perhaps most revealing of the continuing strong feeling about the flag (and the reluctance of many officials to uphold the law), the handful of people who engaged in flag desecration after June 1990 continued very often to face legal reprisals, sometimes under almost certainly unconstitutional (as a result of *Eichman*) state flag desecration laws and sometimes under other legal or administrative pretexts.

The sudden and almost complete disappearance of the flag desecration controversy from general press, political, and public attention after June 1990 was especially surprising because for months Republican and veterans groups' spokesmen and news stories had hammered home the theme that the issue would be a major focus in the 1990 congressional elections and that any incumbent who voted against the amendment would pay dearly at the polls in November. In fact, during the 1990 congressional campaigns, the flag desecration controversy became a significant issue in only a handful of races and did not lead to the defeat of a single candidate; *Congressional Quarterly* reported that the entire issue had proved to be "strictly flash-in-the-pan" and that "hardly a peep on the flag was heard" during the campaign.[1]

During the four years following the 1990 congressional elections, the flag desecration controversy showed no signs of resurfacing as a significant national issue and members of all three branches of the national government indicated little interest in reviving it. The issue disappeared from congressional discussion and President Bush made no attempt to resurrect it. Nominees to the Supreme Court were not pressed during Senate confirmation hearings about their views on flag desecration, and, in decisions that were barely reported in the national news media, the Supreme Court twice (in 1992 and 1994) firmly refused to reopen or reconsider its 1989–90 flag-burning rulings by declining to hear appeals from lower court decisions that had struck down flag desecration–related convictions on the basis of Supreme Court precedents. The Court refused to hear the appeals even though only four votes were required to consider them and all four dissenting members of the *Johnson* and *Eichman* Supreme Courts were still serving.

Why the flag desecration issue went away so quickly and completely, at least as a national issue, until its 1995 revival, can probably be explained by a combination of the same factors that resulted in the comparative diminishment of interest in the issue in 1990 as compared to 1989, plus the additional ingredient of developments in the second half of 1990 that pushed media, political, and public interest in new directions. Among the factors that contributed to diminished interest and support for banning flag desecration in 1990 compared to the previous year, and that continued to move currents in the same direction after June 1990, were the "rerun" (or put more plainly, the boredom) factor; the growing sense that the issue had been seized upon primarily for partisan ends by Republicans; the symbolic power of the Constitution as a countervailing icon to the flag, because, with the striking down of the FPA, the only means of banning flag desecration required amending the Bill of Rights; the growing consensus that more substantive issues demanded attention and that flag desecration was a purely symbolic concern; and even the sense that flag desecration, at least as it had been widely used in eastern Europe during the popular uprisings of late 1989 that helped bring about the downfall of the communist regimes there, could actually serve a positive function. After June 1990, these continuing factors in lowering flag-amendment fervor were significantly supplemented by a shift in attention to at least three highly substantive concerns that, unlike flag desecration, directly affected many Americans in the course of their daily lives: increasing indications that the country was slipping into what turned out to be the 1990–91 recession; growing concern over the budget deficit and adverse reaction to President Bush's abandonment, during the summer of 1990, of his highly publicized 1988 campaign pledge never to raise taxes; and, above all, growing indications during the last third of 1990 that the United States was about to go to war in response to the August invasion of Kuwait by Iraq (as it did in January 1991). Compared to these continuing and growing crises, which could conceivably cost at least some Americans higher taxes, their jobs, or even their lives, concern about flag desecration, which had already been rapidly diminishing, soon faded away as a matter of significant national media, public, or political attention.

Yet while the flag desecration issue disappeared as a national issue after June 1990, during the subsequent year there was plenty of evidence that the legalization of flag desecration had in no way diminished Americans' love for the flag, contrary to many assertions and predictions made by those who disagreed with the Supreme Court's rulings. During the second half of 1990 and especially during the Gulf War fervor of early 1991, flag fashions, flag sales, and flag displays attained extraordinary popularity, perhaps unprecedented in American history. Ironically, many of the flag fashions and patriotic Gulf War flag displays unquestionably would have violated flag desecration laws had they still been in effect—in fact, very similar sorts of clothing and displays had led to numerous prosecutions during the Vietnam War, when they were viewed as ridiculing the

288   DESECRATING THE AMERICAN FLAG

flag, instead of being patriotic. As the *Seattle Times* reported in a June 14, 1991, story about the wave of flag fashions and displays, "What was then desecration is now decoration." The Gulf War also sent flag sales rocketing from levels that had already been stimulated by the 1989–90 flag-burning controversy. Thus, in mid-February 1991, a month after American planes and missiles began bombing Iraq and shortly before the American ground invasion of that country began, a spokesman for the Annin Flag Company in Roseland, New Jersey reported that, "We had good inventories when the fighting began three weeks ago, but that's been wiped out and now we're working on a five- or six-week backlog of orders."[2]

Numerous Gulf War patriotic flag displays would have raised serious legal questions had flag desecration laws remained in effect. For example, the February 1, 1991, *Ann Arbor News* contained a huge picture of a flag at Deerfield High School in Michigan with the slogan, written across the stripes of the flag, "DEERFIELD SUPPORTS OUR TROOPS," and so covered with yellow ribbons designed to express support for American soldiers that they covered virtually all of the flag's stars and thus clearly "defaced" it. Among the scores of other unorthodox Gulf War displays that might well have raised legal questions had flag desecration laws remained in effect was a huge "living flag" created by 3,600 people wearing colored T-shirts in San Diego (what if someone moved or wore the wrong color?); a flag created out of colored lightbulbs (what if some burned out?); and a flag painted on the windows of a college dormitory (what if the window was opened or broken?).

Perhaps the most widespread assumption or prediction made by those who opposed the Supreme Court's 1989–90 rulings was that flag-burnings and similar incidents would increase and that the perpetrators of such acts would henceforth go unpunished. In fact, during the five years following the June 1990 *Eichman* ruling, only about three dozen instances of what could be broadly construed as flag desecration for the purpose of expressing political protest (as opposed to expressing patriotism) were reported in the general press, about the same number of such incidents reported during the fewer than eight months when flag desecration was technically illegal under the FPA between late October 1989 and mid-June 1990.

If predictions that flag burnings would escalate in the wake of the *Eichman* ruling and the defeat of the constitutional amendment proved highly inaccurate, this also proved to be the case with the eminently logical expectation that those who engaged in flag desecration after 1990 would not suffer legal or other penalties. In fact, of the three dozen flag desecration incidents reported between mid-1990 and late 1995, almost half led to arrests and another 25 percent led to various types of noncriminal reprisals and/or threats. In at least eight cases, flag desecrators were arrested under flag desecration laws that had almost certainly been rendered unconstitutional by the Supreme Court's 1989–90 rulings, and in another ten or so cases other, often highly dubious, charges such as arson and inciting to riot were brought, although the real "crime" appears to have been flag desecration. In almost all of these cases the charges were eventually either dropped or those charged were acquitted, but the message that flag desecration would continue to bear a heavy legal cost had still been delivered.[3]

For example, in one particularly bizarre post-*Eichman* flag desecration prosecution, in Youngsville, Pennsylvania, Mark Cox was arrested in June 1991 after a quarrel with his fiancée during which he allegedly ripped down several American flags from a bridge display, threw them at her, and subsequently slapped a woman passerby who had chastised and slapped him for tossing the flags. After pleading guilty to charges of harassment of the passerby and insult to the state and national flags, in the expectation that he would only be fined, Cox was instead ordered in November 1991 by Warren County Judge Robert Wolfe to pay a $500 fine, to serve a jail term of 9-to-23½ months, to undergo alcohol counseling and to read and write a book report about *Man Without a Country,* a fictionalized account of a man who, after denouncing the United States, was banished and required to spend the rest of his life without a homeland aboard ships on the high seas. Judge Wolfe told Cox that he would read the book report to determine if writing it "rehabilitates your attitude towards the flag." Cox served almost four weeks in jail before he was released on parole while he appealed. Warren County officials eventually agreed to drop the flag insult allegations after a Pennsylvania appeals court overturned his convictions in late 1992, without ruling on their substance, on the grounds that Cox had not been given adequate legal assistance and advice at his original trial.

In New York City, charges of violating a municipal ordinance that outlawed setting a fire on any city property, brought against a man named Donald Payne, who was alleged to have burned a flag on three separate occasions in July 1990 outside a city courthouse during a highly publicized trial, were ordered dropped by a Manhattan Criminal Court judge in January 1991, on the grounds that his acts posed no threat to the peace or public safety and were a form of political speech protected by the Supreme Court's flag desecration rulings. Because the city did not allege that Payne had been disorderly, had blocked traffic, or had otherwise threatened any possible government interest in "preventing a public disturbance," the judge declared, "it appears that the primary interest" in prosecuting him was to "suppress the defendant's politically charged acts of burning the flag," a motivation that violated the Supreme Court's ruling in *Johnson* as "inconsistent with the First Amendment."

In a case involving nonprosecutorial harassment of those perceived to be engaged in flag desecration, a Massachusetts condom manufacturer, the Old Glory Condom Corporation, was forced to engage in two years of litigation before the U.S. Patent Office would agree to register as the company's trademark a flaglike image in the shape of an unfurled condom bearing the slogan, "Worn with Pride, Country-Wide," which decorated the exterior packaging of its condoms (which were themselves ordinary latex condoms in single colors of red, white, or blue, with no flag depictions on them). At first a patent attorney had rejected the proposed trademark on the grounds that it would be perceived as "a disparagement of the American flag" that would "scandalize or shock" the general public, even though the Patent Office had previously registered over one thousand trademarks based on flag designs. In another nonprosecutorial case of harassment of alleged flag desecrators, students at Elk Grove High School near Sacramento, California, had to go to court to win the right to paint a mural on the school's walls that included a depiction of a flag burning and textual information about the *Johnson* ruling in an attempt to celebrate American civil liberties. The controversy erupted after school officials had invited student groups in the fall of 1991 to decorate the walls and had approved numerous other murals, including some with controversial contents, such as one that portrayed black militants such as Malcolm X and communist leader Angela Davis. However, after winning their battle in two different California courts and after over two years of negotiations and litigation, the students lost the war when school officials voted in February 1994 to henceforth ban all permanent murals. Subsequently, forty-seven students walked out of school in protest and were suspended for three days each, but the mural was nonetheless painted over, in August 1994.

During the four years following the congressional defeat of the constitutional amendment in June 1990, the only significant effort to resuscitate it was undertaken by the American Legion. Shortly after the 1990 amendment defeat, the Legion quietly organized a drive to obtain resolutions supporting an amendment from at least thirty-eight legislatures, the minimum required to ratify an amendment if passed by both houses of Congress. By mid-1995 the Legion succeeded in gaining such resolutions from 49 state legislatures (all but Vermont, document 14.1). In mid-1994 the Legion publicly announced the formation of a coalition of groups that shared its support for a revived amendment entitled the Citizens Flag Alliance (CFA); the CFA included about one hundred civic, ethnic, veterans, and other organizations with a claimed membership of over twenty-five million (document 14.2).

In the aftermath of the 1994 Republican congressional election triumph, which clearly energized the CFA, the 1989–90 proposed constitutional amendment, whose operative text authorized Congress and the states to "prohibit the physical desecration" of the flag was reintroduced in both houses of Congress in early 1995 (stripped of its original nonoperative preamble—see document 11.6). Under the prodding of the CFA and the Republican congressional leadership, both House and Senate judiciary committees held hearings on the amendment for the first time in five years during the spring, and both subsequently recommended its passage. On June 28 the House of Representatives endorsed the amendment by a vote of 312–120, well over the two-thirds majority required and an increase of fifty-eight votes over those voting for the failed amendment in 1990. However, the amendment was defeated in the Senate on December 12, receiving sixty-three votes, three short of the required two-thirds majority (although substantially more than the fifty-one and fifty-eight votes respectively obtained for the amendment in the Senate in 1989 and 1990); thirty-six senators opposed it.

What was particularly striking about the amendment's greater success in 1995 than in 1989–90 was that the entire controversy received far less press coverage, public debate, and congressional hearings and debate than five years before; that the Clinton administration opposed it whereas the Bush administration had earlier backed an amendment; that public opinion appears to have been considerably less aroused and less favorable toward an amendment than in 1990; and that there were only a handful of reported flag burnings in the country during the two years preceding the 1995 congressional votes, whereas a wave of flag burnings had marked the period between the 1989 and 1990 votes.

The crucial differences between 1989–90 and 1995 were that the 1994 elections had returned a conservative Republican majority to both houses of Congress and that supporters of the amendment had the highly organized backing of the American Legion and the CFA, whereas amendment opponents (beyond the editorial pages of the overwhelming majority of the nation's newspapers), especially in Congress, were relatively unorganized, both compared with amendment proponents in 1995 and with amendment opponents in 1989–90. The Democratic congressional leadership offered no organized opposition to the amendment in 1995 (in sharp contrast to 1989–90); even House Democratic leader Richard Gephardt abandoned his 1990 opposition and voted for it. If the press went overboard in covering the flag desecration controversy in 1989, in 1995 large segments of the press went to the other extreme (at least in their news coverage, if not in their editorial opposition), leaving much of the American public ignorant of the fact that the First Amendment was in grave danger of being altered for the first time in American history. Thus American Society of Newspaper Editors president William Ketter lamented in an October 13, 1995, *Christian Science Monitor* column that the press was suffering from "apathy" in covering the issue. For example, the *Reader's Guide to Periodical Literature* lists thirty-eight articles published about flag desecration during the 1989 controversy and twenty articles printed amidst the 1990 controversy, but a mere six articles published about flag desecration during 1995. Similarly, the ABC evening news devoted two minutes each to reporting the October 19, 1989, Senate and June 21, 1990, House defeats of the proposed flag desecration constitutional amendment, including extensive excerpts from the floor debates. No debate excerpts were presented and less than 30 seconds altogether was devoted to the far closer and far more critical (due to prior 1995 House passage) Senate defeat of the amendment on December 12, 1995, however. Along with the press, flag desecrators clearly also had lost interest in the controversy by 1995: only about ten flag desecration incidents were reported nationwide between mid-1994 and late 1995 (and most of these were only reported in local news accounts and none were apparently organized by any radical groups such as the RCP).

Especially given the paucity of recent flag burnings, the 1995 amendment drive no doubt largely reflected general American insecurities and fears as well as the desire of amendment backers to make a clear symbolic statement rejecting their perception of a trend towards general national, moral, and social disintegration. Numerous studies published during 1990–95 indicated a growing sense of national crisis and a continued economic stagnation in average living standards that had persisted ever since about 1973. For example, in October 1995 an index of the nation's social health developed by scholars at Fordham University reported that, based on sixteen different measures, America's social health had dropped from 77.5 on a scale of 100 in 1973 to 41 in 1993, and that in 1993 the lowest scores ever recorded were reported for six measures, including children in poverty, average weekly earnings adjusted for inflation, and the gap between rich and poor Americans; thus, inflation-adjusted median wages for full-time male workers fell from $34,000 to $30,400 between 1973 and 1993. A study of "leading cultural indicators" published in 1994 by former secretary of education William Bennett reported a wide variety of discouraging trends between 1960 and the early 1990s, including a 500 percent increase in violent crime, a tripling of teenage suicides, a doubling in the divorce rate, and an increase of over 400 percent in illegitimate births. Bennett concluded that unless such "exploding social pathologies are reversed, they will lead to the decline and perhaps even to the fall of the American republic." In November 1995, the National Conference of Catholic Bishops characterized the nation as suffering from a "sense of economic insecurity and moral decline."[4]

In short, just as the flag was the primary symbol of American identity, the perceived need to outlaw flag desecration reflected a sense that the country was undergoing a national identity crisis and something had to be done to remedy this. Backers of the amendment frequently supported it in such terms. For example, at a June 7 HJC subcommittee meeting, HJC chairman Henry Hyde (R., Ill.) termed the amendment "an effort by mainstream Americans to reassert community standards" and declared that the flag desecration issue was less about "the flag itself" than about "a popular protest against the vulgarization of our society." In congressional testimony Northwestern University law professor Stephen Presser said the amendment would allow the American people to establish a "baseline of decency, civility, responsibility and order" and to "reconstruct a dangerously fractured sense of community." William Detweiler, national commander of the American Legion, urged support for the flag amendment in a February 11 letter to the *Washington Post*, which expressed concern that "Americans today harbor real doubts about what we stand for as a nation and who we are as a people," and, although conceding that the amendment might be viewed by some as a "corny idea" and that it "won't even erase all the doubts Americans have about the future" or even "send the stock market into a rally," maintained that "it's a start." In testimony before a SJC subcommittee on June 6, Detweiler made especially clear that many backers of the flag desecration amendment regarded the issue as making a symbolic statement about perceived threats to American unity and patriotism rather than a response to any real threat to the flag itself by declaring that the Legion regarded flag burning as "a problem even if no one ever burns another flag."[5]

Most of the key arguments made on both sides of the 1995 amendment debate echoed those of 1989–90. Opponents stressed that the amendment was a frontal attack on free speech and the Bill of Rights that would harm America's ability to serve as a worldwide model of freedom; that it was motivated by political considerations; that it confused the flag's symbolism with the substantive freedoms it represented; that there was no flag-burning problem to solve; that focusing attention on the issue would only encourage flag burners and divert attention away from real problems; that the amendment would create a "slippery slope" for future erosion of constitutional rights and fail even to increase respect for the flag, because patriotism and love of country could only be brought about by education and solving the country's problems, rather than by mandate; and that the amendment's failure to define "flag" or "desecration" would create legal chaos and endless litigation, especially because each state might come up with their own different definitions (in a futile effort to pick up votes, the amendment's textual provision authorizing the "states" as well as the federal government to ban flag desecration was dropped by its Senate sponsors shortly before the decisive December 12 Senate vote).

Far more than in 1990, most opponents of the amendment attacked it on basic ideological grounds: that it was a frontal assault on free speech. There was far less emphasis in 1995 on the totemic, or sacred and untouchable character (as opposed to the content), of the Constitution as a countericon to the sacred flag. For example, five Democratic members of the SJC minority declared, "If our system of government and our society is to continue to define freedom and democracy throughout the world, it must, as a threshold be a system open to free and diverse debate—that is what separates us from oppressive nations across the world."[6] The HJC minority similarly made strong free speech arguments against the amendment (document 14.3). The most eloquent congressional attack on the amendment on free speech grounds came from Republican representative Wayne Gilchrest of Maryland and from Democratic senator John Glenn of Ohio (documents 14.4 and 14.5). Glenn, a decorated Marine combat pilot in World War II and Korea and the first American astronaut to orbit the earth, was a certified American hero, and his fervent opposition to the amendment played a role in providing "political cover" to other senators much like that played by Senator Robert Kerrey in 1989 (document 11.24). The Clinton administration, in the person of assistant attorney general Walter Dellinger, who had strongly criticized the amendment on free speech grounds while a Duke University law professor in 1989–90, formally opposed the amendment, but with arguments that placed little emphasis on free speech issues; rather, Dellinger stressed that there had not been enough recent flag desecration incidents to justify an amendment and that its text was too vague (document 14.6).

In response to the arguments of amendment opponents, its backers maintained that flag desecration was a form of "conduct," not speech, that could be banned without infringing upon Americans' rights to voice their opinions in an endless variety of other ways; that public opinion overwhelmingly favored providing special protection for the nation's unique symbol; that flag desecration was so heinous that it was irrelevant how frequently such acts occurred, especially as flag burnings were often widely publicized and viewed by millions; that the nation especially owed to its veterans the outlawing of desecrating the flag that millions of them supposedly fought to protect; that the states and federal government could be trusted to come up with reasonable definitions of "flag" and "desecration"; and that giving to the states as well as the national government the power to ban flag desecration was perfectly consistent with the principles of American federalism and democracy. Amendment backers stressed that the American people had made clear, via opinion polls and the forty-nine state legislative resolutions supporting the amendment, that they wanted it, and that in a democracy the public will should be honored. Thus, SJC chairman Orrin Hatch, who served as Senate floor manager for the amendment, told the June 6 SJC subcommittee hearing, "There is more wisdom, judgment and understanding on this matter in the hearts and minds of the American people than one will find on most editorial boards, law faculties and, regrettably, in the Clinton administration."[7] If the single greatest emphasis of amendment opponents in 1995 centered on perceived threats to free speech, the greatest emphasis of amendment backers in and out of Congress centered on the emotional attachment of Americans to the flag and the perceived need to protect this attachment from physical assaults (documents 14.7 and 14.8).

The revival of the flag desecration issue in 1995, considered within the context of earlier, similar controversies in American history, suggests that flag desecration is an issue that has in the past and will in the future go through cycles of increasing and decreasing public interest but is unlikely ever to disappear. The flag is the preeminent symbol of American national identity, and it is therefore not surprising, in a country that has frequently exhibited considerable confusion and insecurity about itself and its self-definition, that recurrently, and especially during periods of increased national insecurity and confusion, frustrations are often focused on those who pour salt into open wounds by assaulting the flag. The 1895–1920 period was marked by enormous tension and confusion about American national identity related to the rapid increase in foreign immigration, fears of radicalism, and a massive and rapid growth in American industrialization and urbanization. The Vietnam War period was another time of enormous national insecurity, as controversy over the war divided the nation to an extent unseen since the Civil War. And the economic difficulties and frustrations of the post–Vietnam War period, marked by stagnant or declining standards of living for most Americans, the end of America's unchallenged international economic supremacy, and perceived threats to American jobs by foreign competition abroad and increasing immigration at home, have also created a fertile climate for targeting flag desecrators, who are perceived by Americans who already feel threatened as symbolically insulting them.

Although flag desecration may have temporarily disappeared again as a national public issue at least in the immediate post-1995 period, all of the ingredients are present for the reemergence of this controversy at any time. Indeed, during the first few months of 1996, numerous, mostly locally publicized incidents related to issues of flag reverence emerged, thereby strongly underlining this possibility. In January, vandals at the C. W. Post campus of Long Island University in Brookville, New York, destroyed a sculpture entitled *Flag Ball*, which consisted of flag fabric wrapped around a seven-foot ball, after Representative Peter King (R., N.Y.) held a news conference along with local veterans to denounce it as a desecration of the flag and to demand its removal. A major controversy erupted at the Phoenix Art Museum during the late winter and early spring in connection with a major exhibit of various forms of artistic depiction of the flag, including a reprise of "Dread Scott" Tyler's 1989 Chicago "flag on the floor" display and a display by artist Kate Millett that included a flag draped over a toilet. Phoenix veterans groups protested the exhibit, and Republican House Speaker Newt Gingrich referred to it as an example of "pathologies" and declared, "They ought to close the exhibit." In February, a Green Bay, Wisconsin, student was suspended for three days and referred to juvenile authorities for possible prosecution for flag desecration for wearing a flag-cape to school with "Star Spangled Lie" written on it. (Further action was dropped after local authorities declared "We've got too many other cases that are more serious.") A nationally publicized controversy erupted in March when professional basketball player Mahmoud Abdul-Rauf was suspended for refusing, on religious grounds, to stand during pre-game performances of the national anthem; he was reinstated only after he agreed to stand while silently praying. In June, Indianapolis authorities arrested two men for criminal recklessness, resisting arrest, and disorderly conduct after they burned a flag to protest a pending execution; the "criminal recklessness" charge was a felony because, the indictment charged, "a deadly weapon, that is: a cigarette lighter and lighter fluid" had been used. In Galesburg, Illinois, police arrested two men for violating the city's open burning ordinance in connection with a July 4 flag burning.

As the 1996 elections approached, the American Legion, the CFA, and presumptive Republican presidential candidate Bob Dole all indicated that they would make the flag desecration constitutional amendment a major campaign issue. Dole denounced the Phoenix art exhibit as a "disgusting display of contempt for the people and ideals of this nation" and on June 14 (Flag Day) he attacked President Clinton for failing to back the amendment, while proclaiming, "I do, I do, I do." The CFA hailed Dole's position, while repeatedly attacking candidates who opposed the amendment; and American Legion national commander Daniel Ludwig termed its passage "absolutely" the Legion's first priority. Two U.S. Senate candidates were booed when they expressed opposition to it at the Legion's Colorado state convention in late June; however, attendee Billy Hightower, an advocate for disabled veterans, lamented, "This flag-burning debate is a big smoke screen that clouds the real issues veterans need to be concerned about."[8]

Document 14.1

Resolutions passed by the Washington and Hawaiian legislatures in 1995 urging Congress to pass a constitutional amendment to outlaw flag desecration.

Source: Congressional Record, 1995, S7632–33.

State of Washington: Senate Joint Memorial 8006
Whereas, Although the right of free expression is part of the foundation of the United States Constitution, very carefully drawn limits on expression in specific instances have long been recognized as legitimate means of

maintaining public safety and decency, as well as orderliness and productive value of public debate; and Whereas, Certain actions, although arguably related to one person's free expression, nevertheless raise issues concerning public decency, public peace, and the rights of expression and sacred values of others; and

Whereas, There are symbols of our national soul such as the Washington Monument, the United States Capitol Building, and memorials to our greatest leaders, which are the property of every American and are therefore worthy of protection from desecration and dishonor; and

Whereas, The American Flag to this day is a most honorable and worthy banner of a nation that is thankful for its strengths and committed to curing its faults, and remains the destination of millions of immigrants attracted by the universal power of the American ideal; and

Whereas, The law as interpreted by the United States Supreme Court no longer accords to the Stars and Stripes that reverence, respect, and dignity befitting the banner of that most noble experiment of a nation-state; and

Whereas, It is only fitting that people everywhere should lend their voices to a forceful call for a restoration of the Stars and Stripes to a proper station under law and decency,

Now, therefore, Your Memorialists respectfully pray that the Congress of the United States propose an amendment of the United States Constitution, for ratification by the states, specifying that Congress and the states shall have the power to prohibit the physical desecration of the flag of the United States; . . .

State of Hawaii, House, Concurrent Resolution 142
Whereas, the flag of the United States is the ultimate symbol of our country and it is the unique fiber that holds together a diverse and different people into a nation we call America and the United States; and

Whereas, as of May, 1994, forty-three states have memorials to the United States Congress urging action to protect the American flag from willful physical desecration and these legislations represent nearly two hundred and twenty nine million Americans, more than ninety percent of our country's population; and

Whereas, although the right of free expression is part of the foundation of the United States Constitution [essentially repeating the text of the Washington state resolution printed immediately above] and

Whereas, as increasing number of citizens, individually and collectively, in Hawaii and throughout the nation, have called for action to ban the willful desecration of the American flag; and to ignore the effect of this decision would be an affront to everyone who has been committed to the ideals of our nation in times of war and in times of peace; now, therefore, be it

Resolved by the House of Representatives of the Eighteenth Legislature of the State of Hawaii, Regular Session of 1995, the Senate concurring, That this body respectfully requests each member of Hawaii's congressional delegation, with the specific purpose of urging the Congress of the United States to propose an amendment to the United States Constitution, for ratification by the states, providing that Congress and the states shall have the power to prohibit the willful physical desecration of the flag of the United States. . . .

Document 14.2

The founding publications of the Citizens Flag Alliance, 1994.

Source: Pamphlets, "Citizens Flag Alliance" and "Protecting the United States Flag: A Historical Prospectus." Reprinted by permission of the Citizens Flag Alliance.

"Every government degenerates when trusted to the rulers of the people alone. The people themselves therefore are its only safe depositories." *Thomas Jefferson*
Burning Our Flag Is Wrong!

A lot of intellectual arguments are being offered about why protesters should be allowed to burn our flag, but nothing changes the fact that it is wrong.

Our flag stands for everything "We, the people" of the United States believe in. It symbolizes our freedoms and opportunities. Can we sit quietly as this symbol of our values and ideals is mocked and defiled?

Our flag stands for our history, our pride and our honor. It has draped the coffins of hundreds of thousands who died in its defense. Are we really willing to give protesters the right to strike a painful blow to their memory?

Our flag stands for our future, our hopes and our dreams. Will our children's nation point to us as the generation that did nothing as this cherished symbol went up in smoke?

We have no choice. We must amend the Constitution. . . . Amending the Constitution won't be easy, nor should it be. But dozens of organizations, American businesses and millions of American citizens are joining together to form the Citizens Flag Alliance. Our goal is to protect our flag by amending the Constitution. . . .

Membership in the Citizens Flag Alliance is open to any citizen who wishes to stand by our flag.

We are asking Citizens Flag Alliance members to sign a petition supporting the amendment, and help us gain more support in your community.

Surveys indicate over 80% of the American people support a flag-protection amendment. Forty-four states have already passed memorializing resolutions to Congress asking for an amendment. Yet Congress has taken no action.

Why?

Because they do not believe the people of this nation care enough to take action. *They are wrong.*

The Citizens Flag Alliance members believe flag burning is wrong. It is not an exercise of free speech. It is a violent act of hate. We, the people, intend to exercise our right to tell our government, "Enough is enough. Amend the Constitution! . . . .

WILL YOU JOIN US?

Protecting the United Flag: A Historical Prospectus

. . . Perhaps more poems and songs and speeches have been written about the flag than any other subject in Americana, with the exception of love. But those writings are, in fact, about love, too. They express our national love of country, of tradition, of idealism, of freedom, of our form of government, and our reverence for those who die defending the values that we, as Americans, hold dear.

The Flag of the United States of America is the one symbol, more than any other, which unites us as a nation. . . .

[The Supreme Court's 1989 decision in *Texas v. Johnson,* document 10.12] not only freed Johnson, but it nullified the flag protection laws in 48 states and the District of Columbia.

Americans were outraged. Public opinion surveys showed three out of four Americans favored protection for the flag, and a similar number believed a constitutional amendment was needed to achieve that goal. . . . Congress responded by passing the Flag Protection Act of 1989 [document 11.8], thinking such legislation would quiet those groups and individuals who were calling for the constitutional amendment. . . .

In 1990, the U.S. Supreme Court, in *United States v. Eichman* [document 12.7], upheld *Texas v. Johnson* and struck down the federal law declaring it in conflict with the First Amendment. . . . It was then obvious to all that the only way to protect the U.S. Flag from physical desecration was through a constitutional amendment. Flag patriots turned once again to Congress.

In June 1990, House Resolution 350, which called for the amendment, failed to get the required two-thirds majority necessary for adoption in the House of Representatives. . . .

The action by the Court and Congress, both narrow decisions, angered the American people. The American Legion and other groups and individuals saw this rebuke of our national symbol as unacceptable. It was viewed as a significant erosion of national values that weakened the moral fabric of the country. Flag supporters vowed to continue the fight to secure protection for the flag by exercising their own First Amendment rights. . . .

An Amendment Solution

There are those who continue to advocate a legislative solution to protect the flag, even though the Supreme Court has rejected all such arguments, saying there is no juridical category in the Constitution providing for flag protection that would overcome First Amendment free speech objections. . . . [T]he Court has sent the message that the only option available to flag protectionists is the ratification of a narrowly drawn amendment allowing the federal and state governments to enact laws to protect the flag.

We cannot accept the Court's decision which allows the U.S. Flag to be set on fire, spit upon, and trampled as a form of political expression protected by constitutional guarantees of free speech. We believe that such acts ARE NOT speech, but are, instead, examples of violent, destructive, and despicable conduct, which recognize no values or morals, and are incompatible with civilized society. . . . [T]he only solution to the problem is to create a constitutional exception for the flag. . . .

Those who drafted the U.S. Constitution realized that changes would be necessary and provided a process [of amendment] to do so. . . . The coalition is [calling for] a narrowly drawn amendment to allow the states and Congress to enact laws to prevent the physical desecration of the United States flag.

The Constitution is considered by many as the most important document ever written. It is also not perfect and never professed to be. It has been amended 27 times, ten times by ratification of the Bill of Rights shortly after it was written. . . .

The Constitution had to be changed to institute the First Amendment freedoms. It had to be changed to provide voting privileges to African Americans, women and 18-year-olds. It can and must be changed to protect our National Symbol.

What would the amendment say? If Congress is consistent with language previously proposed, it may read as follows, although other language might be equally acceptable:

Congress and the States shall have power to prohibit the act of physical desecration of the flag of the United States.

With reference to both the Congress and the States, both would have the power to enact and enforce their own flag desecration statutes. Prior to the

Supreme Court's decision, 48 states had such laws on their books. The amendment would allow those states to reinstitute flag-protection laws.

First Amendment Arguments

The principal argument of opponents to the flag protection movement is that it infringes upon a person's right of free speech. However, freedom of speech is not absolute, nor has it ever been. That's why there are laws against libel and slander. That's why there are obscenity and public decency laws and perjury laws. Our freedom of political expression is also limited. We cannot deface the Supreme Court Building or the Washington Monument, no matter how much we wish to protest a particular government policy or law. . . . Those who oppose government policies, to include protesters and dissidents, may use any number of more reasonable methods to take advantage of the redress option. . . .

Members of the flag coalition believe that Congress should deal with the issue again because Congress was inconsistent in its treatment of the free speech issue when it dealt with the matter in 1989 and 1990. In June 1990, most of the flag amendment opponents stated that their opposition was based upon their concerns over infringement upon free speech. Yet, the overwhelming majority of those amendment opponents voted eight months earlier for a flag protection bill which was more restrictive than the proposed amendment would have been. The flag desecration bill, which became public law in 1989 and later ruled unconstitutional by the Supreme Court, was supported in Congress by a 9 to 1 ratio. Moreover, 90 percent of the people of the United States, through their state legislatures, have asked Congress to let the legislative process work as designed by sending an amendment to the states for ratification. Win or lose, the democratic process is dealt irreparable harm if the will of the people is ignored by their elected representatives.

Generating Public Support

Following the Supreme Court decision in 1989, The American Legion declared the flag's protection to be a priority issue and embarked on a campaign to secure a constitutional amendment. . . . It conducted petition drives and secured over one million signatures in only two months.

The issue became partisan in Congress when President Bush embraced the amendment process and key Democrats spoke in opposition.

Ultimately, the will of the people lost out to the political sparring taking place on Capitol Hill. The amendment issue was put to bed by Congress, but it didn't go to sleep.

On the contrary, The American Legion, along with others believing in flag protection, went to the state legislatures and sought their support in asking Congress to propose the amendment. Undertaking an aggressive campaign to secure memorializing resolutions from the various legislatures. . . .

Although a memorial resolution has no force of law, it does express the will of the people in a particular state. . . . At no time in our history has an issue been memorialized to the extent that flag protection has. . . . Listed below are the [44] states which have passed a resolution [as of May, 1994], . . .

State	Date Adopted
1. Texas	July 10, 1989
2. California	July 26, 1989
3. Utah	February 12, 1990
4. South Dakota	February 22, 1990
5. Tennessee	April 12, 1990
6. New Hampshire	April 19, 1990
7. Pennsylvania	June 19, 1990
8. Nevada	January 1991
9. North Dakota	January 30, 1991
10. South Carolina	February 5, 1991
11. Arkansas	February 20, 1991
12. Wyoming	February 21, 1991
13. Georgia	March 12, 1991
14. Indiana	March 19, 1991
15. Mississippi	March 29, 1991
16. Montana	April 1, 1991
17. Delaware	April 16, 1991
18. Alabama	April 30, 1991
19. Colorado	May 7, 1991
20. Ohio	May 23, 1991
21. Louisiana	May 30, 1991
22. Maine	June 12, 1991
23. Virginia	February 28, 1992
24. Florida	March 13, 1992
25. Wisconsin	April 14, 1992
26. Missouri	May 14, 1992
27. Rhode Island	May 21, 1992
28. Illinois	November 18, 1992
29. Idaho	March 15, 1993
30. West Virginia	March 18, 1993
31. Kansas	March 30, 1993
32. Alaska	May 10, 1993
33. Connecticut	June 7, 1993
34. Massachusetts	November 22, 1993

35. New Jersey	December 2, 1993
36. New Mexico	January 24, 1994
37. Michigan	February 2, 1994
38. Nebraska	February 28, 1994
39. Arizona	March 24, 1994
40. New York	March 24, 1994
41. Maryland	April 5, 1994
42. Minnesota	April 7, 1994
43. Oklahoma	April 20, 1994
44. North Carolina	May 27, 1994 . . .

The Citizens Flag Alliance, Inc. (CFA) . . . evolved from a meeting on May 19, 1994 of over 60 national organizations. This meeting . . . was called by The American Legion for the purpose of organizing the broad-based support needed for the campaign. . . .

Some of the organizations joining the campaign are the American War Mothers, Scottish Rite of Free Masonry—Southern Jurisdiction, AM-VETS, the National Grange, The American Legion and its Auxiliary, Moose International, National Vietnam Veterans Coalition, Fleet Reserve Association and the National Association of Chiefs of Police. . . .

Four different Gallup Surveys taken since the 1989 Supreme Court decision have shown that 78 percent of those asked do not believe such an amendment would jeopardize their right of free speech [and] have consistently demonstrated that more than 80 percent of Americans think the Supreme Court decision was wrong; that flag burning is wrong and that they would, if permitted, vote for a constitutional amendment to protect the flag.

The Citizens Flag Alliance believes the people should have the right to make the decision. . . .

Join the Citizens Flag Alliance. Do your part to protect Our National Symbol.

Document 14.3

Minority views of twelve Democratic members of the House Judiciary Committee, dissenting from the 1995 majority report endorsing a flag desecration constitutional amendment.

Source: Flag Desecration, 104th Cong., 1st sess., June 22, 1995, H. Rep. 104–51, 15–22

We strongly oppose H.J. Res. 79 [the proposed constitutional amendment], which would—for the first time in our Nation's history—modify the Bill of Rights to limit our freedom of expression. Although the motives of the proposition's supporters are well-intentioned, we believe that adopting H.J. Res. 79 is wrong as a matter of principle, wrong as a matter of precedent, and wrong as a matter of practice.

H.J. Res. 79 responds to a perceived problem—flag burning—that is fortunately a rare occurrence in American life today. Moreover, most incidents of flag burning can be successfully prosecuted today under laws relating to breach of peace, thefts, vandalism and trespassing—all fully within current constitutional constraints. . . .

Ironically, H.J. Res. 79 will not even achieve the sponsors' stated purposes—protecting the American flag and honoring America's veterans. History has taught us that restrictive legislation will sadly result in more flag burning in an effort to protest the law itself, and a vaguely worded constitutional amendment such as H.J. Res. 79 may cause such efforts to increase many times over. If we truly want to honor our veterans, it would be far more constructive for Congress to reconsider eliminating cost-of-living increases and health care benefits previously promised to veterans. Thus, while we condemn those who would dishonor our Nation's flag, we believe that rather than protecting the flag, H.J. Res. 79 will merely serve to weaken the Constitutional protection of free expression.

IMPORTANCE OF FREEDOM OF EXPRESSION

Freedom of expression is one of the preeminent human rights and is central to fostering all other forms of freedom. . . . Perhaps the most important function served by a system of free expression is that it allows for free and open exchange of thoughts—referred to by Justice Holmes as the "marketplace of ideas.". . .

The American system of government is itself premised on freedom of expression. . . .

The founding fathers recognized the difficulties in maintaining a system of free expression against the "tyranny of the majority." . . . It is for these reasons that the Constitution not only explicitly protected freedom of expression, but created a judiciary possessing the power of review over all legislative and executive action. These twin safeguards—a written constitution and an independent judiciary—have served to foster in this country the freest society in human history.

H.J. RES. 79 IS WRONG AS A MATTER OF PRINCIPLE

Unfortunately, H.J. Res. 79 detracts from our system of unfettered political expression. The true test of any nation's commitment to freedom of expression lies in its ability to protect unpopular expression, such as flag desecration. In 1929 Justice Holmes wrote that it was the most imperative principle of our constitution that it protects not just freedom for the thought and expression we agree with, but "freedom for the thought we hate." As Justice Jackson so eloquently wrote in 1943 [in *Barnette*, document 5.2]:

> Freedom to differ is not limited to things that do not matter much. That would be a mere shadow of freedom. The test of its substance is the right to differ as to things that touch the heart of the existing order. If there is any fixed star in our constitutional constellation, it is that no official, high or petty, can prescribe what shall be orthodox in politics nationalism, religion or other matters of opinion.

And there can be no doubt that "symbolic speech" relating to the flag falls squarely within the ambit of traditionally protected speech. Our nation was born in the dramatic symbolic speech of the Boston Tea Party, and our courts have long recognized that expressive speech associated with the flag is protected speech under the first amendment.

Beginning in 1931 with *Stromberg v. California* [document 5.1] the Supreme Court has consistently recognized that flag-related expression is entitled to constitutional protection. . . . Those who seek to justify H.J. Res. 79 on the grounds that flag desecration does not constitute "speech" are therefore denying decades of well-understood court decisions.

While we deplore the burning of an American flag in hatred, we recognize that it is our allowing of this conduct that reinforces the strength of the Constitution. . . . The fact that flag burners are able to take refuge in the first amendment means that every citizen can be assured that the Bill of Rights will be available to protect his or her rights and liberties should the need arise.

H.J. Res. 79 will also open the door to selective prosecution based purely on political beliefs. . . . The overwhelming majority of flag desecration cases have been brought against political dissenters, while commercial and other forms of flag desecration has been almost completely ignored. . . .

Almost as significant as the damage H.J. Res. 79 would do to our own Constitution, is the harm it will inflict on our international standing in the area of human rights. Demonstrators who cut the communist symbols from the center of the East German and Romanian flags prior to the fall of the Iron Curtain committed crimes against their country's laws, yet freedom-loving Americans justifiably applauded these brave actions. If we are to maximize our moral stature in matters of human rights, it is therefore, essential that we remain fully open to unpopular dissent, regardless of the form it takes.

H.J. RES. 79 IS WRONG AS A MATTER OF PRECEDENT

Adoption of H.J. Res. 79 will also create a number of dangerous precedents in our legal system. . . .

If we approve H.J. Res. 79, it is unlikely to be the last time Congress acts to restrict our first amendment liberties. . . . Conservative legal scholar Bruce Fein emphasized this concern when he testified [before a HJC subcommittee]:

> While I believe the *Johnson* and *Eichman* decisions were misguided, I do not believe a Constitutional amendment would be a proper response * * * to enshrine authority to punish flag desecrations in the Constitution would not only tend to trivialize the Nation's Charter, but encourage such juvenile temper tantrums in the hopes of receiving free speech martyrdom by an easily beguiled media * * * [The Constitution] will lose that reverence and accessibility to the ordinary citizen if it becomes cluttered with amendments overturning every wrongheaded Supreme Court decision.

H.J. RES. 79 IS WRONG AS A MATTER OF PRACTICE

As a practical matter, H.J. Res. 79 is too loosely drafted and may well open up a "Pandora's Box" of litigation. The terms of the resolution are so open-ended that they give us no guidance as to its intended Constitutional scope or parameter. . . . [T]he amendment's supporters . . . are granting the state and federal governments open-ended authority to prosecute dissenters who use the flag in a manner deemed inappropriate.

The Committee debate highlights the fact that there is little understanding or consensus concerning the meaning of such crucial terms as "desecration" and "flag of the United States." Depending on the state law adopted, "desecration" could apply to cancelling flag postage stamps or use of the flag by Olympic athletes. . . .

H.J. Res. 79 gives us no guidance whatsoever as to what if any provisions of the first amendment, the Bill of Rights, or the Constitution in general that it is designed to overrule. A provision of such untested meaning and scope as H.J. Res. 79 will inevitably lead to confusing and inconsistent law enforcement and adjudication, and it will likely be decades before the court system could even begin to sort out the problems. . . .

CONCLUSION

Adoption of H.J. Res. 79 will diminish our commitment to untrammeled freedom of expression under our constitutional system. We believe we are too secure as a nation to need to risk our commitment to freedom by endeavoring to legislate patriotism. As the Court wrote in *West Virginia Board of Education v. Barnette*:

⟨The⟩ ultimate futility of * * * attempts to compel coherence is the lesson of every such effort from the Roman drive to stamp out Christianity as a disturber of its pagan unity, the Inquisition, as a means to religious and dynastic unity, the Siberian exiles as a means to Russian unity, down to the last failing efforts of our present totalitarian enemies. Those who begin coercive elimination of dissent soon find themselves exterminating dissenters. Compulsory unification of opinion achieves only the unanimity of the graveyard.

If we tamper with our Constitution because of the antics of a handful of obnoxious and thoughtless people we will have reduced the role of the flag as an emblem of freedom, not enforced it. We will not go on record as supporting a proposal which will limit the freedom of expression of the American people no matter how great the provocation, or how noble the motives of its proponents.

Document 14.4

Remarks by Rep. Wayne Gilchrest (R., Md.) in the House of Representatives, June 18, 1995.

Source: Congressional Record, 1995, H6421.

[A]s the House moves closer to a constitutional amendment to ban flag burning, I am reminded strangely enough of the book of Exodus. When the Israelites were given the Ten Commandments, they were warned against graven images as symbols of God. The wisdom of this is obvious. It is easy to confuse the symbol of something with what that symbol represents, and what that symbol symbolizes, so one worships the statue instead of what the statue represents. Mr. Speaker, the House is about to make a similar mistake, confusing the flag with what it symbolizes. I remember when I came home from Vietnam, after spending 4 years in the Marine Corps, I read about incidents where students were insulting servicemen and waving North Vietnamese flags instead of American flags, and I started to think "Is this what I and members of my platoon were fighting and dying for?" It took a few years for me to realize that the right to be obnoxious, the right to be unpatriotic, was the essence of what we are fighting for. Freedom means the freedom to be stupid, just as surely as it means the freedom to be wise. No government should ever be so powerful as to differentiate between the two. I understand the anger and the frustration of people when they hear about malcontents who burn the flag, and most of the time they do that to get attention. I was raised to respect the flag, and I cannot understand anybody that would do otherwise. However, if these malcontents can get us to alter the Constitution, the very premise and foundation of this country, then they have won and we have lost. I read about a southern State legislator who said that nothing is more stupid than burning the flag and wrapping oneself in the Constitution, except burning the Constitution and wrapping oneself in the flag. When we accept the principle of free speech, we have to recognize that it is both a blessing and a curse. We have to understand that the reasoned voices of good men will often be drowned out by the blustering of fools. We have to understand that the government will not be able to protect us from speech which is imprudent or offensive, in most cases, and we accept all of this as the price of freedom. . . .

Document 14.5

Remarks by Sen. John Glenn (D., Ohio) in the Senate, December 8, 1995.

Source: Congressional Record, 1995, 18276–80.

. . . [U]ntil today, I have tended to hold my tongue and have kept my peace about this issue before us because it is no fun being attacked or being labeled as unpatriotic or a friend of flag burners. And I can assure you that I am neither simply because I have doubts about the wisdom of a constitutional flag burning amendment. . . . We all, of course, love the flag, and I would say nobody in this Chamber or this country loves our flag more than I do. . . .

It is now clear that a legislative alternative to amending our Constitution is probably not going to be possible before we have to vote on this. It is now equally clear that those of us who question the wisdom of watering down our Bill of Rights have no choice but to stand up to the political mud merchants in some respects, from some of the comments that have been made, and to speak out against those who would deal in demagoguery on this issue. It is now clear that those of us who remember and care deeply about the sacrifices made on behalf of freedom have a special responsibility, and we do, to point out that it would be a hollow victory, indeed, if we preserved the symbol of our freedoms by chipping away at those freedoms themselves. That is the important choice here. Are we to protect the symbol at the expense of even taking a small chance at chipping away at the freedoms that that symbol represents? . . .

[T]he flag is the Nation's most powerful and emotional symbol, and it is our sacred symbol. It is a revered symbol, but it is a symbol. It symbolizes the freedoms we have in this country, but it is not the freedoms themselves. And that is why this debate is not between those who love the flag on the one hand and those who do not on the other, no matter how often the demagogs try to tell us otherwise. . . . The question is how best to honor it, to honor it and what it represents. Those who made the ultimate sacrifice for our flag did not give up their lives for just a piece of cloth, albeit red, white, and blue, and it had some stars on it. Not just for the flag. They died because of their allegiance to this country, to the values and the rights and principles represented by that flag and to the Republic for which it stands.

Without a doubt, the most important of those values, the most important of those values, rights and principles is individual liberty, the liberty to worship and think, to express ourselves freely, openly and completely, no matter how out of step those views may be with the opinions of the majority. . . . That commitment to freedom is encapsulated, it is encoded in our Bill of Rights, perhaps the most envied and imitated document anywhere in the world. The Bill of Rights is what makes our country unique. It is what has made us a shining beacon in a dark world, a shining beacon of hope and inspiration to oppressed peoples around the world for well over 200 years. It is, in short, what makes America America. . . .

The very first item in that Bill of Rights, the first amendment in it to our Constitution has never been changed or altered even one single time. . . . That Bill of Rights has not been changed even during times of great emotion and anger like the Vietnam era, when flags were burned or desecrated far more than they are today. Our first amendment was unchanged, unchallenged, as much as we might have disagreed with what was going on at that time, as abhorrent as we found the actions of a lot of people at that time in their protests against the Vietnam war. But now we are told that unless we alter the first amendment, unless we place a constitutional limit on the right of speech and expression that the fabric of our country will somehow be weakened. Well, I just cannot bring myself to believe that that is the case. . . .

What we are dealing with is the Bill of Rights, dealing with that first amendment to the Bill of Rights. We are saying for the first time in our country's 200-year history, we are going to make, albeit maybe just a tiny crack, but it will be a tiny opening that could possibly be followed by others. . . . The Supreme Court has held on two separate occasions that no matter how much the majority of us, 99.999 percent of the people of this country disagree, that tiny, tiny, fractional, misguided minority, still under our Bill of Rights they have the right to their expression. . . .

I think there is only one way to weaken the fabric of our country, our unique country, our country that stands as a beacon before other nations around this world. . . . [I]t is by retreating from the principles that the flag stands for—"principles" underlined 16 times—principles that this flag stands for, that if we retreat from those principles that will do more damage to the fabric of our Nation than 1,000 torched flags ever could do. . . . I do not want to see us make some laws, even tiny laws, even the potential of a tiny little crack in that Bill of Rights that would restrict freedom of expression. . . . [W]e can say this time the laws would be about flag burning or flag desecration, to use the exact words. But what will the next form of political expression be that we seek to prohibit, if we start a crack that has not occurred, not in the 200-plus year's history of this country? . . .

And for what? For a threat that, at least in current years, is practically nonexistent? . . .

. . . It has often been said it is possible to detect how free a society is by the degree to which it is willing to tolerate and permit the expression of ideas that are odious and reprehensible to the values of that society. You and I and a majority of our fellow citizens find flag burning and desecration to be vile and disgusting. But we also find Nazis marching in Skokie, IL, or the Ku Klux Klan marching and burning crosses in Selma, AL, to be vile and disgusting. But if the first amendment means anything at all, it means that those cruel and poor misguided souls, many of them I think demented, have a right to express themselves in that manner, however objectionable the rest of us may find their message. . . .

To say that we should restrict speech or expression that would outrage a majority of listeners or move them to violence is to say that we will tolerate only those kinds of expression that the majority agrees with, or at least does not disagree with too much. That would do nothing less than gut the first amendment. What about the argument that flag desecration is an act and is not a form of speech or expression that is protected by the first amendment? Well, I think that argument is a bit specious. Anybody burning a flag in protest is clearly saying something. They are making a statement by their body language, and what they are doing makes a statement that maybe speaks far, far louder than the words they may be willing to utter on such an occasion. They are saying something, just the same way as people who picket, or march in protest, or use other forms of symbolic speech are expressing themselves. Indeed, if we did not view flag burners as something we find offensive and repugnant, we surely would not be debating their right to do so.

Let me say a word about something that has gotten short shrift in this debate, something we should consider very carefully before voting on this amendment. I am talking about the practical problems with this amendment. . . .

[I]f Congress and States are allowed to prohibit the physical desecration of the flag, how precisely are we defining the flag? . . . [D]oes this amendment refer to only manufactured flags of cloth or nylon of a certain size or description, such as the ones we fly over the Capitol here and send out? . . . Does it refer to the small paper flags on a stick we hand out to children at political rallies or stick in a cupcake at a banquet? Those flags are often tossed on the floor or in a garbage can at conclusion of an event.

. . . How about the guy who jogs down the street with a flag T-shirt on and becomes drenched with sweat? . . .

How about a guy that has an old flag with grease all over it, and he wants to destroy it. You are supposed to burn it to destroy a flag. So he holds it up and he is going to burn it and then he says at the same time, "I am doing this because I do not like the tax bill they passed last year, and I am doing it in protest. I am burning the flag because I do not like what they did in Washington." Are we going to lock him up? Remember, the proper way to destroy a flag that is old or has become soiled is to burn it. But what if he does it in protest? What was his intent? . . . What if you take a postage stamp flag and put a match under that thing and it burns up and you say, "There," and you stomp on it? Can you be arrested under the new legislation? . . .

I think history and future generations alike will judge us harshly, as they should, if we permit people who would defile our flag . . . [to] hoodwink us into also defiling our Constitution, no matter how onerous their acts may be. It would be a hollow victory, it seems to me. We must not let those who revile our freedoms and our way of life trick us into diminishing them, or even take a chance of diminishing them. Mr. President, I do not think we can let the passions of the moment stampede us into abandoning principles for all time. . . . If we are going to continue to be the land of the free and the home of the brave, I think we had better be very, very careful. . . .

Document 14.6

Testimony by Clinton administration assistant attorney general Walter Dellinger in opposition to a flag desecration constitutional amendment.

Source: Flag Desecration, 104th Cong., 1st sess., June 22, 1995, H. Rept. 104-151, 9–14.

For five years [since the *Johnson* ruling, document 10.12] the flag has been left without any statutory protection against symbolic desecration. For five years, one thing, and only one thing, has stood between the flag and its routine desecration: the fact that the flag, as a potent symbol of all that is best about our country, is justly cherished and revered by nearly all Americans. . . .

It is precisely because of the meaning the flag has for virtually all Americans that the last five years have witnessed no outbreak of flag burning, but only a few isolated instances, immediately and roundly condemned. If proof were needed, we have it now: with or without the threat of criminal penalties, the flag is amply protected by its unique stature as an embodiment of national unity and ideals.

It is against this background that one must assess the need for a proposed constitutional amendment [that], if adopted, would for the first time in our history alter the Bill of Rights adopted over two centuries ago. . . . [Y]ou are asked to assume the risk inherent in a first-time edit of the Bill of Rights in the absence of any meaningful evidence that the flag is in danger of losing its symbolic value.

The unprecedented amendment before you would create legislative power of uncertain dimension to override the First Amendment and other constitutional guarantees. More fundamentally, it would run counter to our traditional resistance, dating back to the time of the Founders, to resorting to the amendment process. For these reasons, the proposed amendment—and any other proposal to amend the Constitution in order to punish a few isolated acts of flag burning—should be rejected by this Congress. . . .

[O]ur disagreement about the wisdom of the proposed amendment does not in any way reflect disagreement about the proper place of the flag in our national community. The President always has and always will condemn in the strongest of terms those who would show disrespect to the symbol of our country's highest ideals.

The President's record reflects his long-standing commitment to protection of the American flag, and his profound abhorrence of flag burning and other forms of flag desecration. In 1989, after the Supreme Court invalidated the Texas statute at issue in *Johnson*, then-Governor Clinton responded promptly by recommending enactment of a new State law prohibiting all intentional destruction of a flag. . . . As you know, however, the Supreme Court's subsequent decision in *Eichman* [document 12.7], invalidating the Federal Flag Protection Act [document 11.8], appears to foreclose legislative efforts to prohibit flag burning. In the wake of *Johnson*, then-Governor Clinton also instituted a state-wide "flag respect" program to teach school children proper appreciation for the flag. . . .

Because the proposed amendment fails to state explicitly the degree to which it overrides other constitutional guarantees, it is entirely unclear how much of the Bill of Rights it would trump. . . . The text of the proposed amendment does not purport to exempt the exercise of the power conferred from the constraints of the First Amendment or any other constitutional guarantee of individual rights. Read literally, the amendment would not alter the result of the decisions in *Eichman* or *Johnson*, holding that the exercise of congressional and state power to protect the symbol of the flag is subject to First and Fourteenth Amendment limits. . . .

To give the amendment meaning, then, we must read into it, consistent with its sponsors' intent, at least some restriction on the First Amendment freedoms identified in the Supreme Court's flag decisions. What is difficult, and profoundly so, is identifying just how much of the First Amendment and the rest of the Bill of Rights is superseded by the amendment. Once we have departed, by necessity, from the amendment's text, we are in uncharted territory, and faced with genuine uncertainty as to the extent to which the amendment will displace the protections enshrined in the Bill of Rights.

We do not know, for instance, whether the proposed amendment is intended, or would be interpreted to authorize enactments that otherwise would violate the due process "void for vagueness" doctrine. . . . The amendment, after all, authorizes laws that prohibit "physical desecration" of the flag, and "desecration" is not a term that readily admits of objective definition. On the contrary, "desecrate" is defined to include such inherently subjective meanings as "profane" and even "treat contemptuously." . . .

The term "flag of the United States" is similarly "unbounded," and by itself provides no guidance as to whether it reaches unofficial as well as official flags, or pictures or representations of flags created by artists as well as flags sold or distributed for traditional display. Indeed, testifying in favor of a similar amendment in 1989, then-Assistant Attorney General William Barr [document 11.14] acknowledged that the word "flag" is so elastic that it can be stretched to cover everything from cloth banners with the characteristics of the official flag, as defined by statute, to "any picture or representation" of a flag, including "posters, murals, pictures, ⟨and⟩ buttons." . . .

[I]t must be remembered that the amendment at issue here also grants the same power to fifty different states and an uncertain number of local governments. . . . [I]t increases, by at least fifty times, the risk that unduly restrictive or arbitrary legislation may be enacted at some point in the near or distant future, and it virtually guarantees a patchwork of very different state responses. Under these circumstances, Congress has a special obligation to make clear the dimensions of the power the amendment would confer.

I have real doubts about whether these interpretive concerns could be resolved fully by even the most artful of drafting. . . . But even assuming, for the moment, that all of the interpretive difficulties of this amendment could be cured, it would remain an ill-advised departure from a constitutional history marked by a deep reluctance to amend our most fundamental law.

The Bill of Rights was ratified in 1792. Since that time, over two hundred years ago, the Bill of Rights has never once been amended. . . . [O]ur historic unwillingness to tamper with the Bill of Rights reflects a reverence for the Constitution that is both entirely appropriate and fundamentally at odds with turning that document into a forum for divisive political battles.

The Framers themselves understood that resort to the amendment process was to be sparing and reserved for "great and extraordinary occasions." . . . The proposed amendment cannot be reconciled with this fundamental and historic understanding of the integrity of the Constitution. . . .

We come to this discussion at a time when peace among ourselves seems threatened, and national unity an elusive goal. The unity we seek, however, should be of the kind that is freely chosen, because that is the only kind that matters and the only kind that will endure. Americans are free today to display the flag respectfully, to ignore it entirely, or to use it as an expression of protest or reproach. By overwhelming numbers, Americans have chosen the first option, and display the flag proudly. And what gives this gesture its unique symbolic meaning is the fact that the choice is freely made, uncoerced by the government. Were it otherwise—were, for instance, respectful treatment of the flag the only choice constitutionally available—then the respect paid the flag by millions of Americans would mean something different and perhaps something less.

Document 14.7

Remarks by Sen. Howell Heflin (D., Ala.) in the Senate, December 11, 1995.

Source: Congressional Record, 1995, S18353–54.

. . .[W]e have trivialized so many values and symbols that, basically, we no longer have anything that is sacred. I think it is time that we have some matters, including symbols, that are sacred in this United States. We have seen the deterioration of morals, we have seen the deterioration of respect for institutions and for traditions, and I think it is time we look at some of these concerns that are very important to this country. I think the flag is, and I think the flag ought to be sacred. . . .

In my judgment, it is our responsibility to change [the *Johnson* decision, document 10.12] and return the flag to the position of respect it deserves. Few people would disagree with the argument that the American flag stands as one of the most powerful and meaningful symbols of freedom ever created. . . . The flag holds a mighty grip over many people in this country. . . . Thousands of Americans have followed the flag into battle and many, to our sorrow, have left these battles in coffins draped proudly by the American flag. Nothing quite approaches the power of the flag as it drapes those who died for it—or the power of the flag as it is handed to the widow of that fallen soldier. The meaning behind these flags goes far beyond the cloth used to make the flag or the dyes used to color Old Glory—red, white, and blue. The flag reaches to the very heart of what it means to be an American. It would be a tragedy for us to allow the power of the flag to be undermined through desecration. Allowing the burning of that flag creates a mockery of the great respect so many patriotic Americans have for the flag. . . .

Document 14.8

Majority report of the Senate Judiciary Committee in support of a constitutional amendment to outlaw flag desecration.

Source: Senate, *Senate Joint Resolution 31,* 104th Cong., 1st sess., Sept. 27, 1995, S. Rep. 104-148, 1–42.

I. SUMMARY

The purpose of Senate Joint Resolution 31 is to restore to Congress and to the States the authority to adopt statutes protecting the flag of the United States from physical desecration. It reads simply: "The Congress and the States shall have power to prohibit the physical desecration of the flag of the United States."

The American people revere the flag of the United States as the unique symbol of our Nation and the freedom we enjoy as Americans. . . . The American flag represents, in a way nothing else can, the common bond shared by the people of this Nation, one of the most heterogeneous and diverse in the world.

II. LEGISLATIVE HISTORY

. . . On March 21, 1995, Senators Hatch and Heflin, as principal cosponsors, along with a bipartisan group of 45 additional cosponsors, introduced Senate Joint Resolution 31. . . .

This is the same [operative] language of the amendments [defeated] in 1989 and 1990 [document 11.6]. . . . On July 20, 1995, the committee voted 12 to 6 to report favorably S.J. Res. 31. The House of Representatives voted 312 to 120 in favor of an identical resolution on June 28, 1995.

III. DISCUSSION

A. THE FLAG IS A UNIQUE SYMBOL OF A DIVERSE COUNTRY

. . . Congress has, over the years, reflected the devotion our diverse people have for Old Glory. During the Civil War, for example, Congress awarded the Medal of Honor to Union soldiers who rescued the flag from falling into Confederate hands.

In 1931, Congress declared the Star Spangled Banner to be our national anthem. In 1949, Congress established June 14 as Flag Day. Congress has established The Pledge of Allegiance to the Flag and the manner of its recitation. Congress designated John Philip Sousa's "The Stars and Stripes Forever" as the national march in 1987. . . .

Congress, along with 48 States, had regulated physical misuse of the American flag until the Supreme Court's 1989 decision in *Texas v. Johnson*. Indeed, some of these laws originated nearly a century ago.

In 1968, Congress enacted a nationwide flag desecration statute, codified at 18 U.S.C. 700(a) [document 6.1]. . . . These congressional and State actions reflect the people's devotion to the flag; Congress and the States did not create these feelings and deep regard for the flag among our people.

B. THE PLACE OF THE FLAG IN THE HEARTS AND MINDS OF THE AMERICAN PEOPLE

The committee recognizes that members of the Senate need no words from it to explain the special bond between the American people and their beloved flag as a unique symbol of their aspirations to national unity, and the principles, values, ideals, and history of their country. Still, because that bond is the basis for S.J. Res. 31, the voice of the American people in expressing their reverence for their flag are properly heard in this report. . . .

Henry Ward Beecher gave an address entitled, "The National Flag," in May 1861. These are excerpts:

> A thoughtful mind, when it sees a nation's flag, sees not the flag, but the nation itself. And whatever may be its symbols, its insignia, he reads chiefly in the flag the government, the principles, the truths, the history, that belong to the nation that sets it forth * * * [I]t has gathered and stored chiefly this supreme idea: Divine right of liberty in man. Every color means liberty; every thread means liberty. . . .

Henry Holcomb Bennett, born in Chillicothe, OH, in 1863, engaged in ornithology, book illustration, and writing short stories about Army life. In 1904, he published, "The Flag Goes By":

> Hats off!
> Along the street there comes
> A blare of bugles, a ruffle of drums,
> A flash of color beneath the sky:
> Hats off!
> The flag is passing by! . . .

[I]n 1990, the American Legion and other veterans, patriotic, and civic groups, and individual Americans, initiated a grassroots effort to gain support for a constitutional amendment. Many of these groups and individuals formed the Citizens Flag Alliance. . . .

Forty-nine state legislatures have called for a constitutional amendment on flag desecration. According to Prof. Stephen B. Presser of Northwestern University Law School, no other amendment in the Nation's history has had this kind of support in State legislatures. . . .

At the June 6, 1995, hearing of the Senate Judiciary Committee's Subcommittee on the Constitution, Federalism, and Property Rights, Rose Lee, past national president of the Gold Star Wives of America [an organization of widows of Americans killed in battle], testified:

> . . . It's not fair and it's not right that flags like this flag, handed to me by an Honor Guard 23 years ago, can be legally burned by someone in this country. My husband defended this flag during his life. When he died, it was an honor to have this flag cover his casket. But it's a dishonor to our husbands and an insult to their widows to allow this flag to be legally burned. . . .
>
> The flag is a symbol that stands for the freedoms we enjoy as Americans. My husband fought for those freedoms, including one we hear a lot about in this debate, freedom of speech. . . . But burning the flag is not an expression of free speech. It's a terrible physical act. And it's a slap in the face of every widow who has a flag just like mine. . . .

C. NEED FOR AN AMENDMENT

Only a constitutional amendment can restore power to the people enabling them to undertake the legal protection of the flag. The Supreme Court has given the American people and their elected representatives no choice. . . . The proposed amendment does no more than return us to this common understanding and common sense point of view, as most recently expressed by 49 State legislatures. . . .

Congress did enact a facially neutral statute in 1989 with an exception for disposal of worn or soiled flags, as a response to the *Johnson* decision. The Supreme Court promptly struck it down, 5 to 4 [in *Eichman*]. . . .

A statutory response to the *Johnson* and *Eichman* decisions is thus clearly not a viable option. . . . We live in a time where standards have eroded. Civility and mutual respect are in decline. Nothing is immune from being reduced to the commonplace. Absolutes are distrusted. Values are considered relative. Rights are cherished and constantly expanded, but responsibilities are shirked or scorned.

We seek to instill in our children a pride in their country that will serve as a basis for good citizenship and a devotion to improving the country and to its best interests as they can see them. We hope they will feel connected to the diverse people who are their fellow citizens. . . . At the same time, our country grows more and more diverse. Many of our people revel in their particular cultures and diverse national origins, and properly so. Others are alienated from their fellow citizens and from government altogether.

We have no monarchy, no "state" religion, no elite class—hereditary or otherwise—"representing" the Nation. We have the flag.

The American flag is the one symbol that unites a very diverse people in a way nothing else can, in peace and war. Despite our differences of party, politics, philosophy, religion, ethnic background, economic status, social status, or geographic region, the American flag forms a unique, common bond among us. Failure to protect the flag inevitably loosens this bond, no matter how much some may claim to the contrary. . . .

The current movement for this amendment originates with the American people. It is right and proper that their elected representatives respond affirmatively.

SENATE JOINT RESOLUTION 31 IS A SUITABLE AMENDMENT TO THE CONSTITUTION

1. Senate Joint Resolution 31 will effectively restore power to Congress and the States denied them in Texas v. Johnson and U.S. v. Eichman; S.J. Res. 31 does not "trump" the first amendment or any other constitutional provision . . .

[T]he [Clinton] administration [in the testimony of Assistant Attorney General Dellinger, document 14.6] argues, "it is entirely unclear how much of the Bill of Rights it would trump." . . .[T]he amendment *does* overturn the two Supreme Court decisions and empowers Congress and the States to prohibit physical desecration of the flag. [T]he amendment does *not* trump any part of the Constitution.

a. Senate Joint Resolution 31 will effectively empower Congress and the States to enact statutes prohibiting the physical desecration of the American flag

Some critics of S.J. Res. 31 [such as Dellinger] suggest that it may merely be redundant of governmental power to legislate in this area that always has been assumed to exist. The suggestion is ironic since the flag amendment will simply restore power to Congress and the States it was assumed they always possessed. . . .

Simply put, this amendment creates [a] separate "juridical category" for the flag in the Constitution's text, and grants the power to prohibit physical desecration of the flag the Supreme Court took away in 1989. Indeed, any other interpretation of the amendment renders it meaningless. . . .

b. Senate Joint Resolution 31 does not amend the first amendment or "trump" any other constitutional provision

This amendment, granting Congress and the States power to prohibit physical desecration of the flag, does not amend the first amendment. The flag amendment overturns two Supreme Court decisions which have misconstrued the first amendment.

The first amendment's guarantee of freedom of speech has never been deemed absolute. Libel is not protected under the first amendment. Obscenity is not protected under the first amendment. . . . The view that the first amendment does not disable Congress and the States from prohibiting physical desecration of the flag has been shared by ardent supporters of the first amendment and freedom of expression [citing dissents in *Street*, document 8.1, by Supreme Court justices Warren, Black and Fortas]. . . .

Richard Parker, professor of Law at Harvard Law School, testified [at a 1995 SJC subcommittee hearing]:

> The proposal would not "amend the First Amendment." Rather, each amendment would be interpreted in light of the other—much as in the case with the guaranties of Freedom of Speech and Equal Protection of the Laws. . . . Courts would interpret "desecration" and "flag of the United States" in light of general values of free speech. . . .
>
> But, we're asked, is "harmonization" possible? If the *Johnson* and *Eichman* decisions protecting flag desecration were rooted in established strains of free speech laws how could an amendment countering those decisions coexist with the First Amendment?
>
> First, it's important to keep in mind that free speech law has within it multiple, often competing strains. The dissenting opinions [in *Eichman* and *Johnson*] . . . were also rooted in established arguments about the meaning of freedom of speech. Second, even if the general principles invoked by the five Justices in the majority are admirable in general—as I believe they are—that doesn't mean that the proposed amendment would tend to undermine them, so long as it is confined, as it is intended, to mandating a unique exception for a unique symbol of nationhood. . . .

There is no basis for the assertion that the amendment "trumps" or supersedes other parts of the Constitution. Such an assertion is a scare tactic. Nothing in the text of the amendment provides a basis for that fear. . . . As Professor Parker testified, the flag amendment will be read in harmony with the rest of the Constitution, including the first amendment. . . .

[T]here is no basis at all to suggest S.J. Res. 31 trumps the due process clause of the 5th or 14th amendments. . . . [L]egislation under the flag amendment is subject to the void-for-vagueness doctrine. But that doctrine allows Congress and the States to prohibit contemptuous or disrespectful treatment of the flag so long as there is substantial specificity in spelling out what that treatment is—be it by burning, mutilating, defiling, defacing, trampling, and so on. . . .

2. *The terms "physical desecration" and "flag of the United States" are precise enough for inclusion in the Constitution*

The Senate in the 104th Congress should not subject S.J. Res. 31, authorizing legislation protecting the American flag, to a higher standard than the Framers subjected the terms of the Constitution and the Bill of Rights in the Philadelphia Convention and in the First Congress. The terms of the flag protection amendment are at least as precise, if not more so, than such terms as "unreasonable searches and seizures;" "probable cause;" "speedy * * * trial;" "excessive bail;" "excessive fines;" "cruel and unusual punishment;" "due process of law;" "just compensation"—all terms from the Bill of Rights. . . . Legislative bodies will implement the flag protection amendment with the specificity of statutory language which itself, as mentioned earlier, will be subject to constitutional requirements.

Second, the committee does not consider ambiguous the word "desecrate," which in turn is modified by the word "physically." Desecrate means to treat with contempt, to treat with disrespect, to violate the sanctity of something; profane. The committee does not believe these terms are too difficult for our legislatures and courts to handle. . . .

The flag protection amendment does not authorize legislation which prohibits displaying or carrying the flag at meetings or marches of any group—be they Nazis, Marxists, or anyone else. The amendment does not authorize legislation prohibiting derogatory comments about the flag or cursing the flag, nor does it authorize a prohibition on shaking one's fist at the flag or making obscene gestures at the flag, whether or not such gestures are accompanied by words. The amendment does not authorize legislation penalizing carrying or displaying the flag upside down as a signal of distress or flying it at half mast on days not officially designated for such display. . . .

Having said that, under this amendment, there is some flexibility in the legislative bodies in defining the term "flag of the United States." . . .

For example, the term "flag of the United States" could be defined at the narrowest as just a cloth or other substance or material readily able to be flown, waved, or displayed. . . . The flag, of such characteristics and material, could also be defined to be of any size or dimensions. That would be up to legislative bodies to determine.

Another possible definition available to legislative bodies would be to include in the definition of the flag something a reasonable person would perceive to be a flag of the United States meeting the design set forth in the U.S. Code, and capable of being waved, flown, or displayed, regardless of whether it is precisely identical to that design. Thus, under such a definition, for example, physically desecrating a flag with 48 stars, or 12 or 14 stripes, could be covered. . . . .

The choice of what to cover under the term "flag of the United States" should be left up to the sensible judgment of the American people, as it had been for 200 years before the *Johnson* decision.

As to the parade of horribles opponents invoke in opposition to the amendment, there is a straightforward answer: for many years, 48 States and the Federal Government had flag protection statutes on the books. Were there insuperable problems of administration, enforcement, and adjudication under those statutes? No.

Testing the hypotheticals posed by opponents of this amendment about things such as bathing suits, paper cups, and napkins with a picture of the flag, against the history of enforcement of flag desecration statutes, renders these hypotheticals no basis for opposing the amendment. . . .

The committee believes, moreover, that states and Congress will legislate with care, and with the specificity required by the Constitution. . . .

Reliance on the parade of horribles to oppose the amendment would reflect the Senate's fundamental mistrust of the people, acting through their elected officials, to enact reasonable flag protection statutes. . . .

3. *The flag protection amendment is no precedent whatsoever for any other constitutional amendment or statute*

There no "slippery slope" here. The flag protection amendment is limited to authorizing states and the Federal Government to prohibit physical desecration of only the American flag. It serves as no precedent for any other legislation or constitutional amendment on any other subject or mode of conduct, precisely because the flag is unique. Moreover, the difficulty in amending the Constitution serves as a powerful check on any effort to reach other conduct, let alone speech, which the Supreme Court has determined is protected by the first amendment.

It is not the thought we hate which this amendment would allow Congress and the States to prohibit, but rather, one narrow method of dramatizing a viewpoint—one form of conduct. No speech, and no conduct other than physical desecration of the American flag, can be regulated under legislation authorized by the amendment. . . .

Even if one agreed that the *Johnson* and *Eichman* cases were correctly decided under prior precedents, one could still support this amendment— if one believes protection of the flag from physical desecration is an important enough value to override, in the words of Justice Stevens, the trivial burden on expression such protection would entail.

4. *The American flag deserves legal protection regardless of the number of flag desecrations in recent years*

The administration testified that, in light of what it refers to as "* * * only a few isolated instances ⟨of flag burning⟩, the flag is amply protected by its unique stature as an embodiment of national unity and ideals." The committee finds that comment wrong. In the words of Chairman Hatch:

> . . . [A]side from the number of flag desecrations, our very refusal to take action to protect the American flag clearly devalues it. Our acquiescence in the Supreme Court's decisions reduce its symbolic value. As a practical matter, the effect, however unintended, of our acquiescence equates the flag with a piece of common cloth, certainly as a matter of law, no matter what we feel in our hearts. Anyone in this room can buy a piece of cloth and the American flag and burn them both to dramatize a viewpoint. The law currently treats the two acts as the same. . . .

[W]hether the 45 plus flags whose publicly reported desecrations between 1990 and 1994 of which we are currently aware represent too small a problem does not turn on the sheer number of these desecrations alone. When a flag desecration is reported in local print, radio, and television media, potentially millions, and if reported in the national media, tens upon tens of millions of people, see or read or learn of them. . . . The impact is far greater than the number of flag desecrations. . . .

The committee does not believe there is some threshold of flag desecrations during a specified time period necessary before triggering congressional action. . . . If it is right to empower the American people to protect the American flag, it is right regardless of the number of such desecrations. . . .

5. A so-called "content neutral" constitutional amendment is wholly inappropriate

A few critics of S.J. Res 31 believe that all physical impairments of the integrity of the flag, such as by burning or mutilating, must be made illegal or no such misuse of the flag should be illegal. This "all or nothing" approach flies in the face of nearly a century of legislative protection of the flag. It is also wholly impractical.

In order to be truly "content neutral," such an amendment must have no exceptions, *even for the disposal of a worn or soiled flag*. . . . If such an exception is not permitted, however, and burning a worn or soiled flag for disposal purposes is made illegal, the American people would be subjected to the unacceptable choice of letting worn or soiled flags literally accumulate, or breaking the law by disposing of them in a manner already designated by Congress in the flag code. . . .

As former Assistant Attorney General for Legal Counsel Charles J. Cooper testified [in 1995 before a SJC subcommittee]:

> The threshold question that must be answered by proponents of this suggestion is whether anyone *really* wants a "neutral" flag protection statute. Does anyone really want to protect the physical integrity of all American flags, regardless of the circumstances surrounding the prohibited conduct? . . . The act of burning an American flag is not inherently evil. Indeed, the Boy Scouts of America have long held that an American flag, "when worn beyond repair" should be destroyed in a dignified way by burning." Similarly, Congress has prescribed ⟨such disposal for flags no longer fit for display⟩. Nor is the respectful disposition of an old or worn flag the only occasion on which burning a flag might be entirely proper. The old soldier whose last wish is to be cremated with a prized American flag fast against his breast would be deserving of respect and admiration, rather than condemnation.
>
> In contrast, Gregory Lee Johnson's conduct was offensive indeed, reprehensible not simply because he burned an American flag,

but because of the manner in which he burned it. Yet, a truly neutral flag protection statute would require us to be blind to the distinction between the conduct of Gregory Lee Johnson and his comrades and the conduct of a Boy Scout troop reverently burning an old and worn American flag. It would also reach other forms of conduct that honor, rather than desecrate, the flag.

. . . If such conduct is dignified and respectful, I daresay that the American people and their elected representatives do not want to prohibit it; if such conduct is disrespectful and contemptuous of the flag, I believe that they do.

. . . The committee does wish to empower Congress and the States to prohibit the contemptuous or disrespectful physical treatment of the flag. The committee does *not* wish to compel Congress and the States to penalize respectful treatment of the flag. A constitutional amendment which would treat the placing of the name of a military unit on a flag as the equivalent of placing the words "Down with the fascist Federal Government" or racist remarks on the flag is not what the popular movement for protecting the flag is all about. The committee respectfully submits that such an approach ignores distinctions well understood by tens of millions of Americans. Moreover, a constitutional amendment equating the ceremonial, reverential disposal of a worn American flag by burning, with the contemptuous burning of the flag to dramatize this or that viewpoint is as impractical as it is overbroad.

6. *Granting States, as well as Congress, power to protect the flag reflects the constitutional principle of federalism and returns us to the status quo ante 1989*

. . . Concern has been expressed that a "patchwork" of different statutes will develop. . . . While States cannot define the design of the flag, the flag belongs to the people of the several States as well as to the American people as a whole.

If Utahns, for example, want to ban only burning and trampling on the flag as a means of casting contempt on it, and New Yorkers or Congress or both wish to also ban defacing and mutilating the flag as a means of physical desecration, the committee believes New Yorkers and the American people as a whole should have the right to do so.

This is precisely the situation obtaining prior to 1989. Congress and 48 States had flag desecration statutes until 1989. Their lack of uniformity presented no threat to the fabric of our liberties.

Indeed, in restoring power to the States they had held for 200 years, the flag protection amendment reflects the basic constitutional principle of federalism.

Today, some States make unlawful what other States permit, across a vast range of human activity. There is nothing new or startling about this.

Some States legislate the protection of monuments, tombstones, and historical sites differently than other States. States regulate the sale and use of alcohol differently from each other. And on and on.

There is nothing unusual in letting States legislate protection of the American flag, and there was nothing unusual about it when 48 States did so before 1989. . . .

Notes

Index

Notes

1. A Civil War Execution for Flag Desecration

1. For an extraordinarily useful account of changing cultural attitudes toward the flag, see Scot Guenter, *The American Flag, 1977–1924: Cultural Shifts from Creation to Codification* (Rutherford, N.J.: Fairleigh Dickinson Univ. Press, 1990). For more detailed information corresponding to the first nine sections of this volume, see also Robert Justin Goldstein, *Saving "Old Glory": The History of the American Flag Desecration Controversy* (Boulder, Colo.: Westview, 1995).

2. David Eggenberger, *Flags of the United States of America* (New York: Crowell, 1964), p. 136.

2. Origins of the Controversy, 1890–1942

1. See Guenter, pp. 88–103.
2. Sons of the American Revolution, *1904 National Yearbook*, 177.

6. The Dispute During the Vietnam War Era

1. James Brown, preface to *The Flag of the United States: Its Use in Commerce* (Washington, D.C.: U.S. Dept. of Commerce, Trade Promotion Series No. 218, 1941).

2. American Law Institute, *Model Penal Code and Commentaries* (Philadelphia: American Law Institute, 1980), 416; *Handbook of the National Conference of Commissioners on Uniform State Laws and Proceedings of the Annual Conference*, 1966, 176, 427.

3. Hearings Before Subcommittee No. 4 of the Committee of the Judiciary, House of Representatives, on H.R. 271 and Similar Proposals to Prohibit Desecration of the Flag, 90th Cong., 1st sess., 1967, 70–71.

7. Prosecutions in the Lower Courts During the Vietnam War Era

1. *Civil Liberties*, May, 1971, 5.

10. Origins of the 1989–1990 Controversy

1. Information about Johnson's trial is based on an examination of the unpublished trial transcript: *Texas v. Johnson*, No. MA8446013-H/J, in the County Criminal Court No. 8, Dallas County, Texas, Nov. term, 1984. For more detailed information about the material contained in chapters 10–14 of this volume, see Robert Justin Goldstein, *Burning the Flag:*

The Great 1989–1990 American Flag Desecration Controversy (Kent, Ohio: Kent State Univ. Press, 1996).

2. *The Economist,* July 1, 1989.

3. Brief for Petitioner (document 10.9), Brief for Respondent (document 10.10), and oral argument before the U.S. Supreme Court in *Texas v. Johnson* are published in their entirety in Phillip B. Kurland and Gerhard Casper, eds., *Landmark Briefs and Arguments of the Supreme Court of the United States: Constitutional Law, 1988 Term Supplement,* vol. 190 (Bethesda, Md.: University Publications of America, 1990).

11. Public and Political Response to *Texas v. Johnson,* 1989

1. *Newsweek,* July 3, 1989; *Congressional Record,* 1989, S8098.

2. *Time,* July 3, 1989; *Columbia (South Carolina) State,* June 23, 1989; *New York Post,* June 23, 1989; *New York Daily News,* June 23, 1989; *Washington Post,* June 23, 1989.

3. *New York Times,* June 23, 1989.

4. *New York Times,* June 26, 1989; *Washington Post,* June 24, 28, 1989.

5. *Washington Post,* July 20, 1989; *New York Times,* July 20, 1989.

6. Senate Judiciary Committee, *Hearings on Measures to Protect the Physical Integrity of the American Flag,* 101st Cong., 1st sess., 1989, serial no. J-101-33, 115.

7. These data are based on the summaries of network evening newscasts compiled by the Vanderbilt University Television Archives and published as a serial under the title *Television News Index and Abstracts.*

12. Testing the Flag Protection Act in the Courts, 1989–1990

1. Government's Memorandum in Opposition of Defendant's Motion to Dismiss, *U.S. v. Eichman* et al., U.S. District Court for the District of Columbia, Cr. Nos. 89-419/420/421, 1990, 11–12, 15.

2. *U.S. v. Eichman,* 731 F. Supp. 1123 (1990).

3. Brief for the United States (document 12.4), Brief for Appellees (document 12.5), and oral arguments before the U.S. Supreme Court (document 12.6) for *U.S. v. Eichman* are published in their entirety in Philip B. Kurland and Gerhard Casper, eds., *Landmark Briefs and Arguments of the Supreme Court of the United States: Constitutional Law, 1989 Term Supplement* vol. 194 (Bethesda, Md.: University Publications of America, 1991).

13. Second Defeat of the Constitutional Amendment, 1990

1. *St. Louis Post-Dispatch,* June 12, 1990; *USA Today,* June 13, 1990; *Washington Post,* June 19, 1990.

14. The Revival and Defeat of the Constitutional Amendment, 1995

1. *Congressional Quarterly,* Nov. 24, 1990.

2. *New York Times,* Feb. 12, 1991.

3. For more information on the material in this and subsequent paragraphs see two articles by Robert Justin Goldstein, "Whatever Happened to the Great 1989–90 American Flag Desecration Uproar?" *Raven* (1995): 1–30, and "This Flag Is Not for Burning: Snuffing Out Symbolic Speech," *Nation,* July 18, 1994.

4. *New York Times,* Oct. 15, Nov. 5, 1995; William Bennett, *The Index of Leading Cultural Indicators* (New York: Simon and Schuster, 1994).

5. Reuters, June 7, 1995; *CFA Highlights,* June 1, 14, 1995; Associated Press, June 6, 1995; *St. Louis Post-Dispatch,* June 7, 1995.

6. Senate Judiciary Committee, *Senate Joint Resolution 31,* 104th Cong., 1st sess., 1995, S. Rept. 104-148, 74.

7. *New York Times,* June 7, 1995.

8. *Newsday,* Jan. 23, 1995; Reuters, Apr. 1, 2, 1995; *Green Bay News-Chronicle,* Feb. 18, 26, Mar. 8, 1996; *Ann Arbor News,* Mar. 15, 1996; *Indianapolis Star,* June 5, 6, 8, 1996; *Peoria Journal-Star,* July 6, 1996; *New York Times,* Mar. 14, 15, Apr. 29, June 8, 1996; *Tempe (Ariz.) Daily News Tribune,* Apr. 6, 1996; *American Legion Magazine,* June 1996; *Denver Post,* June 29, 1996.

Index

Note: Flag desecration incidents and prosecutions are listed individually and cross-referenced by the state in which they occurred, under the heading "Flag desecration laws, petitions to Congress, and enforcement (by state)." Congressional consideration and passage of proposed flag desecration laws and constitutional amendments, by either or both houses of Congress, are listed under the heading "Congress." Supreme Court decisions are indexed individually. Where documents substantially coincide with the topics of index entries, this is so indicated.